Grace Abounds

"Hunter Coates has written a splendid book on the greater hope. In *Grace Abounds* he covers all the important biblical, historical, and theological bases. Coates's book is a most welcome addition to the growing literature on the doctrine of universal salvation. I recommend it enthusiastically, without reservation."

—AIDAN KIMEL, Orthodox priest and author of *Destined for Joy: The Gospel of Universal Salvation*

"With this book, Hunter Coates has provided an impressive theological, philosophical, and exegetical defense of the universalist hope. If my brother's book—David Bentley Hart's *That All Shall Be Saved*—was a sustained polemic, Coates's book supplies a wealth of study that complements and fills out the former. Convinced universalists will find here a substantial amount of material for encouragement, while those who would argue for a contrary position will likewise benefit from carefully engaging this volume. Coates's research will be especially of interest to studious Orthodox readers, but it should also be welcomed by theologically literate Catholics and Protestants. Altogether, this is a valuable addition to the growing body of literature on the subject."

—ADDISON HODGES HART, retired Catholic priest, author of *The Letter of James: A Pastoral Commentary* and *Silent Rosary: A Contemplative, Exegetical, and Iconographic Tour Through the Mysteries*

"Unqualified universalism is crucial to an acceptable future Christianity that can command both intellectual and popular assent. In this book Hunter Coates explains further why it belongs to the genuine, deep structure of orthodoxy by placing it in clear relation to the Bible, the doctrine of God, the philosophies of free will and the meaning of existence. His case is overwhelmingly accessible and persuasive."

—JOHN MILBANK, Anglo-Catholic theologian, and author of more than fifteen books, including *Being Reconciled: Ontology and Pardon* and *The Politics of Virtue: Post-Liberalism and the Human Future*

"With a down-to-earth and readable voice, Hunter Coates uses careful criteria and a systematic approach to bring critical new points forward in defense of universal salvation. I am especially delighted to see an author who engages with challenging related topics such as the concept of a metahistorical human fall, Constantinople II, and the Harrowing of Hades."

—JESSE HAKE, director of ClassicalU, owner of Orthodox theology blog *Copious Flowers*

"Hunter Coates is a scholarly Christian who has thought deeply about all the issues raised in the modern debate about Christianity and Universal Salvation. The argument presented here moves beyond mere hopeful universalism to a definite universalism which confidently anticipates a glorious progression of all humanity into the ever-expanding vastness of God's love. This book, in important ways, reinvigorates the distinctively Christ centered universalist hope in the early centuries of the church."

—DAVID ARTMAN, pastor, author of *Grace Saves All: The Necessity of Christian Universalism*

"Hunter Coates' *Grace Abounds* is a transformative and deeply moving work that redefines how we understand salvation and reconciliation. With scholarly depth and spiritual insight, Coates dismantles misconceptions about universalism, offering a vision of divine love that extends to all. Grounded in the wisdom of figures like St. Isaac the Syrian and others, this work masterfully illuminates a path to ultimate reconciliation that is both compassionate, restorative and steeped in a holistic understanding of Grace. A must-read for theologians, religious scholars and philosophers."

—MARK GERARD MURPHY, Catholic-Lacanian psychoanalyst, author of *The Direction of Desire: John of the Cross, Jacques Lacan and the Contemporary Understanding of Spiritual Direction*

Grace Abounds

A Holistic Case for Universal Salvation

Hunter Coates

RESOURCE *Publications* • Eugene, Oregon

GRACE ABOUNDS
A Holistic Case for Universal Salvation

Copyright © 2024 Hunter Coates. All rights reserved. Except for brief quotations in critical publications or reviews, no part of this book may be reproduced in any manner without prior written permission from the publisher. Write: Permissions, Wipf and Stock Publishers, 199 W. 8th Ave., Suite 3, Eugene, OR 97401.

Resource Publications
An Imprint of Wipf and Stock Publishers
199 W. 8th Ave., Suite 3
Eugene, OR 97401

www.wipfandstock.com

PAPERBACK ISBN: 978-1-6667-4694-5
HARDCOVER ISBN: 978-1-6667-4695-2
EBOOK ISBN: 978-1-6667-4696-9

VERSION NUMBER 11/22/24

Scripture taken from the New King James Version®. Copyright © 1982 by Thomas Nelson. Used by permission. All rights reserved.

I ask not how remote the day
Nor what the sinner's woe
Before their dross is purged away,
Enough for me to know
That when the cup of wrath is drained,
The metal purified,
They'll cling to what they disdained
And live by Him that died.

—Anne Brontë

The fact that millions of people [...] share so many errors does not make the errors to be truths, and the fact that millions of people share the same mental pathology does not make these people sane.

—Erich Fromm

Contents

Abbreviations | ix
Introduction | 1

Part 1: Establishing a Theological Bedrock
1 What is God | 21
2 Scripture and the Church | 29
3 A Theology of the Incarnation | 38

Part 2: Universalism in Holy Tradition
4 A Preliminary on Eschatology and Hermeneutics | 73
5 A Quasi-Pauline Universalism | 86
6 The Hell That Never Was | 130
7 Christ's Victory Over Hades | 148
8 A Brief Critique of Biblical Annihilationism | 173
9 An Extensive Critique of Biblical Infernalism | 178
10 Constantinople II and its Discontents | 212

Part 3: A Philosophical Defense of Universalism
11 Free Will and Universalism | 257
12 An Interlude on Love | 277

CONTENTS

13 All is Fair in Love and Hell | 284
14 Pavel Florensky's Damning Doctrine | 318
15 Annihilating Annihilationism | 338
16 Shall We Only Hope? | 357

Postscript: Grace Will Abound | 364

Appendix: A Few Thoughts on Ibn Taymiyya and Islamic Universalism | 369
Bibliography | 383
Subject Index | 397
Ancient Document Index | 401

Abbreviations

AHVP	argument from a holistic view of Paul
BCE	before common era
CE	common era
CFW	classical free will
DBH	David Bentley Hart
ECT	eternal conscious torment
ES	(problem) of eternal sin
FEB	fundamental epistemic block
GAS	(problem) of grief among the saved
GC	(problem) of guaranteed certainty
HU	hopeful universalism
KVJAAE	King James Version with Apocrypha
LFW	libertarian free will
LXX	Greek Septuagint
LM	Lewisian model
LW	love web
MWP	masochistic wicked person
NDJ	(problem) of necessary divine justice
NKJV	New King James Version

ABBREVIATIONS

NT	New Testament
OS	(problem) of original sin
OT	Old Testament
PSA	penal substitutionary atonement
PSH	perpetual sin hypothesis
RAG	rebellion against God
SA	status argument
SAWP	set of all wicked persons in hell
TSAWP	total set of all wicked persons in hell in all possible worlds
VC	(problem) of value-correspondence
WP	wicked person

Introduction

WHAT HAPPENS AFTER DEATH? This is one of the most fundamental questions in Christianity. Many books preach about the glorious life that awaits those in heaven, but few are willing to come out swinging with serious arguments about why some should not experience this. I suppose that dreadful torment is not a huge selling point. Regardless of their silence, many of those same books and the Christians who purchase them believe that not all people will experience this. Some will experience precisely such dreadful torment for all eternity and be forever locked out of God's saving grace. This tragedy forms the theological background of the present book.

The author's background should also be mentioned. I do not claim, in any sense, mastery or expertise in the wide range of disciplines and fields I engage with in this book. I also do not claim this book solely as an Orthodox argument favoring universalism. While I predominantly engage with the debate from what I understand to be an Orthodox perspective, at numerous points in the text, I note that what I am arguing in specific instances does not apply to Orthodox Christians and has much more in common with the doctrines that other Christian traditions would accept. I do this to permit a larger audience to enjoy the text and so that I can become more knowledgeable about debates on eschatology outside of Orthodox circles. I came to write this book after having done ample research that I believe is up to date in the relevant fields, but obviously, by no means is this text perfect, nor should it be taken as a dogmatic treatise. Maybe later in life I will come around to attempt that. For now, I ask that all those who are experts in these fields reasonably indulge my engagement with your discipline and judge accordingly.

Salvation for All

Universalism teaches that God will eventually ensure an ultimate joyful reconciliation [*apokatastasis pantōn*] for everyone (Acts 3:21).[1] Universalism does not teach that this reconciliation will be immediate for all people after they die. A common misunderstanding is that the proponent believes in the immediate reconciliation of the damned into Paradise. Much to the contrary, universalists through the centuries have held there to be a form of restorative punishment after worldly death for those who were not saved in life. St Isaac the Syrian writes, "The power of love works in two ways: it torments those who have played the fool, even as happens here when a friend suffers from a friend; but it becomes a source of joy for those who have observed its duties."[2] As a universalist, Isaac believed that this torment, while terrible, would still only be temporary. The torment in hell stems from the feeling of bitter regret on behalf of the soul who did not devote themselves to God in this life.

However, the extent to which restorative punishment lasts cannot be answered convincingly. The Scriptures warn us against speculating about how time in the afterlife functions (2 Pet 3:8), and the philosopher Thomas Nagel put the question about what it is like to experience another mode of consciousness to rest with his famous 1974 paper "What is it Like to Be a Bat?" If humans cannot coherently imagine the experience of being a bat and how a bat would experience time, surely humans cannot imagine the experience of being a soul in the afterlife and how a soul experiences time there. A few minutes in this world may feel like a thousand years for the soul undergoing restorative punishment. For this reason, the restorative process that the damned undergo after their death could be of

---

1. In this book, all Greek and Hebrew—except in extenuating circumstances—is transliterated so as to allow for maximum comprehension on behalf of the reader. When the Greek Septuagint (LXX) is mentioned, chapter and verse numbers of the Masoretic text are adapted to fit this. I note linguistic differences (if any apply) between the two in a footnote under the citation.

2. Isaac, *Ascetical Homilies*, 266.

any temporal duration. Five years? Maybe. Five thousand years? Maybe. Longer? Maybe. The critical point is that it will *not* be everlasting.

Following a basic Christian legal ethic, one can acquire virtue through punishment. So, we should punish mankind to restore their virtue. Divine punishment is not joyful for the present. Still, it produces fruits of righteousness for those trained by it. If we punish mankind to restore their virtue, then once their virtue is restored, they have "paid the toll," so to speak. Once the restoration is complete and their soul is clean, they can presumably enter the conditions of Paradise (Rev 21:27). Accordingly, the time it takes for each person to be clean will differ. I can only assume that a murderous dictator's restorative process is much longer than that of your run-of-the-mill, unrepentant sinner. We could get into the weeds more when categorizing this process, and at points in this book, we will (see especially Chapter 14). But for now, it distracts from the thesis: God will eventually ensure an ultimate joyful reconciliation for all people.

An Ancient Tradition

There is a common misconception that universalism is some sort of new "liberal" Christian tendency that just can't stand to face the harsh truth that Christians have known since the time of Christ. Indeed, there are "liberal" Christians today who do not believe in hell altogether, yet as said earlier, self-identified Christian universalists believe in hell; they just do not believe it's eternal. The universalist who denies the eternality of hell is not the follower of a new fad or a symptom of a dying Christianity. The universalist stands on the shoulders of giants. These venerable men and women are a testament to the ancient tradition of *apokatastasis*. Who are these giants?

The following list, created after detailed research into relevant patristic writings and secondary literature, maintains a relatively conservative heuristic that weighs the respective credence that a figure held to universalism and/or the conclusion of their theology was universalist. If the assigned credence is *likely*, several statements from the figure indicate a universalist vision, and the conclusion of their theology seems to be universalist. If the assigned credence is *very likely*, there are many statements from the figure that indicate a universalist vision, they are known to be influenced by past universalists, and the conclusion of their

INTRODUCTION

theology is universalist. If the assigned credence is *certainly*, the figure was at their death and/or was for some extended point in life a universalist since they explicitly stated their support for positions associated with *apokatastasis* in writing (or, and this is a rare case, there is a trustworthy attestation of their position from an independent source(s)), they are known to be influenced by past universalists, and the conclusion of their theology is universalist. The reason why *very likely* and *certainly* are distinguished is because many figures of the early Church did not explicitly identify their belief in universalism, yet their theology absolutely leads to a universalist conclusion (they very well may have recognized this),[3] and past universalists undoubtedly influenced them in their eschatology. Therefore, the former credence is assigned instead of the latter *only if* there are not any explicit statements in support of *apokatastasis*, but I likewise see the conclusion of the theology as universalist, and they have extensive measurable influence from past universalists. I consider this heuristic charitable and believe that even many non-universalists will grant its validity. If anything, I was too conservative as I could easily adjust the credence of several *very likely's* to *certainly's* without much hiccup. I hope this enlightens interested parties and provides a comprehensive snapshot of the early universalist tradition in the East and West.

In the patristic period (100–451 CE), there's *certainly* the original scribe of *Apocalypse of Peter* (approx. 120), *very likely* St Theophilus of Antioch (unknown–184), *certainly* St Clement of Alexandria (150–215), *certainly* Bardaisan (154–222), *very likely* the original scribe of *Shepherd of Hermes* (approx. 165), *certainly* Origen of Alexandria (185–254), *very likely* St Dionysius of Alexandria (unknown–264), *very likely* St Gregory the Wonderworker (215–270), *certainly* St Anthony the Great (251–356), *certainly* St Pamphilus of Caesarea (unknown–309), *certainly* St Methodius of Olympus (unknown–311), *certainly* Eusebius of Caesarea (262–339), *certainly* St Macrina the Elder (270–340), *very likely* Gaius Marius Victorinus (290–364), *very likely* St Pachomius the Great (292–348), *very likely* St Athanasius of Alexandria (297–373), *likely* St Serapion of Nitria

---

3. This is not mere speculation. Patristic scholars agree that the early Fathers often hinted at their support of certain controversial positions in their writings but were not always willing to stand up for them. Just like their master Plato did in his so-called "unwritten doctrines" mentioned by Aristotle in his *Physics*. As St Clement of Alexandria admits, "At some things my treatise will hint; on some it will linger; some it will merely mention. It will try to speak imperceptibly, to exhibit secretly and to demonstrate silently." Other statements can be found throughout the early Fathers which give similar warnings and disclaimers. Quoted in Behr, "Rational Animal," 219.

INTRODUCTION

(300–360), *likely* St Ephrem the Syrian (306–374), *very likely* St Hilary of Poitiers (310–367), *certainly* St Didymus the Blind (313–398), *certainly* St Macrina the Younger (324–380), *very likely* Titus of Bostra (unknown–378), *very likely* St Gregory the Theologian (329–390), *very likely* St Basil the Great (330–379), *certainly* Diodore of Tarsus (unknown–390), *certainly* St Gregory of Nyssa (335–395), *very likely* St Ambrose of Milan (339–397), *very likely* St Theomitus of Scythia (unknown–407), *certainly* Tyrannius Rufinus (345–411), *certainly* Evagrius Ponticus (345–399), *certainly* St Paula of Rome (347–404), *very likely* St Melania the Elder (350–410), *very likely* St Olympias the Deaconess (365–408), *very likely* Nemesius of Emesa (unknown–420), *likely* St Theophilus of Alexandria (unknown–412), *certainly* St Jerome the Great (at least, before his avowed anti-Origenism, but even then he never denounced his once explicit belief in the *apokatastasis* of all humans, he only renounced his belief in the restoration of the devil; 341–420), *certainly* Theodore of Mopuestia (350–428), *certainly* St Augustine of Hippo (at least, in his long anti-Manichaean years before his explicit self-abandonment of *apokatastasis*; 354–430), *very likely* St John of Jerusalem (356–417), *very likely* St John Cassian (361–435), *very likely* St Eustochium Julia (368–419), and *very likely* St Cyril of Alexandria (376–444).

While these are quite a few names, many of them are highly revered in the Church, and some are the most prolific Christians to have ever lived; there are still (tens of?) thousands more nameless universalists who lived around this time. St Basil, brother of St Gregory of Nyssa and St Macrina the Younger, records that the "great majority" [*hoi polloi tōn anthrōpōn*][4] of his fellow (Eastern) Christians assumed that punishment in the Age to come would only be temporary and not eternal.[5] In this

---

4. The literal Greek reads, "the many of the human race." There is an obvious exaggeration in language here. Basil is only talking about Christians. Also, I specify "Eastern" because it is very unlikely for Basil to have a comprehensive grasp of universalism's acceptance among Western Christians.

5. David Bentley Hart (DBH), *That All Shall Be Saved*, 123. If, as reasonable estimates claim, Christians at the turn of the fourth century made up 5 percent to 15 percent of the population in cities in Asia Minor (with larger numbers in Nicodemia and Eumenia) there were quite a number of universalists in Asia Minor. If Basil is wildly overestimating the number of universalists at the time, these population numbers may not be relevant. Assuming Basil seeks to report the truth, though, he would be a reliable resource (or at least as reliable as one can get for a fourth-century bishop) for such a statistic. Basil is known for his expansive travels to Christians throughout Asia Minor, reaching urban and rural environments. See Trombley, "Christianity and Paganism," 189–91.

remark, he does not explicitly state opposition to or support for universalism. He does show a solid lean towards universalism in other places, but here, he worries about the effect that teaching it may have on a person's desire to obey God and morality. See Chapter 13 for a response to this and other pragmatic arguments against teaching universalism.

Basil was writing in Asia Minor, present-day Turkey. While we should not use this to make blanket statements about the attitude towards universalism in the East overall, this at least serves as a testament that universalism was very popular in areas around Turkey. But it would be odd if Turkey was the only area in the East where universalism was common. It would also be odd if universalism was solely in the East and did not bleed into the West. Blessed Augustine of Hippo was keen to note in the *Handbook to Laurentius*, a late text written after he denounced universalism, that a "great many" [*immo quam plurimi*] of Christians were universalists. He does not explicitly state this as a positive or a negative, but he notes that those who believe this are not in disagreement with the inspired Scriptures.

Universalism seemed to enjoy relative amicability, then, in the first five hundred years of the Church across the East and West (though, seemingly more in the East; see the list above). The American pastor J. W. Hanson first popularized this historical hypothesis at the turn of the twentieth century. Hanson considered himself somewhat of a historian, and while his *Universalism* has many factual improprieties, his conclusion still rings true, albeit with much more nuance than he and other universalists of his day were willing to grant.

Recent texts on the history of universalism tweak Hanson's arguments when necessary but also pay tribute to them. The most notable example is Ilaria Ramelli's 2013 tome, *The Christian Doctrine*. Her text does suffer from its own share of factual improprieties. I recommend reading the appendix of Michael McClymonds's self-acclaimed magnum opus, *The Devil's Redemption*, for a relatively fair critique of her scholarship. I also offer several critiques of my own in this text. While saying this, I do not endorse his text overall. (1) It is worse off due to its limited source gathering. (2) The text lacks a consistent methodology to evaluate the credibility of claims associated with the eschatology a person may or may not hold. (3) The author's thesis that universalism arose from "Gnostic" predilections is utterly vacuous since Gnosticism does not today, nor has rarely ever, been a coherent category that refers to a grounded uniform set

INTRODUCTION

of beliefs held by a person and/or a group.[6] The definition of Gnosticism he uses is, moreover, ironically biblical since St Paul routinely employs dualistic dative comparisons that, while not final, obviously create a distinction between the "good" *pneuma* (spirit) and the "bad" *sarx* (flesh) that modern commentators and English translations of the Bible often try to squirm around. But I suppose that since Paul was a universalist for most if not all his life—as I show in Chapter 5—then it makes perfect sense for McClymonds to claim that universalism arose from "Gnostic" preferences like this. Universalism, at least according to his idiosyncratic definition of Gnosticism, is indeed very biblical! Thus, Ramelli stands strong as a scholar committed to historical and eschatological truth. Both inform us of God's infinite goodness that drags all people to himself (Jn 12:32).[7]

As even a Wikipedia search on the history of universalism can tell you, universalism's popularity in Christianity began to flounder in the sixth century. Before the sixth century, there were signs of wear and tear due to Augustine's explicit statements against universalism. At one point in his famous text *City of God*, he describes seven universalist and quasi-universalist groups popular in the Christianity of his day. Richard Bauckham organizes these groups in a way that Fr Aidan Kimel faithfully reproduces:

1. All, including the devil and his angels, will be saved, after purgatorial punishments.

2. All human beings (but not devils) will be saved, after punishments of varying duration.

3. All human beings (but not devils) will be saved by the intercession of the saints on the Day of Judgment. Thus, no one will be punished at all. Hell is a threat of what the wicked deserve, but mercy will overrule it.

---

6. See a short summary of arguments from recent scholarship on the concept of "Gnosticism" in Gathercole, *Gospel of Thomas*, 169–73.

7. Her follow-up text, Ramelli, *A Larger Hope?: Volume 1* is a shortened introduction to her 2013 text with some new research added as a bonus. The relevant new information leads her to adjust the credence in favor of several figures being universalists in light of recently uncovered documents. The recent discoveries further demonstrate the strong presence of universalism in the early Church up to the sixth century. In an appendix, she responds to McClymonds's criticism of her 2013 text. In another appendix, she applies lengthy criticisms to his *Devil's Redemption*. The critiques I levy here are similar to the ones she brings up. I wrote the bulk of them before reading her appendix.

4. All who participate in the Christian sacraments, including heretics, will be saved.
5. All who participate in the Catholic Eucharist will be saved.
6. All who remain in the Catholic Church (hold the Catholic faith) will be saved, those who lived wickedly after temporary punishment.
7. All who perform works of mercy will be saved.[8]

There are several historical issues with Augustine's categories. Regardless, this list shows that universalism came in many different forms when Augustine wrote in the late fourth and early fifth centuries. As time passed and Augustine's popularity grew over his Eastern counterparts, many began to see *apokatastasis* as flawed, and if not heretical, at least incorrect. This is not to say that the close of the patristic period saw the end of universalism's support in the Church. Looking beyond this period into the rest of the first millennium, there's *very likely* St (Pseudo) Dionysius the Areopagite (sixth century), *very likely* St Maximus the Confessor (580–662), *certainly* St Isaac the Syrian (613–700), *certainly* St John Dalyatha (690–780), *very likely* John Scotus Eriugena (815–877), and *likely* several other notable figures who were universalists. Interestingly, the position was even held with relative amicability in East Syrian (Church of the East) monastic communities and among clergymen up to the fourteenth century. Notably, there's *certainly* Bishop Solomon of Akhlat (thirteenth century) and *certainly* Patriarch Timotheus II (unknown–1332).[9] In addition, several Catholics embraced universalism from the twelfth to the fifteenth century. This included, *certainly* Meister Eckhart (1260–1328), *certainly* John Rusybroeck (1293–1381), *certainly* Johannes Tauler (1300–1361), *very likely* Julian of Norwich (1343–unknown), and *certainly* Nicholas of Cusa (1401–1464). Finally, I would be amiss if I were to leave out those daring figures who began the revival of Origen's image in the West and introduced much of England, for the first time in a long time, to the Eastern Fathers. I am, of course, talking about the "Cambridge Platonists" of the sixteenth century. Those like Henry More, Ralph Cudworth, and Anne Conway were *certainly* universalists; see Chapter 4 for a list of notable universalists in the centuries following. Despite these outliers, with few other exceptions, the number of universalists had significantly diminished across East and West Christendom by

---

8. Kimel, *Destined for Joy*, 154–55.
9. DBH, *That All Shall Be Saved*, 124.

about the sixth century. Chapter 10 studies the role that ecumenical and local councils played in denouncing universalism. Or, more accurately, the role that rumors surrounding what these councils decided played in denouncing universalism. This chapter is the most comprehensive study on the ecclesial reception of universalism on the market today.

Thus, universalist beliefs have been present since the beginning of the Church, were present at all points in the Church's history, and will likely remain present for the foreseeable future. Fr Andrew Louth writes, "The dismissal of universalism as an aberration (however influential) in the Christian dogmatic tradition on Origen's part is less and less defensible."[10] Even if one has disagreements with universalism, one should be able to recognize the broad swath of "universalisms" and not equate them all with one another. This is because universalism, like the Church herself, has evolved over time. To take one person's concept of universalism and apply it to all those who refer to themselves as universalists is borderline incoherent. We must approach each universalist in history and the present with the recognition that they come to the doctrine with a unique outlook that cannot be equated with those who came before them. Sometimes, a person's universalism is similar to that of those who lived around the same time. Other times, a person's universalism is relatively distinct from even someone they would see as a master. There is no exact formula for what constitutes universalism, but I take it that we still have some idea about who is and who is not a universalist. For instance, see my list above.

A Liturgical Analogy

Orthodox liturgical worship is a codified and (relatively) unchanging set of texts and rituals. Some criticize the faith for this reason. Though I ask you, did the Scriptures not tell believers to be like "living stones" in 1 Peter 2:5? We are not a rigid faith, a dead faith. We are a faith of living stones. We are grounded in tradition, but we persist through time. The head of the Orthodox Church is Jesus Christ, and his Word is ever-enduring (Eph 4:14). We refer to our Sunday service as Divine Liturgy for this reason. The content of Divine Liturgy bases itself on the tension between a present providence of salvation and a "not yet" providence of the eschaton. St Paul's eschatology establishes this theme, and the content

10. Louth, "Response to Tom Greggs."

of Divine Liturgy builds off the liturgical theology seen in John's heavenly visions in Revelation.

Liturgy is a cosmic union that unites the past, present, and future into a single moment. Events that happened in the past (such as Christ's victory over Hades; see Chapter 7) are displayed and discussed as if they are happening in the present, and events that occur in the future (such as the eschaton) are likewise displayed and discussed as if they are happening in the present. When we engage with events that occurred in the past or those that will happen in the future, we collapse a chronological order of time and embrace a temporal cosmic union. Time then becomes experienced as if one is standing in a panopticon.

The Great Entry of the priest to the altar allows us to take part in Christ's ascension into heaven, the priest declaring peace upon the people allows us to take part in the ascetic life that many Fathers lived, the Eucharist allows us to take part in the world to come as it transforms the persons involved into the Kingdom that is lying in wait in all of us, and most relevant for our purpose, the closing of the church doors allows us to take part in the eschatological separation between the saved and the damned. Those in the church are experiencing salvation, while those outside are experiencing damnation. But something spectacular happens here. When the church doors are closed during the sermon and the recitation of the Lord's Prayer, they don't remain closed afterward. On the contrary, the doors are opened so those outside the church walls, outside of the saved, can eventually come back in. A hymn recited weekly in the *Liturgy of St John Chrysostom* before the Lord's Prayer reads, "The doors! The doors! In Wisdom, let us be attentive!" I believe this is an apt ecclesial analogy for universal salvation. All people who were once locked out will ultimately be let back in the doors of God's Kingdom in due time. The onus is on them. Mercifully, our Lord has infinite patience to wait for our will to come around. See Chapter 11 and Chapter 13 for more on the philosophical defense of universalism concerning the problem of free will and God's justice.

An Exit and Return to Paradise

The structure of the universalist narrative is necessarily based on the overall creation narrative. The Christian doctrine of creation teaches that creation occurred from God's loving act that sought to order the

INTRODUCTION

primeval sea of chaotic nothingness. However, creation before the Fall is not the same as the creation of today. What God created, how he created, and for what purpose he created, which is told to us in the fragments of Genesis 1–3 along with some further revelation in other places, is not only describing the creation of today, but also the creation of a reality unlike our own. The Fall, that is, the separation of those in Paradise from abiding in God, did not occur on this earth nor even this reality. The Fall occurred in a meta-historical age that exists outside of all known empirical time, history, and science. As the Orthodox theologian Oliver Clément writes, "Science cannot reach beyond the Fall because it itself is part of the fallen state of the world."[11] The idea is not only that this age exists *before* the time we inhabit now but is *beyond* time as we know it.

The temporality of the meta-historical age, like the temporality of the Age to come, is dramatically distinct from the temporality of the present historical age or *chronos*. Time in our fallen world proceeds linearly, from seconds to seconds and minutes to minutes. It is chaotic. It is not ordered. It is a bad infinite, prolonging itself forever into the future. Fallen time tends towards nothingness since it is itself an unceasing movement of decay. Time before the Fall was, one can only assume, dramatically different. Time before the Fall was a continual liturgical production of love and praise directed at God. From our perspective, all occurrences of what seems like the past, present, and future were gathered into one single ongoing moment. Our pious participation in the Divine Liturgy is like looking into a dim mirror compared to the perfect liturgical apperception that beings had before the Fall (1 Cor 13:12). This moment of all-gathered time was spectacular. All existed in the logical fullness of the *aiōnion*, which itself was held together by the infinitely more full, even more ineffable, transcendent Plentitude [*plērōma*] of God in the *aïdios*. This unity between creaturely being and the Godhead, overflowing with love and grace, produced what can only be thought of as utter bliss for those who met its apperception. But it all went awry. The Fall occurred.

As modern science teaches, the observable universe began with a cosmological singularity, such as the Big Bang, almost fourteen billion years ago. According to the meta-historical view, this cosmological singularity is the "first" event after the Fall. The singularity marked the beginning of this age, bringing with it the beginning of fallen time and

---

11. Quoted in Khramov, "Fitting Evolution," 104. Khramov is a Russian paleontologist who takes seriously the theory of Darwinian evolution and the teaching of the meta-historical Fall as passed down through the Eastern Church.

the consequences of the Fall—sin and death (Rom 6:23). Later down the line, humans came along due to evolution. Evolution was a glorious invention, a creative and divine invention, where each step of the way, every newly evolved being grew closer to reaching that perfect liturgical apperception. The driving force behind evolution is the desire to return to union with God, no matter how slight that desire may manifest in some living creatures even today. From slugs to humans, all desire God.

Speaking like this is inexact due to the ineffable nature of this belief; language limits us to speak properly of the magnificent. Personally, I like to think of the meta-historical age, the unfallen cosmos, as best expressed by the description given by Second Isaiah, where the "lion and lamb" feed together (Isa 65:25). This is an event seen in the eschatological future, but perhaps it gives an image, however weak it may be, of the peace which existed in that temporality beyond all known temporalities. A peace where the most virtuous and most evil entities of creation lived in harmony. A peace that we will experience once again, but this time in a truly unceasing manner. The glorified state of being that all things will persist in, more glorious than the cherubim and higher than the seraphim, exists on a paradoxically infinitely long continuum. Only Mary the Mother of God has reached this. And all of us will join her in due time. We will forever pass from "glory to glory" (2 Cor 3:18).

A Patristic Backdrop

The meta-historical view of the Fall has been relatively popular in Eastern Christianity but has yet to find much support in the West. Several of St Augustine of Hippo's early writings endorse the view. This was probably due to the heavy influence that St Ambrose of Milan had on Augustine's early years as a Christian after being the one to baptize him. In his late writings like *Retractions*, Augustine explicitly turns away from a meta-historical view and rebukes those who hold it. Other than Ambrose, the most famous Western proponent was probably the ninth-century mystic John Scotus Eriugena. This makes sense, considering he was also profoundly influenced by the Eastern Fathers and was also *very likely* a universalist (see the list earlier). The first explicit Christian proponent of a position that resembles the meta-historical view was probably Origen of Alexandria, but his understanding may have been flawed. He is said to have claimed that souls pre-exist their bodies, and thus, the

INTRODUCTION

meta-historical age was immaterial in that Adam and Eve "fell" from Paradise due to the first sin that brought them into the material world. Whether or not Origen believed this is debated by scholars.

Regardless, this was certainly not the last word on the view. It took Origen's greatest and most esteemed disciple, St Gregory of Nyssa, to remodel this position and strip it of some of its more questionable elements before it rose to prominence in the Church. As Fr John McGuckin writes, "The survival of so very much [of Origen's work] is a testament to the wisdom of the great fathers who wanted to prune Origen's tree, not uproot it."[12] Gregory's encouragement of the model influenced other beloved Fathers like St Basil the Great, St Gregory the Theologian, and St Maximus the Confessor.

For Nyssa and Maximus, pre-Fall beings were not bodiless souls living in some sort of immaterial realm. Instead, they were beings with angel-like bodies and existed, in some sense, on a physical plane; perhaps in the ilk of the ethereal material that, in Paul's letters, was thought to make up the consistency of the spirit. The Fathers claim that pre-Fall beings had the same powers and potentialities as angels but with one major difference: God created these beings to be immortal and become his sons. Angels are divine cosmic beings, gods appointed for particular offices in serving God and carrying out his will. These pre-Fall beings may have likewise shared with the angels an inability to procreate, an inability to defecate, and an inability to sweat. I mention these (oddly) specific clarifications because the most prominent opponents of this view in the medieval ages—Thomas Aquinas and Peter Lombard—specified that pre-Fall beings could do all of these. This is to say that Aquinas and Lombard were two of the most influential figures in bringing about this materialist view of the Fall that Christians today are unfortunately very fond of. The insights of these figures on the Fall are utterly in opposition to the spirit of the meta-historical view. They read the dying letter of Genesis but failed to encounter its life-giving spirit.

Reading Genesis with Fresh Eyes

Before exploring two Bible verses that arguably favor the meta-historical view, it is worth revisiting what literally occurs in the Eden narrative in Genesis. We know the text has many motifs shared with earlier

12. McGuckin, *Origen of Alexandria*, 94.

INTRODUCTION

Mesopotamian myths, so whatever the text says in the bare literal sense likely has traditions shared with various motifs in that camp. Indeed, there is a chief of the gods (suppose I call this entity "YHWH" for simplicity purposes), other gods who work in part with and serve this chief (Gen 1:26), and a creation that serves this single chief of the gods (Gen 1:28).

A portrait of the literal narrative goes as follows. YHWH and the gods he rules over decided to create a garden Paradise for their creation. If you are to have a unique garden for creation, you must have entities to watch over and cultivate the garden. YHWH created a man first but realized after that he couldn't do it all on his own (Gen 2:20). YHWH then decided to create another servant from the man's body, a woman, since none of the other animals could tend to the garden. Both the man and woman were later given names. Adam was seemingly given his name by YHWH. Eve was given her name by Adam. These servants had the sole purpose of tending to the garden. Unfortunately, these servants grew a bit big for their britches and listened to a crafty serpent in the garden who convinced them that they could join the heavenly realms and unseat some of the gods in the divine council (3:5). This led them to engage in the one activity barred from them: They ate from the Tree that held the knowledge of all Good and Evil (3:6). The gods relied on this as the source for how they knew all good and evil in the everyday sense of knowing what to do and knowing what not to do. The gods became furious at this injunction.

Now that their creation had eaten from the Tree of Good and Evil, their creation was only one step away from achieving immortality. What a tragedy! Fruit from the Tree of Life was next on the list for Adam and Eve (3:22). If they could achieve immortality, they too would become gods since they would now derive their immortality from the same Tree as the gods. This stirred up jealousy and worry among YHWH and the other gods. Turns out, the crafty serpent was telling the truth the whole time. YHWH had lied to them. They would not die from eating the apple. This prohibition was created to ensure that the gods maintained their power and sovereignty over their creation. So, in a fit of rage, seeking to avoid the loss of their power, YHWH and his godly comrades removed Adam and Eve from Paradise. No creature shall unseat those who are the highest of the high. The Eden narrative is a beautiful work of art that combines various traditions and still produces a relatively coherent story with its own plot, sub-plot, climax, and, most notably, downfall.

INTRODUCTION

While there is clearly a downfall in the narrative, a literal reading of Genesis cannot provide a "Fall" in the extreme sense that many today seem to think it teaches. When read in its most wooden (and most bereft of the divine) sense, the removal from the garden was not a loss of innocence or a tale of morality as so many like to claim. This was a removal of two creatures who tried to unseat several gods on the heavenly council. This caused the gods to become jealous and partition a vote of some sort, perhaps to the entity presumably identified as YHWH, for the creatures to be removed from Paradise.[13] Truthfully, one could identify the Fall at several different points in Genesis, and being expelled from the garden is just one of many. Another one could be the murderous act of Cain or the dispersal of language after the Tower of Babel, two more narratives that heavily rely on the Mesopotamian cultural milieu of early Israelite religion. Our attentiveness to ascribe a "Fall" to the events in Eden is a product of later interpretation, as is our attentiveness to claim the divine beings were understood by the earliest hearers to be angels and not a pantheon of gods from the Near East that visually shared much more in common with the Egyptian gods than the angels of later Christianity. Both of these interpretative choices are valid, of course, but we must recognize this.

The Hermeneutics of Eden

Following Hans-Georg Gadamer—the single most influential scholar on the analysis of how modern eyes read ancient texts—the tradition of reading a text is not a permanent precondition that the modern eye encounters but is shaped by the one reading the text who then participates in the evolution of the textual tradition.[14] This is because the person who

---

13. It is still debated among scholars if Yahweh was thought to be the sovereign chief of the gods in early Israelite religion or if there was a higher god, known as El from the Canaanite pantheon, that had dominion over Israel and the world. Pentateuchal texts like Deuteronomy 32:8–9 and others clearly speak of El and Yahweh as two distinct entities. The text says that El Elyon partitioned the land of Israel to Yahweh, and other gods were given dominion over other lands. Over time El's attributes, including El's wife-consort Asherah, became merged into the attributes that were associated with Yahweh. However exactly this process occurred, one can harken it was close to reaching its zenith by Genesis 2–3 where the proper name Yahweh-Elohim is mentioned nineteen times. For a brief overview of how El's attributes became associated with Yahweh, see Hundley, *Yahweh Among the Gods*, 214–15.

14. Gadamer, *Truth and Method*, 293.

engages with the text does so from a relative horizon of meaning from which they interpret it with all their ideological and cultural presuppositions. The person who engages with the text does not stand outside their particular horizon of meaning, so there are always limitations to what they can gather from the text. As such, the reason why the Genesis creation narrative has any sense of being considered divinely inspired is due to the interpretive lens that the Fathers, the liturgical texts, and other outpourings of the Holy Spirit have assigned to it (2 Tim 3:16; see Chapter 2). But despite these mediums all being divinely inspired, none of them are perfect. Like the scribes of Genesis, the figures from these respective mediums likewise come from a particular horizon of meaning that shapes how they engage with and develop the textual tradition. While they smooth out some difficulties with the text and, due to their divine inspiration, draw out further implications of the text that may not have been apparent to earlier generations, there is never a perfect reading of the text possible, at least not from any human, only God can accomplish such a feat.

However faint of a sense it may have been, Paul himself seemed to recognize this. He took an allegorical and spiritual approach to the Eden story and rarely dwelled on it as anything more. This was because the Old Testament books of Proverbs, Wisdom, and Sirach had much more of an influence on how Paul viewed Genesis than the text of Genesis itself. Paul looked towards later tradition on how to interpret the text just as we all should if we want to draw out anything that resembles a cogent theological message from Genesis. Yet he did not just borrow everything from this later tradition. Working under the inspiration of the Holy Spirit, Paul drew out further implications of the Eden story—such as tying Christ in as the New Adam—that the Old Testament scribes simply did not have access to in their respective horizon(s) of meaning. By the end of the first century, a rough method of biblical hermeneutics was developed. Paul set the standard that Christians in the early Church followed. If Christians today would return to the Pauline method of reading Scripture, I like to think that many of these hermeneutical difficulties would be washed away. See Chapter 4 for more on hermeneutics and the "spiritual" approach to the Scriptures that I utilize.

INTRODUCTION

Skins and Angels

Now that a review of the Genesis creation narrative is out of the way, it is worth discussing two key episodes that proponents of the meta-historical view center on. Both take place in Genesis 3. Genesis 3:21 in the NKJV reads, "Also for Adam and his wife, the LORD made garments of skin and clothed them." The phrase "garments of skins" means that Adam and Eve did not have a fleshy existence before the Fall. If they had a fleshy existence before the Fall, they wouldn't have been given garments of skin afterward because they would have already been in this world as fleshy humans. It is due to the Fall, then, that humans have a worldly existence and are subsumed into bodies of flesh or garments of skin because they no longer possess the angel-like bodies they had in Paradise. Genesis 3:24 in the NKJV reads, "So He drove out the man; and He placed cherubim at the east of the garden of Eden, and a flaming sword which turned every way, to guard the way to the tree of life." This verse recalls two episodes: The expulsion from the garden and the provision of a guard to prevent Adam and Eve from entering the garden again. The reason why the meta-historical age ended and why this historical age began must be left as a mystery. Still, the episode of the cherubim guard is worth briefly commenting on. The cherubim guard indicates the cosmic rift that separates our current historical age from the meta-historical age. A rift prevents this cosmos from ever coming into contact with any other existent mode of temporality.

On a grand scale, both verses relay the message that there was a fundamental ontological shift in the nature of reality due to the Fall, and there is no way that we can reach Paradise again on our own accord. This explains why the scribe in Genesis earlier said that the ground was cursed (Gen 3:17) and why Paul in Romans 8:20 likewise refers to the curse of God that has beset all creation. As St Maximus the Confessor was keen to note in several places, the creation of anything in this temporal age was brought into the world already in a state of fallenness. The *logoi*, that is, the view that creation has in the eyes of God—such as its purpose and end—is always perfected in him since he is the eternal source of all being, but the imperfect physical representation of a thing's *logoi*—its existence in this world—is in the state of fallenness. Nothing will exist or has existed in this age that is not already in a decrepit dying state (Rom 5:12), chained to the governance of evil earthly and cosmic powers.

INTRODUCTION

I mention this theological portrayal of the Fall because universalism is the only justified conclusion to the disastrous state of the cosmos. Universalism is the only doctrine that teaches we will all return to union with God. God will allow us to experience the *logoi* of all things just as he, the Logos, experiences them now. This is what it means to be brought into the divine life and become members of the mystical body (Eph 1:23). Non-universalists can try and play semantic-language games to escape this. Still, nothing will shield them from the fact that they refuse to accept a perfect completion of the story of creation. They cannot protect themselves from their implicit agreement that God created beings with the knowledge that their eternal torturous separation (or annihilation) was an ever-present possibility.[15] The beginning will be like the end but more glorious. We will not simply return to our pre-Fall ontological state but will magnify such a state such that the permeation God will have in creation will truly be all in all (1 Cor 15:28). This is the sole reason why God created us: It is our *archē* and *telos*. Eternal damnation was never in the blueprint. We shall be gods (Jn 10:34–35) since we are already of the same race [*genos*] as God (Acts 17:28). Only at this point will we truly comprehend what the Scriptures mean when they say that creation is very good (Gen 1:31) and it is finished (Jn 19:30). In an eschatological context, these refer to the same event: The joyful reconciliation of all things or *apokatastasis*.

---

15. See a further exploration of this argument in Bulgakov, "Apocatastasis and Theodicy."

Part 1

Establishing a Theological Bedrock

1

What is God

An Attempt at a Definition

WHAT DOES IT MEAN when a Christian evokes the word "God?" This question has busied many theologians. Due to the difficulty of defining what this word means, even many who believe in God do not take the time to investigate what they believe in. Is God just a massive guy in the sky who sets moral laws for us to follow, and when we follow them, he is happy? Maybe an uninformed atheist is under the impression that this is what Christians believe, but they would be sorely mistaken. Is God some sort of being that exists beyond our physical universe that is loving, caring, and wants the best for us? We are closer to the truth here but still a bit far off.

"God" is used to evoke the concept of an ultimate reality that is complete, total, and whole. He is the concept of concreteness, of fullness, of completeness. But compared to the existence of things in our universe, he seems to us as beyond all beings. God cannot be reduced to some big guy in the sky or to some sort of thing that exists beyond our physical universe. Paradoxically, God is both out of the universe and in the universe. This is why God is beyond all being yet more being than any other being; the French *plus d'etre* is a fascinating way to express this. Hence, God is not exactly a thing we can point to and say, "Aha! There God is!" When it comes to a chair or a table, we can easily point and go, "There it is!" With God, it does not work this way. This is because God does not have a central point: God is omnipresent. He is everything everywhere, all at once, since he is reality in its fullness. But if God were only omnipresent, if that was the only divine property he had, then he wouldn't be the God that we know and love. He wouldn't be the Father of all creation since to be a Father requires properties of personableness. If God were only omnipresent, he would just be an abstraction. Nobody would worship him, and nobody would love him, and frankly, nobody would talk about him because there wouldn't be much to discuss. Hence, God must be much more than *just* a series of abstract statements; he must have personableness if he is *truly* the God we love and worship. And he is.[1]

Christian philosophers tend to evoke three divine properties other than omnipresence that God has. While we will stray from the terms "divine properties" later in this chapter and involve a description of God that is much more Platonic in language, it may be beneficial for those new to Christian metaphysics to hear the standard talking points before we get more complex. The four divine properties of God are as follows: (1) Omnipresence, (2) Omniscience, (3) Omnipotence, (4) Omnibenevolence. (1) Omnipresence has already been introduced. (2) God is omniscient because the existence of everything at every moment depends on God's existence. (3) God is omnipotent because he has the power to do anything. The function of necessity does not obtain in reference to what God can do. (4) God is omnibenevolent because he has the ground for Goodness in his nature. The way I depict God is not the only way Christians, including pious Orthodox, have and still do depict God. I follow a particular framework that is subject to debate about whether it should be the preferred framework for thinking about God.

On the Names of God

God is Love itself, Being itself, Beauty itself, Life itself, Truth itself, Wisdom itself, and the Good itself. These are the Divine Names of God, formulated by (Pseudo)-Dionysius the Areopagite. During St Paul's mission

---

1. A general point should be made going forward about all masculine pronouns and titles attributed to God: These are not done in the belief that God is *literally* male or a Father, and so on. One could very well substitute "Parent" with Father, and there would not be a theological difference. I refer to God with these male terms because this is how Holy Tradition often, though not always, portrays God. I do not mean to downplay the valiant efforts of womanist/feminist theologians.

work in Acts 17, he met an erudite Greek man named Dionysus, who is said to have joined Paul along the way. (Pseudo)-Dionysius was an anonymous late-fifth-century Syrian Christian who attributed his writings to the Dionysius of Acts. He went beyond just attributing his work to this man as he sought to place himself in the man's life. As scholars often quip, (Pseudo)-Dionysius was not an imposter but rather an identifier. He identified with the Dionysius of Acts to truly become himself. Whoever he materially was, the author, that is, sought an escape from present-day life. (Pseudo)-Dionysius wrote letters that he addressed to various apostles and even described an account of the Virgin Mary's "passing away" or Dormition. Placing himself in this narrative did not lead him to abandon his material identity. Though seeking identification with someone beyond himself, he had no issue referencing, sometimes at length, various paragraphs of fifth-century philosophers and even perhaps hinting at contemporary christological debates of his time. This tension was not a problem or an issue for the author but something he sought to exemplify throughout his work. Suffice it to say that (Pseudo)-Dionysius is one of the most influential figures in Christianity, and his anonymity is one of the most revealing aspects of his presence in Holy Tradition. In Orthodox liturgical texts, the Dionysius in Acts and (Pseudo)-Dionysius are equated as St Dionysius the Areopagite. I shall henceforth refer to the anonymous author this way.

The Divine Names were not randomly drawn from a hat like a lottery pick. These names illustrate what has been revealed about God through Scripture. Dionysius devotes ten chapters of the *Divine Names* to demonstrate how and why Scripture is the ground for his mystical expedition. Everything that exists is at once given through God's goodness, his being, his life, his wisdom, and his love. Everything that exists then participates directly in God's goodness, being, life, wisdom, and love. Hence, when any of these terms are used, the rest are implicitly evoked, but none of them, taken separately or together, perfectly express the nature of God.

The nature of God is beyond human expression and thought. It is remarked in Ephesians 1:21 that after his resurrection, Christ was seated in the heavenly realms, "Above [. . .] every name that is named, not only in this age but the age to come." 1 John 4:12 in the NKJV reads, "No one has seen God at any time. [But] if we love one another, God abides in us, and His love has been perfected in us." Although we cannot know God's nature, we can know him through his love. Accordingly, we can see how

PART 1: ESTABLISHING A THEOLOGICAL BEDROCK

all the Divine Names interlink in the example of love. Love is beautiful, blissful, good, and as 1 Corinthians 13:6 says, love rejoices in the truth. By saying God is Love itself, the other terms are implicitly involved. The nature of God cannot perfectly be expressed in language, as stated, but language can talk about God's attributes in the way that they relate to finite beings. We can say God is Love itself because we know what love is when it comes to finite love, so we have, at least, however small it is, an inkling of what the nature of God as Love itself could be like. Take the concept of love we know and multiply it by infinity, then multiply infinity by infinity, and so on. The result is God as Love itself.

In the fourteenth century, St Gregory of Palamas took a rigorous look at the patristic tradition up to his time. He realized that many Fathers had perhaps unknowingly issued a distinction between how God expresses himself in creation and how God is in himself. Palamas called the former God's energies and the latter God's essence or nature. Although neither Palamas nor contemporary scholarship seems to recognize this, Origen of Alexandria was probably the first to conceptualize a proto-essence/energy distinction. In a very brief and mysterious statement that he does not expand upon in any other writings that I know of, in his commentary on Matthew 11:27 ("No one knows the Father except [through] the Son"), he says that only God himself can teach God. If God's essence [*ouisia*] can only be known by God himself, that is, the Son, then God's essence must be much more divine than the *ouisia* of created things.[2] This seems to mean that whatever we could possibly know about God is different from what God knows about himself. This proto-distinction became more explicit when the fourth-century brothers—St Basil the Great and St Gregory of Nyssa—very influenced by Origen, came to a mutual understanding of the essence/energy distinction. Basil issued a distinction between God's *ouisia* and *energia* (energy). He did this to specifically indicate the action of God is distinct, in a way, from what God is in himself.[3] Gregory followed up with his brother with some remarks about how since God has no form, he has no name. If God has no name, he cannot be thought of as he is in himself. When we predicate terms like *theos* (God) we are naming the divine *energia* of God in his governance of creation.

---

2. See Origen, *New Fragments*.
3. Athanasopoulos and Schneider, *Divine Essence and Divine Energies*, 40.

This distinction does not just appear out of thin air in patristic literature. It has a firm grounding in Scripture. Take the encounter that Moses had with God in Exodus 33.[4] God tells Moses, following the NKJV translation, "You cannot see my face; for no man shall see Me, and live." By doing this, our Lord has distinguished between how he is in himself and how he appears to us. When God refuses to let Moses see his face, going so far as to say that if Moses saw his face, he would not live, this is an overarching statement that creation cannot encounter the *ouisia* of God (also Jn 1:18; 1 Tim 6:16; 1 Jn 4:12).

The divine energies manifest as what we have been calling the Divine Names: Love itself, Beauty itself, Good itself, etc. These energies are uncreated like the essence of God, as they are the eternal manifestation of him beyond the inaccessible essence. As a Platonic analogy common in patristic writings, think of how the sun would still emit rays even if no other matter besides the sun existed in the universe. The rays wouldn't be encountering anything since there is nothing else, but the sun would still emit rays. This is like how, even before the creation of anything, God's energies were the manifestation of his essence, emitting the rays of Love, Beauty, Good, etc. When we speak of God's energies, we often do so in the plural form, but we do not speak of his essence this way.[5] The divine energies abide with and in one another as no single divine energy is independent of all other divine energies. To use the above analogy, we tend to refer to rays of the sun and not a ray of the sun. Hence, we refer to God's energies in their plurality. Like the Divine Names, God's energies have no set amount or limit. They are in infinite abundance.

Apophatic and Cataphatic Theology

Apophatic theology is an ancient tradition that, when taken to the extreme, believes that all we say about God is what he is *not*. We cannot make explicitly affirmative predications of God's being. Apophatic theologians recognize that negation is always an affirmation in a certain sense, but at the same time, they recognize the idea of a "hyper-negation." This negation does not box God in a particular conceptual state but frees God from any conceptual space. It is a negation that is committed to

---

4. St Gregory of Nyssa is perhaps the best patristic exegete of this passage in that he develops its "spiritual dimensions" hidden under the surface of the literal text (see Chapter 4). See Ramelli, "Apophaticism, Mysticism," 563.

5. Bradshaw, *Aristotle East and West*, 241.

perpetual negation. For example, "God is not not in movement." God transcends the finite categories of rest and movement. Though as said above, we must remember that negation retains a sense of affirmation. Sigmund Freud's 1925 psychoanalytic paper "Negation" illustrates this perhaps better than any philosophical treatise. Our psychic processes begin with a negation, a primordial negation for Freud, but with this primordial negation, there must also be an affirmation—the creation of the unconscious. Through further processes of negation, that is, psychic repression, the unconscious affirms content for itself and links various images and memories together, forming a coherent, albeit disjointed, story of the person. For apophatic theology, the affirmation implicit in the hyper-negation is the imposition of divine meaning. Divine meaning transforms one's relationship with God and the world. Divine meaning stretches beyond anything perceivable, permitting one to locate oneself in the eternal timeline. Finally, divine meaning allows people to come to terms with their problems, those gnarly flaws we all have, through remaining in a consistent and ongoing mode of devotion to God.

Unlike the above, cataphatic theology is not so much a tradition of theology expressed in various religions through the ages. It is instead a term used by those who believe their opponent is limiting God in some way. Those who could plausibly be identified as falling under this domain likely see themselves as having a fully rational belief in God. They view belief in God as rational because the concept of God can be accustomed to finite mental categories that humans create. The difference between cataphatic and apophatic theology, then, is roughly that those in the former tend to be more rationalistic, and those in the latter tend to be less rationalistic in matters of faith. These two camps are not black-and-white by any means.

The contemporary Orthodox tradition increased its applause for apophatic theology in the twentieth century due to the rise of the neopatristic movement. A notable theologian in this movement was Fr Pavel Florensky, who is extensively discussed in Chapter 14. The former Anglican Archbishop of Canterbury, Roman Williams, a respected scholar on Eastern Christianity in his own right, explains the rise of this movement as stemming from a highly intellectual laity in Russia that sought to push back against the critiques of Protestant pietists and Catholic polemicists.[6] The movement arose, then, as an Eastern reaction to the influence that

---

6. Williams, *Looking East in Winter*, 162.

Western thought—Protestant and Catholic—was playing in Russia at the time. These theologians believed this influence was stripping Orthodoxy of some key tenets from its mystical tradition. In response, they sought to reclaim the ancient patristic spirit of Orthodoxy by aligning themselves with the stance that they were taking back the Fathers from Scholasticism and its offshoots in Protestant philosophy; hence, the "neo" aspect of neopatristic thought. Although neopatristic thought has rightly been criticized by many in contemporary Orthodox theology for its overreliance on apophatic theology and its somewhat haphazard claim that it was truly a reflection of the early Fathers, it still holds a high status today.

Apophatic theology has gone too far when the idea of God is reduced to a pure abstraction, a collection of mouth sounds that lack a referent. This is why most of Orthodox theology is somewhere between the extreme poles of cataphatic and apophatic theology, leaning towards the latter. A prime example of a supposed cataphatic thinker is the philosopher John Duns Scotus. Scotus made the famous claim that God is univocally predicated as Being itself, and all creation differs from him, not in kind, but in degree of being. By knowing the perfections of things in creation, we can know God's perfection as well; the latter perfections are just superior in degree to the former. The relation of creation's being to God differs by degree and not kind because if it differed by kind, according to Scotus, then the perfections we infer as God's nature would have no relation to the perfections of our world. If there is no relation between the perfections of our world and the perfections of God's nature, then we don't have an epistemic basis to infer about God's nature. As such, if we believe that we can infer about God's nature, and it certainly seems we must accept this, then the perfections of his nature can only differ in degree and not in kind.

Many in Orthodoxy tend to agree with the core proposition of Scotus: Rational beings have epistemic access to God. However, they would differ with Scotus because this is not epistemic access to his essence, what he is in himself. Instead, this is epistemic access to his energies. (A distinction that, granted, is quite haphazard and dualistic in certain phrasings; some may prefer to view this as a formal distinction.) Many also do not opt to use Scholastic terms like "degree" and "kind." These terms are unneeded stipulations that distort the great mystery of the relationship between God and his creation. As such, Orthodoxy often does not take the rationalization of God's relationship with his creatures to the same extent as many Western traditions. This extends to what Scripture's divine inspiration reveals about God and what the natural world reveals about God.

For this reason, Orthodox Christians tend to heavily nuance what is known as natural theology. Natural theology is the field of study that seeks to prove the existence of God by observing creation in the absence of divine revelation and then deducing the existence of God from this. Famous theistic arguments like the cosmological and teleological arguments are in the camp of natural theology. Orthodoxy is not opposed to natural theology, much to the delight of some and dismay of others. However, many Orthodox theologians and saints believe these arguments are not enough on their own. Due to our wariness on natural theology and other aspects of epistemic access to God that many traditions take for granted, the Orthodox often maintain a very humble stance regarding religious epistemology. Orthodoxy is careful not to create a tower of Babel by conflicting with the infinite qualitative and epistemic distance that separates God from us. At the same time, however, it is cautious not to support the infantile belief that God exists somewhere away from his creation. God is absolutely transcendent and absolutely immanent. This paradox of God is as it is because we are finite beings who cannot rationally account for God's infinite plentitude of glory that pours into all things.

2

Scripture and the Church

The Church in Scripture

JESUS SAYS, "HOWEVER, WHEN He, the spirit of truth, has come, He will guide you into all truth, for He will not speak on His own authority, but whatever He hears He will speak" (Jn 16:13; NKJV). Jesus has imparted the Holy Spirit into the Church. The Church, now and forever more, will be guided by the Holy Spirit. Matthew 16:18 in the NKJV says, "And I also say to you that you are Peter, and on this rock I will build my Church, and the gates of Hades shall not prevail against it." Peter in Greek is *Petros*, the masculine form of *petra* or rock. Jesus says here that he will use this rock (Peter) to serve as the Church's foundational scaffolding (rock). Then, in Matthew 18:18, Jesus specifies that all the apostles have the power to "bind and loose" on earth and in heaven. Jesus has appointed all the apostles to serve a leadership role in the Church, with Peter as the leader. The Catholic scholar John Bergsma accurately points out that the "binding and loosing" mentioned in these Matthew verses is a direct reference to the priestly prerogative under the Mosaic Covenant in Deuteronomy 17:8–13.[1] Jesus is bestowing the function of priesthood onto the apostles. In the New Covenant, just as in the Old Covenant, the apostles and their successors have binding and interpretive authority.

---

1. Bergsma, *Jesus and the Old Testament Roots of the Priesthood*, 46.

Second Thessalonians 3:6 in the NKJV reads, "We command you, brethren, in the name of our Lord Jesus Christ, that you withdraw from every brother who walks disorderly and not according to the tradition which he received from us." Here, the importance of apostolic tradition is noted along with the call for those who depart from this to be abandoned. Then, in 1 Timothy 3:15, it is said that the Church is the "pillar and ground of truth." Since the Church is the body of Christ and the Fathers are sometimes called the limbs of the body of Christ, the councils are perhaps like the blood that pumps to the limbs. Ephesians 1:23, if read with the recognition that the Holy Spirit is that which fills all of the Church as the body of Christ, could indicate this. Without blood pumping to the limbs of a body, those limbs will wither. Without limbs for blood to pump to, that blood has no purpose. The councils and the Fathers require one another, but unlike the Fathers who are not inerrant, the councils may be inerrant; see the end of Chapter 10. After all, to play with my tentative analogy again, the blood that pumps in the body sustains the entire body. There is no living body without the pumping of blood. And there is no living Church without the continual flow of doctrine from councils that replenish and pump blood throughout the body. The Church is a living body.

The world has gone through a great deal of struggle in the twentieth century alone, facing powers that are by all means demonic in presence. These have wrought destruction and introduced a level of evil that we have not seen before in human history. But through the vast darkness of the world, there has always been a light that is fancifully glowing (Isa 49:6). This is the light of the Church. The Church is not an earthly institution in the same way as other institutions. This is why the story of the Great Flood takes on an ecclesial meaning in patristic literature. The world was baptized through the Great Flood, just as we are baptized through the Church. The flood was said to cleanse the world of its improprieties, just as baptism ontologically restores the human person. Hence, the flood is "salvation by water." Fr Seraphim Rose of blessed memory writes that the Church is the ark that binds believers away from the wicked world.[2] Those who do not abide by the Church will see the purifying water of the flood become the fire they burn in after death. We practically see this idea already in 1 Enoch 67:13, which speaks to the salvational waters of the flood that became an eschatological fire for those not saved in the

---

2. Rose, *Genesis, Creation, and Early Man*, 260.

ark. There's also Wisdom 14:7, which reads in the KJVAAE, "For blessed is the wood [of the ark] whereby righteousness cometh." The ecclesial meaning is that the waters become the eschatological fire for those not in communion with the Church.

Holy Tradition and Scripture: A False Dualism

The Trinity is true by virtue of the doctrinal declarations of the ecumenical councils that God graciously assigned as being the blood of the body of Christ, that is, the Church. Holy Tradition is a gift from the transcendent God that does not exhaust itself. Holy Tradition is tested repeatedly, but it retains its transcendent nature. A nature that is not of this world but is in this world to bring us all closer to communion with God. However, interpretation is required with Holy Tradition. Scripture is not an exception to this necessity since it is a facet of Holy Tradition. We rely on Holy Tradition to dictate what the words of Scripture mean because the term "Scripture" itself is impossible to specify if Scripture is removed from the context of Holy Tradition. The term assumes the univocality of the text and results in the bind of epistemic circularity. In this context, univocality is the assumption that the Bible has "one voice" and the entirety has a single message that one can garner from the text itself. Since the Bible does not speak with one voice, has evolved in its meaning over time, and contains tensions unable to be reasonably resolved from the text alone, there must be an appeal to a medium outside of the text itself (or rather, an internal medium that mediates the text itself) that illuminates what Scripture is and what to value from it. This is Holy Tradition.

For our purpose here, the primary way to note the necessity of Holy Tradition is by the famous verse 2 Timothy 3:16. This declares that all Scripture is *theopneustos*. English translations render *theopneustos* in numerous ways. The NKJV says, "given by inspiration of God." The most famous and supposedly the most literal translation of this is that "All scripture is God-breathed." A fascinating aspect of *theopneustos* is that the term is only found in 2 Timothy 3:16. No other book of the Bible ever uses this term. This makes it a *hapax legomenon*, which literally means "being said once." The usual procedure that scholars undergo to argue for the meaning of a word in Scripture is to first compare its contextual use in a specific verse with its contextual use in other verses. Of course, this does not end debate, if anything it brings more discussion, but it provides a starting ground from which scholarship can begin. Since *theopneustos* and other terms in the category above are only said once, scholars cannot use this as a starting point. Hence, the term *prima facie* or "on the face of it" tells us almost nothing from the text of Scripture alone. I will return to provide what I understand to be a proper Orthodox definition of *theopneustos* at the end of the chapter.

Due to a lack of starting ground for such a controversial verse, this has just stoked the flames more for those, like many Protestants, who argue that the Bible has a unique ontological status that puts it above every other authority and tradition. To put it in syllogistic form, the hypothetical Protestant argues the following:

1. If x is *theopneutsos*, x is the *only* infallible rule of faith
2. Scripture is *theopneustos*;
3. Therefore, Scripture is the *only* infallible rule of faith.

This is a valid argument, but not sound as I will show. From P1, we are already off to a bad start. There is a sneaky presupposition that whatever is *theopneustos* must be an infallible rule of faith. If Scripture is *theopneustos* and thus an infallible rule of faith, it does not necessarily follow that it is the only authority that is *theopneustos* and an infallible rule of faith. Since there is no claim in Scripture that it is the only infallible rule of faith, one cannot justify Scripture as the only infallible rule of faith from the contents of Scripture alone. Moreover, if Scripture is *theopneustos*, this does not itself mean it is an *infallible* rule of faith, let alone the *only* infallible rule of faith. One could very well imagine a divinely-inspired medium that is not infallible; in some weak sense, practically all Orthodox Christians hold that the great Fathers in their commentaries on the Scriptures are divinely-inspired but not infallible.[3] Suffice it to say, the burden of proof is on the Protestant to procure why Scripture is (a) an infallible rule of faith and (b) the *only* infallible rule of faith on the basis of it being *theopneustos*.[4]

---

3. Canon 2 of the Sixth Ecumenical Council, held in 692, declared that twelve bishops have authoritative (canonical) force in the faith for certain influential writings. Figures like St Dionysius of Alexandria, St Athanasius of Alexandria, St Cyril of Alexandria, St Gregory of Nyssa, and especially St Basil the Great were included in this list.

4. The term "infallibility" and its sister term "inerrancy" can be defined in many ways. Those who hold to this term often define it in such a way so as to avoid obvious problems with the claim that Scripture does not teach factual errors about science, history, and cosmology. Since I am largely addressing Protestants here, when I refer

The issue with the opponent's counter-retort is that even serious Protestant scholars recognize that *theopneustos* in the ancient world was not *only* used in reference to Scripture. In what many consider Lee Martin McDonald's most detailed text, *Biblical Canon*, he says there were many examples of non-canonical authors accepted by others to be inspired by the Holy Spirit in their speaking or writing. There is no historical case that the Scriptures were the only ancient writings that were said to be *theopneustos*, nor is there a historical case that being considered *theopneustos* necessarily entails infallibility.[5] A typical example scholars use to illustrate this point is when St Gregory of Nyssa said that God inspired St Basil the Great's "spiritual" exposition of the creation story in Genesis. A century prior, St Justin Martyr likewise believed in a continued mode of divine inspiration when he said that the prophetic gifts of Scripture have been transferred to us (meaning, to Christians of his time). McDonald's statement a few pages later summarizes his scholarly position on the matter. "From these and many other examples, we see that the ancient Church did not limit inspiration to the Scriptures or even to literature alone." This line reiterates his stance in *The Canon Debate* but with a more definitive stature than before. "The traditional assumption that the early Christians believed that only the canonical writings were inspired is highly questionable."[6] As he learned more about the matters at hand through further research, his position became more solidified that *theopneustos* was not used exclusively for canonical writings.

The late Protestant scholar Bruce Metzger, in his famous *Canon of the New Testament*, writes the following on the matter of inspiration in the early Church. "A writing is not canonical because the author was inspired, but rather an author is considered to be inspired because what he has written is recognized as canonical, that is, is recognized as authoritative in the Church."[7] You would think that a scholar like Michael Kruger,

---

to "infallibility" or "inerrancy" in the rest of this chapter, assume I mean the definitions from the famous "Chicago Statement on Biblical Inerrancy" signed by 300 leading Evangelical leaders of the time. These definitions may be a tad outdated since the document was written in 1978, and the specifics are not affirmed by some Protestants, but the gist is certainly there; it's practically impossible to find a more uniformly recognized definition of these terms. For an academic discussion on how certain Christians have wielded these terms to defend a myriad of (often contradictory) positions, see Young, "Protective Strategies," 1–35.

5. McDonald, *Biblical Canon*, 456.
6. McDonald and Sanders, *Canon Debate*, 437.
7. Metzger, *Canon of the New Testament*, 257.

in his often-cited *Question of Canon*, would respond to these claims from McDonald and Metzger. Kruger sought to provide a well-researched Protestant position that the institutional organs of the Church did not have the responsibility for compiling Scripture. Instead, it was a decentralized effort from many people recognizing what is and is not divinely inspired text. He was undoubtedly familiar with McDonald, perhaps even too familiar as his name appears more than fifty times in the text by my count. And yet, there is not a single response to his stance on the issue of *theopneustos* in early writings outside of Scripture, nor any scholar's stance on this issue for that matter.

This brief overview of the scholarship shows that the early Church undoubtedly viewed individuals and non-canonical texts as *theopneustos*. One should note that for the sake of charity I did not rely on Orthodox or Catholic scholars. The goal is to approach Protestants on their own terms, from within their own wheelhouse, to show why 2 Timothy 3:16 is not a valid verse for *sola scriptura*. Accordingly, this is not an argument against *sola scriptura* as a doctrine since that has been done many times and with, I believe, many successes. This argument mainly demonstrates why 2 Timothy 3:16 is not a valid argument for the doctrine, so Protestants should avoid using it. On the other hand, although this does not argue against the doctrine of *sola scriptura* itself, it deconstructs one of the most common arguments made from Scripture for the principle of *sola scriptura*. Therefore, it could be an argument against the doctrine itself. Since this is, admittedly, by many Protestants, the best candidate for a verse in the Scriptures that could demonstrate the biblical veracity of *sola scriptura*. And if *sola scriptura* is not biblical, yet it is assumed to be the principle that guards doctrinal creation, those who hold to it fall into a performative contradiction: They state the Bible is the highest authority that guards doctrinal creation yet believe a doctrine that itself is found nowhere in the Bible; and as seen in the last chapter's discussion of tradition, seems to in fact be partly against the teachings of Scripture. This is to say that *sola scriptura* is an unjustified doctrine from a biblical point of view. Furthermore, since *sola scriptura* is an unjustified doctrine, yet the Reformation, according to the Protestant theologian Gavin Ortlund, understood it to be the "method" of reforming Christian doctrine, perhaps the Reformation is itself wholly unjustified.[8] But that's a different can of worms that will not be discussed further.

---

8. Ortlund, *What It Means to Be Protestant*, 11.

Since other texts outside of Scripture were regarded as *theopneustos* in the early Church, this seems to indicate that rather than translating the verb into English as God-breathed/"life-given," a better translation is something more like God-breathing/"life-giving." While some may be surprised at such an assertion, there are three key justifications. (a) There is no inherent morphological connotation with the verb that would necessarily render it either way.[9] (b) There is strong attestation that it was rendered both ways among early Fathers and non-Christian Greek writings. (c) There are several uses of the semantic domain "life-giving" being rendered actively in the OT (Gen 2:7; Job 33:4; Wis 15:11; Isa 42:5; Ezek 37:5–10; 2 Macc 7:23) as well as one occurrence in the NT (Acts 17:25).[10] If Scripture is God-breathing/life-giving and not God-breathed/life-given, then the argument that God is continually breathing out his Word in the form of councils and other wellsprings of Holy Tradition, makes a further case for itself. Moreover, since we have demonstrated that other non-biblical texts (and people) at the time were considered divinely inspired, this would indicate that there needs to be some other factor that has led to the canonization of the New Testament as we have it today. Indeed, God has assured us of Holy Tradition.

F. F. Bruce, one of the most influential Evangelical scholars of the twentieth century, can be turned to in his *Canon of Scripture* as an example of how far Protestant scholarship has progressed in this debate in just over thirty years. He claims that in 393, a Church council in Hippo set limits on what books (in at least the West) were considered canonical. Then in 397, the Third Council of Carthage, a provincial council, summarized these proceedings. Both councils did not impose innovations on the churches. Instead, they simply endorsed what had become consensus in the West and most of the East.[11] However, what more recent scholarship has shown from McDonald and others is that while there was a difference of opinion in what books were thought to be Scripture in the NT, there were relative boundaries imposed by the Church that determined just how far this divergence was permitted.[12] The vigorous challenge against "heresy" is a partial testament to this.[13] Another is the local organs of Church governance that rendered certain Scriptures

---

9. Much ink has been spilled in philological debates over the end *-tos* of *theopneustos*.
10. Poirier, *Invention of the Inspired Text*, 15.
11. Bruce, *Canon of Scripture*, 138.
12. Evans and Tov, *Exploring the Origins of the Bible*, 228.
13. McDonald, "Forming Christian Scriptures," 136.

viable for pastoral purposes and others not viable. The texts that were not viable were banned from being taught publicly by the local bishop and instead only allowed to be read privately.[14] Accordingly, the canonization process was, at the very least, *relatively* indebted to the Church. It cannot be thought of as solely a decentralized effort made possible by a multitude of people all feeling the Holy Spirit in the exact sort of way that would lead them to believe the NT comprises the twenty-seven books we know today; the first evidence of such a scriptural list containing all twenty-seven books is St Athanasius of Alexandria's *Festal Letter* of 367.[15] Since the Church imposed boundaries on what can and cannot be openly promoted as Scripture, we can likewise see the imposition of why 2 Timothy 3:16 should be rendered as God-breathing.

We can begin to conclude our discussion of why this text should be rendered as God-breathing by putting the verse in context with the ones that come before it. The author begins chapter three by lamenting the difficult times that will soon endure. "Men will be lovers of themselves, lovers of money, and boasters, proud, and blasphemers. . ." He then calls for believers to turn away from these people as they will just bring them into their worldly ways. The next part is key as it indicates what is to come with 2 Timothy 3:16. It reads in the NKJV, "But you have carefully followed my doctrine, manner of life, faith, longsuffering, love, perseverance. . . what persecutions I endured." Through all the hardships Paul endured, he stayed steadfast in his love and faith in Christ. All the things that Paul taught the people he interacted with and what has made us wise through Jesus Christ is then summed up in 2 Timothy 3:16. When put into context with the verses that come before it, we see how the author tries to indicate that the perilous times that we will endure, should not deter us from love and faith in Christ. We must turn away from these people towards the Scripture that is God-breathing/life giving [*theopneustos*]. The Scripture that has inspired and will inspire other divine authorities for ages to come. Scripture is not the final Word of God, as

---

14. The Orthodox Church has maintained this tradition. Many NT apocryphal texts, like *1 & 2 Clement, Gospel of Thomas, Gospel of the Hebrews, Acts of Peter,* and *Gospel of Peter,* are encouraged to be read privately because they possess wisdom and truth. The same goes with several OT apocryphal texts such as *1 Enoch, Jubilees,* and *4 Maccabees.* Because of this, I feel justified in citing several of these texts in this present book to support my theological arguments.

15. Kyrtatas, "Historical Aspects," 30–32. See a survey and commentary on the wide swath of disagreements among Western and Eastern fathers on the biblical canon in Gallagher and Meade, *Biblical Canon Lists from Early Christianity.*

these difficult times will require God to still breathe his inspiration onto authorities, but Scripture serves as God's Word to inspire all later coming authorities that are themselves imparted with the Holy Spirit.

As such, we read a few lines later that Scripture is profitable for doctrine and instruction in righteousness. Scripture is profitable for its continual and abiding presence that will forever remain relevant because Scripture is God-breathing. Scripture is not God-breathed, the past state of inspiration that will forever be set in stone. Scripture is God-breathing, a vitalist and dynamic doctrine that indicates future authorities will also be God-breathing. Indeed, Scripture is part of Holy Tradition. It cannot be separated as the Orthodox Church compiled Scripture and interprets it with the aid of the Holy Spirit. Holy Tradition is necessary to determine the contents of what qualifies as Scripture and clarify the various controversies concerning the Trinity and the Incarnation of Christ. The latter two will be explored in Chapter 3.

To conclude, what is an acceptable Orthodox stance on *theopneustos* concerning Scripture? I take it that God illuminated the human authors of Scripture to express spiritual truths but within their respective cultural and ideological biases. This influenced the words used, images depicted, and concepts enunciated. There is simply no dogmatic commitment to take every word in the Bible as literal, nor is there any dogmatic commitment to understand the text as a whole to be without error. God illuminated the hearts and minds of these authors in one way or another, and it simply must be left as a divine mystery how precise this influence was and the entailments of this influence. A divine mystery is not simply throwing our hands up like a child when their parent asks who ate the last cookie on the counter. A divine mystery—the Latin *sacramentum*—is a visible thing that points and directs us to invisible things. Scripture is a visible thing that points and directs us to ineffable and invisible things: Divine inspiration. There is no way to know what this influence constitutes in any more exact terms than this. It is a fool's errand to be more confident.

3

A Theology of the Incarnation

THE PURPOSE OF THIS chapter is to contextualize universalism in a robust (though brief) theology of the Incarnation. If universal salvation is taught in abstraction from the belief in the Incarnation of Jesus Christ as the Godman who walked the earth, then one's belief in universal salvation should not be deemed a belief in Christian universalism. Hence, out of the desire to ensure that what I am proposing is indeed a *Christian* universalism and not just an amorphous perennialist universalism, I must spend some time working through the fundamentals of the Incarnation. Much of the content of this chapter is controversial, and I recognize this. So, before diving into the controversy and letting the disagreement fly, it is worth briefly laying down some common ground concerning the Trinity. Don't pick up your pitchforks just yet!

God the Father, Jesus the Son, and the Holy Spirit are three hypostases or persons that are one essence as God. The Trinity itself is beyond the concepts of relation, necessity, and dependence. All the members of the Trinity exist in perfection for eternity. There is no process of becoming in the Trinity that would require God to go beyond himself in the form of creating something outside of himself. There is an interior process of becoming, but only in the sense that the Son is eternally begotten and the Spirit eternally proceeds.[1] God has created all things because he saw

---

1. Depending on your adherence to either Western or Eastern Christianity, you would likely attribute the procession of the Spirit to be from the Father and from the

the creation of them as a bountiful expression of his Goodness and Love since he is the Good and Love itself. His ongoing act of creation is an emptying of all that he is into creation, all the while he remains perfect. There is nothing "lost" of God in his creation because he is the fullness and plentitude of being, and his creation subsides in him and with him (Acts 17:28).

The Forerunner and the Mother of All

To discuss the Incarnation, we must first begin with the roles played by two fundamentally important humans in the cosmic narrative of creation. The first of these is St John the Forerunner (the Baptist). Origen was the first to assign John the title of Forerunner. Mirroring the narrative and theme of the story of Hannah, who longed for a son even though she was very old (1 Sam 1–2), Luke's gospel records that John's mother, Elizabeth, and his priestly father, Zechariah, longed for a child even though they were very old in years. John's pivotal role, as understood in the gospels, was to prepare the world for the coming of Christ. Hence, he is considered the connecting point between the prophets of the Old Covenant and the saints of the New Covenant. He is a bridge to the New Covenant. John has the spirit of the prophet Elijah but is not himself the person of Elijah. John explicitly denies being the person of Elijah, but he is the representative of Elijah through the spirit. Since he is the representative of Elijah, John fulfills a prophecy laid out by the prophet Malachi. In Malachi 3:1, God says that he will send a messenger who will "prepare the way" before his coming. In 4:5, God references his past words and says that he will send Elijah. These prophecies are confirmed not only by what John does but also by Jesus later (Matt 17:10–13; Mk 9:11–13). As Malachi prophesied, John ensured the way was prepared for the coming of Christ by baptizing many in the Jordan River so that repentance and good tides would abound with the revelation of the Godman. In a similar way, this mission was posed to Elijah in 1 Kings 19:11–20 after he spoke with the Angel of the Lord. Both men prepared the people for the coming

---

Son (the Latin *Filioque* clause), or you would attribute the procession of the Spirit to be from the Father (the Greek text of the Nicene Creed). I am not one to get too uppity about this debate simply for the reason that I, following several notable hierarchs of the Orthodox Church and Catholic Church, find it to be a semantic disagreement more than anything. See a balanced Orthodox stance on the *Filioque* in Zizioulas, "One Single Source." For a balanced history of the debate, see Siecienski, *Filioque*.

PART 1: ESTABLISHING A THEOLOGICAL BEDROCK

of God. Both figures now sit as members of the divine council to provide intercession and governing for creation, as do all the other saints.

Historians debate the details of John's life and how much of what the gospels portray about John has its basis in history.[2] What is clear is that he was a very influential and righteous Jew of the time who became Jesus' teacher and taught him everything he knew. Outside of the NT, the first-century Jewish historian Josephus is our earliest source on John the Baptist. He refers to his execution by Herod, which is recorded in the NT, and calls him a "just" man. Several of Jesus' most famous teachings likely come from John. This even includes the "Lord's Prayer," the origin of which Jesus explicitly reminds his disciples of in Luke 11:1. Being a faithful disciple of the Forerunner, Jesus' emphasis on worshiping God as the Father, the coming arrival of the Kingdom of God, and the importance of forgiving each other, stem from John's own teachings. It is unlikely that the exact rendition of the "Lord's Prayer" comes from John, but its themes were taught to Jesus before he started his public ministry. Putting aside the historical debate (since there still really is so little information on his life), it is important to recognize the Forerunner and pay homage to his preparatory work in "smoothing" out the path for the coming of our Lord.

The other fundamental human in the Incarnation is Mary, the Holy Theotokos or Holy God-bearer or Holy Mother of God; more room is required to discuss her than the former. Origen was also the first to assign Mary the title of Theotokos.[3] Mary gave herself to the Lord in an act of pure selflessness that she would bear the Savior. Depicted in iconography, Mary's birth of the Savior unites the heavenly and earthly realms. Mary is the symbol of earth because she is a human and is a beacon for the unity of all humans. Christ is the symbol of heaven because he is God. Together, Christ and Mary stand for the perfect union of spirit and nature. The earliest Marian literature points precisely to her being a symbol of unity for all humans. It was rare for writers to deliberately input their heated theological proclivities in these texts.[4] From St Jacob Serugh (non-Chalcedonian) to St Maximus the Confessor (Chalcedonian), Mary served as a point of unity. Christians put aside their differences to unite in admiration of her.

2. See McGrath, *Christmaker* for a recent study on the historical Forerunner.
3. Shoemaker, *Mary in Early Christian Faith*, 71.
4. Shoemaker, *Ancient Traditions*, 271.

A THEOLOGY OF THE INCARNATION

Due to her love of God and as an expression of her perfect liberty, sin did not act as a force in Mary's will. The blessedness that distinguishes her from all other women is attested to in Luke 1:42. Hence, Orthodox Christians glorify Mary for a few reasons: (1) Mary birthed our Lord and Savior; (2) Mary plays an essential role in salvation through universal intercession by guiding and blessing the Church; (3) Mary's ever-virginity places her in the same category of other post-sexual beings like angels. These motifs culminate in her other crucial title: The Queen Mother of Heaven.

The Queen Mother is a typological motif that draws continuity between the OT and NT. In 2 Kings, the Queen Mother of Israel is King Solomon's mother. When her son is away, she rules in his place. She only has authority because of him. In John 2, this is picked up in the case of Jesus. In v. 5, Mary tells the servants to do whatever Jesus tells them to do. Here, she fills the precise role of ruling when the king is not present. The absence of the king, in the case of John 2, is not literal, but a symbolic absence. The people do not know Jesus is the Messiah yet. At the time of this scene, Jesus has not even displayed his first miracle. For those who deny that Mary is the Queen Mother of Heaven, the onus is on them to explain why Jesus, although being in the Davidic line of kingship through his Mother, would break the pattern of having a Queen Mother, rather than, as he did with most Davidic typology, perfect it. Thus, Mary is the perfected archetype of the Queen Mother. In John 19, Mary is then referred to as the mother of John by Jesus, who says this while on the cross. John is the first "adòpted" son of Mary, but as Holy Tradition informs us, all the disciples saw her as a leader and motherly figure. Just as she was the motherly leader of all the disciples, she is the Heavenly Mother of us all.[5] As the Orthodox theologian Elisabeth Behr-Sigel writes, "[Mary] is the archetype and guide of those men and woman who aspire to give birth to Christ in their hearts and who ask her to intercede for them and to call down on them the gift of the Spirit."[6]

We then see the culmination of the Queen Mother motif in Revelation 12. The woman depicted in the image is symbolically Israel, but Mary is the figurehead as well. Mary's crown symbolizes her ongoing role in our spiritual lives as the Queen Mother. A mother who we can turn to for guidance, just as one can only assume John did after Christ's death

---

5. See Coates, "Toward a Hegelian Mariology," for a creative and speculative paper that ties Hegel's Concept in the *Science of Logic* to a traditional Orthodox Mariology.

6. Behr-Sigel, *Ministry of Women*, 207.

on the cross, and who has a special relation to her Son our Lord. While this is the culmination, it is also the depiction of Mary's ongoing role in salvation history. Her intercessions through prayer are more powerful than any other saint. She is "more glorious than the Cherubim and higher than the Seraphim," as pious Orthodox Christians sing in *Agni Parthene*, who guides the Church towards ever-lasting joy and grace as its members grow closer to the Son.

A number of these motifs, like Mary's ever-virginity, are attested to in second-century accounts like the *Protoevangelium of James*, along with later writings of the Fathers that have been passed down, such as St Maximus the Confessor's *Life of the Virgin*, the first full-length biography of Mary. The *Protoevangelium* is the most influential non-canonical text in Orthodox Christianity. In it, we find a number of motifs that have been passed down in tradition—some of which conflict with Scripture itself—but have grown a life of their own in Byzantine iconography and have maintained wide acceptance for centuries in the East. One of the stories that stands out is that Jesus was born in a cave near Bethlehem, rather than in a manger in Bethlehem, like Luke's account, and rather than just in Bethlehem, like Matthew's account. This was the tradition that St Justin Martyr, who was born a hundred years after Jesus died and lived forty miles from Bethlehem, taught and learned from his elders, as it was simply the accepted tradition of the time. Orthodox icons and liturgical texts used in churches during the Christmas Nativity season still often depict this tradition rather than the canonical narrative. Also in the text, we find attestation, accepted in patristic tradition, that St Joseph, the betrothed of Mary, was a much older man who was an experienced widower. This is important because we can understand the role of Joseph in the birth and life of Jesus. Joseph was the perfect father who raised Jesus with a Jewish background and protected him and Mary from a world that was against them.[7] This is hinted at several times in the canonical gospels, notably the flight to Egypt in Matthew's account.

Moving on from the *Protoevangelium*, one final topic about Mary's role in the Incarnation and salvation history must be mentioned. *The Book of Mary's Repose*, a once lengthy "esoteric" text from the late second century that survives only in fragments, and later texts from the fourth century like the *Six Books Dormition* (that has roots in at least the third

---

7. I take it to be very probable that Joseph's old age at the birth of Jesus corresponds with why we do not see him during any point of Jesus' public ministry recorded in the Synoptics. Joseph died when Jesus was young.

century) should come to mind for what follows. Holy Tradition teaches that eleven years after the death of Christ, Mary died a physical death and was then assumed into heaven. In the East, this is known as the Dormition of the Theotokos. When Christ returns and brings all of humanity into joyful union with the Father through the Son, we will enjoy the ontological status that Mary has now, a status of perfected grace and deification. Stephen Shoemaker, a critical scholar with a specialization in Mariology, wrote the following about fifth-seventh-century traditions of Mary's death. "Mary's final state in this narrative seems more like an assumption than not, since Mary's resurrection in Paradise is clearly both *special* and *enduring*."[8] Although he was specifically commenting on a single narrative in this context, he makes it clear toward the beginning of the book that even many of the earliest traditions did not specify exactly what Mary endured after death but there was a relatively common theme that (1) she died while surround by her loved ones and (2) it was special and distinguished from the fate of others.[9] As the scholar on early Christianity Meghan Henning also notes, the distinguished state of Mary seen in the early Dormition narratives is intrinsically tied to her ability to intercede for the faithful.[10]

However, not everyone is convinced by this. Even some pious Christians have turned away from accepting the historical truth of the Dormition solely due to our first written evidence of it being dated late. Yet it's worth noting that late does not necessarily mean false. And as said, the earliest traditions still have their roots in the third century or earlier. The Trinity is an obvious example where late does not necessarily mean false. The Nicene Trinity (the Persons are consubstantial and coeternal with one another) was not what Paul explicitly taught, nor was it explicitly expressed anywhere in the gospels. A trinitarian-like doctrine is taught, but this is far from mature, reeks of so-called subordinationism, and only grew into the dogmatic definition we have today by means of the Holy Spirit working through the Fathers and later the councils.[11]

---

8. Shoemaker, *Ancient Traditions*, 197. My emphasis.
9. Shoemaker, *Ancient Traditions*, 14.
10. Henning, *Hell Hath No Fury*, 142.
11. See a convincing study of proto-Nicene Trinitarianism in the second-century Fathers; the argument being that Origen was the first to explicitly use (in the proper sense) the proto-Nicene language of *hypostasis* which the Cappadocian Fathers inherited from him, in Ramelli, "Origen, Greek Philosophy," 302–50.

PART 1: ESTABLISHING A THEOLOGICAL BEDROCK

For a secular case, take a text like *Lives*. Plutarch wrote over forty biographies about figures who lived hundreds of years before him, and yet we still view him as one of the main sources for several of these, such as Dion, Pelopidas, and even Cleomenes. Many of the other biographies we do not discount, far from it, but we don't think he gets all the facts right concerning them. We prefer modern sources that can engage more with archeological and textual evidence.

A similar and more relevant point can be made about the traditions presented in the *Acts of Thomas*, a late second-century or early third-century text that discusses the apostle St Thomas's journey to and martyrdom in India. The journey was conducted around 50 CE (there was also very likely an earlier one that began in 40 CE), and his martyrdom occurred around 72 CE. Although the most ancient Church in India found so far only dates to the late first century, the pre-existing traditions that form this text give reason to think Christianity landed on India's shores, likely from Alexandria, Egypt, in less than two decades following the death of Christ.[12] While critical scholars are wary about this text, there is solid archeological evidence that makes a plausible case for the core of it being grounded in historical fact as well as there being an ancient community of St Thomas Christians who have maintained with perfect consistency to this day that Thomas established their community in the first century.[13]

The archeological relevance pertains to piles of coins and several documents found in 1834 in the Kabul Providence that bear the name of the first-century Indian ruler Gondophares; before this, the only known attestation of Gondophares was *Acts*, and so many scholars assumed the author of the text fabricated his name out of thin air to add credence to his tale. Scholars are now not so sure the name was fabricated, and it is becoming harder to explain why this text is the only one that includes the name if the stories in it were fabricated. Another discovery that has emboldened this claim is the discovery of the Taxila Cross in 1935 in the ancient city of Sirkap; due to several archeological discoveries in the 1850s, we learned this was the capital of India under Gondophares.[14] Today, St

---

12. There is a very long and positive history of Alexandrian-Indian Christian relations throughout the patristic period. If Thomas were to have sailed from Alexandria, as *Acts* reports, this may explain why these relations were maintained for so long and the desire in the first place for such relations.

13. McDowell, *Fate of the Apostles*, 169–71.

14. See Kurkilamkatt, "Mission of St Thomas," 55–68 for more on the archeological

A THEOLOGY OF THE INCARNATION

Thomas Christians are split into members of Oriental Orthodox churches and Maronite Catholic churches. Many are located in South India, but there is no mention in *Acts* of Thomas ever visiting South India. This lends even more credibility to their claim of descending from Thomas, considering that it seems to be spurred by an independent tradition. It shows that Thomas's travels in India were more expansive than the text purports, which is expected if he truly traveled to India. Moreover, if Thomas went to India, some traditions claim Indonesia and China too, the absence of his name in first-century writings other than John's gospel (written in the 90s) would make sense. Only when other Christians made their way to India could these traditions become known and compiled in the Syriac text *Acts of Thomas*. Personally, I am convinced that this text is not wholesale fabricated, and there are credible reasons to trust the core narrative that Thomas went to India to spread the gospel and, it seems to me, was killed for his troubles by a king; though, the latter claim has somewhat less evidence than the former. And if it wasn't Thomas, the question then becomes, who (or what) brought Christianity to India to the extent that there was—at least, though on a probabilistic account, likely more—one church there by the end of the first century? An apostolic origin makes a better case for itself than the alternative hypotheses. It's worth remembering the ancient historian Plutarch's poignant words: "It is not astonishing that history, when dealing with events of such great antiquity, should wander in uncertainty."[15]

All this is not to say that we have historical certainty of the Dormition. I take it as a matter of faith more than anything, but arguments that point out how late the earliest extant writings of it are, do not refute the argument, nor are they very convincing. Hence, in accordance with some of the earliest accounts of the conditions surrounding Mary's Dormition, as well as later inspired tradition, she is the first human to reach the state completely beyond death and flesh, but she will not be the last.

---

and epigraphic evidence of Thomas's journey to India.

15. Plutarch, *Lives*, 63. Ironically, Plutarch says this in his biography of Lycurgus, which is notoriously viewed by scholars today to be about a man who perhaps never lived, or at least if there was such a man who reformed the Spartan constitution in the eighth century BCE, nothing else is known about him or his reforms outside of this text.

PART 1: ESTABLISHING A THEOLOGICAL BEDROCK

The Incarnate Godman

How did the Trinity interact to bring forth the Incarnation? When God became man, God truly became man. The Father sent the Son and the Son accepted this and took flesh through the procession of the Holy Spirit from the Father. All three hypostases of the Trinity worked together in order to procure the Incarnation. At the Incarnation, many prophecies of the Old Covenant were fulfilled as Jesus was, in the eyes of first-century Jews, the incarnate Angel of the Lord, Wisdom, and the Son of Man. Other key identifications that first-century Jews attributed to Jesus included the Logos,[16] Son of David, Great Archangel,[17] and god-emperor.[18]

---

16. This is most famously seen in the Johannine texts (John's gospel, 1-2-3 John, Revelation) but was also an identification put forward by Paul several times, explored further by the author of Colossians and Ephesians, and magnified in the Letter to the Hebrews. The prologue to John's gospel is perhaps the most famous expression of the Jesus/Logos identification. Richard Bauckham comments, "By identifying Jesus with an entity intrinsic to the divine identity—that is, with God's Word—they include Jesus in that identity without infringing monotheism." See Bauckham, "Monotheism and Christology in the Gospel of John," 151. Before the NT, much attention was paid to the personalization of the Logos. This was seen among Hellenistic Jews like Philo of Alexandria who, although it is not explicit, positions Logos as a personalization of the God of Israel and several times identifies Logos with the God of Israel. See Hadas-Lebel, *Philo of Alexandria*, 181–88.

17. Drawing from Second Temple Jewish texts that mention Metatron, Michael, and other great Archangels, Jesus is identified with angelic motifs in the NT. Paul does this and it is notably seen in the Book of Revelation; both Paul and the author of Revelation employ other identifications with Jesus as well. The identification of Jesus as an Archangel led some early heterodox groups to consider Jesus as an Archangel and nothing more. On the other hand, orthodox Christians likewise referred to Jesus with angelic motifs but did so with the understanding that he was more than just the Great Archangel. See Hurtado, *One God, One Lord*, 85–88.

18. The identification of Jesus with a god-emperor stems from the earliest days of Christian tradition. The Gospel of Mark begins with an Imperial proclamation, "the Good News of Jesus." This was a common phrase used by carriers who announced the coming of an emperor to a new town (John the Baptist being the carrier here). In the second century, the god-emperor motif was both directed against Christians by pagans like Celsus yet also put forward by Christians like St Justin Martyr. Celsus used this as a polemic, like certain scholars do today, to show that Jesus was just another king (i.e., through his Davidic genealogy) who rose to a divine status among cultists after his death. Justin explicitly identified similarities that Jesus had with the stories of Greek emperors turned gods, which was not to validate their godhood, but to show his Greek pagan audience that they are already sort of familiar with who Jesus is. This was done to enjoin pagans to convert to Christianity. In other texts, Justin employed more orthodox identifications of Jesus as well like Logos and Wisdom, presumably to be read by audiences who were already Christian. See Bird, *Jesus Among the gods*, 225–27 for an overview of Justin's Christology.

A THEOLOGY OF THE INCARNATION

The latter four are not in the purview of my brief study below, but several footnotes are provided for interested readers.

The Angel of the Lord is a recurring title in the OT that refers to an entity whose powers and actions are always distinguished from "an angel" or "angels." The Angel of the Lord is seen in Exodus as who talked to Moses in the burning bush and who led Moses and his people out of Egypt. The Angel of the Lord is seen in Judges as who called out to Gideon (6:11). In v. 14, it says that YHWH turned to speak to Gideon. At first Gideon did not recognize this figure and believed him to be human, but a few verses later, he realized the Angel of the Lord was not human. Only when the Angel of the Lord disappeared did Gideon realize it was YHWH. YHWH confirms this in v. 23 when he says that although the Angel of the Lord has departed, I am still here. The Angel of the Lord is also seen in Joshua 5 as who commanded the Israelite army. Throughout the OT, mentions of the Angel of the Lord often accompany an identification with YHWH. As the Orthodox Jewish scholar Daniel Boyarin writes, "There is, indeed, no clear distinction between YHVH and this special Mal'akh."[19] Jews hearing these stories during the Second Temple period recognized this pattern, but once Rabbinic Judaism came along in the third century CE, they were quick to condemn this as a heretical view. In the NT, Christ is confirmed to be the Angel of the Lord in two notable verses. In 1 Corinthians 10, St Paul says that the rock who was with Moses was Christ. Then in Jude 5, in the manuscripts used by most critical editions of the NT today, it says that Jesus saved a people out of Egypt. In Orthodox icons that depict the Angel of the Lord, Christ is most of the time, if not always, in them.

First-century Jews also identified Christ as the Incarnation of Wisdom. Our first key text in the OT is Proverbs 8:22, which identifies Wisdom as the image of God. The start of John's gospel ties directly into this verse and the opening words of Genesis, which say that Christ was "in the beginning." Then there is Wisdom 1:4, which says that Wisdom will not dwell in a body tainted with sin. This ties into the common motif that Christ was born without sin. Then there is Wisdom 7:28, which says that God loves nothing as much as one who dwells in/with Wisdom. Christ is the Incarnation of Wisdom and God the Father loves nothing more in the world than him. We may also mention the first few stanzas of Sirach, which reiterate that Wisdom is one with God and with him before all

---

19. Boyarin, *Jewish Gospels*, 167.

time. But all these motifs were by no means consistent in the OT. While Wisdom has creative and ruling powers, there is ambiguity regarding whether Wisdom is a divine personification of God or a created entity of God.[20] Sometimes, in the Book of Wisdom and Sirach, for example, Wisdom seems to be a divine personification. At other times, Wisdom is clearly a created entity that is not coterminous or co-equal with God.

Putting this issue aside, the identification of Christ with Wisdom stuck for St Paul and other NT authors. First Corinthians 1:24 in the NKJV reads, "To those who are called, both Jews and Greeks, Christ the power of God and the wisdom of God." First Corinthians 2:7 in the NKJV reads, "We speak the wisdom of God in a mystery, the hidden wisdom which God ordained before the ages for our glory." Then there are the words in Colossians 1:15–17 that refer to Christ as the firstborn over all creation who holds all things together. There is also the identification of Jesus with Wisdom in Hebrews 1:3. This identification was also readily picked up by some of the earliest Fathers like St Justin Martyr and St Clement of Alexandria. Today in the Orthodox Church, several icons identify Christ with Wisdom, such as the Icon of Wisdom. This is commemorated on September 8 and depicts a woman with wings as the Angel of Wisdom who represents Jesus as Holy Wisdom.

The last identification apparent to first-century Jews was Jesus as the Son of Man. The first mention of the Son of Man in the OT is found in Daniel 7. At the end of his vision, Daniel says that he saw "one like the Son of Man" riding on a cloud and this figure was given all sovereignty. The "like" here is crucial because Daniel does not outright identify this mysterious figure as a man. The figure appears like a man but is not a mere man. When put in its proper cultural context, the vision makes sense. In ancient paganism, a figure was identified to be divine when they were depicted as riding on a cloud. This was seen in myths about the Mesopotamian god Ba'al and various early narratives surrounding the Greek god Zeus. Since divinity was signified in this infantile way, it was quite common for contradictory stories to come about in these pagan myths. According to Fr Stephen De Young, the story from Daniel is a polemic or mockery of sorts to the pagan depictions that the author was

---

20. Bird, *Jesus among the Gods*, 97; Hurtado, *One God One Lord*, 42. Hurtado's engagement with Wisdom should be critiqued for not adequately positioning its role in the background of Hellenistic philosophy as well as not discussing the clear parallels that the use of Logos/Wisdom in John's prologue shares with the Logos as understood in the writings of Jewish figures like Philo of Alexandria.

A THEOLOGY OF THE INCARNATION

undoubtedly familiar with.[21] Daniel meant to express two central messages: (1) The Son of Man is divine. (2) The Son of Man is the one who *actually* has power over all things and not the pagan deities like Ba'al. Both of these were picked up in later Jewish literature like *1 Enoch*. In *1 Enoch* 46, imagery from Daniel 7 is used to depict the Son of Man as a heavenly entity who was intimately associated with the actions and knowledge of God but was distinct from the rest of heavenly beings. Since the NT writers were familiar with this text along with the Scriptures, it is expected that they would record stories that involved this motif. Although Jesus rarely refers to himself as the Son of Man, all mentions of the Son of Man in the NT are presumably a self-confirmation by Jesus.

An exemplary case of this is in Mark 14. There are many others, but this shall suffice for the purpose of this chapter. The scene records that Jesus is on trial and he is asked if he is the Messiah. He responds, "I am" and then references the depiction in Daniel 7 by saying that he will come on the clouds as the Son of Man and procure judgment over all. There is an extreme reaction from the official hearing this. He proceeds to accuse Jesus of blasphemy. This may tell us that the Son of Man was believed to be a divine figure of some sort at the time. As the Jewish scholar Alan Segal notes, if we assume this is an accurate portrayal of events, then the official seems to be under the impression that Jesus is confirming that he is YHWH in some sense.[22] There are other confirmations in the NT by Jesus that he is the Son of Man, but these do not provide certainty that the Son of Man was thought to be divine under this context (Matt 24:30; Lk 21:27). Jesus may have been referring to himself in this way for any number of reasons. Regardless, these brief observations make it clear that the NT establishes continuity between the Son of Man motif and Jesus.

The Person of Jesus is not just the Angel of the Lord, Wisdom, or the Son of Man. His presence on earth shows how all these motifs were pointing, in their own way, to the Second Hypostasis of the Godhead. Not exactly, mind you, as Nicene Christology did not develop until the late second century, but certainly, these implicit motifs gave way to the later explicit theological inspirations that identify Christ as the Second Hypostasis of God. First-century Jews who became followers of Jesus picked up on these theological elements, and while they did not hammer everything out in precise brevity, they laid the sketch that later tradition

---

21. De Young, *Religion of the Apostles*.
22. Segal, *Two Powers in Heaven*, 95.

held up by Gentiles would happily fill in; albeit, with some notable bumps on the road to Nicaea and even after.

The Atonement of Christ

For more than a thousand years after the death of Christ, few sought to answer *why* God sent his Son to earth. The Fathers debated the effects of the Incarnation and what has changed in the order of creation, but few came out swinging with a surefire reason for *why* Christ became incarnate. Around the eleventh century, several figures in Catholic circles began to pose this question. Anselm of Canterbury was one of the first to ask: *Cur Deus homo?* (Why did God become man?) Building on Anselm's attempt to answer this, later theologians and then eventually the Reformers gave their own answers. The story of atonement they gave (though it was not what Anselm originally argued) developed into what is commonly known as penal substitutionary atonement (PSA).

PSA assumes a God that is the projection of a judge, the Highest Judge, if you will. Since a judge looks for an exact payment that is fit for a crime if you have wronged a judge through disobeying his law, God looks for an exact payment that is fit for a crime if you have wronged him by disobeying his law. Since we, as humanity, have all wronged him by bearing the brunt of Adam's transgression, God seeks that payment.[23] Since God isn't a finite judge, but he is an infinite judge, any wrong that is done to an infinite judge can never be paid back by an amount that is finite. Hence, God had to pay himself back for the sins of the world by sending himself as his only Son. When God sends himself as his only Son, and then pays himself back, this payment is exchanged by means of wrath being transferred from the Father to the Son. As the Calvinist James Strachan phrases it, which is basically standard across the board, "The Father actively poured out His wrath on the Son [. . .] The Father rendered his Son legally guilty for us in his courtroom, sentencing him to death."[24] As he says later, with no less emotional endearment, Jesus felt the full weight of the Father's just condemnation.[25] The Son was the ransom payment and now that the ransom is paid, there is nothing left for us

---

23. Much of the scriptural warrant for PSA stems from a poor reading of Romans 5:12 that was inherited through the Augustinian tradition. I discuss this briefly in Chapter 5.

24. Strachan, *Warrior Savior*, 34.

25. Strachan, *Warrior Savior*, 170.

to pay God. All we have to do is accept God. The Son took the substitution for the wrath that the Father would have poured out on humanity. The Son saved us all from the Father's wrath. This is why we worship and revere him.

There are several presumptions that must be accepted for PSA to be sound. Many of these are foreign to Orthodoxy and, more importantly, are absurd. Four are worth briefly mentioning here.

First, God must pay himself back. DBH summarizes the problem with this. According to PSA, the fee of sin was a price paid to the Father. The price was paid by Jesus. Jesus is thus like a coin of a circular transaction: God buys off God in order to spare his own displeasure. Think about it in terms of a bank. A bank has issued credit to itself to pay off a debt it owes to itself by employing a currency it has created for this occasion and it certifies the value of this currency on the basis of the credit it is paying off to itself.[26] John Calvin would even agree with a bank-like analogy for the death of Christ as he called it a "wondrous exchange" between man and God. But this analogy is clearly absurd. A bank cannot issue credit to itself to pay itself back in any way that actually creates value in the transaction. This is to say that there is no value created by God paying off the credit he wrote to himself.

Second, substitution should be allowed for punishment. According to PSA, Jesus has put himself in as the substitute to receive the punishment of the Father that should be doled out on humanity for their sins. The problem here is that the notion of substitutional punishment or sacrifice is absolutely nonsensical. If I were a Father and I wanted to punish my son for stealing a cookie from the cookie jar, but then my other son came out of nowhere and volunteered the punishment to be enacted on him, I would not be a good Father if I were to punish my son who did nothing wrong. But humans have done much more than steal from cookie jars, the Calvinist whines. Indeed, suppose then that my son is tried for murder and the state is about to sentence him to death row. Suddenly, his brother, my other son, who is sitting in the back of the courtroom, leaps to his feet and shouts, "Send me to death instead!" There is not a single judge in the entire world who would shrug their shoulders and allow this substitution to occur in a situation *ceteris paribus* or all else equal. (There are some truly comical attempts at responding to analogies like this by pointing out states of exemption in judicial law; for instance,

26. DBH, *That All Shall Be Saved*, 26.

PART 1: ESTABLISHING A THEOLOGICAL BEDROCK

suppose the defendant has a life-altering disability. There are, according to such arguments, certain areas of the industrialized world where judicial laws, specifically property laws, are lenient enough such that an able-bodied volunteer could receive the punishment, say, a fine, instead of the disabled defendant. I hope I don't need to explain the *ad hoc* and disanalogous nature of this argument. I'll leave that for the reader to ruminate on.)

Returning back to the point at hand then, since God is the most good Father, he would not punish the Son for something the Son did not do wrong. And even the Highest Judge, then, would be woefully inept at their judicial practice if they were to allow such a substitution to occur; as Friedrich Nietzsche wrote, one can only assume while fancifully laughing, God the creditor played scapegoat for his debtor, "out of love (can you believe it?)"[27] Yes, somehow, there are (allegedly) cognitively healthy people who do believe this. How that may be is almost as much of a mystery as the Incarnation itself.

Third, God the Father can only punish God the Son in his humanity but not his Godliness. The presumption here is that the Father can subject the Son to an action that only affects his human nature but not his divine nature. The philosophical problem with this is that every action an individual does or is done to them is done by their person or done to their person, not their nature. Suppose there is a person who has a human nature. Suppose the person is driving to work, and a car hits them from behind on the interstate. The person who was hit in their car, is just that, a person. They are human, so they possess a human nature, but their human nature is not *who* was hit in their car. Following this logic, the substitutionary action must be done by the Person of Jesus (the Person of Jesus must die), not his human nature. This must mean, then, that the Godman himself died. And he did. This can be accepted by someone who does not affirm PSA, but it is harder for a proponent of PSA to avoid the logical incoherence that arises from mixing up "person" and "nature." An incoherence that, due to its gravity, was dogmatically condemned at the Council of Ephesus (431) and the Council of Chalcedon (451).

Fourth, the Incarnation was Plan B. Since the Incarnation was done to save the world from its sins, which required a substitution of the Son to bear the wrath of the Father, the PSA proponent must argue that the Incarnation was not eternally planned but rather was a decision made

---

27. Nietzsche, *On the Genealogy of Morals*, 78.

by the Father because of what was occurring in creation. God, then, becomes like a road service worker who visits the scene of a car crash. To put this argument in a cartoonish way, it is as if God the Father were to say, "Dang humans, you guys have caused a lot of sin in the world. There is so much sin that no one human can take on the brunt of my punishment (which I must delve out because I am the Highest Judge or something). Eureka! I shall send my Son, and (somehow) this will solve the problem!" There are two further problems with this presumption. Since PSA posits the Incarnation as Plan B, it contradicts the narrative in Acts 2 and 4 as well as Ephesians 3:11, the latter of which explicitly identifies the plan for the Incarnation as "before all worlds" employing the polysemic adjective *aiōnion* (see Chapter 9 for a discussion on this term). And it is worth mentioning that the idea that the Incarnation was Plan B was generally rebuked both in the East and West until at least the late Scholastic period when it gained prominence. Whether the Fall did or did not happen is of no matter because the Incarnation would happen regardless. The Incarnation was not in the slightest predicated on the entrance of sin into the world.

Any of these presumptions taken by themselves would render PSA dubious. Altogether they make the argument untenable. Suffice it to say that PSA is not a cogent, let alone accurate understanding, of the spiritual meaning behind the Incarnation and death of Jesus Christ.

Orthodox theology is opposed to viewing the Incarnation like this, but some argue that certain early Eastern Fathers like St Athanasius of Alexandria, St John Chrysostom, and St Basil the Great supported PSA. This mischaracterization stems from a reading of these figures that is alienated from how Greek thought developed and the specific language used to convey particular concepts. Moreover, it often reads into the Fathers beliefs drastically distinct from anything they taught. These Fathers and many later ones employed the language of "substitution" but did not think of this as a transaction nor did they think of this as the Father punishing the Son. Anselm, for all the rightly dreadful statements that can be made about his atonement theory, did not even broach such a horrifying claim. Early Fathers like Athanasius and Basil thought substitution entailed that the debt was paid to the condition of our death or, unfortunately, in the case of Origen and St Gregory of Nyssa, Satan. The idea is not that Jesus gave himself as a "ransom" to the Father, rather he overcame human captivity to sin and death through his substitution. In a sense, then, Jesus did give himself as a manumission fee or liberatory fee

PART 1: ESTABLISHING A THEOLOGICAL BEDROCK

[*antilytron*][28] à la 1 Tim 2:5–6, it just wasn't to any Person or entity. While still accepting this basic narrative of substitution, Orthodoxy stands out from the pack by adopting a more hopeful and deeper metaphysical purpose for the Incarnation and death of Christ. The atonement does not only refer to his death on the cross. His entire life on earth is the period of atonement. The central message is that of *theosis* or divinization. This will be returned to after discussing the resurrection below, but the main point is that humans in this life can become divinized through participation in God. The death of Christ redeemed humanity. In a redeemed state, humanity can participate in becoming like God. This is thought in an ontological sense, that is, humans become ontologically more god-like. Humans become more like the One.[29] This redemption brought about through the Incarnation was not merely bestowed on humanity. All of creation is caught up in this ongoing process of divinization. Animals, fish, plants, you name it. All beings are growing in glory. As St Maximus the Confessor refers to it, the consequence of the Incarnation is an ongoing cosmic deifying process.

Way before Maximus, we see an early iteration of this tradition in the second-century text *Acts of Peter*. The text is best understood as an ancient novella—rather than a Greco-Roman biography like the Synoptic gospels (Matthew, Mark, Luke), see the next section—since it mixes a core historical narrative with clear legendary embellishments to form an entertaining story for a respective audience. At one point, it famously records that when St Peter was taken to be crucified in Rome, he asked to die upside-down on a cross. Some doubt the historical accuracy of this account due to the so-called legendary elements surrounding it, such as miracles. Some also doubt its historical accuracy because the narrative can be seen to fit a clear apologetic purpose. As Candida Moss notes, from the perspective of a historian, associating Rome with martyrdom aided Rome in bolstering its claims about being the center for grievances

28. Many English translations wrongly render this "ransom," which only supports the PSA hypothesis. This makes it seem like Jesus was given as a ransom payment to the Father or, on some early accounts, to a malevolent demonic force.

29. As Fr Andrew Louth notes, the association of "oneness" with "atonement" tracks back to the earliest etymological meaning of similar verbs in Middle English. Atonement itself, used in a theological context, only dates back to William Tyndale's translation of the Bible. Atonement is one of the very few theological terms that originated in the English language. However, Middle English verbs etymologically associated with "to atone" date back much further. Verbs that are similar to "to atone" literally mean "one-ment," that is, becoming one with God. See Louth, "Eastern Orthodox View," 19–44.

and persecution against Christians.[30] The prerogative for dying in this way makes at least theological sense, even if you do not buy that Peter was crucified on specifically an upside-down cross (less deny he died in Rome). Since the cosmos was already being redeemed through Christ's death on the cross, a right-side-up cross, if Peter was to experience crucifixion like his Savior, he wanted to experience it in an upside-down way. He wanted to approach the world upside-down since the world was turned upside-down by the nature of sin. This view of the cosmos was a symbol of the world before Christ and this allowed Peter to edify his faith even more in the cosmic redemption efforts of Jesus.

Moving away from this text, the idea of divinization should also lead us to recall the theme of "rest" in Scripture. To be at rest is the enshrined goal for all creation. Deuteronomy 12:9 in the NKJV reads, "For as yet you have not come to the rest and the inheritance which the Lord your God is giving you." Psalm 127:2 in the NKJV reads, "He grants rest to those He loves." Throughout the NT and later apocrypha, a similar concept can be found. In Matthew 11:28, Christ tells those with burdens to come to him because he gives rest. Hebrews 4:10 indicates a similar point. A saying of Jesus in the early *Gospel of the Hebrews* goes so far as to tie together the kingly status of "reigning" with that of rest.[31] Those who receive the kingly status will rest. Rest is the cosmic *telos*. Rest, in this sense, does not mean literal rest, as everything in creation stops moving. When creation is fully divinized, nothing will feel the spiritual sense of struggling between Good and evil because evil will no longer be present.

God did not have to give himself to us in order that we would become like him. The Incarnation was not propagated by necessity. As early as the second century, great theologians like St Irenaeus of Lyon argued that God became incarnate due to his love that seeks to make us become like him.[32] God sent his Son as a pure gift of peace and reconciliation. When a good person gives a gift, they do not expect payment back. Since God is the Good itself, he did not expect payment back. Even the proponent of PSA knows that our payment will never be enough to appease God. Accordingly, the Orthodox view strips away all talk of payment. The death of Christ is a *gift* without a receipt (Rom 6:23).

30. Moss, *Ancient Christian Martyrdom*, 78.
31. Elliot, *Apocryphal New Testament*, 6.
32. Irenaeus, *Scandal of the Incarnation*, 56.

PART 1: ESTABLISHING A THEOLOGICAL BEDROCK

To use Heideggerian language as a change of pace, the death of Christ is the Clearing [*Lichtung*] to the Truth of cosmic reconciliation. Having lived and wrote for much of his career in the German Black Forest, Martin Heidegger knew the sublime exuberance of seeing a clearing in the forest—the sun shining on a plot of land that is otherwise encircled by foreboding trees and shadows—and he incorporated such an experience into his phenomenology of Dasein; the human being with an openness and connectedness to Being as such. The Clearing for Dasein is their everyday accompaniment of new experiences and perceptions that they embark upon; yet in some sense, Dasein is itself the Clearing since Dasein is the being that brings out entities and objects so that they may emerge out of the concealment of reality. It is these moments in our lives, those where a Clearing has occurred, that feel as if a light has shone down on the shadows of our world and brought with it the potential for new knowledge and experience.

The crucifixion is the archetype and epitome of the Clearing. The crucifixion has unconcealed everything that was once concealed. The eternally persisting relationship between humanity and God (say, call it Sophia) has been revealed, and humans are no longer to be viewed as, in Heideggerian language, "standing-reserves," that is, servants of a God who is indifferent to them and uses them as he wishes; far from it. Humans are to be viewed as infinitely valued participants in the story of creation. Irenaeus writes, "At the beginning of our formation in Adam the breath of life which comes from God was united to what had been formed, animated man, and showed him to be a rational animal, so, at the end, the Word of the Father and the Spirit of God, united to the ancient substance of Adam's formation, made man living and perfect, capable of knowing the perfect Father."[33] Hence, this is why we reject the legalistic PSA: The death of Jesus was not an exchange, a simple bank transaction between God and man. The coming of Christ made the process of deification for the entire universe possible—a process that is not in some far-off eschatological plane of existence—but rather has always-already been occurring since the Incarnation.

---

33. Irenaeus, *Scandal of the Incarnation*, 58.

Christ Has Risen!

It is here where the importance of the resurrection comes into play. Christianity without a resurrection story is an empty faith (1 Cor 15:14). Many apocalyptic rabbis lived in first-century Judea, were rejected by the majority of Jews, and killed by Jewish officials with institutional support from the Roman state. Many of these rabbis traveled to various cities and claimed they could perform miracles. Yet only one of these preachers resurrected from the dead and then ascended into heaven. From the beginning, Christianity has always been a "resurrection religion." Indeed, this is what the apostles who were martyred (five is a fair estimate) went down proclaiming. But the ascension is not the conclusion of Jesus' ministry on earth. The ascension is instead the commencement of his Kingly ministry. The resurrection is a story of hope, an unconditional promise. The promise that because Jesus has risen, our sins are forgiven. Because Jesus has risen, we may experience a life of sacrifice, but we should never fear losing ourselves. The gospel, through the resurrection story, offers an unconditional promise that we know will be fulfilled at the end of days when we are resurrected into our spiritual bodies, described by St Paul in various places.

Some theologians like William Lane Craig approach the resurrection from a historical framework, what is often known as "positivistic" historiography. They believe that the actual event of the resurrection can and should be justified by an appeal to the historical tools that historians use on a daily basis. He writes, "The historical evidence for the resurrection of Jesus consists primarily in the evidence supporting three main facts: The empty tomb of Jesus, the reported appearances of Jesus to his disciples, and the origin of the Christian faith."[34] The issue with Craig's and any other scholar's historical approach to the resurrection is that the scholarly consensus changes over time. When Craig wrote this text towards the end of the 1980s, the consensus in scholarship was that there indeed was an empty tomb. However, in the last five years, several prominent scholars have rescinded these claims and are now skeptical of the empty tomb narrative. This is largely due to Paul's omission of this in his letters. For reasons like this, Orthodoxy tends to avoid this whole debate and leave the event of the resurrection as a holy mystery. A holy mystery does not mean we cannot make any historical claims about the event of the resurrection, but it does mean that we don't tend to focus

---

34. Craig, *Son Rises*, 39.

on doing so. Rather than make historical claims and then bicker with secular authorities who seek to disprove the Christian story, we leave it as a mystery.

But let's back up for a second. In general, when establishing the exact historicity of events in the gospels, it is best to proceed with caution. Did Jesus say exactly this or that? Did Jesus go to this place at this specific time? What the sayings of Jesus provide in the Synoptic gospels is a summary of content that is rolled up into a number of texts that share common motifs. As James Dunn put it, the gospels should be studied for their ability to recover the "very own voice" of Jesus, even if his "very own words" are impossible to verify.[35] Still, sometimes the texts may be very close to what Jesus said. After all, disciples of rabbis during the time of Jesus were expected to memorize the Scriptures front-to-back so that they could then become rabbis and teach others. Compared to the length of the Torah, which is hundreds of thousands of words, the gospels are only about thirty thousand. There is certainly a likelihood that stories of what Jesus said could have been authentically passed down by word-of-mouth and then written down eventually. There are many literary devices that show a memorized account that was controlled, though relatively loosely, by members of the early Jesus movement.

A transmission like this makes sense if, indeed, as I tend to argue, the authors of the Synoptics had access to multiple eye-witness testimonies, especially Mark and Luke;[36] as well as Matthew and Luke having relied on that early lost collection of sayings [*logoi*] known as Q, that at times intersects with Mark's gospel and at other times provides new information unknown by Mark, that Luke and Matthew were able to use. The Q-hypothesis probably derives its greatest evidence from the fact that we

---

35. Dunn, *Jesus Remembered*, 226.

36. Luke's historical acumen is well-acknowledged by scholars. While there are some skeptics who doubt Luke sought to fairly compile past sources about Jesus' life together (and the life of the early apostles), most scholars, even if they do not think Luke was a successful historian, do not doubt that he sought to be a successful historian; as attested to in Luke 1:3. At the very least, most scholars concur with Martin Hengel. "Luke is no less trustworthy than other historians of antiquity." Hengel, *Acts*, 60. This is not to say, as some like Richard Pervo have argued, that Luke *borrowed* information from historians like Josephus, which would necessarily entail that Luke was writing sometime after the 90's. I believe this argument has been shot down definitively. See Armstrong, *Dating Acts*, 84–94. Luke was a reliable historian trained in some informal or perhaps even formal capacity in historiography. To see a defense of Luke's account of the shipwreck narrative (Acts 27), which skeptics routinely put in favor of him being an unreliable historian who relied on Homeric motifs, see Keener, *Acts*, 3555–67.

still have early copies of *logoi* gospels such as the *Gospel of Thomas*, which dates to either the early or mid-second century, as well as a citation from Paul, written down by St Luke, of what he understood to be a Jesus saying that is found nowhere in the gospels we have today (Acts 20:35). I am not one to flat out disagree that at least some of the sayings attributed to Jesus in the *Gospel of Thomas* could very well be authentic, as some certainly come from an independent Aramaic oral tradition to the Synoptics, and share many parallels with Synoptic materials from Matthew, Mark, and Luke.[37] The influence of John is certainly present as well, especially in the most "esoteric" and monistic statements the text attributes to the mouth of Jesus. Likely, then, the Q source that Matthew and Luke used was similar in structure to this collection of sayings.[38]

Some sayings Jesus probably repeated over and over, such as the parables. This would track with what we know about typical practice between rabbis and their students during this period. Sayings that are constantly repeated are much easier to memorize than statements that Jesus made once or twice. This shouldn't be surprising at all. Jesus certainly did not make up new sayings every time he went to a new town. The disciples were well-equipped to memorize his sayings due to their familiarity with hearing them for, if we take the estimate in John's gospel as historically authentic, around three years. But, before I get too controversial here, I must remind the reader that paraphrased motifs are certainly not grounds for rejecting the historicity of the gospels. Scholars of all theological stripes accept that the Synoptic gospels are the greatest existing source for the life of Jesus. There are just many disputes about what precisely is historical in those texts.

A very liberal but still serious scholarly position today might read as follows: What we can historically know about Jesus is that he lived as

37. For a negative evaluation of the significance of *Gospel of Thomas* for study on the historical Jesus, see Gathercole, *Gospel of Thomas*, 177–84. Gathercole is right to note that the text displays a lack of knowledge about the geography, currency, and daily life of Judeans at the time of Jesus. Still, I believe there is a historical core.

38. See Kloppenborg, *Q*, 106–11 for an overview of the textual similarities between Q and *Gospel of Thomas*; this does not necessarily mean one relied on the other, but rather that both were following similar oral traditions like the Synoptics. Many passages in *Thomas*, even if they are claimed to be from the mouth of Jesus, cannot possibly stem from before the creation of monastic culture in Christianity. Much more attention is paid towards the importance of monasticism than would be expected if it were early; and there are proto-Gnostic elements from the beginning of the text onwards that do not find parallel in any of the Synoptic materials, and thus were almost certainly not said by the historical Jesus of Nazareth.

PART 1: ESTABLISHING A THEOLOGICAL BEDROCK

an impassioned apocalyptic preacher who was baptized by the renowned Jew John the Baptist and who later traveled from town to town with a number of disciples, and was known for his miraculous healings and speaking memorable wisdom-sayings, and at some point in his life began to see himself as a messianic figure who would save Israel; and after clearing out a good portion of moneychangers from the temple (which occurred at the end of his ministry, not the start or both), he was arrested, imprisoned, and then crucified on a cross that bore the words "King of the Jews," and was thought by his closest followers to have risen from the dead when reports soon after began to circulate that he was alive, which were subsequently picked up by those inside and outside Jerusalem, several of whom were martyred for testifying to the truth of this message in the years following. Long gone are the days of liberal scholars claiming, like Rudolf Bultmann famously did in the 1940s, that all we can historically know about Jesus is that he lived, preached, and died by crucifixion. Or even the days of the Jesus Seminar in the 1990s, whose members confidently drew a black marker through any verses in the gospels that they thought were totally ahistorical (crossing out all but four verses in John's gospel); such a methodology, even with their more nuanced categories, now defies what we know about the spread of the gospels through collective oral tradition, as it is far too much of an atomistic approach that we would never use for any other ancient document.

A very conservative but still serious scholarly position might hold that the gospels follow a "reportage model" and overall accurately transcribe the words and deeds of Jesus with rare literary embellishments on behalf of the author. This means that what we can historically know about Jesus corresponds very substantively to the narrative described in the Synoptic gospels (with likely several or more details added in or removed based on traditions from John's gospel). I tend to identify more with scholars who responsibly flirt with positions in both camps, less on the extremes of either. In any case, like all ancient Greco-Roman biographies, the focus of the gospel authors was less on figuring out what *exactly* happened, as you may find in a contemporary historical text, but rather on establishing a common theological narrative, developing the story around a single protagonist who is the primary subject of the main verbs of the book, and developing the character traits of both the figures involved who surrounded the protagonist in their life and the protagonist themselves.

A THEOLOGY OF THE INCARNATION

In the words of the second-century BCE historian Polybius of Megalopolis, who probably innovated on the historiographical standards of the fifth-century BCE historian Thucydides, a bare historical account of facts without a narrative to go along with it is an "accomplished essay, but not a lesson, and while pleasing for the moment [...] is of no possible benefit for the future."[39] Whether or not the authors of Matthew and Mark were knowledgeable of ancient historiographical standards is debatable. In the case of Mark, that answer may be negative, but there is no doubt that Luke was very aware of these standards and sought to employ them in both his gospel and Acts. Put more succinctly, Luke sought to record a historical account to the best of his ability while maintaining a theologically driven narrative. Overall, this attitude of leaning into a theological narrative as well as developing the traits of your characters is what we see in the accounts of Jesus' resurrection. No account in the NT rejects the event of the resurrection. There are just different accounts of what exactly occurred in light of the core truth that Jesus unexpectedly rose from the dead.[40] Because of this, I embrace Origen of Alexandria's so-called "polymorphic" understanding of the risen Jesus. He writes, "Jesus was not seen in the same way by all who beheld him."[41] This leaves open all sorts of possibilities regarding how Jesus appeared and what he did when he appeared, even going so far as to allow contradictions between claims of the risen Christ; after all, why should we expect our fallen minds to coherently categorize such a miraculous event? Perhaps Jesus appeared much more as a fleeting apparition to some while as a substantial-bodied figure to others, and perhaps not even the same substantial-bodied figure to everyone.[42]

---

39. Polybius, *Histories*, 3.31.

40. N. T. Wright aptly notes, "It is not that someone believes in Jesus' resurrection and now finds an empty tomb to confirm that belief; it is, rather, that they have found an empty tomb and are offered the startling and totally unexpected explanation that Jesus has been raised." Wright, *Resurrection of the Son of God*, 628.

41. *Contra Celsum*, 2.64.

42. Celsus's Christian source that Origen is dealing with in *Contra Celsum* claims that Peter encountered Jesus in a dream. There are no known literary texts related to this tradition. This can mean it either originated from that person (which is unlikely), or it can mean that it was a known tradition that person inherited from an older generation (this is more likely). More interestingly, the *Acts of Peter* records a tradition that the disciples who gathered did not all see Jesus in the same way. Everyone saw the Uncreated Light, but in the Light, some saw Jesus as an old man, others saw him as a young man, and still others saw him as a boy who touched their eyes. To the author of the *Acts*, this contradiction was of no worry since Peter then begins praising the Lord all

With all that said, I take a historical reconstruction of the resurrection to be along the lines of the following. Early in the morning, three days after Jesus was crucified, several female followers of Jesus went to the tomb of Jesus, hoping to anoint the body, but did not find the body in the tomb. They did not find the body of Jesus because Jesus had risen. Jesus first appeared to St Mary Magdalene. Over several episodes, Jesus spent time with his twelve disciples, first spending time with certain ones (perhaps not all) individually and then with all of them, as well as engaging with them in several activities. He later appeared in front of a crowd with at least five hundred people; men and (very probably) women were included in this count.[43] Many other events involving the risen Christ very well could have occurred either before or after the appearance to the five hundred; John 21:25 states an obvious truth in hyperbolic language. Finally, how long Jesus remained on earth before his ascension should remain an open question due to the many diverging traditions in the early Church. I hazard a modest guess at anywhere between forty days and more than a year.

In the eyes of contemporary scholarship, the resurrection appearance in front of the crowd is the most trustworthy historical data we have from some of the so-called legendary accounts in Scripture. By my lights, this reasoning is based on three strong points. (1) The impossibility of multiple people experiencing the same hallucination involving more than a single sense;[44] (2) The sheer number of people involved in this

---

the same. Why should it be a worry to us today? We shall praise the Lord all the same.

43. See arguments about how to interpret *adelphois* here, taking into account the standard Pauline use, in Graieg, *Resurrection Remembered*, 56–60. Graieg considers it "likely" that women were included in the credal tradition recording of the appearance to the five hundred. After considering the tendency of the Synoptic materials to document the participation of women in resurrection appearances (a criterion of embarrassment for ancient readers; see below), I conclude that this argument holds a lot of evidential weight.

44. I argue that the most devastating argument against the hallucination hypothesis is that there has never once been a single recorded case of hallucination which has involved more than one sense at a time and that was also shared in the same way by more than one person. As we see in the gospel accounts, and perhaps vaguely in the credal record of 1 Corinthians 15, more than one sense is being used at a given time and those same sense-experiences are often being shared by more than one person. Many Christian apologetics arguments go awry in the claim that multiple senses cannot experience hallucinations at the same time. Recent psychological work has done a lot to debunk this myth, but it prevails in the public consciousness. The rare phenomenon is now known as "multimodal hallucinations" where two modalities or senses are affected by hallucinations that stem from one source. For more on this phenomenon, see Montagnese et al., "Multimodal Hallucinations," 237–48. For an empirical study

attestation (said to be still alive at the time of Paul's writing, which presumably was said so that the receiver of the letter could verify this with them if they so pleased); (3) The early date assigned to this oral tradition. Paul reports on the appearance in 1 Corinthians 15:3–7. Mike Licona does well to argue the priority that historians should (and often do) give to Paul's account:[45] (a) Paul is the earliest known author to mention the resurrection of Jesus. (b) The letters of Paul are the only verifiable reports by a verifiable eyewitness of the risen Jesus. (c) Paul's account was from the position of someone who was an extreme enemy of the Church at the time. His account is distinct from an account of an already believer who claims to have experienced Jesus. The plausibility of bias on Paul's part in favor of the hope for a resurrected Jesus is quite null; if anything, it is almost the opposite of bias in favor of a resurrected Jesus.

The creed is identified by practically all NT scholars, critical and otherwise, as a pre-Pauline tradition. This means that it is a tradition passed down by word-of-mouth in the early Jesus movement. At the beginning of the creed, Paul states his reception of the tradition. There are few prominent scholars who claim the creed is older than ten years after the death of Jesus. There are many prominent scholars who claim the creed is around five to ten years after the death of Jesus. There are even several prominent scholars who claim the creed is one to three years after the death of Jesus. James Dunn argues it was likely information conveyed to Paul during his introductory catechesis.[46] Even Bart Ehrman, a notorious, highly regarded critical scholar, has to somewhat concede an early date.[47] Ehrman leaves it as an open question just how early the creed is, but he openly admits that the story of Jesus appearing to the five hundred tracks back very early to the years following Jesus' death.

On a brief closing note, I believe the existence of an early tradition like this, which attests to such a widespread miracle, is the *single best* argument in favor of Christ's resurrection. When read in the original Greek, this especially reads like a memorized list. (I, an intermediate student of Greek, took the time to memorize most of it myself to see how easy it was. This certainly would have been even easier for a person in a

---

(perhaps the first ever) that demonstrates how multimodal hallucinations are more common in psychotic patients than we once thought, see Dudley et al., "Prevalence and Nature," 1–6.

45. Licona, *Resurrection of Jesus*, 437.
46. Dunn, *Jesus Remembered*, 854–55.
47. Ehrman, *How Jesus Became God*, 100.

PART 1: ESTABLISHING A THEOLOGICAL BEDROCK

first-century Greek environment who was used to memorizing religious statements in their native language.) Yet, I still don't go as far as many "Pauline fundamentalists" who take Paul as the final word on authentic resurrection accounts. It is common among scholars to see the credence for a particular piece of evidence in relation to the resurrection highly determined by whether Paul himself mentions it. This is because the consensus in scholarship today is that Paul's letters written in the fifties are the earliest texts we have in the NT. You see this with how scholars discount the evidence for St Joseph of Arimathea's aid in the burial, whether Mary Magdalene had an experience of Jesus,[48] whether there ever was an empty tomb,[49] among other traditions in the gospels. This is almost solely because Paul does not mention these explicitly in his letters. As Dale Allison points out, this is poor practice for the following reason: Paul never wrote a Greco-Roman biography about Jesus. Rather than a biographical dictation, what we see in Paul's letters are musings here and there about events related to Jesus. Paul is almost entirely disinterested in the miracles that Jesus did, and never once does he mention the public ministry of how Jesus healed the sick.[50] It would only make sense to view Paul as highly authoritative on the resurrection accounts and the life of

---

48. For why the tradition about Mary Magdalene's experience is reliable, see Allison, *Resurrection of Jesus*, 49–53. Allison rightly points out that there seems to be a censorship of Mary Magdalene's role in the resurrection and a bolstering of Peter's role in the resurrection as the gospel traditions develop over the years. This is unfortunate. Eastern liturgical tradition considers Mary to be *isapóstolos*, or "equal to the apostles," because she was the first to witness the risen Jesus.

49. While there is much debate about whether Paul knew of and/or believed in an empty tomb, since it is not explicitly included in any of his letters, I consider it very likely that he both knew of and believed in the empty tomb. This is implied by Paul's received tradition in 1 Corinthians 15 that "[Jesus] was buried." See Graieg, *Resurrection Remembered*, 37–41. Contra Allison, Paul did not "pass over" the tradition of the empty tomb (presuming it existed at the time he was writing) because he had an androcentric bias, and the empty tomb tradition involved women. Rather, Paul assumed his readers would know of the empty tomb (both through their prior knowledge of the Jesus tradition and his specific grammar in the 1 Corinthians creed). Mentioning St Justin Martyr's similar silence on the women at the empty tomb does not bolster Allison's point here either. Justin often sought to relate to his pagan audiences with his portrayal of the Gospel. As we see in Origen's *Contra Celsum*, his debate opponent, Celsus, criticized Christianity precisely for being a religion whose first followers were women. It is not wild speculation to think that Justin and Paul were dealing with similar opponents. Leaving out the dangerous information that women were the first to reach the empty tomb was perhaps an advantageous move to promoting evangelism. See Allison, *Resurrection of Jesus*, 51.

50. Allison, *Resurrection of Jesus*, 92

Jesus overall if he penned a biographical account rather than a series of letters intended to bolster the faith and piety of the hearers. Since Paul did not, one cannot assume that just because he failed to mention a given post-resurrection event from the gospels, there is no longer enough evidence to add it to one's favored chronological account of the resurrection. Therefore, I encourage a polymorphic and synergized but tentative chronology of the resurrection that responsibly takes into account Paul's claims and the gospel traditions.

The Christian story, a meta-narrative about the contours of history itself, is null if you deny the resurrection.[51] We must remember the edifying words of St Symeon the New Theologian. "What is here and now [...] leads us more readily into faith than if we had seen and heard [Jesus] then." Symeon was responding to those who liked to imagine, as many secularists do today, just how much easier it would have been to believe in Jesus if they lived in first-century Judea and witnessed his miracles, his resurrection, and so on. In a moment of historical clarity, Symeon makes it clear that if we did live in the time of Jesus, the likelihood that we would not have believed him and followed him is much greater than if we lived in the present time because he appeared as an "insignificant man" but, through the witness of Holy Tradition, it is clear that he has been proclaimed to us as the true God.[52] Writing in the eleventh century, so much of Holy Tradition had already been laid out through the Scriptures, councils, and the Fathers. Now, think how much more of a deposit we have to work with in the twenty-first century. Let us rejoice in the unconditional and living promise that Christ has given us!

---

51. The French Marxist philosopher Alain Badiou identifies the resurrection of Jesus as the ultimate Event. I defined the Event as follows: "The Event is said to be when the inconsistent multiplicity inherent to a social order, appears to society, and undergoes a retroactive realization, after the 'empirical' event has already occurred." See Coates, *Conspiracy and the Subject*, 123–26 for more on the Event. This is to say that for Paul, the Event of the resurrection opens up new potentialities that would not have been apparent to him otherwise; namely, this is seen in the redeemed union between the Jew and Gentile in Galatians 3:28. There is nothing stopping any Jew or Gentile from maintaining fidelity/faith to the Event of the resurrection. All are one in Jesus. This is also seen in Paul's "fundamentalist" attitude towards the resurrection: There is no debate, argument, or mediation when it comes to the resurrection. There is no proof needed because the Event itself is the proof. See Badiou, *Saint Paul*, 49–50.

52. Quoted in Stamps, "St Symeon the New Theologian."

PART 1: ESTABLISHING A THEOLOGICAL BEDROCK

God's Gift of Divinization

We shall all eventually be in union with the divine family, the Trinity. This ongoing process and end goal of creation is known as *theosis* in Greek. This term can be translated into English as deification or divinization. First Corinthians 15:28 in the NKJV reads, "Now when all things are made subject to Him, then the Son himself will also be subject to Him who put all things under Him, that God may be all in all." All in all. That is what God will be. As St Maximus the Confessor stresses to us, it does not say God will just be all in all people. This verse extends divinization to a cosmic scope. All of creation will rejoice when Christ is all in all at the end of the Age. Yet divinization is not only available at the end of the Age. The Fathers show us where Scripture indicates this truth.

St Gregory of Palamas gives three examples of divinization in *Triads*: Exodus 34:29, Matthew 17:2, and Acts 7:55. In Exodus, the face of Moses glowed as he came down from Mount Sinai. In Acts, St Stephen reached divinization before he was martyred and stoned. In Matthew, perhaps the most obvious case of divinization, Christ was transfigured on Mount Tabor, and the three disciples who saw him in his state of transfiguration reached divinization. Those disciples were St Peter, St James, and St John. According to many Fathers like St Basil the Great, St Maximus the Confessor, and St John of Damascus, the transfiguration of Christ displayed Christ in his true form. The glowing ray of light that is the transfigurated Jesus was hidden from the world up to this point in his life, but it was always the true emanation of Christ's presence on earth. From the womb to the cross, Christ was fancifully glowing in a perfected state of glory. The world was blinded from seeing this because it was not ready. A veil covered their hearts. Only those who were worthy of seeing Christ in his true form could glance upon his divinity and experience an ontological change in the constitution of their being. All members who witnessed the transfiguration took an active, not passive, role. Since Peter, James, and John were said to be the pillars of the Church by St Paul (Gal 2:9), and we know that at least Peter and James took a leadership role among the disciples in Acts, it is fair to say that they were chosen for a reason to be the ones to see the transfiguration of their Messiah, just as several of the disciples were individually called by Jesus as shown in the gospels. The veil was removed from their hearts. At this moment, they began to know as they are known (1 Cor 13:13).

A THEOLOGY OF THE INCARNATION

Paul duly reminds us in 2 Corinthians 3:7–8 that the whole truth of divinization cannot come to fruition in our finite lives. By using the exact story of Exodus 34:29 and comparing it with the Age to come, Paul writes, "How will the ministry of the Spirit not be more glorious?" He then answers himself. "The ministry of righteousness exceeds much more in glory." The veil that Moses applied to himself so that the children of Israel would not gaze upon his glowing face is removed through Christ. This is because Christ is entirely divine and entirely human without any confusion. Verse seventeen of the chapter then finishes the account. Through the result of the Incarnation of Christ, the living image of how the transcendent and immanent are unified, we now stand to God as a mirror of him, with an unveiled face, and are being transformed in a way that takes us from "glory to glory." When we accept Christ and begin the path to divinization, we shall be able to experience this glory. According to the Greek text, we are thus *being* transformed into the image that Christ is, that is, being transformed into a divine image; a present participation in the divinity of Christ. What Paul does is spectacular here. He does not use the future tense "will be transformed" but "being transformed" [*metamorphoumetha*]. Some Christians who reject divinization have trouble with these passages. Yet, as one can see, this really is quite clear in the Greek.

In all three accounts of divinization mentioned earlier, a miraculous event involved a sheer outpouring of light experienced by one or more finite beings. We associate this image of light, invoked in many verses such as Numbers 6:25; Habakkuk 3:4; John 1:5, as the *penultimate* display of God to creation. Once we realize that God's display of himself to creation is the light he emits as evoked in Scripture and that all the experiences of divinization noted involve light, the reasoning from Orthodoxy that we can become like God begins to make more sense. But the Fathers are very clear that divinization will not be experienced by Christians who shy away from humility and self-sacrificial discipline toward God. Only humans like Moses, those three disciples, and St Stephen, who were so loyal and steadfast in their worship that they undertook great struggles, may experience divinization in this life. This is not to say they are the only humans who have experienced divinization. As we know, many Fathers have reached this final stage whereby they gaze upon the uncreated light of God.

In the account from a disciple of St Seraphim of Sarov, Seraphim's eyes shone like lightning and while the disciple could feel the hands of

Seraphim holding onto his shoulder, he could not see his hands nor his body because Seraphim appeared as an incomprehensible "blaze of light." In the famous account from Joanna Reitlinger, who was with Fr Sergius Bulgakov during the last days of his sickness and life, the onlookers and parishioners who were by his side (medical professionals included) were struck with wonder at how his face had become completely illuminated by light.[53] The features of his face were perfectly preserved in this light; the light illuminated his expressions and features more powerfully than ever before. Reitlinger, backed by several other eyewitnesses, claimed this miracle lasted two hours. Hence, divinization is the stage where the light of God is not a fleeting ecstasy that reaches us in prayer but a stage where the light of God is the light that forever is noticed in our conscious apprehension of reality. To put the concept of divinization in the Platonic language that Palamas often invokes, we can shed our earthy shadows and become nearer to the light of Christ.

Accordingly, the Scholastic criticism of divinization—that it involves a pantheistic logic—can be dismissed. Christians who dispute the truth of divinization see the hope for divinization as the passed-down struggle of Adamic man in his fallen nature. Whereby man has a selfish desire to become like the Creator. Needless to say, the truth of divinization could not be further from this. Divinization is about the self-sacrificial giving to God. From this giving, God, due to his incomprehensible nature, may gift man with a divinized state so that we may participate in him. God does not need to give man divinization but he does so as a pure gift that we cannot understand. The difference between Adam trying to become God through partaking in the divine fruit and divinization is that the latter is entirely about humility towards God rather than the self-centered wish to become like him.

Although all of creation will become divinized, including the plants, rocks, and snails on this earth, there is still a fundamental anthropocentric worldview that seems to underlie Christianity. St Gregory of Nyssa claims there is a reason why humanity was created last in Genesis 1. According to his reading, this is so that we would be royalty to the "lodging" of the cosmos.[54] The land, the seas, and all the animals were set forth before the creation of man occurred. While I reject the insipid literal interpretation of Genesis that supposes the world was created six thousand

---

53. Reitlinger, "Final Days," 45.
54. Gregory, *On the Making of Man*, 168.

years ago, as should any serious person, there is a spiritual meaning in the Genesis creation story and in many other religious texts that parrot a similar development: Creation bends its will towards man and man's sacred history is the basis of creation's history.

This is why Gregory and many other Fathers consider man to be the royalty of creation. According to Gregory, the nature of the hypostasis of Christ has eternally had the totality of the human image in him. He reads this from Genesis 1:26–27 as a deeply communitarian truth that the Holy Spirit gives to us. This is to say that there is an ontological bond between humans because the collective human image, an image of our nature that is made up of all individual persons to have ever lived, is already in a perfect state in the fullness of time. It is hard to grasp what this means due to our state of fallenness. We are bogged down by thinking of time as a linear development, that moments pass into moments, but this is not the experience of time in its perfected state. There is a temporality beyond our fallen one, or rather, a temporality that marks the fullness of our fallen one, where all humans who have ever lived already exist in that perfected state of glory (see Introduction). When God becomes the concrete meaning of everything to everyone, humanity as a concrete whole will pass into this image and be in complete communion with the Trinity. As a saying of Jesus reads in the *Gospel of Thomas*, "When you make the two one you shall become sons of man. . ."[55] All humans who have ever lived will experience the ontological bond that runs through us all as all souls are glorified into ever-greatness. We see this precise scene play out in John 20:17.

Per Gregory's interpretation, the Son goes to the Father and presents the Father the entire image of humanity and gives it to the Father by fully and completely submitting himself to the Father since this image is already in the hypostasis of Christ as the Logos. St Dumitru Stăniloae of blessed memory reminds us that this must occur because the joy of Christ can never be completed—since his joy is of being begotten—until his whole body submits into joy. If we are all members of him, since the Logos became incarnate and the totality of human history is already in the hypostasis of Christ, then so long as members of his body are not submitted to the Father, Christ himself is not entirely submitted to the Father.[56] All members must, however that may occur, joyfully submit

---

55. Elliot, *Apocryphal New Testament*, 146.
56. Stăniloae, *Eternity and Time*, 19.

to the Father. At the point of complete and total union with the Father, creation will be born again, cast away its fleshy existence, and take on its ever-lasting spiritual body in the eschaton. All fleshy bodies desire to be brought into their proper *telos* as the spiritual body (2 Cor 5:2). Paul writes, "As we have borne the image of the man of dust, we shall also bear the image of the heavenly man" (1 Cor 15:49; NKJV).

Humanity was born from dust, but through Christ, who will conquer death and evil itself at the end of the Age, we will concretely inhabit the image of humanity eternally in the Son's hypostasis. Adamic man shall be no more because flesh and blood cannot enter the Kingdom (1 Cor 15:50). The "garments of flesh" (Gen 3:21) we inherited from the Fall will melt away like wax melts before a flame, that is, the fiery all-consuming, all-glorifying, and all-cleansing presence of God (Heb 12:29). All shall return to God because all came from God, he who is the Alpha and the Omega. This is the doctrine of *apokatastasis* or universal salvation that the rest of this book will argue in favor of.

Part 2

Universalism in Holy Tradition

4

A Preliminary on Eschatology and Hermeneutics

A Fresh Start

DEBATES OVER CHRISTIAN ESCHATOLOGY have reached their highest popularity in the past twenty years. Those involved in the debates have many intricate views. The two most widely held positions are universalism and infernalism. Universalism is the postulation that all people will eventually be saved. Infernalism is the postulation that some people will not be eventually saved, and those who are not saved will endure everlasting torment in hell. Other positions in the debate include hopeful universalism and annihilationism. Hopeful universalism is the postulation that while we should not claim certainty that all people will be saved, we should hold out hope that all people will be saved. Annihilationism is the postulation that some people will not be eventually saved, and those who are not eventually saved will cease to exist at some point.

Those in universalism could hold to a few positions, two of which I can comment on. Some believe that all will be immediately saved after death. Those in this camp do not believe that hell or any sort of purification exists at all. Most believe that all will eventually be saved after those who are not originally saved at worldly death undergo a period of purification. I hold the latter position. Those in infernalism could hold to a few positions, two of which I can comment on. Some believe that eternal hell is a requirement for retribution purposes, and those that have been sent to eternal hell have been sent there because God deems them to be unjust people deserving of his wrath. Most believe that God has not damned those sent to eternal hell per se, rather they have sent themselves to hell through their unjust actions in life. The latter position is the most held by infernalists today in Orthodoxy, Catholicism, and Protestantism. Other distinctions exist in the infernalist camp as well, such as whether or not eternal hell is a physical place of somatic torment, a psychological condition of torment, and whether hell is an existential separation from God. The majority of infernalists in Orthodoxy, Catholicism, and Protestantism seem to hold to the position that eternal hell is a psychological (not somatic/physical) condition of eternal conscious torment (ECT) and an existential separation from God.

The most favored contemporary model of ECT in infernalism is often referred to as the Lewisian model (LM). The LM derives largely from how C. S. Lewis depicts hell in his bestseller, *Great Divorce*. Lewis disposes of any physical concept of hell that corresponds with the belief that the damned are separated from God's presence. There is not a place over here called Heaven and a place over there called Hell. What Lewis does, and what most infernalists do today, is believe something along the lines of the following: When the soul dies in their physical body, they are damned to hell and remain in hell for eternity because they continue to damn themselves while in hell. The famous phrase to express this is, "The gates of hell are locked from the inside." The damned who are in hell are in hell because they freely choose to reject God in their earthly lives and continue rejecting God in the afterlife. He is not the first to propose something like this, but he certainly was the one who made it famous, at least in the West. Much of what the remainder of this book will respond to is the LM, even if I do not always specify this. Though different iterations exist of it. The LM was popularized in contemporary Orthodox theology by Met Kallistos Ware of blessed memory. This model holds that all people experience the presence of God as fire, as Scripture depicts, but this consumes some into torment while others are illuminated by it. God does not determine the way we respond to the fire, rather it is determined by how we live our lives on earth. How we live will determine whether we experience the holy fire as love or torment. Wicked souls experience torment. Virtuous souls experience love. Catholics and Protestants tend to add their own iterations upon the LM, but the core foundation of it remains throughout most forms of contemporary infernalism: God does not damn us, rather, we damn ourselves.

When it comes to the view that hell is a material lake of fire, I do not even entertain this possibility. Although millions of Christians genuinely believe this, I consider the stance so infantile that I completely disregard it. If you believe that hell is a material place, I must then ask, where the hell is hell? I doubt few Christians alive today (even the most insipid of the bunch) would propose the eighteenth-century hypothesis of an English empiricist like Thomas Swinden, who claimed that hell is located in the sun. I also assume that few would adopt the view that hell is quite literally under the earth in the fiery core that sustains the deepest layers. If both views are outrageous, then where is hell located?

The presuppositions here are wrong. Hell isn't located in a material geography but rather a spiritual geography. It is constituted by the existential separation from God, the fiery torment of the wrath of the damned soul being reflected back onto themselves, along with the suspension in a hyper-timeless void-like existence. Hell is the self in the absence of predication. Hell is the Luciferian embrace of ontological individuation taken to the extreme. Hell is the actualization of the egotistical bounds in nature. This is what I mean by hell throughout this book.[1]

Salvation Outside the Church?

The Orthodox Church has never affirmed a dogmatic statement on where the Holy Spirit resides. We know that the Church has the Holy Spirit, but we will never claim that your church does not have it. And on an individual level, the Church never says who is and who is not saved. As such, those who are heterodox to the faith may still be immediately saved and brought to union with God. First Corinthians 5:12 in the NKJV reads, "For what have I to do with judging those also who are outside? Do you not judge those who are inside?" Fellow Orthodox Christians are already judging those inside the canonical Orthodox bounds. If we are already judging our fellow Orthodox brothers and sisters and struggling to avoid doing so, why should we turn to the outside and judge them as well?

---

1. Much of the scrapped material for this present book (totaling well over 100 pages) was centered on developing an intricate topological and phenomenological understanding of hell by employing Lacanian Psychoanalysis, a Kantian theory of personhood, and Heideggerian phenomenology. These couple sentences serve as an extremely summarized version of those "lost" pages.

Exactly, we should not. Let us avoid those who do this and not cast a wandering eye on the heterodox. As Paul says in the next verse, God will judge those outside. It is not in our hands as a Church nor in the hands of any single bishop or patriarch.

Since the Orthodox Church does not make dogmatic statements about which other church does or does not have the Holy Spirit, there are likewise no dogmatic statements about who outside of Christianity altogether will or will not be saved. Many assume, for simplicity purposes, that all those outside Christianity will be damned. This is not an accurate statement. And I'm not even saying this because of *economia* whereby the rigidity of the canons is suspended, such as when Jesus told the murderer on the cross that he will be with him in Paradise (Lk 23:43). This is not an accurate statement because so-called pious pagans exist; below, I use Plato as an example. Moreover, I admit, I have a leniency towards the practices of other faiths, but so do many other Orthodox Christians, even if they don't admit this. A stellar example of outside influence is the ascetic practice known as hesychasm. This is a state of silent prayer that achieves inner silence. When practicing this mode of prayer often, one eventually forms a hesychastic lifestyle. This is a lifestyle where one attempts to make room for God in their life by maintaining constant awareness of his presence. Since a hesychastic lifestyle is very God-oriented, it tends to be associated with Orthodox monks, but it is actually open for all to engage in. Orthodox Christians around the world enter into this mode of prayer daily.

Normally, this is entered by first repeating the Jesus Prayer aloud or in one's head. The Jesus Prayer reads, "Lord Jesus Christ, Son of God, have mercy on me, a sinner." As the Christian undergoes repetitions of this prayer, the world starts to fade away as their connection to fallen worldly beings begins to diminish. The Christian's consciousness of the world is not absolved, rather the world is taken up with the person in their moment of prayer. A change in consciousness is undergone as the Christian feels the stillness of being in God's presence. The recognition of this led several "traditionalist" Catholic theologians in the nineteenth century to discredit hesychasm as a pagan ritual and far Eastern. Indeed, hesychasm involves breathing exercises meant to relax the Christian as they pray. This may lead some, on first thought, to leap into a frenzy. But, despite its probable inheritance from Buddhism, the tradition of hesychasm has even deeper roots in what is known as Chariot Mysticism. This branch of Second Temple Jewish mysticism grew popular

A PRELIMINARY ON ESCHATOLOGY AND HERMENEUTICS

in the first century BCE and coined its name from the prophet Ezekiel's chariot vision. Ezekiel saw the divine chariot-throne in the heavens from which God governs creation and a figure sitting on that throne known as the Angel of the Lord. The tradition inspired many later visions that involved a participant venturing into the heavenly domains, sharing discourse with angels, and sometimes even gazing upon the Uncreated Light of Glory. To receive these visions, a deep mode of contemplative prayer practice was developed known as *Shema* which drew from various prayers in Deuteronomy. St Paul was well associated with this tradition. His vision of being brought into the "third heaven," along with his famous experience on the road to Damascus, attests to this. The depiction in Revelation of the throne-room scene where the angelic council surrounds God also attests to the popularity of this (Rev 4). The *Shema* said by Second Temple Jews laid the groundwork for the Orthodox concept of hesychasm and especially the Jesus Prayer.

While I am not a strict religious exclusivist, this does not mean that I believe most who are not Christians will be immediately saved. I don't see how we could believe Christianity is the Way, the Truth, the Life (Jn 14:6), and yet believe that all people will immediately be saved. Although more syncretically minded Christians often make arguments that what other faiths are worshiping is always the Christian God, even when they don't realize it, I am not entirely convinced by these. On the other hand, I do believe that those in other religions who claim to have experienced the divine should not have their claims tossed out. Claims related to the experience of God are utterly distinct from worldly experiences and have a few set commonalities across all cultures and times. Those who claim experiences of God must be taken seriously. Moreover, a universal evolutionary model of religion, routinely inspired by post-Lutheran musings on the nature of religion as transitioning from a model of concrete symbolism to abstract piety, is something I reject. More and more evidence shows that indigenous peoples (particularly in the Australian continent and nearby) were monotheistic; that is, they devoted all worship and sacrifice towards a single deity who they believed created everything and instilled moral laws for their people to follow.[2] Anthropological and ethnographic observations like this make dubious any claims that posit a universal evolutionary model of religion, and they make dubious any claims towards strict religious exclusivism.

2. An enlightening book to read on this topic that nicely compiles ethnographic work from the nineteenth century is Corduan, *In the Beginning God*.

PART 2: UNIVERSALISM IN HOLY TRADITION

It doesn't take a genius to see the commonalities here with what we see in the Scriptures and what the Church teaches. As such, it would be utterly irresponsible of me to say, for instance, that God cannot appear to a Chinese man living in the fifth century BCE even if the man is ignorant of the Israelite religion. As St Nikolai Velimirovich controversially stated in *Agony of the Church* before he was forced by his hierarchs later in life to retract the statement, "Better is unbaptized saintliness than baptized earthliness." This led him to argue that many saintly individuals outside the Orthodox Church should be officially canonized. For him, this included St Hermes, St Pythagoras, St Buddha, St Krishna, St Lao-Tse, St Confucius, and St Abu-Bekr; he also argued that certain Catholic saints like St Francis of Assisi and St Theresa of Ávila should be canonized by the Orthodox Church. As Hieromonk Damascene more cautiously argued in *Christ and the Immortal Tao*, it may well be true that some of the great ancient Chinese thinkers were divinely inspired due to their striking overlaps with Christian doctrine at times. While I do not agree entirely with either one of these authors, especially the latter's superiority complex when it comes to the Christian revelation, they provide a great deal of legroom for pious Orthodox Christians to ruminate on our relation to heterodox Christians and other religious traditions.

If this isn't enough, it was a prevalent belief among early Christians that Plato, at least, was working under some sort of divine oversight. The hypothesis first came from the Jewish philosopher Philo of Alexandria, who argued that Moses was learned in Egyptian wisdom and taught Pythagoras, who eventually taught these divine teachings to Plato. The hypothesis became more developed by St Justin Martyr (who referred to Socrates as a "martyr"), Athenagoras of Athens (who exquisitely traced back the model of the Trinity to Plato's philosophy),[3] St Clement of Alexandria, Origen of Alexandria (who was more balanced since he had to deal with non-Christian Platonists like Celsus), and others around the second century who argued, somewhat inversely, that Plato read the books of Moses or was divinely inspired with similar ideas by the Holy Spirit.[4] Much of this attitude was snuffed out by the fifth century, with the denunciation of Plato from St John Chrysostom and St Gregory the Theologian (although the latter most certainly took a great deal of influence from Plato in all realms of his thought, as did the former, explicitly

---

3. Radde-Galwitz, "The One and the Trinity," 54.
4. O'Leary, "Socrates and Plato in the Fathers," 195–98.

with his demonology), but even then, St Didymus the Blind,[5] Blessed Augustine of Hippo, and later St Cyril of Alexandria continued to put forth the importance of Plato in Christian tradition; it is unlikely that Cyril accepted Philo's or Martyr's hypothesis, but Augustine and Didymus may very well have.[6] Of course, one cannot provide historical evidence to prove or disprove that a writer was or was not divinely inspired—this is simply out of the scope of what history can tell us—but history can tell us that there is no hard evidence (or even circumstantial, frankly) that Plato ever read Hebrew or traveled to Israel. I happen to believe Plato and perhaps several of the other figures I named earlier were divinely inspired independently from the Hebrew scribes.

There is a telling hagiographic account that may indicate the inspiration of at least Plato. St Anastasios of Sinai famously relayed an account given to him by an elder at a monastery at Sinai. Before bed every night, the elder would curse Plato because he believed that Plato's influence on Orthodoxy was the greatest blight on the faith. Eventually, after some time, Plato himself appeared in a dream to this elder and said, "Man stop cursing me; for you are merely harming yourself. I do not deny that I was a sinner; but, when Christ descended into hell, no one believed in Him sooner than I did."[7] (In Chapter 7, I discuss more about Christ's descent into hell, but for now, I can note how this account is one of great acuity and brevity. I personally trust it, and in terms of Plato declaring himself a sinner, this does not itself rebuke claims of inspiration since it is understood that all people are sinners.) The relevance of this account is that Plato must have had something special about him to be one of the first sinners to confess themselves when Jesus descended into hell.[8] Returning to the point, since the Orthodox Church does not make any dogmatic statements on who will be included or excluded, an Orthodox universalist should not claim certainty on who will reach immediate inclusion or exclusion. This is because all people are along what St John Climacus refers to as the "Ladder of Divine Ascent" or ladder of *theosis*. John was explicitly not a universalist—even though his theology leads to this conclusion—but this image of a ladder has become very prevalent in Byzantine iconography, and for good reason. The icon depicts a golden ladder with many men on it, some closer to the top, others closer to the

5. Radde-Galwitz, "The One and the Trinity," 72–73.
6. O'Leary, "Socrates and Plato in the Fathers," 201–2.
7. Louth, *Greek East & Latin West*.
8. As Plotinus phrased it in *Enneads* 4.8: *o theios Platōn* (the godly Plato).

bottom. At the top, Jesus is holding his hand out to pull those up off the ladder. At the bottom are a bunch of men in hell. While men are climbing up the ladder towards Jesus, winged demons are plucking them off. Towards the bottom, there are many demons plucking people off. Towards the top, there are fewer demons but still some that pluck people off. Although there is debate about whether John intended the people on the ladder to refer to only Christians, many later Fathers understood it to refer to all people. And I wholeheartedly agree with this. All people are either being divinized or are being plucked off the ladder and carried further towards non-existence. Nobody will in fact reach this state of destruction, but being carried further away from Jesus leads one to this perilous result. This ladder provides a lasting image of *theosis* and the process of salvation for all people.

Nobody is excluded because all are somewhere along the divine ladder. Some will be stuck in the middle or even towards the bottom for a long time. Yet even those unfortunate souls will eventually make their way up. Demons are only so powerful as finite contingent beings. Those unfortunate souls will make their way up because their love for God and movement towards the Good overrides all worldly passions and selfish desires. Salvation is not guaranteed for those outside the Church, but all will receive it, perhaps not immediately, but eventually, when all finally touch the hand of Christ who pulls them off the ladder; once one has reached the top of the ladder they cannot fall back down, after all, the top of the ladder is the perfect union with God. Nobody who experiences this even once could resist it. Reaching the top is not the end of growing in the Lord but a new beginning, a beautified beginning, as one begins from the state of perfection, and from there, one can only grow more perfected in glory.

A Proper Biblical Hermeneutic

Whether you are Orthodox, Catholic, or Protestant, I am sure you would like to think that Scripture informs many of the theological positions you take. But when we approach Scripture and use it as a tool to form our theology, we always do so from a holistic lens. Take the Trinity. If I were to ask you for a specific verse or even several put together where the post-Nicene Trinity (consubstantial and co-eternal Persons) is detailed, you would be unable to fulfill this request. This is because the ecumenical councils that dogmatized the Trinity did so from the position of a holistic reading. In taking a holistic reading of the Bible, the councilmen noticed the status of Christ in the NT seemed to be that of the Father at times, and the status of the Spirit of God likewise seemed to be the same as the Father at times. As well, the common evocations of the Angel of God in the OT and the Wisdom of God point to some sort of pre-existent unity-in-multiplicity in God. In Christian eschatology, likewise, we cannot rely on a single verse to "prove" whatever position we hold. We can and should use verses as a staging area for our stance on eschatology. However, a single verse in the NT is not the sole necessary and sufficient condition to constitute proof *for* or *against* a position.

Moreover, English readers of the Bible approach the text from a translation that always has an ideological and theological bias. What you so often find in these English translations is that the people doing the translation know little about the culture in which these texts were produced. It is probably the first and most important rule of translation that one must have a strong grasp of the cultural context surrounding the concepts and ideas expressed. For the NT, this means that the text must be translated using terms that would convey conceptual categories that made sense to Second Temple Jews and the traditions they were aware of. Yet even if one successfully does this, which rarely happens in the first place, a translation is still inherently an ideologically loaded medium that involves aspects of thought not found in the original author's intentions. Even good translations, like the NKJV and New American Bible, that genuinely try to reproduce the original author's intentions will always fall short (not to mention the grotesque "translation" ironically called *The Message*). Perfect translations do not exist, but we often forget this. As the Anglican universalist Thomas Allin puts it, "The Bible was not written by some Englishman in the nineteenth-century, for his fellow Englishmen. It comes to us from very distant ages; in many parts; the work of very many minds, but one and all writing from an oriental standpoint, saturated with oriental habits of thought, and in oriental phrase and style."[9] This seems so obvious yet so difficult to wrap our heads around. Although we may think certain verses indicate a specific meaning, this could be and often is due to the ideological biases of the translators who rendered them in this way. St John Chrysostom and later St Photius of Constantinople pointed this out in the many differences

---

9. Allin, *Christ Triumphant*, 51.

between the Hebrew Scriptures and the Greek Septuagint regarding the words used in certain Psalms. The same goes for English translations of the Bible.

Let me also add that as an Orthodox Christian who disagrees with the Protestant implications of 2 Tim 3:16 (see Chapter 2), there is simply no dogmatic commitment to inerrancy. Orthodoxy has never had a dog in this fight. Due to this lack of a theological commitment towards inerrancy, I disagree with a number of universalists with evangelical commitments like the Anglican Fr Robin Parry, who affirms that we must find a way to hold every text in Scripture together.[10] But despite Parry's commitment towards inerrancy, even he eschews those in the debate who get "bogged down" by particular verses.[11] My goal, then, is not to get caught up in the minutia but also not to overlook the importance of establishing a biblical warrant for universalism. This is a tricky heuristic to maintain but one that Orthodox Christians in all domains of theology often embrace. Primarily, this will be accomplished through a hermeneutical approach to Scripture.

I approach the Bible through George MacDonald's "hermeneutics of love."[12] MacDonald was a Scottish nineteenth-century Protestant minister known by many for his fiction, but few are aware of his rich theological writings. I consider MacDonald and several other universalists like father-son duo Johann & Christoph Blumhardt, Thomas Allin, Edward Plumpre, and Anne Brontë, and before these six, in the eighteenth century, Johann Alrecht Bengel, F. C. Oetinger, and Elhanan Winchester, to be in a relatively exclusive group of Protestant thinkers who although were influential in shaping the theologies of acclaimed twentieth-century Protestant systematic theologians like Karl Barth and Jürgen Moltmann, never took the time to be systematic thinkers themselves. What a shame. At least Anne Brontë became famous for her lovely poetry.

In *Unspoken Sermons*, MacDonald argues that when we read Scripture, we should do so only from a view of God's self-revelation revealed in Christ. He then goes on to say, "I acknowledge no authority calling upon me to believe a thing of God, which I could not be a man and believe right in my fellow-man."[13] He is certainly not the first to say

---

10. Parry, "A Universalist Response," 48.

11. Parry, "A Universalist View," 102.

12. To my knowledge, Fr Aidan Kimel is the one who coined this term to refer to MacDonald's hermeneutical method.

13. MacDonald, *Unspoken Sermons*, 39.

A PRELIMINARY ON ESCHATOLOGY AND HERMENEUTICS

something so "radical" along these lines. Origen of Alexandria wrote the following in the third century. "But even the simple-minded of those who claim allegiance to the Church have supposed that nothing is greater than the Creator, while yet entertaining beliefs about him of a sort that they would not harbor regarding a human being of the utmost savagery and injustice."[14] St Gregory of Nyssa in the fourth century adopted much of Origen's biblical hermeneutics and wrote, "If we come to a halt at the [Old Testament] for its bare events, [this] does not provide us with the exemplars of a good way of life."[15] He goes on to say that if these historical events can be proven with good evidence then we should consider them as fact but if they cannot, why must we trust the "letter of the law?" Origen expressed a similar sentiment, albeit less explicitly.[16] In saying this, Gregory refers back to St Paul: "The letter kills, but the Spirit gives life" (2 Cor 3:6; NKJV). Paul himself took an allegorical and spiritual reading to be the obvious interpretation of the Scriptures. If we rely on the "letter," that is, the literal text alone, we accuse God of evildoing. By relying on the Spirit, that is, a spiritual meaning which goes beyond and sometimes altogether rejects historical happenings if they conflict with what we know about God, we arrive at a far greater truth. Gregory implements this stance throughout the *Life of Moses*. A key example is his outright denial that God ever killed the Egyptian firstborn in Exodus. This is rather a typological description that when a person is consumed by evil, the beginnings of their vice must be destroyed. This type of hermeneutic became *one* of the most prominent in the East. We see a rejection of naive literalism as well, more cautiously, in St Augustine of Hippo's ofttitled *A Literal Reading of Genesis*. In general, a rejection of literalism is the *primary* mode for interpreting Scripture throughout the Fathers.[17] I seek to show my acceptance of this hermeneutic tradition throughout the present text.

And, on a side note, even holy Fathers in the Antiochian school who opposed Origen's "over-spiritualization" of the Scriptures were clear that there is always a spiritual dimension that rises above the literal historical

14. Origen, *On First Principles*, 489.

15. Gregory, *Homilies*, 2–3.

16. Origen and St Gregory were both not too keen to outright deny biblical events. They both believed in a historical Exodus from Egypt led by Moses, but they focused on the spiritual and allegorical meaning of the events involved rather than trying to pinpoint when and where they happened. Personally, I leave the question of a historical Exodus to archeologists. This has no bearing whatsoever to my scriptural concerns.

17. Swinburne, *Was Jesus God?*, 152.

correspondence to what happened; they just thought Origen went too far. Take the text *Selected Quotations* from the ninth-century East Syrian Ishō bar Nūn. This heralded exegesis of the OT that engages with Syriac, Arabic, Hebrew, and Greek manuscripts and figures is organized like a "question-and-answer" where Isho asks an exegetical question and then provides an answer, largely basing his answers on the writings of St Basil the Great as well as Theodore of Mopuestia (known as the "Blessed Interpreter" in East Syria) and St Ephrem the Syrian. A clear example of his literalist approach to the Scriptures is when he eschews those who say that Genesis 1:2 refers to the Holy Spirit going over the face of the waters since, when read literally, the Hebrew *ruh* is just air or wind; he cites Basil in support of this. Later in the text, however, he holds that four people were brought into the ark rather than any other number because the number four corresponds to the number of elements in the world. Four people were to make the world anew, just as the four elements made the world anew. It is clear, then, that even those in the Antiochian school did not only read the Scriptures literally.

When reading Scripture properly by rejecting naive literalism, a more holistic stance should be considered. The Bible is produced and developed through and by liturgical texts; hence, the purpose of Chapter 7. Since the Divine Liturgy centers around breaking the bread and serving the Eucharist, our approach to Scripture should also center on this event. All of Scripture must be read through the self-revelation of Christ, as said, but this takes on a proper liturgical sense that MacDonald did not spell out earlier. Luke 34:30–31 in the NKJV reads, "Now it came to pass, as He sat at the table with them, that He took bread, blessed and broke it, and gave it to them. Then their eyes were opened and they knew Him; and He vanished from their sight." This scene recalls one of Jesus' post-resurrection appearances. Earlier, the disciples met Jesus on the road but did not recognize him; see Chapter 3 for more on polymorphic Christology. Only after Jesus physically served them communion, that is, only after they experienced his real presence in the Eucharist, did the disciples recognize him. At this moment, the Church changed into the Eucharist.

These verses have a profound meaning. We can only fully recognize Jesus by partaking in the Eucharist, that is, serving in the life of Jesus' wedded Church. Worship is incomplete unless we are in the Church and participating in the wedding ceremony that eventually leads us to partake in the Eucharist; the crescendo of every Divine Liturgy. It is for this reason that all the great Orthodox liturgical theologians of the twentieth century understood the Eucharist to be like the "present" entrance into the eschaton; such that it is a hint, a mighty powerful hint, of the permeation of grace that will abound in the eschaton, when everything is itself made (or, realized) into the body of Christ. Hence, concerning Scripture, the self-revelation of Jesus Christ in the NT, through the Eucharist, is the only proper way to grasp the spiritual richness of the text. Theology is not just an academic exercise. Any other approach to Scripture that refuses to read backward, that is, see the elements and prophecies of Christ in the OT, as well as later tradition in the Bible overall, is doomed to fail from the start.

5

A Quasi-Pauline Universalism

A STRANGE PATTERN HAS developed across the history of Christianity concerning eschatological statements in the NT. The metaphorical language that the NT uses to describe eschatology is taken as literal, while straightforward statements are disregarded or given an array of other excuses to explain away their meaning.[1] When verses talk about an impending harvest, fiery ovens, and worms eating flesh, these are taken far more seriously to describe hell than those that talk about a peaceful reconciliation eventually occurring where all people will confess their faith in Jesus Christ. The former's linguistic devices have a purpose, but they do not point us to a concrete conclusion. This is in comparison to verses which, as I will argue, express a universalist message. Universalist statements in the NT often point us to concrete conclusions that are joyful and peaceful and express the full revelation of God's love as promised by the coming of Christ. This does not mean we are left with an either/ or here: Either embrace metaphorical statements as literal or disregard them altogether. As the Catholic theologian Karl Rahner duly notes, it is theologically unacceptable to entirely de-mythologize eschatological assertions in Scripture.[2] If I were to deny, as some do, the eschatological assertions and claim they are merely about worldly events such as the fall

---

1. DBH, *That All Shall Be Saved*, 94.
2. I cannot find where exactly I remember reading this in Rahner, *Theological Investigations: Volume 4*.

A QUASI-PAULINE UNIVERSALISM

of the Second Temple in 70 CE, then I would be operating with a theologically unsound hermeneutic. Yet Rahner fails to say that it is equally theologically unsound to overemphasize metaphorical assertions over ones that concretely point toward an eschatological conclusion. Infernalists and annihilationists tend to do precisely this.

I do not believe that the number of "proof texts" you cite is worthwhile in determining the credibility of your position. So, I shall mainly focus on defending the following verses in this chapter. These make the most plausible case for universal salvation from a biblical point of view. The four or so verses I will provide a detailed exegesis of are as follows: 1 Corinthians 15:22; Romans 5:18; Philippians 2:10–11; Colossians 1:20. As an informed reader of the Bible can tell, all of these texts are at least *Quasi*-Pauline. I say "Quasi" because Colossians may not have been written by Paul but rather by a later admirer of Paul. This will be explained much later in the chapter. Regardless, it is clear that all the texts mentioned were written with at least an undisputable Pauline influence.

I grant that I am open to criticism by focusing my biblical exegesis on the letters attributed to Paul and overlooking the eschatological references in the gospels. Am I not overlooking the words of our Lord? There is no easy answer I can give. The sayings of Jesus in the gospels do not have a singular and cogent eschatological vision. This was simply not the focus of his ministry. To our knowledge, Jesus did not spend his days on earth preoccupied with the thoughts of divine punishment. Jesus focused on restoring the hearts and minds of Israel through a compassionate socio-political doctrine that emphasized, above all else, the importance of obeying God the Father and overturning the oppression experienced at the hands of the rich to prepare for the coming apocalypse. See Chapter 9 for more on how to interpret the eschatological sayings of Jesus.

In contrast to the gospels, I argue that the letters attributed to Paul *may* have an eschatology that shares continuity. But even this must be nuanced. Ilaria Ramelli writes, "In Paul, remarkably, the most important passages that could inspire the supporters of the doctrine of *apokatastasis* are found in Romans, 1 Corinthians, and Philippians, that is, letters whose authenticity is undisputed."[3] I concur with Ramelli, then, that *at least* the undisputed Pauline letters have a universalist eschatology. I also found there to be a confident universalist sentiment in Colossians. Other texts in the NT that plausibly indicate universal salvation to the degree

---

3. Ramelli, *Christian Doctrine*, 41.

that they at least deserve a brief mention, in order of ascending book, are as follows: Luke 16:16; John 3:17; 12:32; Romans 11:32; 2 Corinthians 5:14; 5:19; Colossians 1:28; Ephesians 1:9–10; 4:10; 1 Timothy 2:3–6; 4:10; Titus 2:11; 2 Peter 3:9; 1 John 2:2; 4:14. The most plausible of these are probably: Luke 16:16; Romans 11:32; 2 Corinthians 5:19; Ephesians 1:9–10.[4] A study of these is not in the purview of my exegesis here, though I cover Romans 11:32 in Chapter 9 and mention most of the others in passing. Unfortunately, I can't discuss everything in one book.

The Universal Involvement

First Corinthians 15:22 (NKJV): "For as in Adam all die, even so in Christ all shall be made alive."

The first important matter that determines the interpretation of this verse is if the "all" in both cases means "without exception." The "all" in the first case is in reference to the fact that due to Adam's sin, all humans are condemned to a finite life in this world.[5] To doubt this involves all humans without exception means to say that some humans are not "in Adam." If some humans are not "in Adam," those humans have eternal life in this world. Since no humans have eternal life in this world, it is safe to say that the first "all" is not hyperbole and indicates all humans without exception. The second "all," I argue, likewise indicates that all are given life without exception.[6] It is unlikely that a parallel would be drawn between all those in Adam and all those in Christ if there were all people in Adam but only some in Christ. The parallel between the two indicates that both uses of all [*pantes*] denote the same group. This group is all humans and was understood to be so by some of the greatest early Christian exegetes, including Origen of Alexandria, St Dionysius of Alexandria, St Gregory of Nyssa, and so on. The other important matter is to determine whether "in Christ" denotes just people who are Christians in the present or if it denotes all people at the coming of Christ. To

---

4. On a brief note, Luke 16:16 is a fascinating case. Origen is the first to argue that the verb *biazetai* is not active but rather passive. This makes the verse, contra most modern English translations, read something like: "Since [that time of the prophets] the kingdom of God is preached, and every man is being violently pushed into it." Or ".And every man is being pushed into it [with force]."

5. See my later exegesis on Romans 5:12 for context on what Paul means here.

6. See my later exegesis on Romans 5:18 for responses to those who criticize the parallel here.

read this as the former does not make that much sense as the phrase "in Christ" does not modify "all," it is rather an adverbial phrase that modifies "shall be made alive." So, if we take this understanding that all shall be made alive in Christ, what does this entail?[7]

For one, we have good reason to believe that "shall be made alive" [*zōopoiēthēsontai*] lacks any indication that some who are made alive are just made alive to eternally suffer or face annihilation. Although [*zōopoiēthēsontai*] is a *hapax legomenon*, the root *zoopoieo* and other iterations of this are found numerous times in the NT and are *only* ever used to express a positive outcome.[8] Many times, even a glorious one. Take John 6:63. "It is the Spirit who gives life [*zōopoioun*]; the flesh profits nothing."[9] Take 2 Corinthians 3:6. "For the letter kills, but the Spirit gives life [*zōopoiei*]."[10] Another positive and glorious demonstration. Due to the meaning of *zoopoieo* in the NT, it is highly unlikely that if all are made alive in Christ, some, and for that matter, the vast majority of humanity, will not be met with a positive outcome. Let's examine verses 20–24, skipping v. 22 for now.

> First Corinthians 15:20–24 (NKJV): "But now Christ has risen from the dead, and has become the firstfruits of those who have fallen asleep. For since by man came death, by Man also came the resurrection of the dead. . .But each one in his own order: Christ the firstfruits, afterward those who are Christ's at His coming. Then comes the end, when He delivers the kingdom to God the Father, when He puts an end to all rule and all authority and power."

This clears up some controversies but also brings about many questions. Verses 20–21 are about how Christ was the first to be resurrected, but in the eschatological future, others will be as well. Since Christ is the "New Adam" it shows that others will follow his lead. Onto vv. 23–24. Even universalists dispute the meaning of this seemingly tri-fold schema of a salvational process. Thomas Talbott argues that first Christ is resurrected, then he comes again and all Christians are resurrected, and then

---

7. Alain Badiou is very clear about what this parallel entails. He writes, "There is no place here for vengeance and resentment. Hell, the roasting spit of enemies, holds no interest for Paul." See Badiou, *Saint Paul*, 96.

8. Also, Romans 4:17; 8:11; 1 Corinthians 15:36; Galatians 3:21; 1 Timothy 6:13; 1 Peter 3:18.

9. First Corinthians 15:45 uses *zōopoioun* to denote "life-giving."

10. John 5:21 uses *zōopoiei* to denote "life giving" or "gives life."

at some temporal moment that is unspecified and unknown, all the rest of humanity is resurrected into God's kingdom since they are now believers (having undergone some sort of post-mortem purification).[11]

Talbott makes this argument by disagreeing with the traditional English translation of *to telos* as "the end" in v. 24. Instead of "the end," he argues there is enough credence for translating this as "the remainder." Fr Robin Parry argues that "the end" is the most likely translation and points out how this makes more sense in context to the deliverance of the kingdom to God the Father in v. 28.[12] I concur with Parry on translating it as "end," but I would add an important stipulation: The *telos* in *to telos* should be read in the proper philosophical way. As Paul was familiar with Platonism and Stoicism, he knew the implications of *telos*. In this sense, I argue, Paul's schema is a narrative account of what creation is destined for by nature (the logic of this is explained in verses 25–28). This is why Paul splits the resurrection into three stages; the end goal is only accomplished at the final stage. But back to Parry. The implication of translating *to telos* as "end" is that Paul does not mention a universal reconciliation in vv. 23–24. Instead, Christ is resurrected, he comes again, all Christians are resurrected, and then they are delivered to God the Father. There is no mention of what happens to those who are not Christians.

However, this does not mean universal reconciliation is off the table. Verse 22 is in favor of the universalist hypothesis. It could be the case that Paul was not focused on talking about non-Christians in vv. 23–24 for whatever reason. He talks about it in the prior verse and does not draw the implications of this into the next verse. Although Paul does not mention non-Christians in the context of the schema in vv. 23–24, he also does not mention anything about ECT for non-Christians or the destruction of their souls. If he believed that non-Christians would certainly endure ECT even after the resurrection, or if he believed that non-Christians would not exist after the resurrection, he failed to mention this. To argue that since Paul did not mention the resurrection of non-Christians in this schema entails that non-Christians will not be resurrected in a joyful state (see v. 20) is an argument from silence; those rarely turn out well. We will return to this later. For now, let's examine vv. 25–28, which fill in Paul's gap of an explicit universalist sentiment.

---

11. Talbott, *The Inescapable Love of God*, 60–62.

12. McDonald, *Evangelical Universalist*, 77. Gregory McDonald was an early pseudonym of Fr Robin Parry.

A QUASI-PAULINE UNIVERSALISM

First Corinthians 15:25-28 (NKJV): "For He must reign till He has put [*thē*] all enemies under His feet. The last enemy that will be destroyed is death. For 'He has put all things under His feet.' But when He says, 'all things are put under Him,' it is evident that He who put all things under Him is excepted. Now when all things are made subject to Him, then the Son Himself will also be subject to Him who put all things under Him, that God may be all in all."

This ends the eschatological narrative of the cosmos that Paul has set out. This also fills in the universalist gap of vv. 23-24. The end will not come until Christ's victory and triumph are complete.[13] Hence, v. 25 tells us that all the enemies of God must be put under "His feet." The verb *thē* denotes the absolute sovereign ability of God to ensure this occurs. The enemies referred to in this verse are the evil (heavenly) rulers, (heavenly) principalities, (heavenly) powers, and death; the first three were mentioned explicitly in v. 24. Death is a new addition and is listed on its own because of how much power it has over the present Age. Some argue this mention of "enemies" also refers to damned human souls.[14] Suppose we grant this for hypothetical purposes. Put aside the fact that this is baseless, and there is no indication in the text that humans are entailed in the referent. I have two concerns. One is a broader theological concern. The other is based on the context of these verses.

God indeed sees us as his enemy until we begin to believe in him (Rom 5:10). This, however, cannot possibly mean that our personhood is itself an enemy to God. What this must mean, if we are indeed made in his image (Gen 1:26) and made to be loved (1 Jn 4:19), is that our sinful lifestyle stands as an enemy to God. If God knows everything that will ever and has ever happened to us, why would God create beings in his image that are his enemy? Isn't it also a common theme in the gospels to emphasize how important it is to love our enemies? It seems that if we are told to love our enemies, it would follow that God also loves his

---

13. Talbott, "Pauline Interpretation," 26-27. Talbott responds to those who disagree with his controversial interpretation of *to telos* and reasonably argues that even if we take this as "the end," universalism may still be entailed by verses 23-24 in virtue of verses 25-28.

14. Even many early infernalist commentators on this verse, like St John Chrysostom, argued it to indicate only that of devils/angelic evil powers. It is much more of a modern view to believe this verse has anything to do with human beings; for instance, as claimed by Jewett, *Romans*. See a defense of the former position in Bowens, *An Apostle in Battle*, 168-70. Also, De Boer, *Defeat of Death*, 230-31.

PART 2: UNIVERSALISM IN HOLY TRADITION

enemies. Indeed, "enemies" [*echthrous*] is used over ten other times in the NT, including the token verses we might think of, like Matthew 5:66 & Luke 6:35. These two, in particular, speak to the importance of loving the enemy as oneself. However, loving the enemy as oneself, in the case of God, seems to falter if we suppose that he sees all of mankind as his enemy. It would make much more sense for v. 25, if it is referencing "the damned" which I disagree with anyways, to still mean something along the lines that God sees our pre-Christian sinful lifestyle as an enemy to his goodness. More particularly, God sees sin itself as the enemy, and since sin governs our lives in this context, our sinful life is God's enemy. A pre-Christian sinful lifestyle is an enemy to God, but the person practicing this lifestyle is not, in their personhood, an enemy to God.

The contextual issue I have with this argument involves the supposition that "put under His feet" necessarily entails annihilation or ECT. The verb *katargeō* was used in verse 24 to either mean nullify or destroy in context to "all rule and all authority and power." By my lights, 1 Corinthians 1:28 offers the best case in the NT where *katargeō* means "to annul" and not "to destroy." However, I could see the argument that the meaning of *katargeō* should be left as an open question. Hebrews 2:14 seems to indicate that *katargeō* means "to destroy," as it is in context to the devil. On this point, I would respond that Hebrews 2:14 only seems to indicate "to destroy" if you already agree that the use in 1 Corinthians 15:24 means "to destroy." On the other hand, if you believe that evil entities will not be destroyed in the eschaton but will be made entirely powerless, then you would likewise interpret the use in Hebrews 2:14 to mean "to nullify." In estimating the level of credence these opposing interpretations have, I argue that 1 Corinthians 1:28 is clearer in meaning "to nullify" than Hebrews 2:14 is clearer in meaning "to destroy." Since Paul wrote 1 Corinthians and did not write Hebrews, it seems that if we are trying to determine what Paul meant by *katargeō* in 1 Corinthians 15:24, we should probably go with "to nullify" since that meaning is more clearly expressed in 1 Corinthians 1:28. As such, Paul likely meant "to nullify" in 1 Corinthians 15:24 just as he did earlier in 1:28.

If we interpret v. 24 as meaning that the rulers and powers are not destroyed per se; rather, they are rendered powerless, the enemies of God could likewise be thought of as being rendered powerless. Suppose we once again assume that "damned souls" is implicitly suggested in this (though, again, this is baseless). Even in that case, the damned are thought to be rendered powerless but, contra annihilationists, are not destroyed. In this sense, "put under His feet" can be analogized to turning a lamp on in a dark room. When we turn a lamp on, the darkness is not destroyed or annihilated but rendered powerless. The darkness no longer has power because it no longer has a presence as darkness. Perhaps this analogy can make more sense when put into context with v. 26. If death is just destroyed or annihilated as some would have it, what does this genuinely mean? The meaning is quite fuzzy. Again, in this case, it makes more sense to view this as a follow-through of v. 24's use of *katargeō* as "to nullify" or "to annul." If we read v. 26 this way, death is nullified or rendered powerless by eternal life. Eternal life snuffs out the presence of death. Verses 27–28 can now be brought into this.

Verse 27 is *prima facie* straightforward, but there is a debate over what the referents are in the verse. The debate largely centers on whether the allusion to Psalm 8:6 (8:7 in LXX) and 110:1 (109:1 in LXX) is enough to depict that Christ is the one to whom all things are subjected or if all things are subjected to the Father. The text makes much more sense when read that all things are subjected to Christ just as he is subjected to the Father. This is supported by the allusions to this in vv. 24–27, the allusions to this in Ephesians 1:20–22, and on a much more tentative note, the allusions to this in Hebrews 2:6 (even though Paul may not have written Ephesians and certainly did not write Hebrews).

In any case, v. 28 is the crescendo of the universalist message to draw from 1 Corinthians 15:20–28. Once all are subjected to Christ, Christ will entirely give himself to the Father. We see a similar scene to this play out in John 20:17. In line with the interpretation of this verse from St Gregory of Nyssa, supported by St Gregory the Theologian and St Ambrose of Milan, Christ goes to the Father and presents him the entire image of humanity, that is, every human who ever was. In subjecting this entire image of humanity to the Father, Christ subjects himself in turn since the entire image of humanity is already in his hypostasis. Gregory of Nyssa *certainly* (and *very likely* the other two) were proud universalists. They understood the radical implications of this. If the entire image of humanity is handed over to the Father through the Son, likewise subjecting himself to the Father, no remainders face torment or annihilation.

Regardless of how well this verse from John matches up with the depiction in v. 28, the universalist interpretation is still justified for the following reason: Paul provides the example of Christ to show that *even* the Son will be subjected to the Father, implying that certainly everything else will be subjected to the Father in some way. Andrew Hronich notes,

"Would Jesus truly be subject to His Father if His will was opposed to the Father, but He merely lacked the power necessary to overthrow His Father?"[15] He makes a good point. In being subjected to the Father, the will of the Son must be in line with the Father's will. But this does not lead Jesus to a lack of will. Jesus still has his will. His will is just entirely in line with the Father. Likewise, when all things are subjected to Christ, all beings will still have their will. Their will is just entirely in line with Christ. As Gregory of Nyssa and Gregory the Theologian interpret this verse, since all beings still have their will, this is a freely made submission.[16] In this sense, Christ is subjected to the Father the same way that all things will be subjected to Christ. And since Christ is perfectly in the Father, all things are perfectly in Christ. The final unity of *apokatastasis* is a unity of wills that comes about through the free choice of all beings. This is why God is said to be "all in all" in v. 28.

The English phrase "all in all" is translated from the Greek *panta en pasin*. In English, this is wonky. In Greek, it is a bit ambiguous as well. Some translations clarify this by saying something like "so that God may be everything to everyone." This helps some since it, likely unintentionally on their part, reiterates that there will be a unity of wills in the *apokatastasis*.[17] Early commentators on this phrase, like Origen, argued it indicates the teleological purpose of creation: To be made divine and returned to its proper order. St Gregory of Nyssa was very clear about the universalist message of this verse and can be quoted. "Either God will not be in all if some evil will be left in beings, or, if it is necessary to believe that God will really be in all, then, together with this conviction, it is demonstrated that there will be no evil. For it is impossible for God to be found in evil."[18] Gregory's commentary acts both as an affirmation of universal salvation and an argument in favor of it. This clear sentiment has similarities to a statement from his commentary on Psalm 150: "All will become one body, and one spirit, through one hope to which they were called."[19] For Gregory, the Psalms form a coherent whole and thus

---

15. Hronrich, *Once Loved Always Loved*; see commentary on 1 Corinthians 15.

16. Ramelli, *Christian Doctrine*, 39.

17. Several translations that do this include the Revised Standard Version, the Contemporary English Version, and the Amplified Bible.

18. Berghaus and Drecoll, *Gregory of Nyssa*, 454. This argument relies on the view of evil as a privation of good. Most Christians hold this view so the assumption shouldn't be a problem.

19. Quoted in Ludlow, *Universal Salvation*, 74–76.

the 150th Psalm serves as a final eschatological statement that emphasizes the beauty, glory, and love that will be given to all "breathing things."[20] All breathing things were quite literally created for this eventual purpose to be realized.

St Augustine of Hippo focused more on the possible consequence of this phrase, which is that Jesus will give up his Sonship to the Father. He believed that despite the heavy-handed language of the verse, we should not understand this in a literal way. Although Augustine did not support universalism at this point in his career, the commentary he provided can indeed be read in a universalist light. Indeed, Jesus will not give up his Sonship to the Father, but his will will be totally united to the Father, just as the individual wills of humans will be totally united to Christ. St John Chrysostom devoted much time to what he believed this phrase could indicate and came up with a few meanings, one of which can be mentioned. He believed that *panta en pasin* could mean that all things will be dependent on God. Although many of his fellow bishops at the time were universalists, John was not. Despite this, his commentary here likewise seems to point in the direction of a universalist conclusion. I take it that all things will be dependent on God because God will replenish and restore the great condition of Paradise in Eden. All things will be dependent on God because our recognition of our dependence on the Father is seen to be in the nature of humanity. We are all called to this recognition. Eventually, this universal call will be actualized. Putting aside my universalist expansions to Augustine and John's commentary, there is no denying that v. 28 means that the wholeness of divinity will permeate, in some sense, all of creation. As John Scotus Eriugena crucially notes, the intention of saying this is not that the substance of God will be destroyed, but that "there will be an ineffable return to the pristine and perfect state that is union with God."[21] Only God will appear in human nature, just like when the air is illuminated by the sun, it is only the sun's light that shines through, but this does not negate the substantial being of air. This completes the *telos* of air, such that it is in the substance

---

20. Note that St Gregory of Nyssa is sometimes ambiguous (and this is one of those cases) about whether universal salvation involves all entities or just humans. I argue that, overall, he does believe even demons will be brought into this universal reconciliation. This sentiment is found in multiple texts. See Ludlow, *Universal Salvation*, 80–82. For this reason, Gregory's universalism is even more radical than Origen's, who denied on multiple occasions that demons will be saved. That is to say, a canonized saint is more of a universalist than an allegedly condemned heretic.

21. Quoted in Villanueva, "Apocatástasis," 30. My translation.

of air to be illuminated by the sun and provide this function for the sun. In the same way, God appearing in human nature does not negate the substance of human nature, it completes its *telos*. God, as the sun, shines through his sons and daughters.

What Paul does not indicate here and cannot be garnered from a sober reading of the text is that the vast majority of entities, or even just some entities in creation, will not be subjected to Christ. Indeed, following the LM, God being "all in all" could entail the existence of damned souls who experience the all-ness of God as everlasting torment. I have heard this many times over from infernalists. Yet, in light of the above, where there is a parallel between the subjection of Christ to the Father and humanity's subjection to Christ, this reading doesn't hold up. As the hopeful universalist Met Kallistos Ware admits, "The phrase 'all in all' (*panta en pasin*) definitely suggests not ultimate dualism but an ultimate reconciliation."[22]

The annihilationist interpretation likewise falls short but, I will say, is stronger (at least biblically, not philosophically per se; see Chapter 15) than the former in this case. The annihilationist may agree that all existing entities are subjected to Christ; this is true because the only entities that will exist at this point are the saved. The damned will have been destroyed, obliterated, rendered non-existent. For this reason, it is true that God is "all in all" because he is all in all, in those that have not been annihilated. The proponent might further argue that since I even admit that vv. 23–24 do not mention non-Christians, they would regard this neutrality in their favor through an argument from silence. Perhaps an argument from silence is better than no argument, so some say. Yet this does not hold much water because the universalist and infernalist can likewise make an argument from silence here. All three are relatively dubious.

In what follows, I provide a hypothetical argument from silence from the position of a universalist and then an infernalist. The universalist argues that even though Paul does not mention what happens to non-Christians in vv. 23–24, we can assume with relatively high credence that if v. 22 indicates a universalist conclusion, then vv. 23–24 should be assumed likewise to have a universalist conclusion. To disagree with this would entail a tension in the text or that Paul has failed to track the argumentative logic of v. 22 to vv. 23–24. In light of the text's non-existent

---

22. Ware, *Inner Kingdom*, 197.

evidence for infernalism or annihilationism, we should conclude that universal salvation is the teaching of vv. 23–24, even though it is never spelled out explicitly.

The infernalist argues that even though Paul does not mention what happens to non-Christians in vv. 23–24, we have it on good credence that Paul believed in ECT. If he did not, he would have mentioned another outcome. We can only assume that Paul was familiar with those in his day who believed in infernalism since Second Temple Jewish texts like 2 *Enoch* seem to teach ECT, as do several Qumran scrolls (see Chapter 6). Since Paul did not mention another outcome yet was familiar with texts that taught ECT and those who followed the doctrine, we should conclude that infernalism is the teaching of vv. 23–24 and reconcile this somehow with v. 22.

In comparing the strength of these arguments from silence, I admit that the annihilationist reading of specifically vv. 23–24 seems the strongest, the universalist reading seems the second strongest, and the infernalist reading seems the weakest. However, this ranking is only true if you disregard the surrounding context. Since v. 22 & vv. 27–28 in this set are universalist, the annihilationist reading is only the strongest when disregarding all this. This is to say that the annihilationist exegesis of vv. 22–28 is only strongest when cherry-picking two verses, but when these are put in their broader context, the annihilationist exegetical narrative falls apart. (See also Chapter 16's philosophical critique of the annihilationist's interpretation of v. 28.) The infernalist reading is the weakest because it must interpolate the idea into the text that those who are not mentioned in vv. 23–24 are not mentioned because they are undergoing ECT. This is not indicated or even hinted at.

Regardless of where these views are ranked based on their level of justification, in the grand scope of things, even the strongest argument from silence does not mean much due to the weak argumentative standard that an argument based on the absence of countervailing evidence has.[23] So, annihilationism doesn't really score any relevant points here. For these reasons and more, I shall leave vv. 23–24 as neutral in that they should not play a decisive influence in our interpretation of v. 22 and vv. 27–28. The infernalist and annihilationist cling to these because v. 28 is

---

23. See McGrew, "Argument from Silence," 215–28 for a philosophical study of the logical structure of an argument from silence and why these arguments should almost always have a very weak influence on human reasoning.

unambiguous about a positive universal union with God, and this clearly informs the way one should, and many Fathers did, read v. 22.

In 1 Corinthians 15:20–28, Paul shows his universalist feathers, but here we are only parsing the tea leaves. If God is all in all, all entities are in Christ in the same way that Christ is subjected to the Father. Freedom remains intact and eternal life is given. This is the ultimate eschatological victory. Any other result would be an absolute failure.

The Universal Gift

> Romans 5:18 (NKJV): "Therefore, as through one man's judgment came to all men, resulting in condemnation, even so through one Man's righteous act the free gift came to all men, resulting in justification of life."

Romans 5:12–20 shares a very similar theme with 1 Corinthians 15:20–28. Like the latter, I argue this set has a universalist message. Many commentators focus on one or the other and then assert that the one they did not talk about is basically saying the same thing. For some, this may be a fine methodology, but I do not wish to mince words about what these verses do and do not mean. In the following exegesis, I focus mainly on what v. 18 entails, but I put it briefly in context with the surrounding verses.

The most important matter in interpreting this verse is determining if the "all" [*pantes*] evoked both times, just like in 1 Corinthians 15:22, denotes a parallel referent. Paul has identified a single class (all men), and this class includes every sinful descendant of Adam. All the members of this single class (all men) are then said to receive justification and life. *Prima facie*, this is a parallel. Early commentators like Origen recognized this. "[Paul] said merely 'condemnation' in order, obviously, to demonstrate how much more abundant the gift to *all* is than the transgression."[24] The renowned Methodist theologian Adam Clarke made a particularly eye-opening statement about the parallel. "Now, leaving all particular creeds out of the question, and taking in the scope of the apostle's reasoning in this and the preceding chapter, is not the sense evidently this?"

---

24. Origen, *Commentary on the Epistle to the Romans*, 340. Origen, along with most early Fathers, interpreted v. 19 as a reiteration of v. 18. For Origen, Paul used "many" instead of "all" in v. 19 in order to hedge his bets and not upset those who wanted to keep everyone in fear of eternal hell. The infernalist St John Chrysostom would also later look past the "many" and view it to be synonymous with "all."

A QUASI-PAULINE UNIVERSALISM

I appreciate Clarke's honesty. However, you would not be surprised to learn that there are modern infernalist critiques of this. One of the most common critiques is exemplified by Douglas Moo. It is true that "all" does not always mean "without exception," as discussed earlier. So, it is plausible that the first "all" means all people without exception, and the second all only denotes a limited group of people. Moo supports this argument with the fact that at other points in Romans (8:32; 12:17; 14:2; 16:19), Paul says "all" but certainly does not mean "without exception."[25]

Despite not saying this, it is clear that Moo is following his Protestant forefathers in his exegesis. This was the reading that most early Reformers took. John Calvin strictly follows this. John Wesley does as well but is less certain with his interpretation because his reading of "many" in v. 19 entirely informs his reading of "all" in v. 18. Albert Barnes is one the few early Protestants who stood out since, in line with many early Fathers, he viewed the "many" in v. 19 to be synonymous with the "all" in v. 18. This is to say that he read the "many" through the lens of the "all" which is a universalist reading and the opposite of Wesley's exegesis. The problem with the traditional Protestant reading that Moo inherits is that while Paul does use "all" multiple times without the connotation "without exception," none of these verses pertain to the context of eschatology, nor do any of these verses indicate two "all's" that leave open the gates for a supposed parallel. You would assume that if there was such a verse where Paul is clearly haphazard in his language to the extent that he uses *pantes* twice, but it has two clear different referents, and moreover that it is even in the context of eschatology, that Moo would provide this. The failure to provide such a verse is quite telling, and I have come up short in my own investigation.

Another response some give is that the second "all" is only about those who are offered the gift of grace, whether they are Jews or Gentiles.[26] This argues that the first use of "all" does apply to all people, but in virtue of v. 17, which supposedly speaks to "those who receive," the second "all" is in reference to how all the people who receive God's grace, whether they are Jews or Gentiles, will be justified. This reading is *prima facie* plausible because the claim has continuity throughout Paul's writings (for example, Gal 3:28). He was very concerned with emphasizing that Christ has offered himself to all kinds of people. This theme is likely

---

25. Moo, *Letter to the Romans*, 344.
26. Witherington and Hyatt, *Paul's Letter to the Romans*, 150. Douglas Moo argues v. 17 in favor of his position as well.

PART 2: UNIVERSALISM IN HOLY TRADITION

even an undercurrent in Romans 5. But this interpretation still suffers from some glaring issues. As Andrew Hronich notes in line with Frank Thielman, "A careful study of Paul's use of *lambanō* (receive) reveals man's passive role in verse 17."[27] Due to Adam's sin, the consequence of his action is what humanity received. The consequence of Christ's act must also be received by humanity in this way. This does not indicate a believing acceptance. Rather, this indicates us being made recipients. Our acceptance of Christ is, in the end, no more voluntary than our acceptance of Adam's sin that brought a finite worldly life to all creation. If v. 17 can no longer be used in the argument for this interpretation, there is no contextual basis to say that Paul's theme of Jew-Gentile relations bleeds into v. 18. Or at least that it bleeds into this verse to such an extent that an obvious parallel is not obvious. Since there is no contextual basis to say that this theme bleeds into the verse, the argument is unlikely to be true.

A response similar to the last is that the second "all" does not mean "without exception" it just means "without distinction."[28] Robert Jewett argues the second "all" means that all *kinds* of people will be justified. The focus from Paul in the second "all" is not on an individual basis for who is and who is not justified; he is just expressing that many *kinds* of people will be justified. I suppose that Paul's language here is thought to be how we might say, "All *kinds* of people like ice cream." The *kinds* of people who like ice cream include young people and old people. There is an exception for those who like ice cream in those groups, but there is no distinction. They all like ice cream. Following Jewett, the *kinds* in Paul's statement refers to the Jew-Gentile theme mentioned earlier and has something to do with those who are believers. All *kinds* of believers, whether they are Jew or Gentile will be justified. The glaring issue with this argument is that Jewett provides no justification, be it linguistic, patristic, or otherwise, which adds credence to his claim that v. 18 means this. If Paul had wanted to say that the "free gift" had been given to all *kinds* of people, he probably would have said this or at least given a modicum of indication that he meant this (the Greek *tupos* or even *eidos* to qualify "all" would not have been a bad idea). Since he did not do either of these, it is safe to disregard this argument.

27. See commentary on Romans 5 in Hronich, *Once Loved Always Loved*.
28. Jewett, *Romans*, 384–86.

A QUASI-PAULINE UNIVERSALISM

The final argument non-universalists arrive at to avoid the obvious parallel is that the text depicts a parallel between Adam and Christ. Though, due to Paul's statements in other verses regarding the destruction or eternal torment of the damned (pick your poison), we must assume he is either inconsistent on eschatology across his writings or that the true meaning of whatever Paul was getting at is lost to time. This is a position taken up by few in general and especially few Protestants.[29] Clearly, this is a last resort, and rightly so. I assume that all universalists, infernalists, and annihilationists would like to think not only that Paul is in their camp but that Paul always has been in their camp. The annihilationist James Spiegel humbly admits that even if the non-universalist wants to use this argument, they must accept the entailment that there is at least a "tension" in Paul's thought, if not a contradiction.[30] To admit that Paul may have switched positions at some point in his life or that he is simply inconsistent leaves a very unsavory taste in the mouth of many pious believers. As someone who disregards claims of biblical inerrancy, this is not a huge deal personally, but it is practically unthinkable for many others. Paul evolved in his theological sensibilities over time? And his letters reflect a change in his thinking? Oh, the horror!

> Romans 5:12 (NKJV): "Therefore, just as through one man sin entered the world, and death spread through sin, and thus death spread to all men, because [eph'hō] all sinned."

One of the big general debates concerning v. 12 is over the prepositional phrase *eph'hō*. Two positions on this can be noted. The first is the interpretation made popular by Blessed Augustine of Hippo. This takes *hō* as masculine with *henos anthrōpou* as the antecedent. A few other interpretive decisions are made, which basically renders the end of v. 12 to read: "In whom [Adam] all sinned." This was the standard translation in Catholicism throughout the medieval ages and was accepted by practically all the Reformers. The theological consequence of this interpretation was that the doctrine of original sin involved the concept of original guilt. Adam becomes the head of the race of humanity, and through his Fall, all of humanity has sinned and is guilty as a result. What would seem to be similar to the Orthodox stance on this verse and the one most favored by contemporary scholars, takes *hō* as neuter and the

---

29. Some broach this as a possible get-out-of-jail-free card to Romans 5:18. See, for instance, Boer, *Defeat of Death*.
30. Spiegel, *Hell and Divine Goodness*, 27.

phrase *eph'hō* as a causal conjunction.[31] This reads: "because all sinned," as mirrored in the NKJV translation above. Due to the original sin of Adam, the sin we inherit as humanity is a finite life; we inherit a finite life and physical death. This brief background provides context to v. 18. Much more can be said, but now we know more about the judgment [*paraptōmatos*] on humanity.[32]

> Romans 5:15 (NKJV): "But the free gift is not like the offense. For if by the one man's offense many [*polloi*] died, much more the grace of God and the gift by the grace of the one Man, Jesus Christ, abounded to many [*pollous*]."

Skipping to verse 15, we are given a lead-up to v. 18's encapsulation of the universalist message.[33] Origen reads the parallel here in Aristotelian terms. Adam is a type of Christ in that he is similar in genus but contrasting in species. The species is in contrast because the transgression of Adam made men sinners but Christ will make men righteous. St Erasmus of Formia and other early Fathers liked this formula. What is of note here is that almost no early commentators expressed controversy with the "many" used in both instances. Likewise, few contemporary commentators take issue with Paul's use of *polloi* and *pollous*. Even those like Douglas Moo, who disagree with the Adam-Christ parallel in v. 18, recognize the universal effects of death in v. 12 are synonymous with the "many" in v. 15. Moo argues that "the many" depends on the context at hand and in this case, it is clear that "many died" and "all died," are synonymous.[34] However, Moo goes wrong since he argues that "those who receive" in v. 17 should inform how we understand the second "many" in v. 15. I already responded to this earlier in the context of v. 18, so it should not concern us here.

Contrary to Moo and other infernalist commentators who inform their understanding of the second "all" in v. 18 with the second "many" in v. 15 & v. 19, I propose we read this the other way around. What if the

---

31. This is not to say that "because all sinned" is favored by every contemporary scholar. Probably the most detailed treatment in favor of the majority view is in Moule, *Idiom Book of New Testament Greek*, but there are some serious scholars who argue other positions. I might also note that the Orthodox stance on this verse, at least from some early Greek Fathers, has taken *hō* as masculine to maintain the "through Adam" theological point rather than "through man" in the neuter.

32. The phrase "sin entered the world" is borrowed from *4 Baruch*.

33. Verses 13–14 are irrelevant, so I pay them no attention.

34. Jewett, *Romans*, 336.

second "all" in v. 18 is what Paul really meant the whole time? If v. 12 is the start of the set, v. 18 is the conclusion, and what comes after is more so Paul restating himself and expanding on the nature of sin. We should inform our understanding of the conclusive parallel with the same parallels given throughout this set. Verse 15 gives us precisely this Adam-Christ parallel. That parallel is then expanded on, and the implications of this are drawn out a bit in vv. 16–17, leading to another parallel. But this time, the parallel is conclusive and is given a poetic diction. In this sense, Paul does not give an argument, flesh out some propositions, and then arrive at a conclusion. Paul has the conclusion from the start, and he lays the groundwork for this conclusion to make sense. We could only fully understand the entailments of this conclusion if we were first provided with a beginning. Adam is the beginning and Christ is the end. Therefore, from Adam to Christ is the *telos* of all humanity. However, this *telos* is not only reserved for us. Paul later indicates in Romans 8:22 that the creative order will be redeemed through Christ. (See Chapter 9 for a universalist reading of Romans 9–11.) Salvation is a gift to all.

The Universal Confession

> Philippians 2:10–11 (NKJV): "In [*en*] the name of Jesus every knee will bow of those in heaven, and of those on earth, and of those under the earth, and that every tongue will confess [*exomologēsētai*] that Jesus Christ is Lord, to the glory of God the Father."

Philippians 2:5–11 is known as the "Christ Hymn." The Hymn in full will be briefly addressed later as it is unnecessary to grasp the eschatological meaning of vv. 10–11. Let us begin with the debate over "every knee will bow" [*pan gony kampsē*]. The act of kneeling can represent the acknowledgment of an entity with a higher authority and/or status. This is seen in Matthew 15:25 and 3 Maccabees 2:1. On the other hand, the act of kneeling can be used as a mode of mockery to an entity that believes it has a higher authority and/or status.[35] This is seen in Matthew 27:29; Mark 15:18; and John 19:3. All three accounts relay how Roman officials mocked Jesus by kneeling for the "King of the Jews." The earliest commentaries on vv. 10–11 lacked a shadow of a doubt that it indicates universal reverence towards Jesus. Origen writes, "Every kind of creature

---

35. Bird and Gupta, *Philippians*, 86.

now reveres him."[36] St Cyril of Alexandria writes, "He worships as one who has assumed the worshiping nature of humanity." Several of the Reformers understood this in their commentaries as well. Martin Luther writes, "This Lord [. . .] to whom everything is subjected even according to his humanity."[37]

Many contemporary commentators agree with the sentiment that *pan gony kampsē* entails universal reverence.[38] Though some doubt this. A scholar would doubt this because the grammatical construction employed in v. 10 is unique, and thus it becomes far more difficult to determine an exact referent. Whenever the verb *kampsē* is used with *gony*, meaning "to bend the knee" as a sign of religious devotion to someone, the object of this devotion is often, perhaps in all cases, expressed by "to" and the accusative (Eph 3:14) or by the dative alone (Rom 11:4).[39] In v. 10, however, "in" [*en*] is employed along with the dative. In this sense, Paul denotes that "every knee will bow" will be a voluntary action of some sort of religious devotion. In the eschatological paradigm here, a voluntary action of religious devotion is precisely the image of universal salvation. This is how St Gregory of Nyssa reads v. 10 as well. Even commentators who doubt the voluntary nature of this action, however wrong they are, are less likely to be concerned that v. 10 indicates a prophecy

---

36. Origen expands the domain of those who worship beyond the confines of humanity alone. He notes that all beings are included in this prophecy. Some commentators like Grant Osborne disagree with this interpretation since Isaiah 45:23, where this phrase originates, clearly indicates only humans. However, Osborne is certainly in the minority, and more importantly, I believe he is wrong on this. Most scholars have now put to rest this controversy in light of Martin, *A Hymn of Christ*, 258. The three plural adjectives ("of heaven and of earth and of under the earth") are what R. P. Martin refers to as a "rhetorical pleonasm." Paul uses poetic license to say that Christ's victory is all-embracing. I argue that Martin's argument holds up. After all, Paul clearly has no problem with adopting Isaiah 45:23 to fit his theological purposes. He does this in another case by denoting Jesus as Lord and substituting "in me [YHWH]" in Isaiah 45:23 with "in the name of Jesus."

37. Quoted in Tomlin, *Philippians, Colossians*, 52–54.

38. To name a few in the last twenty years, see Campbell, *Pauline Dogmatics*; Osborne, *Philippians*; Cousar, *Philippians and Philemon*; Hansen, *Letter to the Philippians*; Silva, *Philippians*; Fowl, *Philippians*. Campbell is a fascinating case because he considers Paul to be a universalist at times and an annihilationist at others. This still leads Campbell to the conclusion that Paul was implicitly a universalist even if his letters do not portray him this way at all times; it is worth noting he considers ten Pauline letters to be genuinely penned by Paul, which I believe plays a large factor in leading him to this conclusion. Also note that for Osborne, as explained above, he limits this reference to humans.

39. Hawthorne and Martin, *Philippians*, 127.

A QUASI-PAULINE UNIVERSALISM

that will be fulfilled. This is often understood by taking "will" as an aorist subjunctive, which indicates that a definite outcome is to be caused by a prior action stated. However, some stragglers resist this reading, as there always are with even the most obvious cases.[40] Regardless, this is not one of those cases where Scripture says that God hopes x will obtain, but Scripture does not indicate that x will obtain. This is a prophetic announcement of, I claim, the universal reconciliation that will occur.

The use of *en* here has significant theological consequences that further demonstrate why v. 10 teaches universal salvation. The phrase "every knee will bow" is borrowed from Isaiah 45:23. In Isaiah, the phrase expresses YHWH's victory over the nations. It is significant that Paul would opt for a verse with the sole message of promoting YHWH as the one true God and apply it to Jesus. Isaiah 45:22 in the NKJV reads, "For I am God, and there is no other." Hence, although the grammatical construction of v. 10 is unique, Paul asserts that the homage is paid *to* Jesus as Lord and not *through* Jesus as Lord; Jesus is not an angelic mediator. It is unlikely that Paul did not know what he was doing by structuring the verse this way. Isaiah 41–45 has four verses (41:13; 42:8; 43:11; 44:6) emphasizing the uniqueness of the divine name. Paul is likewise asserting that "every knee should bow" *in* Jesus.

This is one of the rare moments in the NT where an author may be expressing that Jesus is on a very similar status of authority as God the Father. If every knee is bowing *in* Jesus, then this implies a deep level of intimacy that the text would not communicate if "to" was apt. You can bow *to* a king in a forced show of reverence, but you cannot bow *in* a king, that is, in a king's intimate status, if you do not share a symbolic, or in the case of Jesus, ontological intimacy. This is indeed an argument supported by mentions of Jesus' name in other parts of Scripture. Matthew 18:20 in the NKJV reads, "Where two or more are gathered in My

---

40. Some choose instead to render this as future indicative. Verse 10 is then split off from v. 11, leaving two independent clauses. But as Hawthorne points out, this still leaves you with the universalist conclusion. Hawthorne argues we must leave the right way to take this as an open question since Paul believes in eternal damnation. However, Moises Silva sufficiently illustrates how Hawthorne's argument is flawed. (1) Hawthorne equivocates on God's "purpose." (2) Hawthorne takes [*exomologēsētai*] in v. 11 to be merely subjunctive. This series of verses is just about the lofty hope that God has. God hopes all will bow and confess. As Silva notes, this does not follow in light of the decisive language of Isaiah 45:23 that vv. 10–11 borrows from. This also does not follow in consideration of verses like John 3:16, which opts for "may save" as a subjunctive but is traditionally held to be a firm statement. See Silva's commentary on Philippians 2:11 in *Philippians*.

Name, I am there." Would anyone seriously argue that Matthew 18:20 denotes anything but confessional intimacy? I would hope not. The universalist message of v. 10 has been demonstrated to the extent I consider necessary. Verse 11 is even more explicit with the message of universal salvation.

Following from v. 10, every knee will bow, and now we learn that every tongue will confess as well. The relevant debate surrounding v. 11 is over the phrase "will confess," which comes from the strong Greek verb [*exomologēsētai*]. This verb can mean a number of things. Infernalist commentators often argue the verb in v. 11 *only* means "acknowledge."[41] According to this argument, Paul says that every creature will only acknowledge that Jesus is Lord. An acknowledgment is certainly not the same as the NKJV translation of "confession." By limiting this verb to only indicate "acknowledge," the infernalist commentator can easily skirt any question of an eventual universal reconciliation. Those undergoing ECT will acknowledge Jesus is Lord, but this does not indicate they will joyfully confess that Jesus is Lord. After all, one can easily acknowledge that Jesus is Lord from the fiery pits of hell.

However, this argument is weak when we consider the use of verbs that fall in the relevant semantic domain in other parts of Scripture. Other than in this verse, the verb is used many times in the Septuagint, the NT, and rarely, if ever, denotes anything but respect, praise, and thanksgiving.[42] I argue that Paul follows this tradition closely and likewise uses [*exomologēsētai*] to denote respect, praise, and thanksgiving. If he indeed means that all creation will confess with praise that Jesus is Lord, as I claim he does, then Paul's message is universalist.

Let's examine two verses from the Septuagint and two verses from the NT to demonstrate this. First Chronicles 29:13 reads in the NKJV,

---

41. Hawthorne and Martin do not even consider the other meanings of [*exomologēsētai*]. They simply assume that the verb in Philippians 2:11 only means "acknowledge" since this is what the most conservative use of it can mean. See *Philippians*, 129. Ben Witherington III in Witherington, *Paul's Letter to the Philippians*, considers the hypothesis that [*exomologēsētai*] may refer to thanksgiving and praise but argues it "need not imply this." While correct that the connotation is not inherent, his argument is relatively lackluster since he minces a controversial interpretation of Philippians 1:28 (few render this "destruction" nor should they) with a poor reading of Isaiah 45:24 that seems to completely omit the theme of redemption associated with the text.

42. Considering these uses in the Septuagint and the NT, Osborne admits that Philippians 2:11 *clearly* denotes joyful confession for all creation. However, due to his belief that Paul is an infernalist, he says this must be a tension in the text and cannot literally mean what it says. I suppose some are willing to bite this bullet.

"Now therefore, our God,[43] we thank You and praise Your glorious name." Surely, the author is not simply acknowledging that God has higher authority than him. This is clearly a giving of praise and thanks. Psalm 30:4 (29:5 in LLX) in the NKJV reads, "Sing praise to the Lord, you saints of His, and give thanks at the remembrance of His holy name."[44] Surely, the psalmist is not just telling his audience to acknowledge that God exists and is the highest authority. The psalmist is praising God out of a feeling of voluntary exuberance. Perhaps it is a foretelling of universalism that the psalmist follows this up with, "His anger is but for a moment, His favor is for life." All people have eternal favor with God.

Now, take two examples from the NT. Matthew 3:6 in the NKJV reads, "And [they] were baptized by [John the Baptist] in the Jordan, confessing their sins." Are the people being baptized by John simply acknowledging his presence and higher authority? No, of course not. The people are overjoyed at the baptism rite, leading them to confess their sins. Now imagine if we could see how the use of [*exomologēsētai*] in the NT denotes praise and thanksgiving in context to God. We can. Turn to Matthew 11:25 in the NKJV. "I thank You, Father, Lord of heaven and earth, that You have hidden these things from the wise and prudent and have revealed them to babes." Are you seriously going to claim that Jesus is simply acknowledging the existence of God the Father's higher authority in this verse? No, of course not. This denotes praise and thanksgiving in relation to God.[45] But suppose that, I'm sure some infernalists are thinking, Paul may use the verb differently in his own writings. Indeed, multiple words are employed one way in the gospels but are employed a different way by Paul. This is for several reasons, one of which is relevant to mention. Compared to some of the gospel writers, Paul was more skilled at writing and hence had greater knowledge of how to manipulate the Greek language to go beyond the wooden and literal implications of the text.

For this reason, we should examine the use of [*exomologēsētai*] in Paul's letters. Romans 15:9 in the NKJV reads, "For this reason I will confess to You among the Gentiles, and sing to Your name." This verse begins with language drawn from Psalm 18:49 (17:50 in LXX). Paul uses this to communicate the image that the psalmist and all the Jewish people are praising God with the Gentiles. Once again, this is another use that

---

43. The Septuagint uses "Lord" instead of "God."
44. Or, "holiness" instead of "name."
45. Bird and Gupta, *Philippians*, 86.

indicates respect, praise, and thanksgiving and certainly goes beyond mere "acknowledgment." Even in Paul's writings, then, the verb does not seem to have a distinct meaning from that of the Septuagint and gospels. The argument that [*exomologēsētai*] does not only mean "acknowledge" in v. 11 is strengthened further when we look at 1 Corinthians 12:3.[46] Paul writes, according to the NKJV, "No one speaking by the Spirit of God calls Jesus accursed, and no one can say that Jesus is Lord *except* by the Holy Spirit." Following v. 11, all are either *just* acknowledging Jesus is Lord or confessing that Jesus is Lord. If all are *just* acknowledging this, then all beings have the Holy Spirit. If all are confessing this, then all beings have the Holy Spirit. Those who have the Holy Spirit are always said to be those who have faith and love in God. Since this is true, all cannot *just* be acknowledging that Jesus is Lord in Philippians 2:11. All *must* be *confessing* that Jesus is Lord in joyful praise.

By my lights, infernalists have seemingly two responses in light of this. (1) Admit that Philippians 2:11 is a difficult verse to square with ECT and leave it as a tension in the NT. (2) Argue that saying "Jesus is Lord," for some reason, means two distinct things when one is in an eschatological sense and the other is in a more present sense.[47] Unfortunately for the infernalist, these collapse into a single untenable response. Consider Romans 10:9 in the NKJV. "If you confess with your mouth the Lord Jesus and believe in your heart that God has raised Him from the dead, you will be saved." This verse is very useful for the argument as not only are we given a mouth metaphor like in the case of Philippians 2:11 (every tongue), we are given the line of confessing "Lord Jesus," which is synonymous with Philippians 2:11's confessing "Lord Jesus Christ," and we are given an eschatological overtone like in Philippians 2:11. The infernalist must now admit *at least* four glaring tensions in the text to maintain that Philippians 2:11 does not teach universalism. (1) Philippians 2:11 and Romans 10:9 are in tension. (2) Philippians 2:11 and 1 Corinthians 12:3 are in tension. (3) Romans 10:9 is in tension with Paul's infernalist eschatology (in virtue of (1)). (4) 1 Corinthians 12:3 is in tension with Paul's infernalist eschatology (in virtue of (2)).

---

46. Hunsinger, Philippians, 67.

47. This response may even be entirely discounted by the fact that Paul's famous "already/not yet" formula is throughout the epistles. If anything, I keep (2) as a choice here just so the infernalist can see how both responses collapse regardless of which one they choose.

A QUASI-PAULINE UNIVERSALISM

After considering all this, the infernalist makes their final battle cry by pointing out how since Paul explicitly borrows language from Isaiah 45:23, then if Isaiah 45:23 is infernalist, Philippians 2:10–11 may not be universalist after all. Let's examine the passage.

> Isaiah 45:20–25 (NKJV): "Assemble yourselves and come; draw near together, you who have escaped from the nations. They have no knowledge, who carry the wood of their carved image, and pray to a god that cannot save [. . .] And there is no other God besides Me, a just God and a Savior [. . .] I have sworn by Myself; The word has gone out of my mouth in righteousness, and shall not return, that to Me every knee shall bow, Every tongue shall take an oath. He shall say, 'Surely in the Lord alone I have righteousness and strength. To Him men shall come, and all shall be ashamed who are incensed against Him. In the Lord all the descendents of Israel shall be justified, and shall glory.'"

I have no intention of providing a full-length exegesis of this, but some brief notes can be made. The beginning of the series is about God calling all the idol-worshiping nations to turn away from their idols and worship him instead. This is a common theme in Isaiah and can be seen in other surrounding verses from the scribe Second Isaiah, like 42:17 & 44:9. In Isaiah 45, God then calls the nations to turn away from their idols by swearing on himself that every knee shall bow and every tongue shall confess allegiance to him. As DBH explains, "This is why the Septuagint renders the Hebrew [*tissaba*] into [*exomologēsētai*] and why Paul then uses this language in Philippians 2:11. There is a joyous confession because all creatures have answered the call they were destined to receive from the beginning of time."[48] Despite this, infernalists will often center on the language of v. 24. "All shall be ashamed who are incensed against Him." However, and I think this is such a basic question that for some reason is rarely addressed, as so many unfortunately are, why must the shame of idol worshippers equate to ECT? Indeed, idol-worshippers *should* be ashamed when they first turn to God. Consider Ezekiel 16:63 in the NKJV. "That you may remember and be ashamed, and never open your mouth anymore because of your shame, when I provide you an atonement for all you have done, says the Lord God." God tells the people of Israel that after they pass through a period of idolatry, they *will* be redeemed, and they *will* feel ashamed of their past idolatrous ways. There

---

48. DBH, *You Are Gods*, 119.

is no indication that this shame is synonymous with ECT. The shame is in tandem with redemption.

The other line of attack from an infernalist is to claim that even if all the idol-worshiping nations are taking a bow and oath, this does not rule out a forced submission. However, as Fr Robin Parry argues, there does not seem to be the forced submission of enemies in Isaiah 45:20–25 for a few reasons.[49] First, as we have seen, God has called all the nations to turn to him and be saved. This is the context in which God swears an oath by himself. Second, swearing oaths in YHWH's name is something believers in him do and not his defeated enemies. Third, those who confess YHWH then go on to say, "Surely in the Lord alone are righteousness and strength." This sounds like a cry of praise, not a wretched whimper from a defeated enemy. To argue that not all people will be saved does not follow from this. In fact, Paul's use of Isaiah 45 seems to confirm the universalist reading rather than rebuke it. We can now turn to the overall structure of the Christ Hymn to see how the message of universal salvation is the cherry on top that completes the hymn.

> Philippians 2:5–11 (NKJV): "Christ Jesus, who, being in the form of God, did not consider it robbery to be equal with God, but made Himself of no reputation, taking the form of a bondservant, and coming in the likeness of men. And being found in appearance as a man, He humbled Himself and became obedient to the point of death, even the death of the cross. Therefore God also has highly exalted Him and given Him the name which is above every name, that at the name of Jesus every knee should bow, of those in heaven, and of those on earth, and of those under the earth, and that every tongue should confess that Jesus Christ is Lord, to the glory of God the Father."

Scholars refer to this as a V-shaped trajectory.[50] Jesus Christ began with the highest of glory, descended unto earthly existence (Jn 1:14), went even lower than this in the humiliating death on the cross, and then will receive the highest exaltation possible when all of creation bends the knee and confesses his glory.[51] A worry of this reading is that it can often

---

49. See McDonald, *The Evangelical Universalist*, 94–96 for more of an explanation and support to this augment.

50. Bird and Gupta, *Philippians*, 78.

51. I disagree with Bart Ehrman who argues, in line with many liberal scholars, that Paul portrays Christ's Incarnation to be that of the descent of a high angel. See Ehrman, *How Did Jesus Become God*, 252–69. While Paul often attributed angelic motifs to Jesus, it is clear on other occasions that he thought Jesus to be divinely superior to all other

separate each part of the V-shape into a distinct stage when this is not what Paul intended. The series is meant to flow together as one poem, and the beginning of the series is retroactively justified by the end of the series. This means that we can only really grasp what Paul means in v. 6 when we reach v. 11. These two verses flow into each other; in both cases, the hero (Jesus) enjoys the highest glory and status in heaven. Verse 6 identifies Jesus as equal in some sense to God the Father.[52] In v. 7, then, what we see is an analogy between a king and a slave. Jesus fell to such a lowly place (earth) from such a highly glorious place (heaven) that it is almost like a king became a slave. The King over all became the son of a carpenter, a disgraced trade; the King did not become an earthly king with political powers.

Early Fathers like St John Chrysostom were keen to harp on the identification of the Christian and Christ with the slave. The king motif is justified in virtue of v. 6 & v. 11, that is, a retroactive justification. Verse 8 is about how the ultimate act of obedience from Jesus was his death itself. This ultimate act of obedience was not only to God the Father, following Pauline theology, it was given to many. Once again, if we read this retroactively, the death that was made for all in service of the Father is the eternal life that will be given to all, through the Son, who is in service of the Father.

However, v. 9 institutes a radical change in the Hymn. So far, Jesus has been the active subject. Jesus was the one who brought himself to earth, he was not brought to the earth. Jesus has total sovereignty over his pre-existence. Now, Jesus shifts to become the passive subject. His humiliation experienced on the cross leads directly to his exaltation on behalf of the Father. This exaltation is a victory as the Son returns to the Father. The Suffering Servant no longer suffers as the Servant is exalted into the title of Lord. The slave who was once a king becomes a king again. And with kingship comes responsibility and dominion. Yet his Kingship is not

---

heavenly beings. There are no times in Paul where other angels are praised for the sake of themselves, or given their own judgment day, or are positioned with a heavenly throne seat, etc. Jesus was understood by Paul to be divinely pre-eminent in some sort of way where he had the status of the Father and bore the full glory and image of the Father while still not being a different being than the Father. Put otherwise, Pauline Christology became organized more precisely by Origen and others into what we now call the Nicene Trinity. See Bird, *Jesus Among the Gods*, 60, 351–52, 374–76, for a christological summary of the Philippians Hymn.

52. The key phrase here is "in the form of God" or *morphe theou*. This is a heavily debated phrase, but I confidently hold that it indicates that Jesus is in some way equal to the Father (obviously not in the exact Nicene sense).

solely about dominion and responsibility. His Kingship brings with it the self-giving love that magnifies through the cosmos. This self-giving love is seen on full display in vv. 10–11.

Due to God's ineffable, infinite, and self-giving love, all will bend the knee and confess that Jesus Christ is their Lord and Savior. The power of the cross is eternal, like God's forgiveness. Some may take a long while before they bend the knee and confess, but all will eventually joyfully confess. Joyful union with God is in our nature and there is no way around it.

I shall close this discussion on the Christ Hymn with a few stanzas from John Milton's (in)famous *Paradise Lost*.[53] This can roughly tie the eschatology of Philippians 2:10–11 to 1 Corinthians 15:28. When all have bent the knee and confessed that Jesus is Lord, God will be all in all.

> To glorify thy son, I always thee,
> As is most just; this I my glory account,
> My exaltation, and my whole delight,
> That thou in me well pleased, declar'st thy will
> Fulfilled, which to fulfill is all my bliss.
> Scepter and power, thy giving, I assume,
> And gladlier shall resign, when in the end Thou shalt be all in all, and I in thee.

The Universal Reconciliation

> Colossians 1:20 (NKJV): "And by Him to reconcile [*apokatallaxai*] all things to Himself, by Him, whether things on earth or things in heaven, having made peace through the blood of the cross."

This verse and its surrounding context will serve as a close to our examination of *Quasi*-Pauline universalism. I title this chapter "Quasi" because the verses we have studied so far are from epistles that lack controversy when it comes to establishing genuine Pauline authorship. Colossians is more controversial. It is often referred to as "Deutero-Pauline" in contemporary scholarship. According to Bart Ehrman in 2020, 60 percent of NT scholars think that Paul did not write Colossians.[54] After examin-

---

53. Milton, *Paradise Lost*, 189. Unfortunately, Milton spoils this beautiful message a few stanzas down.

54. Ehrman, "Did Paul Write Colossians?"

ing the arguments in favor of a Pauline forgery in an earlier 2013 text, he writes that the letter is written by someone who wants his readers to think he is Paul.[55] Although 60 percent is certainly not a vast majority, it is a majority opinion, and that probably should mean something. In light of this, I will leave it as an open question whether or not Paul wrote Colossians. On principle, I have no issue with being in a camp that only has 40 percent of NT scholars. After all, I am probably in the minority camp or close to it on the question of whether Jesus is identified in the NT as being, well, pre-eminently equal to God the Father in some vague sense.

In any case, I am leaving this as an open question because I do not believe the evidence reaches the level of justification that would necessitate me to declare a position either way. I will say, however, that many who doubt the authenticity of Colossians *severely* overestimate the credible reasons to think it is inauthentic. Margaret MacDonald's hypothesis can shed some more light on this. "If we think of the authorship of Pauline works as a communal enterprise undertaken by Paul and his entourage, the sharp distinction between authentic and inauthentic epistles is significantly reduced."[56] I quite like the notion of a "Pauline school," not a literal school where Paul is teaching a class of some sort, but a group of people who worked and knew Paul well and sought to advance his theology in one way or another.

This is indeed what scholarship on Johannine literature, including the gospel and 1–2–3 John, have come to note.[57] In the case of John's gospel, it was likely the work of two scribes and a final redactor. The former is indicated by the conclusive statements at the end of chapter 20, which read like an epilogue to the gospel. This is the first scribe closing his gospel. Then we pick up in chapter 21 with several post-resurrection

---

55. Ehrman, *Forgery and Counterforgery*, 315–20. Ehrman does not spend nearly enough time examining the external evidence in favor of Pauline authorship. He centers on the internal evidence such as the letter's theology along with linguistic, grammatical, and syntactical choices of the author. In my extended view, the external evidence (citations from early commentators, plausible locations for it being written, and so on) is certainly in favor of genuine Pauline authorship while the internal evidence is lacking in this department, but it isn't even *that* lacking! The side that strongly opposes Pauline authorship tends to offer little positive external evidence in favor of Deutero-Pauline authorship. In consideration of all this and more, I leave the authorship of this epistle as an open question.

56. MacDonald, *Sacra Pagina: Colossians and Ephesians*, 57.

57. See De Boer, "Story of the Johannine Community," 63–83 for a recent title in this pervasive scholarly debate. I disagree with several claims of De Boer. My brief discussion above has less to do with his work and more with my own research.

PART 2: UNIVERSALISM IN HOLY TRADITION

accounts, a clear apologetic against those downplaying Peter's role in the formation of the Church, and an account that portrays Jesus' foretelling of Peter's glorious martyrdom in Rome. This is the second scribe. The existence of a final redactor is indicated by the first person plural *oidamen*, "we know," in 21:24, which indicates a singular person speaking on behalf of others, verifying that the gospel is from the "beloved disciple;" this cryptic honorary title was perhaps not original to the gospel and was an edit of the final redactor that replaced whoever's name was the "beloved disciple" to maintain secrecy, exude humility on behalf of the main scribe of the text, and to not distract the reader/listener from the narration of events. Yet the scribes agreed with the theological portrayal of Jesus. There is a clear literary unity; they worked in a close-knit community à la, the "Johannine community," and likely read off each other's notes and remained in close contact throughout the composition process of the gospel. The final redactor, then, likewise worked closely with the main scribe of the gospel, perhaps also the second scribe, or he may have lived longer than the main scribe (or both) and hence stood as a final testament to the truth of the "beloved disciple." Much is obviously up in the air. In 1–2–3 John, the last two letters were very likely written by the same person, but a different scribe from the Johannine community may have wrote the first. Similar theological motifs abound when comparing 1–2–3 John with the gospel; the beginning of 1 John is basically a rehashed form of the prologue in John's gospel. This is all to say that if we accept the hypothesis of a Pauline school, then the categories of genuine and Deutero-Pauline may disappear altogether, or at least it would become very difficult to differentiate between them. Still, in light of the fair arguments on either side, I think it's best to leave the authorship of Colossians as an open question.

It is important to state this controversy at the start of this exegesis because the debate over the authorship will become very relevant later. Arguments favoring a universalist or an infernalist interpretation often assume Pauline authorship, allowing them to draw a respective continuity between Colossians and genuine Pauline writings. In this exegesis, I argue that regardless of whether you ascribe authorship to Paul himself or someone else whom Paul influenced, the universalist interpretation still makes the most plausible case for itself. With these introductory words out of the way, we can properly examine the text.

The first relevant debate over v. 20 concerns the use of the crucial verb *apokatallaxai*. The author of Colossians and Ephesians may have coined this specific verb as it appears nowhere else in the Bible or known literary Greek.[58] The verb indicates that a previous state of hostility, estrangement, or alienation has been overcome and restored into a friendly relationship.[59] What exactly the hostile or alienated state is in v. 20 is debated, but v. 13 mentions a "power of darkness," and v. 16 mentions the division into powers and principalities. Putting aside questions of a Pauline demonology here, it is clear that all things were not united for a common purpose, but Christ has united them all.[60] This unity, however, is not completed in the Incarnation. Hence, we see Paul's already/not yet formula displayed here. There is a sense in which the previous state of hostility has *already* been overcome. On the other hand, this union has not *yet* reached its completion and will only reach its completion when Christ returns and reconciles all things to himself. Let's now examine *apokatallaxai* in more depth.

This specific verb only occurs in Colossians 1:20, 22; Ephesians 2:16 and the related word group appears in genuine Pauline writings like Romans 5:10, 11; 11:15; 1 Corinthians 7:11; 2 Corinthians 5:18, 19.[61] Peter O'Brien, a respected infernalist commentator, notes that in all references, the ground of reconciliation lies in the "gracious initiating activity of God."[62] We can examine a few of these to see if his statement holds up.

First, Ephesians 2:16 in the NKJV. "And that He might reconcile them both to God in one body through the cross, thereby putting to death the enmity." This verse is situated in the context of the author explaining a standard Pauline theme of how Christ fulfilled the Jewish law and now believers follow him. The verse says that when someone holds faith and love in Christ, they are reconciled towards God as they are made into new men. Following the entailments of reconciliation above, the new believer has overcome a previous state of estrangement towards God, and now there is a unity between them and God. Reconciliation

---

58. Dunn, *Epistles to the Colossians and Philemon*, 102.

59. Dunn, *Epistles to the Colossians and Philemon*, 102–3; Bird, *Colossians and Philemon*, 57.

60. One should heed MacGregor's call whenever thinking about Paul's demonology. "We shall never get inside the mind of Paul until we take seriously [. . .] [what is] in the primitive Christian proclamation of the Gospel." See MacGregor, "Principalities and Powers," 17.

61. See the entry for Colossians 1:20 in Pao, *Colossians and Philemon*.

62. See the entry for Colossians 1:20 in O'Brien, *Colossians, Philemon*.

obtains as clearly a "gracious initiating activity of God."[63] O'Brien's statement is justified so far.

Second, Romans 5:10 in the NKJV. "For if when we were enemies we were reconciled to God through the death of His son, much more, having been reconciled, we shall be saved by His life." In great depth, I examined later verses in Romans 5, but v. 10 was left unmentioned. To some who are *really* stretching the biblical case for universalism, this may seem to be in favor of the doctrine, but I cannot argue this with good faith. Regardless, the verse is not explicitly against universal salvation, and it is clear that Paul is once again arguing for reconciliation to be obtained as a "graciously initiating activity of God." An activity that overcomes a past estrangement to bring forth a new friendly relationship. This further justifies O'Brien's remark.

Third, 1 Corinthians 7:11 in the NKJV. "But if she does depart [her husband], let her remain unmarried or be reconciled to her husband." This is in the context of Paul declaring the importance of keeping your marriage vows unto death. I suppose someone could claim that this verse breaks the continuity of O'Brien's remark, but this would be a wildly uninformed stance. Paul's discourse about marriage isn't because he personally likes marriage. If anything, we know Paul stressed that marriage is not a necessity. Marriage is important because it is in line with God's commandments. Hence, if a woman who has departed from her husband decides to reconcile herself to him by remarrying him, this is also a reconciliation between her and God. A past estrangement in the worldly context between the wife and husband and, in the divine context, between a sinner and God has been overcome. O'Brien's claim stands firm here as well.

Finally, 2 Corinthians 5:19 in the NKJV. "God was in Christ reconciling the world to Himself, not imputing their trespasses to them, and has committed to us the word of reconciliation."[64] This verse is in context to another one of the "already/not yet" formulas. Paul uses this to say that when we follow Christ in this life, our old character passes away. We become new people in Christ because he helps us shed our transgressions and past sins. This aptly fits Paul's story as a Pharisee

---

63. It is worth noting that Ephesians 2:16 diverges from some depictions of reconciliation in the Scriptures. Such as 2 Maccabees 1:5; 5:20, where God is reconciled to humans, rather than humans being reconciled to God.

64. DBH believes this verse is in favor of universal salvation. See DBH, *That All Shall Be Saved*, 97.

who became "new" in Christ. But humans becoming "new" in Christ in this life is not God's fully completed purpose. Creation as a whole must overcome its estrangement from the divine and become "new" in Christ. This is indicated by the end of the verse, "committed to us the word of reconciliation." Creation is not yet made new in Christ. Thus, there still is a remaining state of estrangement that will eventually be overcome, and those involved will be brought into a friendly relationship with the Father. This clearly supports O'Brien's statement.

After examining four selections from the use of words in the word group of *apokatallaxai* in the NT, I conclude that O'Brien's statement is supported by internal textual evidence. I also conclude that my indication of what the verb entails at the beginning of the exegesis is supported by internal textual evidence.[65] It is now time to examine the debate over the verb *eirēnopoiēsas*, which in English is translated as "having made peace" or "make peace."

This is another particularly difficult verb to parse out because it is a *hapax legomenon* in the NT, though "made peace" is broken into two words in Ephesians 2:15. In the Greek Septuagint, it appears only in Proverbs 10:10. The adjective form of the exact verb, however, appears in Matthew 5:9 during the Sermon on the Mount where Jesus classifies those who seek peace over violence as "blessed." Some commentators against a universalist interpretation employ external evidence to determine that *eirēnopoiēsas*, in the context of Colossians 1:20, involves a type of forced pacification. After concluding that "make peace" means forced pacification, they can then use this to inform their interpretation of *apokatallaxai*. This leaves them with the conclusion that Colossians 1:20 does not promote universal salvation since God forces the damned people and evil powers to be pacified.

Charles Talbert gives the most detailed account of this argument. Biblical evidence is put on the back burner as external evidence is the focus. He lays it out as follows. For those hearing the letter to the Colossians in the context of being under Roman imperial rule, an act of pacification would supposedly entail a sense of subjugation required to "make peace." Talbert cites the ancient historian Plutarch, who comments on Alexander the Great in the following way. "Those whom he

---

65. Peter O'Brien's statement on what the verb (and its related word group) entails, as well as the indication I laid out earlier, is also supported by the use of "reconciliation" in some apocryphal texts: *Jubilees* 1:29; 23:26–29; *1 Enoch* 91:17. Note that, in my view, not all of these depict a universal reference to all entities on heaven and on earth.

could not persuade to unite with him, he conquered by force of arms, and he brought together in one body all men everywhere."[66] Peace will be ensured, whether people want it or not. Then, in the recital acts of Emperor Augustus, we see the language of "peace" mentioned precisely as a result of violent pacification. "The provinces of the Gauls, the Spains, and German [. . .] I reduced to a state of peace." He cites two other sources written or at least compiled roughly around the first century CE. In light of these citations, he remarks that peace does not necessarily come from nonviolence in the Roman world. Peace came from conquest. He concludes that the author of Colossians did not necessarily promote universal salvation through the language of "make peace." Since the author was not necessarily promoting universal salvation in the second half of the verse, we can then read into the first half and hypothesize in tandem with other Pauline writings that "reconcile" must also denote something other than what it seems to say on a first look.

Talbert's argument begins on reasonable grounds. The language of warfare is certainly the context surrounding v. 20. The language of "blood" and "cross" are used here, not in the familiar Pauline fashion. In Romans 3:25, along with 1 Corinthians 11:25, "blood" evokes the symbolism of a bloody sacrifice, harkening back to the Levitical sacrifices done by earlier generations of Jews. The "cross" in Paul often evokes the humiliation and shamefulness that Jesus experienced, as evidenced in Galatians 5:11; Philippians 2:8. The "blood" and "cross" in Colossians 1:20, however, suggest the blood of battle, and the cross is the instrument by which peace is achieved.[67] This is a battle cry of sorts. However, this battle only ends in forced pacification if you assume that the meaning of *eirēnopoiēsas* is entirely uninformed by the adjective *eirēnopoioi* in Matthew's gospel.[68]

According to Talbert's argument, the author of Colossians takes this adjective and turns it into a verb that denotes peace-making through *literal* violence/forced pacification. There are decently strong reasons to

---

66. Quoted in Talbert, *Ephesians and Colossians*, 196. Talbert is one of the only commentators who makes this an explicit argument against the universalist interpretation. A few others mention this in passing.

67. Dunn, *Epistles to the Colossians and Philemon*, 103–4.

68. I should also refer the reader to a study on a handful of early Jewish sources written around the time that use the language of "peace" in a cosmic sense, but do not denote violence. This muddies the waters of Talbert's straightforward claim. See Davies, *Setting of Sermon on the Mount*.

think that the author of Colossians read Matthew.[69] Supposing that the author of Colossians read Matthew, it is unlikely he would adopt a word used to denote the call for making peace without violence, into a call for cosmic peace to be made only through violence. This is not simply a little change on a random verse in Matthew; if it were that, I would have to leave this plausibility open in good grace. This is the Sermon on the Mount, one of the most famous scenes in all the gospels that remained in the collective consciousness of many early Christian groups. Most importantly, this is an entire inversion of the meaning of Christ's words. Since the author of Colossians was a follower of Christ, it is unlikely he would twist the words of Christ like this, so much so that they quite literally mean the opposite of what Jesus called for in one of the most famous scenes of his life.

The credence of my response is even higher if we suppose Paul wrote Colossians. This works against Talbert and many other infernalist commentators who tend to adopt a confident stance on traditional Pauline authorship. We know a lot about how Paul traditionally draws out new meanings in words borrowed from the gospels. What we don't see often, if ever, is Paul inverting a word used in the gospels to mean something entirely different from what it originally meant. As such, it seems unlikely that, in a vacuum, Paul would entirely invert the meaning of a word used only once, and that usage is from one of the most famous scenes in the gospels. In the specific case of inverting the meaning of *eirēnopoioi* to become *eirēnopoiēsas*, this is magnified tenfold. A word used to denote the "blessedness" of those who abstain from violence somehow becomes inverted as a word that speaks to the necessary cosmic violence that must

---

69. Many on the critical side of NT scholarship contest that the author of Colossians could have read Matthew if the author was Paul since Matthew was written after 70 CE. For reasons that are too complicated to detail in this text, I firmly believe that Matthew was written sometime in the early to mid-fifties, twenty years prior to the fall of the Second Temple. Many of my infernalist opponents across Christianity agree with this conclusion. Hence, I do not feel the need to justify why it should be granted that if the author of Colossians is Paul, and we know he read Matthew, this is relevant to the debate. Also, why it should be granted that if the author of Colossians is a student of Paul (or a student of a student of Paul), and we know he read Matthew, this is relevant to the debate. In the latter case, if the author was not Paul, scholarly estimates range anywhere from 70–90 CE for when Colossians could have been written. At the latest, scholars have put Matthew's final composition in the 80s; most put it in the mid-70s. This leaves a decent time frame for the anonymous author of Colossians to have read Matthew.

PART 2: UNIVERSALISM IN HOLY TRADITION

occur before peace. Hence, this is even more unlikely than if we presume the author of Colossians is anonymous.

What about the warrant of external evidence in favor of Talbert's interpretation? Frankly, it doesn't concern me much. This is a last-ditch effort to avoid concluding that Colossians 1:20 has a universalist message. We can respond to this with a few thoughts, but by no means should any of these be taken as a full argument. The sources that Talbert draws on are fine as they are relatively close in the context of ancient history to when Colossians was written. Yet the first issue I see is that he does not cite any Greek text or even transliterated Greek text of the English translations he provides. I should note he cites Greek and transliterated Greek in many other parts of the commentary and on pages near his commentary of Colossians 1:20. If external texts use the language of "peace" to denote forced pacification, and my argument is that this language is similar to the language evoked in Scripture which denotes "peace" such that the language in Scripture might also denote forced pacification; surely, you would expect me to provide the language that allows the reader to determine if the meaning corresponds to that of *eirēnopoiēsas*. It seems to be a scholarly responsibility that if I am backing a linguistic argument using language in an external text, I should provide the original language of the external text. Without the language of the original text, we lack the tools to proficiently study the Greek words involved, dampening any proper analysis.

Moving on from a methodological critique, I would like to briefly turn to the analogy itself employed by Talbert. A military general living in or near the first century CE has a pretty standard goal when they enter battle: Destroy the enemy by any means necessary and take over the land so that it can be used in trade, which will glorify the emperor's power. However, God is not a military general. A cosmic battle for God need not entail the utter defeat of those who are against him, so much so that their defeat leads them to be eternally punished. A cosmic battle for God could very well consist of peace that occurs when, to use the language of warfare, all things on heaven and earth surrender to him. Contrary to traditional warfare, this surrender is not caused by a knife to the throat but perhaps a recognition that the other side (God) was right all along. A recognition that, as we see in the language of St Maximus the Confessor, is primordial in that it remains dormant in all created beings (which includes spiritual beings) until that point at which it is actualized. This does not occur at the same time for everyone. And for some it may be a long time before they come to this recognition. In the end, though, when the evildoers on heaven and earth are defeated, this defeat will come of their own volition. It will come out of their own volition because they will now prize God over their own selfishness. This is total cosmic victory in the only way that would befit God's glory.

I grant that this response to Talbert's external evidence is not very explanatory, but I am confident in leaving this as is because the linguistic argument I made earlier has a very high credence. To harp on this, it is *unlikely* that if Colossians was written by someone other than Paul, then that person would invert the meaning of a word from such a pivotal scene in Jesus' life. And if Paul wrote Colossians, it is *very unlikely* that he would invert the meaning of a word from such a pivotal scene in Jesus' life. Whatever way you flip it, it remains *at least unlikely* that the adjective "peace-makers" would become the verb "forced pacification."[70]

However, suppose we grant for whatever reason that "make peace" is synonymous with "forced pacification." For now, assume that the author of Colossians is anonymous. If we then take this conclusion and use it to inform our interpretation of "to reconcile," this leaves us with a major problem. Two conclusions about "to reconcile" were arrived at earlier. (1) This word entails that a previous state of hostility or estrangement has been overcome and restored into a now friendly relationship. (2) This word entails a "gracious initiating activity of God." These statements were supported by suitable biblical evidence. Hence, if we grant that "make peace" is synonymous with "forced pacification," there seems to be a dire inconsistency. How is there a friendly relationship if there is also forced pacification? It seems unlikely that, in light of the truth of (1-2), it would also be true that the author tries to denote a forced pacification in the second half of the verse. Since this is already *prima facie* unlikely in virtue of what we know about the entailments of "to reconcile," this becomes even more unlikely when we consider the biblical evidence I provided against "make peace" suddenly taking on an inverted violent

---

70. If one does not wish to accept this, the (weaker) argument can then be that the Greek adjective used by the author of Matthew to denote Jesus' message in the Sermon on the Mount is clearly used positively to denote "peace-making." Since Colossians was also written in a Greco-Roman context, it makes sense that, regardless of whether the author knew of the content in Matthew's gospel, the author would be using *eirēnopoiēsas* in a similar fashion since this accords with the literary-linguistic standards of the time. For Paul or whoever to adopt an entirely opposite meaning of the word is unlikely, even accounting for the secular citations that Talbert draws on (which, again, he irresponsibly does not provide the original text of).

meaning in contrast to the use of the adjectival form in Matthew 5:9. In consideration of likelihood in the last paragraph, I argued it was *unlikely* that the allegedly anonymous author of Colossians meant *eirēnopoiēsas* to be understood as "forced pacification." I will now alter my credence in light of what is said here. I now consider it *very unlikely* that the allegedly anonymous author of Colossians meant "make peace" to be understood as "forced pacification."

Suppose the author of Colossians is Paul. The four verses used earlier to back the argument for statements (1–2) being true were four genuine Pauline verses. These four genuine Pauline verses take on even more argumentative force if we grant that Paul wrote Colossians. Since Paul uses "to reconcile" in this way many times, it would stand to reason that Colossians 1:20 likewise uses "to reconcile" in this way. If Colossians 1:20 uses "to reconcile" in this way, then Colossians 1:20 has the message of universal salvation as entailed by the truth of (1–2). If we then add in the stipulation that we should read "to reconcile" retroactively from the interpretation of "forced pacification" in the second half of the verse, we are left with the same inconsistency. In this case, the inconsistency itself is the same, but the likelihood of the inconsistency being true is raised. If we grant even relative linguistic continuity in Paul, there is an even lower credence that "make peace" should be read as "forced pacification" in the case of genuine Pauline authorship. Indeed, it follows from earlier that the credence is raised in favor of universal salvation if Paul wrote Colossians. Since this follows, and I have now adjusted my argument for the likelihood that the allegedly anonymous author meant to denote a "forced pacification," it stands to reason that I should also adjust my likelihood under alleged Pauline authorship. The former was declared to be *very unlikely* in light of the further justification given. I now declare the latter *extremely unlikely* in light of the further justification given here.

Hence, although we cannot be certain that "make peace" entails something that is close to the adjectival form given in Matthew 5:9, it is at least *very unlikely* that "make peace" is synonymous with forced pacification. The *at least* arrives from my statement that if the author of Colossians is anonymous, then it is *very unlikely* for "make peace" to be synonymous with "forced pacification." If the author of Colossians is Paul, then it is *extremely unlikely* for "make peace" to be synonymous with "forced pacification." Since most infernalist commentators seem to ascribe genuine Pauline authorship, this works against their favor. And even if they do not ascribe genuine Pauline authorship, their argument is

A QUASI-PAULINE UNIVERSALISM

still quite unlikely. Overall, I believe this turn towards external evidence is, for the most part, an *ad hoc* approach. The infernalist commentators who do this realize the lack of biblical evidence for their position and the mounting evidence against it. Upon recognizing this, they turn towards another medium in which they can find an inkling of proof that "make peace" is somehow synonymous with "forced pacification."

Instead of focusing on external evidence, the vast majority of infernalist commentators base their argument on the internal evidence of Paul's writings.[71] I shall refer to this as the argument from a holistic view of Paul (AHVP). The argument goes that since Paul doesn't believe in universal salvation, which is indicated by several of his other writings, we have high enough credence to deny that Colossians 1:20 indicates universal salvation. There are several issues with this, as expected.

The first problem with AHVP is that the infernalist commentator must implicitly assume that "reconcile" has a double meaning in v. 20. For believers, reconciliation is a joyful eternal union with God. For the damned humans and evil powers, reconciliation has the entailment of forced subjugation. This is nowhere in the text and cannot be assumed into the text with good grace without an overhaul of ideological bias. The likelihood that "reconcile" would take on a double meaning here begins to decrease even further when we consider some of the past arguments we looked at from infernalist commentators about precisely this issue. In 1 Corinthians 15:22, we examined the debate for why both uses of "all" [*pantes*] obviously have the same referent. The referent is that "all people," each and every single one, will die a worldly death because of Adam's sin but will eternally live in Christ. In this case, there was at least an argument, albeit a weak one, that the second "all" refers to a more restricted group than the first. However, in the case of Colossians 1:20, the debated word "reconcile" is used just once.

Hence, the infernalist must accept the following logic to maintain the argument: The author of Colossians sought to indicate that only some people and entities—those who are already believers in Christ at a specific time before the eschaton—will be saved. The author does not at any point use "reconcile" twice to indicate this, rather he expects his audience

---

71. For instance, see Moo's brief commentary on Colossians 1:20 in Moo, *Theology of Paul*. Also, his more detailed commentary in Moo, *Letters to the Colossians and to Philemon*. The following argument does not rely on the acceptance of an early date for Matthew. It addresses *all* infernalists regardless of whether they accept an early date (though many do, as mentioned).

to implicitly know there is a double meaning in the text. Again, this is an even weaker argument than the one in 1 Corinthians 15:22. The same is true in Romans 5:18, where "all" is used twice to indicate an obvious parallel between Adam and Christ. The infernalist who quibbles that the two uses have different referents must grant the following logic for Colossians 1:20: Although "reconcile" is used once, the author expects his audience to know there is a double meaning assumed here. Believers experience joyful unity. The damned and evil powers experience eternal torment. Once again, this is even weaker than the argument that "all" has two distinct referents in Romans 5:18. The assumption of an implicit double meaning in v. 20 is lackluster at best and baseless at worst.

Furthermore, to argue AHVP, the infernalist commentator seems to presuppose that Colossians is a genuine Pauline writing. They rely on prior conclusions about Pauline verses to back a contextual linguistic argument about Colossians 1:20. If Colossians is not a genuine Pauline writing, then AHVP becomes even weaker. Even if Colossians was written by a student of Paul or a student of a student of Paul, this does not guarantee that the contextual distinction allegedly made by Paul in 1 Corinthians 15:22 and Romans 5:18 would likewise be made by the author of Colossians. Much less than a guarantee, this does not even deserve a high credence. Students of the students of spiritual teachers can employ far different language uses in their writings due to influences from other teachers and their own creative innovations. (Look at the Origenist faction of Palestinian monks known as the Isochrists, which I will discuss in Chapter 10, who were influenced by Origen, Evagrius Ponticus, St Dionysius the Areopagite, and others). Moreover, disagreement from ancient and contemporary commentators on the referent of the second "all" points to just how mysterious the entailments of 1 Corinthians 15:22 and Romans 5:18 may be. Hence, if it is true that Paul did not write Colossians, the argument that the context entails a double meaning is even more baseless than if we assume Pauline authorship and that this authorship necessarily entails an infernalist eschatology. In other words, AHVP lacks high credence even if it is granted that Paul is an infernalist who wrote Colossians.

However, in consideration of my exegesis, we should not assume that Pauline authorship entails an infernalist eschatology. For AHVP to be sound, it roughly relies on two propositions to be true: (1) Texts like 1 Corinthians 15:22, 28; Romans 5:15, 18; Philippians 2:10–11, are infernalist.[72] (2) Paul wrote Colossians. If Pauline verses like these and others are infernalist and Paul wrote Colossians, then it seems AHVP is due a level of credence that Colossians 1:20 is also infernalist. The first, however, has been suitably refuted and proven false. Paul seems to be a card-carrying universalist. Since I left the second as an open question, I shall once again leave this as an open question. In light of my prior exegesis and regardless of my humility in determining authorship, it seems clear that whether or not an infernalist accepts Pauline authorship, they cannot reasonably employ these texts to argue against the claim that universal salvation is taught in Colossians 1:20. Let's now examine the surrounding context and see how this plays into the message of universal salvation.

> Colossians 1:15–18 (NKJV): "He is the image of the invisible God, the firstborn over all creation. For by Him all things were created that are in heaven and that are on earth, visible and invisible, whether thrones or dominions or powers [. . .] And He is the head of the body, the church, who is the beginning, the firstborn, the firstborn from the dead that in all things He may have the preeminence."

This is similar to the Christ Hymn that we saw in Philippians 2. The core ideas of both were likely circulating around before the period in which this was written. I believe the most plausible theological background for the Hymn is a high christological interpretation of Genesis 1:1 that may borrow language from the Wisdom tradition in the OT as well.[73] The notoriously debated Hebrew compound word, *bereshith* (in the Beginning), is polysemous with "firstborn" when taken as *reshith*, the non-compound word. As St Athanasius of Alexandria defended against the heretic Arius, Jesus is regarded as "firstborn" in terms of status, not

---

72. By a stroke of luck, perhaps divine luck, the verses I examined earlier are the exact ones that commentators often trot out in defense of AHVP. See Moo, *Theology of Paul*; Talbert, *Ephesians and Colossians*; O'Brien, *Colossians, Philemon*. Talbert mentions a few of these after his warrant with external evidence. For another older but still cited source in contemporary scholarship, see the commentary on Colossians 1:20 in Bruce, *Epistles to the Colossians*.

73. Michael Bird notes a similar argument for the most plausible theological background in Bird, *Colossians and Philemon*, 48–49. However, I argue that Bird diminishes the influence of Wisdom a little more than I would. It seems he believes the choice is either/or: Either you affirm the influence of Wisdom or turn to genuine Pauline writings like 1 Corinthians 8:6. Why not both? Whether Paul wrote Colossians, we can still say on good ground that the author of Colossians was aware of both 1 Corinthians and the Wisdom tradition. He then sought to incorporate both of them into his own Pauline outlook.

in terms of time. The influence of the Wisdom tradition probably comes from Wisdom 7:26, where Wisdom is said to be the "image" of God's goodness. Then there is also Proverbs 8:22 in the NKJV, which references a Wisdom motif. "The Lord possessed me at the beginning of His way, before His works of old. From the beginning, before there was ever an earth." Parallel language is also in Sirach 1:4; 24:9, and other places. The main sticking point made by Peter O'Brien that points him away from overemphasizing the indebtedness of the Wisdom tradition on the Hymn is that nowhere in any writings on Wisdom is Wisdom said to be the goal of all creation.[74] I concur. This common Pauline and/or Deutero-Pauline motif must come from an original christological interpretation. Seemingly, the only text that could plausibly push against this statement is in *4 Ezra*, but even this says that the world was created for "Israel," and there is some reason to doubt it was even written by the time of Colossians. Hence, it seems unlikely that the link between Genesis 1:1 would be made here if this Hymn does not depict a high Christology.

We see both the link to Genesis and the Wisdom tradition emphasized more in v. 16. The language that "all things were created" links to the language of John 1:3–4, which is purposefully meant as an identification of Christ with Wisdom. This identification of Christ with Wisdom, which ascribes to him to have done certain divine activities similar to the depiction of Wisdom in the OT, is a common motif seen later in Hebrews 1:3. But again, Christ is not equated with Wisdom as such. Jesus Christ was born in the flesh. Many people saw him, spoke with him, and participated in physical activities with him. In this sense, what the author seems to denote, as did Paul many times over, is that Jesus is the Incarnation of Wisdom. Also in this verse is the famous phrase, "visible and invisible," which was dogmatized into the Nicene Creed. This phrase logically leads the author to discuss a few angelic orders, many of which are mentioned numerous times in Paul's writings and stem from Enochic literature. These are the "invisible things" that, as we saw at the start of the exegesis, play into the idea that creation is in an estranged relationship with God. Verse 16 concludes and picks up with another Wisdom motif in v. 17. Verse 18 involves the language of "the church," which is used here for the first time in the Hymn. It also has a distinct ecclesial concept of "the church" not found in undisputed Pauline writings. In Romans 12:4 and 1 Corinthians 12:30, the Church is the body of Christ. Only here and in

---

74. See the commentary on Colossians 1:15 in O'Brien, *Colossians, Philemon*.

Ephesians is Christ the head of the Church.[75] This is a break from Pauline ecclesiology in a way, but it can be informed from the depiction in 1 Corinthians that Jesus would later be regarded, by a future student or an older Paul, as the head of the Church.

In an eschatological context, the mention of "the church" is very relevant to how we must read Colossians 1:20. First, it is clear that the Church is referring to the true believers in Christ. Second, it is clear that the Church is given a fundamental role in the economy of salvation. Salvation will only be guaranteed to those who are members of the Church. Third, the Church plays an important role as a mediator between man and God. Everything said here is in line with Orthodox dogma. Orthodoxy holds that the Church, through the giving of her Eucharist to believers, plays a fundamental role in how we worship God. Worship itself is incomplete until we share a meal with God. Hence, the eschatological relevance of this is twofold: Salvation is only guaranteed to those who are believers and those who accept the Church as a mediator. Upon hearing this, some infernalists may jump for joy as seemingly any shred of universalist hope is removed from the context of Colossians 1:20.[76] However, they fail to realize that universalism completely agrees with this statement. Until one accepts Christ and is brought into the Church, salvation is not guaranteed. However, as shown in my earlier exegesis, the universalist knows that all will eventually be brought into the Church. This is just one of many unfounded inferences on behalf of infernalist commentators. The ecclesial language of v. 18 does not derail the message of universal salvation in v. 20.

> Colossians 1:19-21 (NKJV): "For it pleased the Father that in [the Son] all the fullness should dwell. And by Him to reconcile all things to Himself, by Him, whether things on earth or things in heaven, having made peace through the blood of the cross. And you, who once were alienated and enemies in your mind by wicked works, yet now He has reconciled in the body of His flesh through death, to present you holy and blameless, and above all reproach in His sight."

Verse 19 begins with the language of "fullness" [*plērōma*]. This is to say that the Father's Word, Wisdom, glory, and authority were imbued into the Son. When brought into the previous context of the

---

75. See the commentary on Colossians 1:18 in Pao, *Colossians and Philemon*.

76. For instance, see the commentary on Colossians 1:20 in Wright, *Colossians and Philemon*.

Wisdom-Genesis synthesis that I briefly laid out, it is relatively clear that the Son's "fullness" was not imbued in the current Age. Despite being one of the leading verses cited by defenders of Nicene orthodoxy, this type of language paved the way for the christological heresy of adoptionism. This taught that Jesus became the Son of God only at some point during his time on earth. Some thought this was when he was baptized in the Jordan River. Others thought this was when he was resurrected from the dead. The use of this language likely arose from a still confused doctrine concerning the Godhood of Jesus while he was on earth. These confusions were mostly smoothed out by the Council of Chalcedon in the fifth century. However, even after, the adoptionist heresy was well-regarded by various sects of Arabian Christians into the sixth and seventh centuries. The prominence of adoptionism in Arabia and parts of Syria may have led to a few statements in the Qur'an that seem to explicitly push back against the idea that God can adopt sons (10:69; 19:93–94; 25:2; 39:4–6). It is not entirely clear if the Qur'an was only responding to pagans or also to Christians who held the adoptionist heresy. However, two pointed statements in the Qur'an seem to rebuke the Nicene Trinity or at least a doctrine similar to this (4:169–71; 9:30). Mohammad and his early followers seemed to have been under the mistaken impression that many, or at least a good proportion of Christians, held to the adoptionist doctrine so much so that a polemical argument against it should be included in their holy book.

Putting this aside and returning to Colossians, there is a relevant eschatological point to draw from v. 19: Jesus was given personal agency in the process of reconciliation due to the "fullness" that was in him. The personal agency of Jesus is on full display in v. 20. To review, all are reconciled to him as the Son, through his death, has already overcome the estranged and alienated relationship between God and his creation. The estranged relationship between God and creation has now become a friendly relationship guaranteed by the war-like sentimentality of Christ's death on the cross. This process of overcoming, however, is not fully completed by the death on the cross. There still must be a total "fullness" of all things in Christ. All things must be reconciled once and for all. From here, we are led into v. 21.

Verse 21 is a follow-through of the reconciliation obtained in the last verse. Although "you" may, in a vacuum, seem to be only referencing the person or group receiving this letter, in light of the cosmic reconciliation of the last verse, the author seems to be drawing the people of Colossae into this reconciliation. They, like all of creation, will be involved. Where once the people of Colossae were alienated from God due to their evil deeds, they are now saved: Already/not yet. They are already saved since the truth of Christ has come to them, but this salvation process is not yet complete. Cosmic reconciliation has not yet been obtained where flesh is discarded as all creatures take on spiritual bodies. The people of Colossae still possess the flesh that holds them back from being perfectly holy and blameless. Only through an eschatological cosmic reconciliation will all be made well. All inequities will be alleviated, and all stains will be washed away. God will be all in all (1 Cor 15:28). The gift of salvation will be embraced by all as all are now made alive in Christ (Rom 5:18). Every knee will bow, and every tongue will gratefully confess that "Jesus is Lord" (Phil 2:10–11). And all will be reconciled to the Son in joyful reunion just as he is reconciled to the Father (Col 1:20). These verses tie into each other as the theme is fluent throughout: Universal salvation.

Many universalist authors have examined these verses before, but this section has gone above and beyond what usually qualifies as an acceptable biblical warrant. Still, however, this exegesis could be better. Then again, an exegesis will always be flawed as the field of biblical scholarship is constantly evolving. For this reason, I tried to pay close attention to the work I cited and ensured that the vast majority of scholarship was written in the past twenty years. In the case of texts written prior to this, I only cited them if I believed they offered valuable insights that either (a) contemporary scholarship is highly indebted to or (b) they offer arguments that contemporary scholarship does not sufficiently account for. Even when working under this standard, however, I am sure that something fell through the cracks. Something always does. Maybe in the future I will write more on this topic, but I basically consider this a done deal. Save your comments for the gallows (or an angry book review). I pray that the work produced here is life-giving to universalists who seek to write their own biblical warrant. I also pray that for those who believe a scriptural warrant is necessary for a theological position, this has convinced you of universalism or has at least increased your amicability towards the position. Finally, I implore all to use my warrant as much as they please. What good is the gospel if we don't spread it?

6

The Hell That Never Was

MUCH TO THE SURPRISE of many English-speaking Christians who have solely relied on a copy of their translated English Bible to distill spiritual truths hidden before all ages, there is not a *singular* word employed in the Bible to reference "hell." Hell, as a singular term that is all-encompassing, is a figment of the modern imagination.[1] There is nowhere in the OT or the NT that provides a detailed and clear vision of what happens to those who find themselves in this devastatingly unfortunate situation. And if it even needs to be said, there is no hint of the Miltonian fantasy that hell refers to a kingdom controlled by demons with Satan as the all-mighty ruler. Rather, the OT and NT provide clues that, when pieced together with later revelation through Holy Tradition, can only then become salient. Hence, the salience of hell as a concept is not in virtue of the Scriptures alone but through the imparting of wisdom on behalf of the Fathers and other bearers of divine truth.

When examining the Scriptures, several terms stand out as what may seem to correspond to the modern vernacular of "hell:" Sheol/Hades; Gehenna; Tartarus. These terms, albeit insufficiently, lay out a blueprint

---

1. The NKJV is the only prominent English translation to translate Hades, Gehenna, and Tartarus as "hell." The New International Version, New American Standard Bible, and many others, translate Gehenna and Tartarus as "hell" but leave Hades in transliterated Greek. The New American Bible never uses "hell" once in the translation itself; the term appears once in reference to the Latin Vulgate in a footnote. It often translates Sheol and Hades to "netherworld" but always leaves Gehenna as is.

for how the Christian mind eventually came to understand some sort of post-mortem punishment. This chapter will study these terms in enough detail to conclude that we should not haphazardly group all these terms into the singular all-encompassing concept of hell. We must consider the author's purpose and what the early audience of the oral tradition then text was likely to have understood as the connotation of these terms. Only then can we paint a clearer picture of what OT and NT authors believed about hell and, most importantly, what Jesus and his audience may have believed about hell. It will become very clear that turning towards what the Scriptures say about some sort of post-mortem punishment and trying to construct a complete narrative that does not have any tensions in the text is impossible. This is why I conclude that while the Scriptures should point us in a certain direction when it comes to eschatology, they cannot be the sole principle for how we come to eschatological commitments about hell. If they were, then not a single living Christian today would be justified in their eschatological commitments.

Sheol/Hades: Realm of the Dead

The concept of Sheol in the OT derives from the belief of ancient Jews in a realm of the dead. Almost all the people who have ever lived, regardless of how good or bad they were in life, end up in Sheol.[2] The few exceptions are Moses, Enoch, and Elijah, as they were said to be assumed into heaven. Sheol, then, is certainly not the Anglo-Saxon rendition of "hell" that so many want to read into the OT. There is no clear indication of torture or torment of any kind happening to those in Sheol, although there are times when Sheol is rhetorically used as a punishment by scribes.[3] Above all else, in many texts, Sheol is synonymous with the underworld. The geography of Sheol as the underworld, quite literally under the earth, tracks with the three-tiered cosmological descriptions given in the OT. In Job 11:8; Psalm 139:8; Isaiah 7:11, it is seen to be cosmologically and geographically opposed to heaven. Heaven is above, the earth is below, and Sheol is below the earth.

---

2. This has basically been the scholarly consensus since critical studies on the OT began in the nineteenth century.

3. Johnston, *Shades of Sheol*, 73; Henning, *Educating Early Christians*, 140–45 for a chart of all the times in the OT where Sheol is used rhetorically as a punishment against a particular group or person.

PART 2: UNIVERSALISM IN HOLY TRADITION

Some of the common motifs to refer to Sheol, that we will see in Chapter 7 when examining the Harrowing of Hades mentioned in 1 Peter 4:6, is the language of "no return" (Job 16:22), "bars" (Jonah 2:6), and gates (Isa 38:10).[4] This language is meant to emphasize to the Jews of old that there is no escape from Sheol. Everyone goes there and everyone remains there. However, there are some obvious tensions with verses like these. Scholars since the 1960s have pushed back on what used to be the standard interpretation: Everyone is destined for Sheol and remains there forever. This is because other verses may indicate that only the destiny of the wicked is for Sheol (Isa 5:14; Ps 9:17, Job 21:13) and the righteous are not destined for Sheol. Where are the righteous destined to? That is never said in exact terms. Other verses indicate that sinners (Job 24:19) and/or the immoral (Prov 5:5; 9:18) are destined for Sheol. There is no mention of where the righteous are destined.

The indication that all the dead in Sheol remain there forever is especially pushed back on by verses like Isaiah 26:19. The Rephaim mentioned in this verse are thought to be either a particular clan of Nephilim (giants) that the Israelites faced in battle or they are sometimes referred to as synonymous with the Nephilim as such. Jonathan Yogev comments on this verse with an exquisite parallel, "God's dead shall rise, but the Rephaim shall fall."[5] It is clearly stated that a general resurrection awaits all souls in Sheol other than the Rephaim. This type of despair about the future of the Rephaim is also referenced in Psalm 88:11 to indicate the psalmist's own perilous feeling about the agony he is suffering in life. He has numbered himself among the dead and not just any dead, but the most damned of the dead who will never rise. Yet even here, the motif that there will be some who are not resurrected eventually is not without tension. In short, there are three claims about Sheol and a general resurrection in the OT: (a) All inhabitants are resurrected; (b) Most inhabitants are resurrected except for giants (maybe Rephaim in particular or Nephilim altogether); (c) There is no general resurrection.[6]

---

4. Johnston, *Shades of Sheol*, 76.

5. Yogev, *Rephaim*, 157.

6. Recent scholarship has also come to recognize that some mentions of Sheol in the OT are so absurdly anthropomorphic (for instance, Isa 38:18) that, in fact, Sheol may have been the name of an underworld deity at some point in Israelite (or proto-Israelite) history. If true, this classification became entirely absent in later Jewish history once YHWH became the only deity worshipped and recognized. This is why I don't mention it in the main text. See Koisor, "Underworld," 29–40.

When it comes to everyday life in Sheol, the OT is once again sparse on details. There is seemingly no social interaction for the souls here. Scholars often describe it as a "shadowy existence" that could only presumably be constituted by an ultimate boredom short of non-existence. As Meghan Henning writes, it can hardly be said that those in Sheol are "alive" in any meaningful sense.[7] However, there is some indication that the souls in Sheol can be influenced by the actions of living humans, which must mean they are alive or at least "potentially" alive in Sheol. In the books of Leviticus and Deuteronomy, contacting the dead in any way is outlawed. If you outlaw something, there is certainly a sense that you believe the activity could happen. After all, we don't have laws that impose dreadful sentences on those who time travel and teleport. Then there is the famous story where Saul tries to contact Samuel, who is dead, and we are given a bone-chilling line in 1 Samuel 28:15. "Why have you disturbed me by bringing me up?" Scholars debate whether the depiction of Sheol as a shadowy existence would fit here, considering there seems to be a sense that Samuel was experiencing something during his time in Sheol.[8] What was there to experience? This is unknown. Regardless, there is no question that the author of 1 Samuel believes the dead can be contacted and, perhaps if taken literally (and this is justified in context), rise again; note that this is in tension with later Jewish traditions, such as Wisdom 2:1.

The most thought-provoking interaction between living humans and the inhabitants of Sheol is found in 2 Maccabees 12:45. The KJVAAE reads, "It was a holy and good thought. Whereupon he made a reconciliation for the dead, that they might be delivered from sin." There is a very different concept of contacting the dead here compared to the Pentateuch. Leviticus 19:31 outlawed the contact of the dead using wizards. Deuteronomy 18 outlawed contacting the dead through casting spells and other forms of magic. But in 2 Maccabees, contact with the dead is not made for the sake of the living—a selfish reason—the contact is made to restore the dead to a place of good grace. The contact is also not made with pagan magic and other pagan mediums; it is made through

---

7. Henning, *Educating Early Christians*, 20–22.

8. Recent archeological evidence since the 1950s has indicated that at times in Jewish history, ancestral veneration and contacting the dead in this way was not seen as off-limits. 1 Samuel 28 might be an account from a time where this was attempted, and according to the text, succeeded. See Overton and Friedman, "Death and the Afterlife," 39–42.

the belief of God's chosen people. Since Orthodoxy considers this text to be canonical, we believe that praying for the dead is beneficial for the dead. We don't entirely know how, and we don't pretend that we must know how.[9] In the context of the OT, this reference clearly indicates that the destiny of those in Sheol could possibly change. Where would the souls who exit Sheol go? This is not said. As mentioned in Chapter 2, we cannot presume univocality between the assortment of voices and authors in the OT nor presume there was an attempt to create a coherent eschatological vision.

This introduction does not constitute a suitable study of Sheol. However, it should provide enough context to grasp the depictions of Sheol in the NT. It should also provide enough context to see how the depictions in the NT largely just borrow this concept. The main message to drive home about the discussion of Sheol in the OT is that the Hebrew writers had little interest in what was going on in the realm below and who was in there. They focused on emphasizing the fear of God in their worldly lives rather than academically explaining the details of the afterlife. This theme will change a bit in the NT as authors take more interest in spelling out the details of Sheol, but even then, not to a great extent.

In the NT, Sheol is never once called Sheol. Sheol becomes Hades as this is a translation of the Hebrew word into Greek. Going forward, I shall refer to Sheol as Hades in context to its use in the NT. Hades is depicted in a very similar way to its depiction in the OT. Most of the dead, with a few exceptions, are said to be sent there, and it is sometimes employed rhetorically as a punishment. In the NT, Hades is explicitly mentioned *ten* times: Two times in Matthew (11:23; 16:18), two times in Luke (10:15; 16:23), two times in Acts (2:27, 31), and four times in Revelation (1:18; 6:8; 20:13, 14). Like in the OT, Hades is under the earth (or sea, perhaps; Rev 20:13). Like in the OT, Hades is often depicted as the destiny of sinners and those who are unjust in some sort of way. Like in the OT, not much information is given about what precisely goes on in Hades. Finally, if these mentions are all taken together, like in the OT, we have tensions in the text that portray a non-uniform understanding of the afterlife among the NT authors.

---

9. Personally, I like Fr Sergius Bulgakov's insistence that since Orthodoxy recognizes praying for the dead is a valid way the damned can be saved (though we don't know exactly how), hell can very well be referred to as "universal purgatory" or in the Russian *"vseobshchee chistilishche."* See Bulgakov, *Bride of the Lamb*, 361.

For instance, observe how Matthew 11:23 and Luke 16:23 depict Hades. The context of the Matthew verse is Jesus talking about how since the city Capernaum did not change its heart even after Jesus displayed his powers, it will descend to Hades; and it will be more tolerable for the inhabitants of Sodom on the day of judgment than Capernaum. The point being that if Jesus showed his powers to such a vile city like Sodom, they still would have been more repentant than Capernaum. This use of Hades, then, seems to correspond well with the motif of wickedness and immorality that respectively we saw in Isaiah 5:14 and Proverbs 9:18. Donald Hagner says, "It is difficult to make the application of the first rhetorical phrase to Capernaum more precise, but it seems to refer to an unwarranted, prideful confidence in an exceptional degree of eschatological blessing."[10] In this sense, the immorality and wickedness motifs perhaps come together in the use of Hades in Matthew 11:23. The key motif, however, is pridefulness on behalf of Capernaum. Moreover, this use of Hades does not tell us whether or not most of the dead will end up here. Once again, as with the OT, there could be another destination where some of the most righteous will end up.

The depiction in Luke 16:23, perhaps the most famous depiction of Hades (thought especially here to be a univocal concept of "hell" by many), offers a slightly different take on the constitution of Hades but still retains the OT theme about it generally being a realm for the dead. This takes us to the parable of Lazarus and the rich man. Lazarus is a beggar near the gate of the kingdom. The rich man is, well, a rich man who wears fancy clothes. When Lazarus died, he was carried off to the bosom of Abraham. When the rich man died, he was sent to Hades. While in Hades, the rich man looks up and sees Lazarus far off in the bosom of Abraham. The rich man then calls out to Abraham for mercy. Abraham responds that while the rich man received all the good things in life, he failed to help those who did not. Abraham then says there is a "great chasm" between Lazarus and the rich man that can never be crossed. Infernalists often employ this verse as an argument for ECT, but one cannot garner such a conclusion from the text.

While some may believe this use is more in line with a traditional "heaven vs. hell" motif, this displays a poor grasp of what particularly the "bosom" is. The Greek here is *kolpos*. Interestingly, DBH makes the argument that it is better to think of it as referring to a sort of "hidden

---

10. See the entry for Matthew 11:23 in Donald Alfred Hagner, *Matthew 1–13*.

place" set apart from the rest of Hades while still being in Hades.[11] We must remember that Hades is just the Greek of Sheol, and so the geographical and cosmological location is under the earth. In that sense, the bosom is a sort of shelter given by God to Lazarus in exchange for Lazarus undergoing trials and tribulations throughout life that the rich man did not go through. The modern Anglo-Saxon concept of "hell" is quite removed from a concept like this. Moreover, although it may not be clear on a first reading, Lazarus and the rich man are *both* in Hades, the realm of the dead, yet they are separated as the "great chasm" language evokes. Where the "great chasm" comes from is a mystery in terms of its correspondence to the OT, but it wouldn't be off base to say this may be an attempt by the gospel authors to detail more about how Hades is actually organized; it also likely stems from several ruminations in *1 Enoch*. Perhaps the authors realized that a single realm for the dead without any distinction of where people are situated leaves a bit of a bad taste. This indeed seems to already be the path that later Second Temple Jewish writings were leaning towards. If the teachings of Christ (especially in Luke's account) harp on the importance of being charitable to others, it would make sense to document teachings that show what happens in the hereafter to those who are not charitable. This may track with the later authorship date of Luke over Matthew, where Luke's narrative was more theologically privy to speculate on eschatological matters. If so, this would also track with the increasing level of detail paid to eschatology that we will see in other mentions of terms translated as "hell." Perhaps Luke was the first to jumpstart this by centering more on the idiomatic sayings of Jesus that tried to overturn the simpler OT concept of Sheol. The finale of Sheol is then seen in 1 Peter 3:18, which will be addressed in Chapter 7. Regardless of speculation, it remains clear that the same concept of Hades is not uniformly depicted between Matthew 11:23 and Luke 16:23.

As modern Christians who read the Bible, we cannot presume that the mentions of Hades in the NT correspond with what we believe to be a complete eschatology. The NT does not offer a water-tight eschatology. Rather, as you probably realized in Chapter 5, it offers a few continuous themes that can be plucked out and adapted to fit later traditions in the Church. The first later tradition is that we believe in praying for the dead (2 Macc 12:45). Another later tradition is that we believe the Harrowing

---

11. DBH, *New Testament*, 156.

of Hades (1 Pet 4:6) was a historical event, along the same vein of the resurrection, where Jesus freed the inhabitants of Sheol. This is why we can maintain that the depictions of Sheol in the OT and NT are true. They are not perfectly laid out, prim and proper, like we may want an eschatology to be, but this is why later tradition is so important. Only through the other elements of Holy Tradition are we able to make sense of these often contentious depictions of Sheol (OT) and Hades (NT). Hence, the literalist interpretation of Scripture, once again, utterly fails. A secular scholar may throw up their hands here because these tensions become too much for them. How can it all be brought together under the unconditional promise of Jesus? I suppose that if you believe that each biblical text should be interpreted in a vacuum, then certainly none of this comes together. However, to reference St Paul, a veil still covers both their hearts (2 Cor 3:15). We read the Bible through Christ and his Church.

Gehenna: A Symbol for Post-Mortem Punishment

The concept of Gehenna, or rather, the Valley of Hinnom, is probably the closest concept in the entire Bible to the modern idea of hell, but even this is not 1:1. The Valley of Hinnom is a physical valley located southwest of Jerusalem, that over time in Jewish history became a symbol for post-mortem divine punishment. This is the most likely meaning for most mentions of Gehenna in the NT. A lot of mystery surrounds precisely why this location became associated with divine punishment over any other place in Israel. Still, a few indications in the OT and Jewish apocrypha paint a rough history. The first mention of the valley is in Joshua 15:8, where it is called the "Valley of the Son(s) of Hinnom." There is never any mention in the OT or later Jewish literature of who Hinnom is, but supposedly his son(s) owned this valley at some point. Later in Jewish history, the "Son(s) of Hinnom" was dropped, and the valley became known as Hinnom's own valley, which later became known as Gehenna. Gehenna is the term we see in the NT. The most likely reason why this valley became associated with divine punishment is due to the mentions in 2 Kings, Isaiah, and Jeremiah.[12] However, there is not a single time in the OT where Gehenna is used as a symbol related to

---

12. Second Chronicles 28:3 could also be mentioned, but I don't consider it necessary since it just reiterates the point about child sacrifice. There is no original tradition contributed. Nehemiah 11:30 also doesn't need to be examined because it just uses Hinnom in a brief mention to divide the land.

post-mortem divine punishment. The earliest text where Gehenna takes on this moniker is *1 Enoch*. This section will briefly study the Gehenna tradition in the OT and its eventual use in the NT.

Second Kings has a prominent mention of Hinnom in 23:10, which reads in the NKJV, "And he defiled Topheth, which is in the Valley of the Son of Hinnom, that no man might make his son or daughter pass through the fire to Molech." In the OT, Molech was often spoken about as a Canaanite deity who was worshiped by means of human sacrifice. Many scholars today recognize that this was a misunderstanding on behalf of the OT authors. They argue there is no evidence that Molech was ever a deity but rather was the name for a type of sacrifice.[13] Putting this debate aside, there is suitable evidence to conclude that the Canaanites indeed performed child sacrifice. Whether the sacrifice itself is Molech or they are sacrificing to Molech and/or other gods is irrelevant here.

The claim that Canaanites performed child sacrifice is attested to by prominent non-Jewish ancient historians including Plato, Plutarch, Cleitarchus, Diodorus Siculus, Lucian, and others. Few claims were so broadly attested in the ancient world. Several modern anthropological excavations have likewise determined that the Canaanites (or, as the more proper historical and geographical name for them, the Phoenicians) and their nearby neighbors sacrificed children to their gods. In a 2014 collaborative paper that involved scholars from all over the world, Oxford researcher Josephine Quinn writes, "It's becoming increasingly clear that the stories about Carthaginian child sacrifice are true."[14] She goes on to say, "What we are saying now is that the archaeological, literary, and documentary evidence for child sacrifice is overwhelming and that instead of dismissing it out of hand, we should try to understand it." If child sacrifice was thought to and did occur in a specific region, it isn't far off to think that later Jews would begin to associate the location with a demonic moniker. Indeed, the Valley of Hinnom became seen as an unholy place that was devoid of God's goodness. When it comes to the mention of Topheth, this is another term often seen in verses of the OT and connected to the Valley of Hinnom in some way (Isa 30:33). Topheth either refers to the stand above the fire where the child was placed for sacrifice or the hearth and stand as a whole. Regardless of its

---

13. See a review of the debate in Dewrell, *Child Sacrifice in Ancient Israel*, 8–27.

14. Editors, "Ancient Carthaginians Really Did Sacrifice Their Children." For more on child sacrifice in ancient Canaan, see Dewrell, *Child Sacrifice in Ancient Israel*, 37–68.

precise referent, Topheth, as early as some Levitical traditions, became associated with the place where child sacrifice occurred in service of the god Ba'al.[15]

In Isaiah, a prominent mention of Gehenna is found in 66:24. The depiction is of a valley near Jerusalem that is filled with dead bodies being consumed by worms and fire. The worm will not die and the fire will never be quenched. As Friedrich Nietzsche quips, "To the worm a corpse is a pleasant thought, and to everything living a worm is a dreadful one."[16] The verse likely points to judgment-day imagery, but not in a far-off eschaton; it is a physical last battle waged on Jerusalem. The enemies of the Jews will wage a final battle, but they will lose, and their bodies will fill the valley to the southwest of Jerusalem.[17] This may also indicate a general disposal of bodies that are unfit for proper burial. This may also indicate that garbage in general was disposed here. Likely, the choice to opt for Hinnom over another geographical location is to build on the theme that Hinnom is completely neglected by God's goodness. Thus, Gehenna is associated with three motifs in the OT: (1) Location for human sacrifice; (2) Location for dead bodies of Israel's enemies; (3) Location for general disposal of garbage.

In Jeremiah, the Valley of Hinnom is mentioned several times. One of the most relevant ways that this book builds on the history of Gehenna is that in chapter 19, the valley is renamed the "Valley of Slaughter." This plays into the tradition identified as (1) above. This also plays into the tradition, developed earlier in Isaiah 66:24 and identified as (2) above, that Israel's enemies will be slaughtered through battle in this valley. In chapter 31, it is said that dead bodies pile up in the valley and are burned. This also may seem to associate the valley with (3), a place where garbage in general was disposed of and burned.

According to the legend started by the renowned thirteenth-century Jewish rabbi David Khimi in his commentary on Psalm 27, garbage was indeed disposed of in the Valley of Hinnom. Scholars from all theological stripes and several Christian universalists have run with

---

15. Ba'al is a bit of a complicated term because it denotes a title and a deity at different times. In Aramaic, Ba'al means "Lord." When Ba'al or Ba'al worshippers are singled out in the OT, the reference is to some sort of foreign deity that those people are worshiping. However, when God refers to himself as having once been Ba'al (Hos 2:16) but now is referred to as husband, this is in reference to the title alone.

16. Nietzsche, *Untimely Meditations*, 24.

17. Parry, *Four Views on Hell*, 117–19.

PART 2: UNIVERSALISM IN HOLY TRADITION

Khimi's claim. The prominent Anglican infernalist N. T. Wright voiced support for this multiple times.[18] The universalist Sharon Baker does as well.[19] DBH voiced plausibility for this in his NT translation and his text on universalism but never explicitly supported it in either case.[20] If proven to be true, this should dramatically shape the way we view the statements about Gehenna in the NT. Maybe it was never really a symbol of divine punishment! Maybe Jesus is just talking about a place where bodies decay!

I wish it were easy to say either that this claim is utterly baseless or that it has a strong credence, but neither one of these is true.[21] According to some, the claim lacks evidence and solely reflects a long-held Jewish legend. But there may be at least a *little* reason to doubt such a confidently blanket claim. In the 1970s, the prominent archeologist Gabriel Barkay made some surprising discoveries at a dig site in the Valley of Hinnom. While digging under the remains of a Byzantine church, Barkay and his team discovered several cooking pots that contained crushed and burnt bones. He concluded this indicates Roman cremation tombs were built here, and these can be dated to the period of 70 CE onwards.[22] Certainly, this was after the time that Jesus died, and so this alone should not lead us to believe that the audience Jesus is speaking to is under the impression that Gehenna refers to the burning garbage outside the city. On the other hand, this date already places us in the first century.[23] The credibility of this evidence increases when we consider that Barkay and his team also mention the more than twenty burial caves that were in use from the seventh century BCE to the early sixties CE. In light of this evidence, it seems incredulous to confidently claim that Gehenna was not used as a garbage disposal that was routinely set on fire to make room for more garbage. Still, it would be irresponsible to say this is decisive evidence. Hence, it can be left as an open question whether Gehenna indeed functioned this way historically, but what should not be left as an open question is that

18. Wright, *Surprised by Hope*, 175. This is a restatement of Wright's earlier and more scholarly dealings with the topic in Wright, *Jesus and the Victory of God*, 180–85.

19. Baker, *Razing Hell*, 129.

20. DBH, *New Testament*, 449–50; *That All Shall Be Saved*, 113–14.

21. See also Brad Jersak's helpful scholarship in Jersak, "Gehenna."

22. Barkay, "Riches of Ketef Hinnom," 26.

23. Referencing the account from Josephus about Gehenna having been a burial ground for the dead during the fall of the Second Temple, David Artman adds credence to the view that, at least by the end of the first century, Gehenna was used in this way. See Artman, "Hell."

there certainly seems to be a belief held by Jews around the time of Jesus that Gehenna did function this way. This may lead us to conclude that the Jewish audience that Jesus taught also believed this.

First Enoch is the first text in Jewish history where Gehenna is explicitly used as a symbol of post-mortem divine punishment. The text was written a century or so before the time of Jesus. The author identifies themselves as Enoch, the great-grandfather of Noah, which led to many fascinating hypotheses from early Fathers regarding how exactly the writings of Enoch survived the Great Flood. St Jerome believed that Noah must have had a copy of the text on the ark. Other Fathers came up with their own theories, but St Augustine of Hippo was the first to remark that *1 Enoch* was probably not written by the Enoch in Genesis. He was right. In *1 Enoch* 27, Uriel, a popular angelic figure in Enochic literature, responds to Enoch who asks him a question presumably about the Valley of Hinnom. "This accursed valley is for those who are accursed forever [. . .] here they will be gathered together, and here will be their place of judgment [. . .] in the last days there will be the spectacle of righteous judgment on them in the presence of the righteous forever." This mention is starkly distinct from the canonical OT mentions but clearly built upon the older tradition. (Refer to the list above.) In *1 Enoch* 27, the valley is said to be accursed because of the history of child sacrifices, the resting place for Israel's enemies in the final battle, and perhaps because it is thought to be the location where bodies in general, are discarded. By taking all three of these motifs, the author then expands on the concept of Gehenna by divesting it, in a way, from its physicality in this world as it becomes a harrowing symbol for the next. After *1 Enoch*, the theme of Gehenna as a post-mortem punishment became relatively popular in Second Temple Jewish texts but was never explained in detail and was often highly malleable (also, see *1 Enoch* 54:1–2; 67:4; *4 Ezra* 7:36).[24]

In the NT, Gehenna is only ever referred to as Gehenna. By this time in Jewish history, any tradition about a Valley of the Son(s) of Hinnom or even Hinnom's valley itself had been shortened to Gehenna. Despite this, DBH's NT translation renders all mentions of Gehenna into English as "Vale of Hinnom." It seems he does this for two reasons: (a) He wants to retain a reference to the physical valley of Hinnom since this would certainly be on the minds of those Jesus is preaching to. If this reference is erased altogether, it becomes hard for modern readers to remember the history behind this reference, which does, in some sense,

24. See Jersak, "Gehenna."

PART 2: UNIVERSALISM IN HOLY TRADITION

inform how Jesus uses the term. (b) The choice of "Vale" over "Valley" is to maintain a sense of other-worldliness that accompanies the mentions of Gehenna. Even though Gehenna is in some sense referring to a physical valley to the hearers of Jesus, it also is in some sense referencing an otherworldly punishment of some sort.[25] These are fair reasons, but I keep all references here as Gehenna since this is the more recognized term in scholarship.

Gehenna appears *eleven* times in the Synoptic gospels: *seven* in Matthew (5:22, 29, 30; 10:28; 18:9; 23:15, 32), *three* in Mark (9:43, 45, 47), and *one* in Luke (12:5). This term appears only *one* more time in the rest of the NT, in the Letter of James (3:6). The mention in James is uncontroversially a figurative use and thus has no bearing in how Gehenna is portrayed in the NT. We do not know what James thought was the actual nature of Gehenna, and so I do not engage with the text here. Also, it is worth noting that this term never appears in any writings attributed to Paul or any of the Johannine texts, including Revelation. Whatever Paul and others thought about post-mortem punishment was expressed in different language. In the Synoptic gospels, Gehenna is often depicted as a symbol of post-mortem punishment. This is most clear in Matthew 18:9; 23:15. There is also likely some implicit undercurrent in the mentions of Gehenna that harkens the audience back to the known Valley of Hinnom as the physical place where demonic activities unfolded and Israel's enemies were slayed. This is most clearly expressed in Mark 9:43, which borrows language from Isaiah 66:24. The other mentions in Matthew and Mark (the one in Luke is a repeated motif, with some revisions, from Mark 9:43) are not as clear and can be argued as either referencing the valley itself and the "final battle" motif or perhaps a form of post-mortem punishment. This is unclear from the text, but what we know from the Fathers is that these verses often have multiple meanings. There could very well be an eschatological reference in the verse in tandem with a "final battle" motif of some kind.

Take Matthew 5:22, which comes from the Sermon on the Mount. Here, Jesus decries those who call others "Fool!" and says they will go to the Gehenna of fire. Are we seriously going to argue that Jesus means anyone who says "Fool" is going to undergo post-mortem punishment?[26]

---

25. DBH, *The New Testament*, 452.

26. Charles Talbert considers the mention of Gehenna here to be *entirely* hyperbolic. Perhaps this is a little reductive. See his commentary on Matthew 5:22 in Talbert, *Matthew*.

Jesus in Matthew 5:22 seems to use Gehenna in the way that English speakers say, "go to hell!" when someone insults us, and this causes us to be riled up. If you constantly degrade someone's intelligence by calling them a fool, this will eventually lead them to become angry, and this may cause some sort of conflict. Furthermore, in the context of first-century Judaism, name-calling is even more of an offense than it is today. What your name was and what others called you, especially publicly, mattered greatly. Your name was inextricably tied to your personhood. For this reason, it may be apt to compare the connotation of this verse with Jesus in Matthew 16:23, who says, "Get behind me Accuser (Satan)" to Peter. By comparing Peter to an Accuser, one who brings tribulations to the disenfranchised Jewish people by oppressing them both spiritually and through keeping them as literal debt slaves, Jesus strikes a fundamental blow to the personal character of Peter. This helps us see the purpose of Jesus' name-calling in Matthew 5:22 as well. Those who engage in name-calling are deeply insulting to others, and it is like they need to be told to "go to hell," so to speak. On a tentative note, there may also be a more general belief being expressed here concerning what happens to those who constantly degrade the intelligence of others. If you spend your life insulting others, calling them fools, then you yourself will be made the ultimate fool by God at death. There could be an inversion, then, in what Jesus expresses. The one who calls others "Fool!" will become the ultimate fool when God sends them to Gehenna. In any case, it is probably best to consider the use of Gehenna in Matthew 5:22 along the lines of both a figure of speech and an uncertain eschatological reference.

When we try to determine what connotation the term Gehenna has for both Jesus and his audience, we should also take into account the common parlance concerning Gehenna in the Qumran texts and Rabbinic schools of the time. The eschatology in the Qumran texts written by the Essene Jewish sect is not consistent across the board. Some texts mention the destruction of all the nations, others mention the suffering of all the nations, and yet still, others speak of a redeemed Jerusalem that all nations participate in after a period of suffering.[27] The final is a redeemed state of being where all humans are exalted to the status of angels, shining like stars in the heavens, which ties in with Daniel 12:3, among several later Jewish texts.[28] Due to these diverging traditions, it

27. Nanos, "Question of Conceptualization," 105–10.

28. See Bird, *Jesus Among the gods*, 200–202 for a review of this eschatological motif in Qumran texts and the NT.

PART 2: UNIVERSALISM IN HOLY TRADITION

makes it difficult to speak with certainty about what eschatology the Essenes held. A similar theme is seen in the Rabbinic traditions at the time of Jesus. Some promoted Gehenna as final destruction, others promoted Gehenna as a place of punishment, and still some others thought it to be more along the lines of purgatorial readjustment, which cuts off the suffering of the inhabitants at some undefined point. Much of this was speculation and was not thought to have been divinely revealed. The two leading schools, the Shammai and Hillel, both taught that Gehenna is a place of punishment, and that the wicked in Gehenna will either remain there eternally or some sort of final judgment will eventually surmise and then something else will happen to them. Perhaps along the lines of a complete annihilation. Suffice it to say that the Essenes and even the orthodox Rabbinic schools did not have very borne out eschatologies, but in both cases, even still, there was certainly universalist sentiment to be found; particularly, this was seen in Rabbinic prayers and texts that centered on the restoration of Israel with the whole world whereby all the nations would acknowledge and worship God, rather than just the restoration of Israel by itself.[29]

Whether you found yourself part of an orthodox Rabbinic school or the mystical Essenes, as a first-century Jew, you were inundated with Hellenism wherever you went. All Rabbinic schools and outside groups were deeply indebted to the Hellenistic philosophical imports centuries prior, which influenced their eschatology, such as the innovation of Tartarus in Enochic literature and images of the underworld being associated with fire. As Jacob Taubes wrote in context to the Hellenistic environment that Jews lived in, "One could sing it to a Gentile tune, this apotheosis [. . .] one could sing it in Roman, and one could sing it in a Jewish way."[30] The intermingling of Judaism and Hellenism in Second Temple contexts has practically become a tautology in scholarship since Martin Hengel released his famous study *Judaism and Hellenism* in 1974.[31]

These Essenian, Rabbinic, and Hellenistic considerations may point to certain conclusions regarding what Jesus and his audience may have believed, but these conclusions are still very speculative.[32] Anyone who

---

29. Reif, "Some Notions of Restoration," 301–2.
30. Taubes, *Political Theology of Paul*, 23.
31. Though, see a needed critique of some radical interpretations of this when it comes to Paul's relationship to Judaism in Foster, "An Apostle too Radical," 1–11. Scholars must allow Paul to be an original thinker.
32. See Jersak, "Gehenna."

claims certainty about what Jesus meant by Gehenna or what his audience believed about Gehenna is simply not respecting the nature of a contentious topic like this. Several of Gehenna's mentions could very well just be thinly veiled metaphors that reference the location of demonic activity and garbage fires. But more likely, I believe, these OT motifs are implicitly employed while the eschatological reference for Gehenna— drawing from Enochic literature—becomes the primary connotation in the NT. These motifs may have even led to the eschatological connotation being primary. So, what exactly is Gehenna's eschatological reference? We genuinely do not know. It surely is some sort of post-mortem punishment, but beyond that, the picture gets quite fuzzy. Because of this, we should act with great caution when staking claims that the gospels teach anything that can amount to coherent eschatological doctrines, let alone that there is a single coherent eschatology to be parsed from Jesus' sayings in the gospels. There simply isn't. At this point, I shall end the section with a short message summarizing what has been learned.

In the OT, mentions related to the Valley (of the Son(s)) of Hinnom can be roughly organized into the three categories from earlier: (1) Location for human sacrifice; (2) Location for dead bodies of Israel's enemies; (3) Location for general disposal of garbage. Likely, these motifs became implicit in the first eschatological connotation of Gehenna found in *1 Enoch*. Refer to this motif as (4). (4) then becomes more explicit in the Essenian and Rabbinic traditions around the time of Jesus. In the NT, we are presented with an array of mentions that seem to correspond well with (2); (3); (4). The primary connotation in the NT is likely (4), but we would be diving into pure speculation if we tried to determine what exactly (4) involves. A secondary connotation of Gehenna in the NT involves figurative/hyperbolic language. Unlike the mentions of Hades in the NT, there are not many prominent Orthodox traditions drawn from specifically the use of Gehenna. As mentioned, it is absent in Pauline and Johannine texts and only makes one appearance in the Letter of James (3:6), a figurative one at that. The primary purpose that Gehenna serves in tradition is that it (however haphazardly) lays out several motifs like "destruction" and "lake of fire" that, over time, became subsumed into the eschatology of infernalism. Some recent Orthodox infernalist theologians have also used it to refer to hell after the Final Judgment, such that all the beings in hell before the Final Judgement are not said to be in Gehenna, but after the Final Judgment, Gehenna will be permanent. This

PART 2: UNIVERSALISM IN HOLY TRADITION

has not caught on broadly in the Orthodox world, though several recent saints have seemingly borrowed this language.

Tartarus: A Prison for Evil Spirits

The explicit term for Tartarus does not appear in the OT. There are several references to motifs that would track with Tartarus in 3 Maccabees and one in *Jubilees*, but none of these are explicit. By my count, even in known Jewish apocrypha, the term only explicitly appears *twice*: Both times in *1 Enoch*. In chapter 10, the "prince of demons" tells Solomon that he controls all those who are bound in Tartarus. In chapter 20, Uriel the angel is mentioned as having control over the world and Tartarus. The concept of Tartarus comes from Greek pagan lore and is *very* distinct from both the OT portrayal of Sheol and the Enochic portrayal of Gehenna. Tartarus does not refer to post-mortem punishment for wicked humans. It is the deep dark place thought to be under Sheol (which, again, is itself underground or under the sea or both) where the fallen angels remain chained up and where the demonic giant-offspring of the fallen angels, the Nephilim, remain till the end of days. Tartarus is the prison of the underworld.

The term is explicitly used only *once* in the NT. 2 Peter 2:4 in the NKJV reads, "For if God did not spare the angels who sinned, but cast them down to Tartarus and delivered them into chains of darkness, to be reserved for judgment. . ." Although almost every English translation, including the NKJV, renders this as a noun, "to Tartarus," the term is actually employed as a verb in Greek; it means something more like "they were tartarized. . ." Regardless, this is a clear reference to the Enochic portrayal of Tartarus. The author uses the concept of Tartarus to condemn the false teachers who introduce error into the Church and says they will be like those in Tartarus. This is not meant in a literal sense as Tartarus was not created for wicked humans. There are also a few motifs of Tartarus that appear in the NT but without referencing the term itself, noun or verb. For instance, Luke 8:31 says that the demons begged for Jesus not to send them into the abyss. The language of *abysson* tracks with the Enochic portrayal of Tartarus as well. Whatever the case may be regarding what other gospel authors thought about Tartarus, it seems that Luke believed this motif was useful.[33] But this word and concept

---

33. Jersak, *Her Gates Will Never Be Shut*.

is absent from Paul and the vast majority of the NT. The final reference beyond a shadow of a doubt about Tartarus can be found in Jude, where the author either quotes or knows of a tradition from *1 Enoch* related to Tartarus but still does not explicitly name the location.

To many, this term does not contribute much to Orthodox tradition but rather stands as a weirdly Hellenistic element mixed into the NT. One that I am sure many would like to forget is even in there. While Tartarus is Hellenistic in origin, we should not assume that Luke and Peter believed in the literal Tartarus described in Greek mythology. Rather, they were borrowing from the Enochic portrayal and Hellenistic language to convey a message that can be read into the OT as a nifty location for the Nephilim to be, but is nowhere explicitly in there; moreover, as pointed out earlier, there are multiples times in the OT where the Nephilim and/or the Rephaim are explicitly said to be in Sheol, which makes this very hard to synthesize with the OT and clearly shows a later tradition. For our purpose, the mention of Tartarus conveys a spiritual truth corresponding to what we may call a spiritual geography. Tartarus is not literally under the earth, but in some way, it does exist. Indeed, I must move beyond the confines of historical scholarship here, which necessarily requires one to engage in "phenomenological bracketing" to state a claim that is unprovable by nature.[34] There is no definite answer I can provide or even wish to provide on what exactly Tartarus is, but I have confidence that the motifs described do point to a spiritual geography. There is, in some sense, a mental prison that God keeps certain spirits in, which restricts them from ultimate freedom in some way. What this spiritual geography constitutes further, as with most questions, I leave the answer to divine mystery and our Lord's sovereign knowledge.

---

34. The philosopher Edmund Husserl used "phenomenological bracketing" to mean an investigation into a person's experience of phenomena without regard to whether or not the phenomena is real. Historical scholarship forces one to discuss the experiences and perceptions of others without bias to the existence or non-existence of the phenomena. Here, I break the illusion of "bracketing" and assert an unprovable claim.

7

Christ's Victory Over Hades

THE GOSPELS DETAIL MANY significant moments in the life of Jesus. There is the miraculous birth of Christ, the Transfiguration on Mount Tabor, the crucifixion on the cross at Golgotha, the resurrection from the dead, as well as all the public miracles he performed on earth. The gospels provide crucial insight related to events like these, but there is one event that the gospels do not mention explicitly: The Harrowing of Hades. The Harrowing was a miraculous overthrow of the realm of the dead in which Christ descended to Hades and utterly made waste to the prison where almost all souls, other than at least Moses and Enoch, were held. Although this common name only stems from the beginning of the second millennium, the earliest recitations of the tradition date back to at least the Apostles Creed, which famously reads, "And He descended into hell. . ."[1] Several Protestant denominations exclude this part because it is not found in records of the Apostles Creed before the third century, but it is explicitly clear in the great Anglican *Book of Common Prayer*. "As Christ died for us, and was buried; so also it is believed that He went down into Hell." Orthodox and Catholic Christians likewise observe this event as a historical and eschatological truth.

---

1. One of the earliest attestations we have to the Old-Middle English term "Harrowing" being used to describe this event is Aelfric of Ensham's *Homilies* written at the turn of the eleventh century. In scholarship, the event is commonly known as this, so I shall refer to it with this title.

CHRIST'S VICTORY OVER HADES

This chapter briefly overviews relevant scriptural, apocryphal, and liturgical texts discussing the descent into Hades. I argue the Harrowing of Hades is a precursor to the peaceful universal reconciliation (Col 1:20) that occurs when all God is all in all (1 Cor 15:28) and all bend the knee to confess that Jesus is Lord (Phil 2:10–11) because we are of the same race as God (Acts 17:28) and have been given life through Christ (Rom 5:18).

The Harrowing in Scripture

The only *explicit* mention of the Harrowing in the NT is found in 1 Peter 4:6, which reads in the NKJV, "The gospel was preached also to those who are dead, that they might be judged according to men in the flesh, but live according to God in the spirit." The narrative for this event goes as follows. After the death on the cross, the body of Jesus was in the tomb for three days before he was resurrected. While Jesus was in the tomb, he did not simply lie there in wait until three days had passed. On the contrary, Jesus spent this time evangelizing and presumably freeing those in Hades. Those who, according to Genesis 6:6, were the ones that God was sorry for creating. Often commentators wrongly assume that 1 Peter 3:18–20 is referencing the same event, the evangelization of the dead, but this refers to Jesus preaching to the disobedient spirits only; this refers to the Nephilim—the race of giants—that were discussed as being imprisoned in Tartarus at the end of Chapter 6. If we base our theology of the Harrowing solely on the explicit mention in 1 Peter 4:6, then Jesus preached to all people and offered them salvation regardless of what they did in their earthly lives. Whether all people joyfully answered to the preaching of Jesus is not said.

While the Harrowing occurrence may find its only direct expression in 1 Peter, there are several OT prophecies and events that point to the eventual descent into Sheol/Hades.[2] Three are discussed below. While this will not be discussed further, there is already a portrayal of a descent into the underworld found in *1 Enoch*. Enoch travels to an underworld in complete darkness with a river of fire. This is not exactly like the Hades depicted in the NT or later apocrypha since it seems to be influenced more by Homeric motifs than motifs associated with Sheol in the OT. There are also a number of indirect mentions in the NT that reference the descent. Several are discussed below: Matthew's gospel has

2. Bremmer, "Descents to Hell," 343–44.

two mentions, Acts has *two* mentions, Ephesians has *one* mention, and Revelation has at least *one* mention.

The first relevant prophecy is found in Ezekiel 37. In this chapter, the prophet explains a vision where he is placed by God in a valley full of dry bones. The question is posed as to whether these bones on the ground can live, and Ezekial responds that only God knows. God then asks Ezekial to issue a command to make the bones come back alive. Ezekiel does this and the bones come back to life as people with flesh. In v. 11, it is said that these bones are the people of Israel. The second prophecy is the chronological narrative of Jonah. Jonah was kept in the body of the whale for three days. Matthew tells us in 12:40 that to parallel this, Jesus was kept in the heart of the earth for three days. The third OT prophecy is found in Hosea 13:14, which reads in the NKJV, "I will ransom them from the power of the grave; I will redeem them from death." These three OT prophecies, even without the parallel given by Matthew, point to Christ's descent and conquering of Hades (also Job 38:17; Ps 15:10).

The first NT mention has already been stated, but the other one in Matthew relates more specifically to who exactly was freed during the descent. In chapter 27, it is said that the tombs were opened and the bodies of the saints were released after the crucifixion of Christ. Then, when we turn to Acts, we see a clear attestation in 2:22–24 that the descent into Hades was a historical event of some kind. Peter's famous speech on the day of Pentecost mentions how Jesus was not abandoned to Hades and his flesh did not see corruption. He entered Hades but was not abandoned to it and while he was absent from his body, his body did not decompose but remained in perfect condition in the tomb. This mention in Acts cannot be overlooked because it clearly shows that the apostles believed in the Harrowing, and this was not a mere metaphor or figure of speech. The other plausible indirect mention in Acts comes from 13:34–37, where it is said that David was raised from the dead without corruption. Turning to Ephesians, we see an indirect mention of the Harrowing in 4:9, where it is said that Christ descended into the lower parts of the earth so that when he ascended, he would fill all things. Out of all the indirect mentions, this is perhaps the *most speculative* and eschatological. Finally, in Revelation 20:10, it is said that Christ will cast Hades and death into the "lake of fire." This builds on the earlier motif from Revelation 1, where Christ says he holds the "keys of Hades and Death." His descent and destruction of Hades demonstrated the authority that Christ, as the Son of God, had over Hades. A destruction that is complete with tossing them into the lake of fire. That is, per Deuteronomy, the all-consuming fire of God (Deut 4:24).

By my lights, mentions of the Harrowing in the NT leave us with four relevant conclusions. These theological motifs crop up in the liturgical texts we will examine below: (1) The Harrowing of Hades was historical. (2) Jesus preached to all souls in Hades and thus offered salvation. (3) There is no clear answer as to whether all souls accepted salvation. (4) Jesus declared (at least) partial victory over Hades and Death.

The Harrowing in Early Christian Apocrypha

Central to the Orthodox stance regarding the divine inspiration of Holy Tradition is an unwillingness to declare that Christian apocrypha is utterly baseless and lacks inspiration from the Holy Spirit. While many in other traditions have no problem decrying all Christian texts outside of the twenty-seven books in the NT as nothing more than early Christian superstition and legend, Orthodoxy has always taken a more reserved stance. Several apocryphal texts play a fundamental role in how the details of the Harrowing of Hades evolved through Eastern liturgy and thus deserve an examination. When Holy Tradition borrows motifs from this or that text, however, this does not entail a full endorsement of the text. While many in other Christian traditions believe divine inspiration is a one-size-fits-all, Orthodoxy has always maintained that aspects of texts can be divinely inspired while other parts of the text can be completely rejected. This is important to note because the texts mentioned in this section involve some theological elements that are anti-Christian and certainly anti-Orthodox. The confirmation of which elements from these texts are inspired and which elements are to be sorely rejected is found in the liturgical tradition we will examine later. In general, the apocryphal texts provide much more detail regarding what exactly occurred in Hades. The most relevant point to consider for our purpose is: Who was saved, and who (if any?) was not saved. These narratives related to the Harrowing vary in origin as well as content, but they maintain the four theological motifs mentioned above and, importantly, shed more light on specifically (3).[3]

3. This section, "The Harrowing in Early Christian Apocrypha," was presented in an edited form at the National Conference for Undergraduate Research in April 2024 held in Long Beach, California, under the title, "The Harrowing of Hades in Christian Apocrypha and the Controversy over Universal Deliverance."

PART 2: UNIVERSALISM IN HOLY TRADITION

In this section, I argue that the earliest apocryphal traditions related to the Harrowing describe an occurrence in which Jesus Christ breaks into Hades, frees all souls in Hades, and grants them salvation which brings them to Paradise. Later apocryphal texts seized this narrative of universal salvation and twisted it to such an extent that it either entirely disappeared as a restrictive salvation narrative came into play or later texts left the issue of who is saved as entirely ambiguous. The evolving apocryphal narrative that leads away from viewing this as a universal event is in line with the evolving narrative in the Fathers that turned away from viewing this as a universal event. However, the latter is not in the purview of this section. This section will summarize two of the earliest and most detailed apocryphal texts that explicitly indicate that Christ led a true victory over Hades and freed all people. These are *The Questions of Bartholomew* and *The Gospel of Nicodemus*.[4] These texts, the first being the earliest, explicitly reference that all souls in Hades were freed by the Harrowing led by Christ. The destruction of Hades was not conditional or partial, it was total.

The earliest traditions relevant to the Harrowing found in the *Questions* date well back to the second century.[5] But the text is found in only six manuscripts. Two each in Greek, Latin, and Slavonic. These were written sometime between the third and fifth centuries.[6] Each manuscript's narrative is similar in the core theme that there was a Harrowing of Hades, but the details differ given which manuscript is being examined. All text manuscripts roughly detail the following core

---

4. The *Questions* is often mixed up with the lost *Gospel of Bartholomew* which is referenced by a number of sources including St Jerome the Great. It is unknown whether these are identical texts. The *Questions* is also often mixed up with the *Resurrection of Jesus Christ by The Apostle Bartholomew*. These are two different texts and are in no way identical.

5. There are certainly late traditions in the *Questions* such as what is likely a Nestorian portrayal of Jesus' nature later in the text. This places the christological background of the second section probably around the fifth century. Still, there is large agreement from scholars that specifically the Harrowing narrative can be dated back to the second century.

6. A tangentially unrelated but fascinating point to make on the theological background of this text is that it contains a very mature Mariology. Mary is seen as both the keeper of divine knowledge who teaches the apostles, and veneration is paid to her in the face of suffering, primarily by Bartholomew. This is perhaps the first text which explicitly has both of these theological motifs and it is remarkable that it can be traced back to the third century, if not earlier, since the predominant consensus in Western scholarship for many years was that Marian devotion only began in the fifth century. See Shoemaker, *Mary in Early Christian Faith*, 95.

narrative: Jesus was crucified on the cross and once all the other disciples left the scene, only Bartholomew, the disciple identified as Nathaniel in John 1:46, was left. While he was paying close attention to Jesus, Jesus suddenly disappeared. Bartholomew then heard voices coming from under the earth and felt an earthquake. Bartholomew is puzzled about this. In the discussion that follows, Jesus explains how he left the cross to provide salvation to those in Hades. At this point, the continuity between the six manuscripts begins to unravel.

In the oldest Latin manuscript and supported by the two Slavonic manuscripts, it says in v. 9 that Jesus delivered Adam and all the prophets to salvation.[7] The fate of other souls is not mentioned. However, the oldest surviving Greek manuscript in v. 9 says Jesus went to save Adam and all who were with him.[8] Throughout the NT and apocrypha, Adam is a symbol of the fallen human race as a whole. The fact that the text specifies not only "Adam" but also those who were with him, that is, his descendants, clearly points to a universal deliverance from Hades. However, a few tensions in the Greek text play into the relevant narrative. Verse 20 seems to be in tension with v. 9 because, in the former, it is said that Jesus led "all the Patriarchs" out of Hades. There is nothing said about the non-Patriarchs here. That same Latin manuscript earlier also has a tension in the text here because it provides a universalizing change to the statement made in v. 9. No longer are only Adam and the prophets delivered but also "all who were detained in the same place." This presumably means that all souls in Hades are delivered as well.

The most overbearing tension in the manuscripts probably concerns their treatment of v. 21. Both Latin manuscripts indicate that Jesus liberated all souls from Hades, but then they say that once the dead arose and worshiped Jesus, they returned to their tombs. "I saw you again, hanging upon the cross, and all the dead arising and worshiping you, and going up again into their sepulchers."[9] This is a very odd textual addition, considering it makes almost zero sense. Jesus raised all people from the dead so they could worship him and then sent them all right back to (presumably) Hades. Why did he bring them out of Hades in the first place? In accordance with Bart Ehrman, I consider this corruption to be a purposeful attempt by (two?) later Latin scribes who sought to erase the connotation of universal deliverance from the earlier tradition that

7. Ehrman, *Journeys*, 221.
8. Alfeyev, *Christ the Conqueror*, 27.
9. Elliott, *Apocryphal New Testament*, 657.

eventually developed into this verse.[10] The archetype of which they were drawing traditions from likely omitted the narrative point that the dead went back to their graves. Instead, the original tradition or something close to it probably ended with "and all the dead arising and worshiping you." That is a universal deliverance whereby Jesus empties Hades of its contents and brings all to worship him as Lord in peaceful exuberance. This erasure of universal deliverance from apocryphal texts by later scribes is seen on an even greater display when we consider that the Greek manuscript entirely omits the Latin/Slavonic narrative in v. 21 where the dead arise and worship Jesus and then return to their tombs. It is quite simply not there.

When piecing together the genealogical development of this text, a few elements stick out and should be considered. Although v. 9 in the surviving Greek seems to indicate an obvious universal deliverance/salvation, the same surviving manuscript utterly omits v. 21, which would, if ended at "and all the dead arising and worshiping you," further support the motif of universal salvation. The choice to omit this may seem nonsensical from our point of view (and it is if you are trying to put forth a narrative of universal deliverance), but it makes sense when we consider just how serious later Christians were about trying to erase any shred of evidence that universal salvation was a popular position in early Church history. These later Christians were so dead set on removing any shred of universal deliverance that they would sacrifice implementing tensions in the text and randomly scrap verses just to avoid any of their audience discovering the original connotation. And if the Greek was indeed later than the Latin manuscripts, as Ehrman and I argue, this would be an expected outcome.

Roughly then, I believe the transmission history can be summarized as follows: The Latin derives from an original second-century tradition regarding the descent, which taught that Jesus saved all people from Hades. From the Latin, came the Slavonic, which borrowed many traditions handed down from the Latin but with some of its own innovations. In v. 21, it is said that Bartholomew saw angels while Jesus was still on the cross, but it omits the nonsensical narrative that the dead returned to their tombs after worshiping Jesus.[11] From the Slavonic finally comes the Greek, which tries to lay the final smackdown on any hint of universal

---

10. Ehrman, *Journeys*, 223–24.
11. Elliott, *Apocryphal New Testament*, 657–58.

salvation. It does this successively by omitting any hint of the "dead arising and worshiping you" in v. 20. Still, it fails to do this in v. 9, which seems to indicate a universal salvation or deliverance from Hades. A rough genealogy like this paints a sordid picture: Non-universalist Christians sought to cover up earlier traditions by corrupting texts and rewriting them in an attempt to fit an infernalist eschatology. After all, as any rational person could admit, if indeed all people were raised from Hades and brought into Paradise, why is it implausible that all people who are not currently in Paradise will again be raised at the Second Coming and brought into Paradise? Thus, later non-universalist Christian scribes of the *Questions* made a committed and prolonged attempt to, put bluntly, erase history.

The *Gospel of Nicodemus* has the most detailed account of the Harrowing out of all the apocryphal texts. The traditions that formed it come soon after the account of the Harrowing in the *Questions* and are influenced by them. Almost all future accounts of the Harrowing from apocrypha and Eastern liturgy incorporate one or more key themes from this text. The work is structured as follows. Part one is often coined as the "Acts of Pilate." Part two discusses the descent of Christ into Hades. Part three discusses the resurrection of Jesus. Scholars debate just how early the text is since there are elements that certainly cannot be before the fourth and fifth centuries. And during the Middle Ages, the text (specifically Latin A)[12] enjoyed wide appeal and authority that leveled even the canonical gospels. Before this, there are few direct citations.[13] But on the other hand, some elements undoubtedly date back to apostolic times. Having examined many sources in favor and against the early dating of this text, I concur with Met Hilarion Alfeyev that the core themes developed no later than the middle of the third century.[14] This places it around a century from its predecessor, the *Questions*. There were once hundreds of manuscripts of this text in many languages (Latin, Greek, Coptic, Syriac, Arabic). Like the *Questions*, the versions differ in the core theme we have been studying: What is the extent of Christ's salvation effort in Hades? Compared to the *Questions*, however, there is not much contention about which recension of a complete manuscript (all three parts) is chronologically first. The oldest recension with all three parts dates back to the sixth century and was written in Latin. But there are

12. Izydorczyk, *Medieval Gospel*, 47.
13. O'Ceallaigh, "Dating the Commentaries," 22; Izydorczyk, *Medieval Gospel*, 15.
14. See Alfeyev, *Christ the Conqueror*, 30–31 for many resources on the debate.

spurious mentions of a text resembling "The Acts of Pilate" or perhaps early iterations of the text itself in second-century St Justin Martyr's *Apology* and Tertullian.[15] Regardless, Latin A is the earliest manuscript, which puts the compilation of the written text at the beginning of the sixth century.[16] The other two most cited manuscripts in scholarship, Latin B, and the Greek, respectively, come later.[17]

The relevant part of *Nicodemus* is part two, which discusses Christ's descent into Hades. All narratives seem to have a common theme: Hades and Satan are personified as two entities in dialogue with each other in concern of the coming Savior who will overturn their power, lay waste to their dwelling, and free (at least) some of their prisoners. From here, the narratives lose continuity and consistency. We will first examine Latin A, then Latin B, and then the earliest Greek manuscript (M).

Latin A is very clear about its connotation of universal salvation. Hades says, "If [Jesus] is so powerful in humanity, of a truth I say to you, he is all-powerful in divinity, and no one can resist his power." Satan responds that he has tempted the Jews to kill Jesus so that Jesus will hopefully be delivered to Hades. This, however, does not work out so well for Satan and Hades. Jesus surely arrives in Hades, but this arrival is more like when the Kool-Aid Man bursts through a wall. As they are conversing, v. 21 tells us that a "voice of thunder" says, "Lift up your gates, princes; and be lifted up your everlasting gates, and the King of

---

15. Elliot, *Apocryphal New Testament*, 164–65. St Justin Martyr mentions the "Acts compiled during Pilate's time." This would indeed indicate an ancient dating of the first century ("Pilate's time") but a number of scholars like Izydorczyk consider whatever Justin referred to as not existing and he was mixing up his referent with something else related to a "Passion" proof. I don't think Justin mistakenly attributed a tradition to a non-existent text as this would be quite foolish and not something we would expect from him. Likely, we simply do not have this text anymore and whatever it said or didn't say that was similar to the manuscripts of *The Gospel* we have, is unknown.

16. Elliot, *Apocryphal New Testament*, 166; Izydorczyk, *Medieval Gospel*, 3.

17. Jeffrey A. Trumbower agrees with the conclusion that as *Nicodemus* developed, universalist elements were removed, but he disagrees with this specific chronology. For Trumbower, the Greek text was first, then came Latin A and B. I argue this is misguided because the Greek (what I refer to as M) is an attempt by a later scribe to synthesize A and B. Trumbower's analysis of *Nicodemus* overlooks what I later argue to be universalist motifs in Latin A. Although he overstates some universalist motifs in Greek M, he rightly considers Latin B to be non-universalist. I seek to illustrate how, like in the later manuscripts of *Questions*, the connotation of universal deliverance from Hades was taken out overtime and rewritten with a non-universal deliverance. This may have been done for a number of reasons that I will touch upon at the end of the section. See Trumbower, *Rescue for the Dead*, 105–8.

Glory shall come in."[18] Then, the prophet David says he recognizes this voice because he has "prophesied through the same spirit." Suddenly, the Lord descends into the eternal darkness in the form of a man. This type of "hook-line" approach to the narrative would become prominent in commentary on the Harrowing from St Gregory the Theologian, St John Chrysostom, and many other Fathers (as well as Eastern liturgical texts) through the centuries. Hades was tricked by Jesus because he could not sense the hypostatic union of Jesus. He perceived Jesus to be merely a man. This is the "hook" that Satan bites, which leads him to allow Jesus into Hades. This allowance leads to the downfall of Satan and Hades. It is then said that Jesus breaks the "indissoluble" chains and visits "us" who were sitting in the deep darkness of trespasses and "in the shadow of death." I have not seen any commentators mention this, but by my lights, the "shadow of death" phrase comes from Psalm 23 (22 in LXX). The psalmist (presumably David) speaks to the fact that God will always walk with us in the shadow of death. In the Harrowing narrative, David references his prophecy and tacks it onto Christ as he who walks with us in the "shadow of death." And as Ehrman notes, the message of universal deliverance is seen in the language of "indissoluble" and "us."[19] The chains that were thought to be forever in place on all prisoners of Hades have been broken by Christ. If we then add to this my tie-in with Psalm 23, the chains are broken for all people because Jesus reaffirms his status as God and his status as forever remaining with those who were in Hades. Even when they were believed to be prisoners, they always had Jesus with them. Now that Jesus has descended and freed them, they are perfectly in Jesus.

The message of universal deliverance is emphasized by v. 22, which goes so far as to say that through the death on the cross, Jesus has "perhaps [received] dominion over the whole world." This is said after a band of demons cry out, "[You] attempt in addition to deliver everyone from our chains?" But, I hear some argue that this verse's subjunctive language may show that the writer is apprehensive about a complete destruction and deliverance. After all, the statement ends with a question and then says "perhaps" which would indicate uncertainty on behalf of the writer. This would be a fair critique if a few statements in v. 23 weren't there. For

---

18. Elliot, *Apocryphal New Testament*, 193–94.
19. Ehrman, *Journeys*, 226.

instance, Hades then says, "The human race no longer fears us," referring to himself and Satan.

The nail in the coffin that shows Latin A preaches universal deliverance is indicated by the following statement: "Why without reason did you dare unjustly to crucify him in whom you knew there to be no fault, and bring to our realm an innocent and righteous man, and release the guilty, wicked and unrighteous of the whole world?" Although this ends with a question, it is an emphatically clear sentiment addressed to Satan by Hades. Hades is wondering why Satan ever allowed Jesus to be crucified in the first place.[20] Satan then wonders why Hades allowed Jesus to enter the realm of the dead and "release the guilty, wicked and unrighteous of the whole world." I consider this not only the most direct statement of universal deliverance found in *Nicodemus* but perhaps even the most direct statement of universal deliverance found in apocryphal texts overall. It is then said in v. 24 that Jesus stretched his hand out. "Come to me, all you my saints that have my image and likeness." The "image and likeness" is obviously a reference to Genesis 1:26 and indicates all humans. All humans were made in the image and likeness of God. The culmination of the Harrowing is seen later in v. 24 when Jesus makes the "sign of the cross" on Adam and all his saints and then ascends from Hades.[21] Verse 25 makes it clear that they ascend to Paradise. The saints are now identified as all humans who are delivered regardless of how wicked or unrighteous they were (see v. 23).

Thus, Hades is destroyed as a prison for the dead, and Satan is left alone to struggle against the pressing weight of God that will, in the end, eventually overwhelm him. Moreover, as Ehrman argues, the universal deliverance from Hades did not only affect the humans there at the time, according to the text, but also had everlasting and timeless consequences.[22] A statement in v. 24 reads, "O Lord, set the sign of the victory of your cross in Hades that death may no more have dominion." Hades, Satan, and Death have completely lost their right to dominion over the fallen. Those who are now in hell will eventually be brought into Paradise. The Lord has dominion over those in hell and he is all-powerful. The will of

---

20. This may indicate a reference to Luke 22:3 and/or John 13:27, where Satan entered Judas. This led to Judas reporting Jesus which led to the crucifixion.

21. A mention of the "sign of the cross" tells us that the tradition which became this verse comes from no earlier than the early third century when Tertullian and several others mention the sign.

22. Ehrman, *Journeys*, 227.

CHRIST'S VICTORY OVER HADES

Christ and the power of Christ is greater than that of Hades, Satan, and Death. The love of Christ is more powerful than any worldly attachment or demonic possession. All people who have passed since the Harrowing will once again be freed and brought into Paradise in due time.

Latin B is against any message that teaches Jesus ensured a universal deliverance from Hades, but some scholars like Zbigniew Izydorczyk downplay the extent of these purposeful omissions. However, again, this would track with the later date of it and the hypothesis that later Christian scribes sought to erase away the history of universal salvation. We can find an anti-universalist statement almost immediately at the start of the descent narrative. "The gates of death and darkness have been destroyed, and the saints have been brought out of there, and have ascended into heaven along with Christ the Lord."[23] So, the "saints" are brought out, but there is no mention of anyone else. Latin B does contain the similar phrase, "Lift up your gates you princes;" and it soon follows up v. 19 with Satan saying, "All my dungeons now lie exposed." But the first does not in any way indicate universal salvation; it indicates that Christ descended into Hades with a destructive entrance. The second, I claim, may point us to that type of universalist remnant we saw in later manuscripts of *Questions* as well. Here, it seems that the (Christian?) scribe left this phrase for whatever reason, even though it plausibly could be taken as universalist if placed in the proper context. In comparison to Latin A, the dialogue between Satan and Hades on this point is shortened as there is less expression of fear and trembling towards Christ but more of a focus on preparation for the coming Christ. "[They began] to fasten the locks and iron bars." This language was found in Latin A, but it is just more emphasized here. Verse 20 provides another anti-universalist sentiment. "And the kingdom of those who have believed in him will endure for ever." There is nothing said about those who did not believe. Again, however, we see remnants of universalism four verses later when Jesus greets Adam and says, "Peace be to you, Adam, with your children, through immeasurable ages of ages."[24] Perhaps the scribe believed this was ambiguous enough so he did not feel the need to edit out this sentiment. A more direct omission in v. 24 is the removal of the "image and likeness" language. In Latin A, this language indicates that all humans are saved and not only the saints. Perhaps the scribe did not add this

---

23. Elliot, *Apocryphal New Testament*, 200.
24. Elliot, *Apocryphal New Testament*, 203.

language because he realized how the early scribe (and third-century tradition) explicitly preached a universal deliverance; the saints are not the only ones with the "image and likeness" of God.

The final relevant statement against universal deliverance is found in v. 25, which leads to the culmination of the Harrowing in v. 26. "Then the Savior [. . .] immediately threw some down to Tartarus and led others with him to the world above." This sentiment is nowhere in Latin A and is essentially a textual addition made by a scribe for ideological reasons. Unequivocally, this tells us that Latin B does *not* teach universal deliverance. "Then all the saints asked the Lord to leave as a sign of victory, the sign of his holy cross in the underworld." In comparison to Latin A, the sign of the cross is made here to bar the demons and Satan from taking back those whom Christ had saved.[25] The sign is not meant to declare complete and total victory over Satan, Hades, and Death. But, I hear some say, v. 26 also includes a statement about Tartarus but does not mention humans being sent there: "Then we all went forth with the Lord, leaving Satan and Hades in Tartarus." Indeed, the scribe does not mention any prisoners of Hades being sent to Tartarus, and if this alone was what v. 26 said, then it seems the culmination would somehow involve salvation for all prisoners in Hades. Unfortunately, the statement right before this is clear that "some" will be sent to Tartarus. In short, the later scribe who composed Latin B not only made small omissions and additions here and there. The later scribe, in essence, rewrote the Harrowing narrative of Latin A to invert the beautiful universalist message by morphing it into a message of restrictive deliverance.[26]

The Greek M manuscript of the Harrowing derives from a translation of the Latin A manuscript and was likely written at the end of the ninth or tenth century.[27] For our purpose, the key question remains the same: What was the extent of Christ's effort of salvation? The answer in Greek M is far more ambiguous than the two Latin versions: Latin A is certainly universalist and Latin B is certainly non-universalist. In

---

25. Ehrman, *Journeys*, 229.

26. Recognizing cases like these in textual traditions is important because it further deconstructs the myth that scribes of ancient texts saw themselves as mere copiers who sought to reproduce word-for-word the meaning of sentences they were translating into their respective languages. Rather than viewing this as a series of scribal "mistakes" or "errors," this was the scribe's creative voice with all their cultural, theological, and political biases being imputed into the text. For more on the creativity of scribes in early Christianity, see Moss, "Curators of the Word."

27. Ehrman, *Journeys*, 230.

Greek M, the focus is shifted a bit from the salvation effect to the effect of Christ's preaching. The scribe emphasizes that Christ preached to everyone, but whether everyone is saved or not is unclear. Maybe, as Ehrman argues, this version attempts to compromise between the two very distinct pictures found in the Latin manuscripts. If the Greek M is indeed a translation from Latin A, and it seems it is, then perhaps the later Greek scribe was dissatisfied with the universalist message in Latin A and the non-universalist message in Latin B. The scribe sought to unify the two by remedying them so that aspects of both could be preserved. In the case that the scribe of Greek M did not have access to Latin B (although there is reason to think he at least looked off notes), then perhaps the Greek scribe sought to nuance Latin A by moving the emphasis on universal salvation to an emphasis on universal preaching. In either case, Greek M stands as a nuanced version of the Harrowing.

We can see a universalist sentiment in places like v. 20. Hades says to Satan that he is worried that all prisoners will be freed with the coming of Christ. "None of the dead will be left." Then, there are two notable universalist statements in verse 24. Jesus is said to have cast them out of Hades after he reached his hand out to Adam and all the "others." But earlier in the text, such as in v. 18, we see a more nuanced position.[28] Jesus mentions to the prisoners of Hades that it is time for them to repent because there will come a time when this is not possible. The latter time is never specified, but it is reasonable to assume the scribe means the period after Jesus ascended from Hades. So, if the prisoners in Hades do not repent now, they will not have a chance once Jesus leaves Hades. Due to v. 18, we are left with a question: Did all prisoners in Hades repent according to Greek M? Going off basic probability, more than likely not. If we assume that all people who have died (other than Moses, Enoch, and possibly a few others) before Jesus' Harrowing are in Hades, then it seems only probable that at least one person chose not to repent. At least one person decided that their hatred for Christ and love for idols (in the case of pagans) was more important to maintain. On the other hand, Hades is certainly not a great place to be (even by this early period in Christianity, Hades was already merging into motifs associated with Gehenna). Is it really such a logical leap to think that everyone in Hades would indeed like to be saved from this treacherous place? Both arguments can be made with relative success, but I think that, unfortunately,

---

28. Ehrman, *Journeys*, 231.

if we are seriously trying to determine what the scribe may have wanted to indicate, it seems that Jesus did not save all prisoners from Hades. In any case, this is all speculation, and it is quite difficult (if not impossible) to get into the mind of an anonymous scribe who lived over a thousand years ago. What we can say for certain is that Jesus preached to all people in Hades according to Greek M. Whether all responded joyfully is not said in the text.

This section leaves us with a conclusion that may seem conspiratorial at first but begins to make sense when some necessary rejoinders are provided: The oldest texts of *Questions* and *Nicodemus* are universalist in nature. Some of the later texts of both are not universalist in nature. The latest texts of both are certainly not universalist in nature. If I were to leave the conclusion at this, I would have to accept the accusation of conspiratorial thinking. At the start of my last text, I defined conspiracy as "an attempt to explain events as mediated and contingent on a non-lacking Big Other which doubles itself in the subject's assumption of Deception on behalf of the Big Other."[29] To mercifully spare the reader from a lengthy explanation of psychoanalytic terminology, a conspiracy theory develops when a person believes an authority is purposefully deceiving them of the truth of a narrative, and they are one of the few, if not the only ones, who can see through the ideological charade. In context to our discussion here, the alleged conspiracy developed is as follows: Although it may *seem* like the various additions and omissions of these texts do not have an overarching political and ideological bias, if you look deeper into the transmission history, there is a purposeful effort over many years by committed individuals who sought to erode the message of universal salvation which was the standard in early manuscripts. This is indeed what many commentators on the Harrowing narratives seem to be arguing without much nuance. Overall, this type of mindset is relatively common among scholars. How ironic it would be for an author who wrote a text analyzing the structure of conspiracy theories to posit a grand conspiracy like this.

Ironic indeed, but there are reasons to think that such a textual development took place among multiple scribes. I will not be able to go in-depth with these as that itself would take a chapter, but a brief explanation is in order. I estimated the time frame for the earliest compilation of both these texts to be roughly around the second to the fifth century. The

---

29. Coates, *Conspiracy and the Subject*, 8.

CHRIST'S VICTORY OVER HADES

Questions was compiled in the second century, and the earliest complete (all three parts) manuscript of *Nicodemus* was probably compiled by the fifth century. Constantinople II was held in 553. Allegedly, this council condemned *apokatastasis* and thus universalism as a whole when it anathematized Origen of Alexandria in its Canon 11. This canon served as a sort of culmination to the growing distaste for Origen's universalism that had been building steam for several centuries by this point. The earliest of both apocryphal texts mentioned were compiled before the council. These early manuscripts were far more universalist than the ones that came later. Perhaps the growing distaste that eventually led to the council in 553 contributed to the feeling of need by Christian scribes to edit old traditions that had now gone out of style. This would track with the growing number of Fathers who had come out against *apokatastasis* in centuries leading up to this, the most notable being St Augustine of Hippo. This would also track with several local councils in the fifth century that began to come out against Origen. Since these texts were compiled in the period leading up to the alleged condemnation of universalism as a whole, Christian scribes felt that the onus was on them to ensure later compilers of traditions were not confused as to why the Harrowing was at first preached as a total deliverance and destruction. As mentioned earlier, if the Harrowing was a total deliverance, why can God not ensure a total deliverance once again? The scribes may have recognized precisely this.

A more Marxian analysis may focus on power and authority's role in religion. If religion is the "opiate of the people," in the sense that it makes their lives more enjoyable and functional all the while they become addicted to the illusion it creates, then a religion that teaches all people who once were bad were then delivered from their miserable state into a higher esteem of happiness, will be a religion that struggles to maintain power and authority. This type of message strips away the power of the state and Church to command people to follow their will. A much better way to ensure that the state and Church have command over people is to posit that many of those wicked souls who lived miserable lives will endure an even more miserable life in the hereafter. And you, too, if you do not obey their authority, will endure this everlasting misery, i.e., hell. Hell reflected the Roman penal code and punishments that victims were already associated with. Early Christian texts like the *Apocalypse of Peter* explicitly did this, as did St Augustine of Hippo in his *City of God*. Megan Henning writes, "The suffering of bodies in early

PART 2: UNIVERSALISM IN HOLY TRADITION

Christian hell was part of the culture of surveillance meant to ensure productivity and good behavior in a system pervaded by the power of domination."[30] People become addicted to bliss, but the opium comes with a cost: Follow the proper authorities or you will lose the opiate and endure a miserable existence forever.

The philosopher Hannah Arendt took a similar view to this. She notes how the doctrine of hell was something the few could hold over the many to maintain moral and political control. She goes on to say, "The point at stake was always the same: truth by its very nature is self-evident and therefore cannot be satisfactorily argued out and demonstrated."[31] Throughout her career, Arendt was critically focused on how political and religious authorities use the framework of truth as a bludgeon. Hell was obviously the most grotesque invention one could create to maintain such political and religious authority. She shows her prowess in patristic studies by citing St Gregory of Nyssa and Origen as those who saw past the bludgeoning attempts by those in power. Those who manifested the teachings of Jesus better than anyone else of their time. Those who recognized the Harrowing and moreover the entire Christian eschatological vision for what it truly is: The preaching of the Good News. The most relevant point she makes in the essay is that the doctrine of eternal hell in both the East and West grew to prominence after the downfall of Rome and the gradual rise of the Papacy's temporal power. While I reject such a sweepingly secular view of history, there is a great kernel of truth here: Power structures in society saw the narrative of universal salvation as a detriment to their ideological biases and thus sought to erase this narrative and provide a substitute that matches more with their proclivities of power and domination over all people but especially minority groups.

Whatever the reason these plot-altering edits were carried out over the years, I think it's safe to say that for Orthodox Christians who pride themselves on having an ancient faith, we should put aside these later manuscripts and turn towards the earliest ones. It is worth noting that no ecumenical council ever condemned the belief in a universal deliverance from Hades. Blessed Augustine of Hippo was the only early Father to state this as "heretical." Even the other infernalist Fathers of the time never went this far. It has always been left as a *theologoumenon*. Some say that since the ecumenical councils anathematized universal salvation,

---

30. Henning, *Hell Hath No Fury*, 38.
31. Arendt, *Between Past and Future*, 131–32.

CHRIST'S VICTORY OVER HADES

the belief in a universal deliverance from Hades has also been anathematized. Yet whether or not the ecumenical councils did the former—I show in Chapter 10 they certainly did not—this still has no bearing on whether the councils anathematized a belief in a universal deliverance from Hades. The belief in the total and complete destruction of Hades is fine for an Orthodox Christian to accept. Perhaps this is even expected if liturgical texts should inform our theology, as will be discussed below.

I shall summarize the relevant motifs present in the *Questions* and *Nicodemus* as follows. These should lead us to recall the four conclusions related to mentions of the Harrowing in the NT. (1) The Harrowing was a historical event. (2) All souls were preached to by Jesus and thus offered salvation. (3) There is disagreement over whether all souls accepted salvation. (4) There is disagreement over whether Jesus declared partial or total victory over Hades and Death.

The Harrowing in Orthodox Liturgical Texts

The Harrowing of Hades plays a paramount role in Orthodox liturgy, both historically and today. Christ's descent is mentioned more than a hundred and fifty times on Sundays throughout the year.[32] It may seem odd from a Catholic or Protestant perspective to involve elements from Pascha (Easter) in your standard liturgy, but for Orthodox Christians, every Sunday is like a "little Pascha." This is why there is an annual selection by the Orthodox Church of eleven resurrection accounts that are read on a repeating cycle.[33] Every liturgy provides a time to recall the glorious promise our Lord brought to us through his resurrection and destruction of Hades. While certainly not infallible, liturgical texts are one of the various doctrinal authorities that play a necessary role in the formation of our theology. Hence, when considering a proper Orthodox stance on the Harrowing, it is only just to approach what liturgical texts say about this event.

However, before we do this, it would be worthwhile to briefly lay out what I consider a suitable analysis of the liturgical structure. The basis of the following is the philosopher Paul Ricœur's three stages of mimesis. Ricœur is not a believer, and the theological backdrop he writes in is due to his thoroughly Reformed upbringing, but I believe there is a

32. Alfeyev, *Christ the Conqueror*, 155.
33. Klaassens, "Reformed Tradition in the Netherlands," 467–68.

worthwhile dimension to draw out of his theory of mimesis.[34] (a) Imitation: A text is, in some sense, an imitation of life. (c) Portrayal: A text influences those who read it. (b) Transformation: A text transforms the lives of those who engage with it. These are straightforward for the most part, but I find that they exemplify a basic structure of liturgy. Liturgy is not meant to merely imitate events in tradition but rather influence the hearers and thus allow for the texts to serve as a transforming force in the believer's life. The use of symbolic language like "Adam" to signify the human race, fallenness as such, and perhaps the actual figure "Adam" brings those hearing the liturgical texts into the liturgy by identifying them with known liturgical characters. The use of language like "dead" signifies all those who are dead and even reminds us of our own existentially looming time of expiration. More examples exist, as you will see, but the main point is that liturgy is a living tradition that we do not just hear but engage with and actively participate in.

The liturgical hymns sung throughout the year are known as the *octoechos* or "Book of the Eight Tones."[35] This collection is traditionally attributed to St John of Damascus, but it was written by many more figures. The theme of the Harrowing is developed in the *octoechos*. The development of this theme incorporates the motifs mentioned, but for our purpose, I have chosen to select the ones that relate to (2), (3), and (4) above. A few examples can be provided: (a) "Oh Christ you destroyed the misery and wretchedness within the gates and stronghold of hell." (b) "Hades was emptied and made helpless by the death of one man." (c) "The Redeemer has opened the tomb and taken Hades captive." (d) "For our sakes you endured the Cross and burial, O Saviour, but as God you slew death by death." (e) "The tyranny of hell has ended, and its reign has finally been abolished." The sentiment from hymns like these speak to a total and complete destruction of Hades because Christ has preached to all people and emptied Hades of its prisoners. The language involved here may lead us to recall a few statements from *Nicodemus* that reference the slaying of "death," "the opening of tombs," and the recurring motif of destruction expressed in Latin A towards Hades.

However, like in the NT and apocrypha, the portrayal is more complicated than this. There is no consistent answer in the *octoechos*

---

34. Ricœur, *Time and Narrative*, 54–71.

35. All translations of liturgical hymns are from Alfeyev, *Christ the Conqueror*, 158–78. Note that when the liturgical text uses "hell," I edit this to "Hades" for continuity with the NT tradition.

that tells us who was delivered from Hades. Alfeyev has estimated that in almost five out of one hundred cases, the hymns preach that Christ *only* led the righteous out of Hades.[36] Two examples can follow: (a) "You liberated the souls of the pious from [Hades]." (b) "Pitiful Hades spewed out the souls of the righteous." This portrayal is similar to the one at various points in the Greek manuscript of the *Questions* and Latin B of *Nicodemus*. It is exceptional how rare this narrative is in the *octoechos*. Moreover, the question arises: What constitutes righteousness? St John Chrysostom argued that righteousness meant to not worship idols and to worship the true God. If this is true, did all idolaters from the nations remain in Hades? Did such idolaters get a second chance, which allowed them to become righteous by virtue of their potential response to Christ's presence? Considering the vision experienced by the Sinai elder about Plato's response to the Harrowing, the second is, at the very least, true (see Chapter 4). In any case, for such a commonly assumed truth concerning the Harrowing, Orthodox Christians should note that this type of portrayal is very rare.

One of the most frequent portrayals of the Harrowing in the *octoechos* is that Christ raised Adam out of hell. Like in the NT and apocrypha, Adam is not a singular person (he may be that also), but "Adam," when evoked in the liturgy, is primarily a symbol for humanity as such and the condition of fallenness. If a hymn mentions that Adam is raised/freed from Hades, then all prisoners in Hades are freed. Matthew Emerson, an Evangelical opponent of the idea that Christ saved all people, writes that many early Christian interpreters portrayed in writing and iconography that when Christ brought Adam and Eve up from Hades, this was interpreted as teaching that Christ's descent has "healed all of humanity."[37] Emerson is right, although he probably wishes he was not. As we will see, many early Fathers and the Orthodox liturgical texts make Adam synonymous with all of humanity since he is the figurehead of sin and fallenness.

A few notable examples of this are as follows: (a) "Girded with power you ascended the Cross and came to grips with the tyrant, and as God hurled him from on high; but Adam you raised up with your invincible might." (b) "You despoiled death and smashed the gates of hell; while Adam, the prisoner, was released and cried out to you: your right

---

36. Alfeyev, *Christ the Conqueror*, 164.
37. Emerson, *'He Descended to the Dead,'* 177.

PART 2: UNIVERSALISM IN HOLY TRADITION

hand has saved me, O Lord!" (c) "Adam fell into the depths of hell; but being God and Merciful by nature, you went looking for him, carried him on your shoulders and resurrected him with you." (d) "Fearful you appeared, O Lord, as you lay in the tomb; but rising on the third day in power you raised with yourself Adam." These liturgical texts clearly show that Adam (all of fallen humanity) was raised from Hades. If raised, where did they go? Well, I think it's quite obvious. Unless you are one of the Latin scribes of *Nicodemus* and think all were raised just to be sent back to Hades, then all people were raised and brought into Paradise. I happen to think that the rational compilers of our holy liturgical tradition do not teach that all were raised just to praise the Lord and then were sent back to Hades. All prisoners were raised after the destruction of Hades and brought to Paradise!

There are some hymns which discuss the universal significance of the Harrowing. The descent into hell was not a one-time thing where Christ descended, raised all (or some), and then life carried on as is. The descent into hell was a universally significant event that has forever altered the history of salvation and continues to alter the history of salvation. In the words of the Catholic theologian Hans Urs von Balthasar, "From now on, even hell belongs to Christ."[38] A few examples can be provided: (a) "Let the heavens be glad and let earthly things rejoice; for the Lord has wrought might with his arm. He has trampled down death by death and become the firstborn of the dead. From the belly of Hades has he delivered us and granted the world great mercy." (b) "Glory to your Rising, our Saviour, for you, as the Almighty One, have saved us from the hell of corruption and death." (c) "O Christ, by descending into hell you despoiled death, and by rising on the third day you raised us with you." (d) "Glory to your Rising on the third day, through which you have granted us eternal life and forgiveness of sins." I recognize that a few of these clearly identify the Church as "us," and so a non-universalist can argue that these hymns do not teach that all will be saved in the eschaton. However, when paired with the hymns in prior paragraphs, it seems more likely that this follows a similar connotation: A total deliverance from Hades has ensured universal salvation. The likelihood for this increases when we consider the origin of this theme, arguably found in Latin A of *Nicodemus*. Earlier I cited v. 24. "O Lord, set the sign of the victory of your cross in Hades that death may no more have dominion." Satan, Hades, and Death no longer control those who have fallen asleep.

38. Quoted in Jersak, *Her Gates Will Never Be Shut*.

CHRIST'S VICTORY OVER HADES

Since the liturgical theme of a significant and universal meaning being attached to the Harrowing (at least in part) derives from the universalist sentiment of Latin A, there is certainly reason to believe that the hymns in this context teach universal salvation as well. Hence, those who are currently undergoing a type of post-death purification, however it may occur, are under the dominion of God. His ever-lasting love will ensure they eventually choose him over their own selfishness.

The *most frequent* portrayal in the *octoechos*, which Alfeyov estimates occurs in forty out of one hundred cases,[39] is that the "dead," "those who have passed away," "the human race," or "the race of Adam" are the ones who Christ led out of Hades. These phrases are synonymous with one another and signify that all people were brought out of Hades. Several examples can be provided: (a) "You rose from the tomb, all-powerful Savior, and seeing the marvel hell was struck with fear, and the dead arose." (b) "He raised the prisoners from the tombs." (c) "Having fallen asleep as a man, as God did you raise through your invincible power those sleeping in the tomb." (d) "By descending into Hades you freed those enchained from every age, granting incorruption to the human race." (e) "When the Savior went down as mortal to the prisoners, the dead from every age arose with Him." (f) "When you rose from the dead by your power, O Saviour, you raised up with you the human race, granting us life and incorruption." (g) "When you had taken captive the kingdom of Hades and raised the dead." From these, it is clear that Christ did not leave a single prisoner.

The message that Christ raised all people out of Hades is what we find in several verses in the apocryphal texts we examined. Verse 9 of the oldest surviving Greek manuscript of the *Questions* says that Adam was raised, and the whole race followed behind him. The universal language in v. 23 of Latin A's manuscript may also come to mind. "Why without reason did you dare unjustly to crucify him in whom you knew there to be no fault, and bring to our realm an innocent and righteous man, and release the guilty, wicked and unrighteous of the whole world?" On another note, we see a concern answered here that I did not touch on earlier. At least two of the hymns above directly rebuke the argument that only the dead from a certain period of time were delivered out of Hades. This is important because some claim that "the dead" mentioned in 1 Peter 4:6 only refers to those who were dead before a certain period of time. The frequency of language like "from every age" and "the human race"

---

39. Alfeyev, *Christ the Conqueror*, 170.

in these liturgical texts should lead those who claim that the Harrowing only ensured salvation for a certain group of people living in a specific historical time to abandon this claim; that is, if they believe liturgical texts should help shape their theology. It's fairly clear that around forty percent of the relevant hymns in the *octoechos* teach that all prisoners of Hades were delivered into Paradise.

The time has come to determine the central message to draw from these portrayals. If we want to synthesize these to produce a compelling starting point for theological dispute about the Harrowing, we must find a *central agreement*. I concur with Alfeyev that nowhere in the *octoechos* is it ever said that Jesus failed to preach to every prisoner in Hades.[40] Several hymns teach that Jesus only freed certain groups of people, such as the righteous. Still, there is not one statement that should lead us to think Jesus *only preached* to certain groups. The *central agreement* that should be the undisputed bedrock of any Orthodox view on the Harrowing is that Jesus preached to everyone in Hades.

This nuance should remind us of the portrayal in Greek M of *Nicodemus*. In v. 18, Jesus tells all the prisoners that the time to repent is now because they will soon be unable to repent. It was this verse that made us drastically reconsider how to approach Greek M as a whole. Other verses surely teach a universal deliverance, but since this verse does not, we must factor this into our hypothesis. Indeed, a similar conclusion must be reached here but with some stipulations. In Greek M, it was not said with exact precision who was and who was not saved. This was left as an open question. We may want to also leave this as an open question in the *octoechos* as Alfeyev does. Although all people were preached to, it is infrequently said that only the pious and righteous are saved. Did all people become pious and respond joyfully to the coming of Christ? I argue they did. This does not in any way contradict the *central agreement* above. The hymns *never once* say that some people turned away from Christ and decided to remain in Hades. The hymns simply leave us with the question above that cannot be answered from the hymns alone. Hence, my belief that all people were indeed freed from Hades because they responded righteously to the Lord's presence agrees with the *central agreement*. It just takes it further than some.

For this reason, the Orthodox philosopher David Bradshaw's critiques of total deliverance are misplaced.[41] His thesis is that the response

40. Alfeyev, *Christ the Conqueror*, 178.
41. Bradshaw, "Patristic Views," 197–98.

made by prisoners in Hades was determined by their character formed in life. The repentance permitted to prisoners in Hades was "weak" in that it only involved repentance for errors committed in ignorance. A "strong" repentance would be repentance that involves a complete disavowal for every action done in opposition to God's will. This leads him to conclude that only the righteous could have been saved in Hades. But nowhere is it argued that repentance in Hades functions the same way as repentance in our lives. Bradshaw is well aware of patristic views on how time, space, and actions in spiritual geography do not operate in the same way as they do in our earthly lives. He cites St Basil the Great's concept of a "hyper-time" that divine beings live in and a statement that there may be a kind of quasi-temporality in the afterlife.[42] Yet, he still concludes that there is no way "strong" repentance can be undergone after death.

I struggle to see how one can admit there is a divine mystery regarding how actions, space, time, etc., are organized and yet be so certain that "strong" repentance is impossible. I would rather skirt this language of "repentance" altogether and say that however the prisoners of Hades were freed is not my focus. They were freed. This is what matters. Did they repent in any sort of way that constitutes what we refer to as "repentance?" Maybe, but that isn't a hill I'm willing to die on. For Bradshaw's argument against total deliverance, this must be true. His argument also necessitates a libertarian view of free will; as will be shown in Chapter 13, this is faulty. And indeed, as Alfeyev notes, the idea that Christ freed all people in Hades is the most widely referenced interpretation in Orthodox liturgical texts overall; Bradshaw seems to skirt this fact.[43] And he seems to skirt by the constant invocation in liturgical prayers of prayers for *all* the dead; regardless of whether *you* personally believe that a specific person you are praying for will be saved, it is still canonically and liturgically advised to pray for them. If I, as a universalist, can so easily turn to our holy liturgical texts to support my position, but you, as an infernalist, must instead turn towards "proof-texting" Fathers, and in so doing, entirely skirt the topic at hand as well as push an idea that—from a pragmatic lens of what has actually occurred in Orthodox churches around the world for almost two thousand years—nobody follows, one of us needs to have a serious look in the mirror. Just who is really the

---

42. Bradshaw, "Patristic Views," 211.
43. Alfeyev, *Christ the Conqueror*, 204.

PART 2: UNIVERSALISM IN HOLY TRADITION

one acting outside the tradition of the Church? I personally feel quite comfortable where I am.

Christ's descent into Hades does not correlate to our usual ideas about justice, retribution, punishment, and fulfillment of duty. This was an extraordinary and miraculous event. Whatever exactly took place beyond the legendary depictions in apocrypha and hymnography was magnificent and exceeds that of our finite understanding. If Christ only showed mercy to those like David, St John the Forerunner, and the good thief, this strips away the significance and mercifulness of this event. Jesus saved all those who had always believed in him because they were illuminated by the Holy Spirit while on earth. So much for a fascinating divine mystery because we just solved it. Gladly, the Orthodox liturgical tradition is not accustomed to answers like this, nor should it be. The Papal Magisterium has historically placed far less hope on the belief in a universal deliverance. The "traditional" Catholic stance, made popular by Thomas Aquinas, is that Jesus only descended to the top layers of Hades, which housed virtuous pagans and faithful Jews who did not have the historical opportunity to become followers of Christ. Christ descended to them, and because they were already virtuous and faithful, they were obviously saved and followed him. Everyone in the lower layers of Hades remained there. Orthodox liturgical texts serve less to provide easy answers and rather to function as theological boundary zones: What can I responsibly believe in line with Holy Tradition? The texts may lead to inspiration and debate, but they rarely provide easy answers. The Harrowing of Hades is an exemplary case of this. I argued that a theological bedrock, or *central agreement* as I called it, is that all Orthodox Christians must believe, at the very least, that Jesus preached to all people in Hades. Wherever you go from this is your prerogative. I shall close with the ending lines from DBH's graceful poem "The Theotokos Visits Hell."[44] Our Holy Mother continues to pray for the salvation of all those still in hell.

> For in the graceful bearing of your form
> The ancient rift between the worlds is healed,
> If for a moment, and a mercy glimpsed
> By eyes that find in dark their only comfort.
> And, even gone, the sight of you recalled
> Becomes a song that breaks upon this silence
> Like a storm of glory, shattering hell,
> And lifting up the dead in ceaseless supplication.

44. DBH, "The Theotokos Visits Hell."

8

A Brief Critique of Biblical Annihilationism

ANNIHILATIONISTS ARGUE THAT WHEN the Bible and related texts discuss the concept of hell, it is rarely or perhaps never in a sense where the torment of the damned is eternal. Rather than ECT, annihilationists argue that the conscious torment of the damned will come to an end when their souls are entirely destroyed. The damned are destroyed, and the saved are given blissful immortality. Some annihilationists propose this as a punishment of a lesser degree than that of ECT, but others believe this is actually a greater punishment to the damned than ECT would ever be. Infernalists and annihilationists go back and forth on this issue. Frankly, I think it is obvious (as should everyone) that being annihilated is leagues better than being in perpetual torment. The argument often given in opposition to this is that when a soul is annihilated, they are forever unable to experience the joy of living, and even that joy of living, despite the torment being endured, still weighs higher than not feeling the joy of living. The most likely proponent of this argument would be a Thomist who considers being as such, the state of existing, as always more preferable than the state of not existing. But again, this is a ludicrous argument, and perhaps the exact case of infernalism vs. annihilationism demonstrates just how absurd it really is.

When it comes to a biblical justification, annihilationists often trot out a few verses that *prima facie* indicate the destruction of the damned. I am poised to agree with DBH, who says, "[Annihilationism] [. . .] appears to accord somewhat better [than infernalism] with the large majority of scriptural metaphors."[1] Several statements from Jesus fit under this, as do several from Paul. Bart Ehrman agrees with the above and even goes so far as to state that it is *likely* that Jesus and Paul teach annihilationism, it is *unlikely* they teach universalism, and they *do not* teach infernalism.[2] In light of this, I will examine what I take to be the most cited text from defenders of annihilationism: Matthew 10:28. Those who are Orthodox rarely, if ever, hold this view. Hence, I do not feel the need to spend much time responding to an eschatology that finds almost all its proponents at Evangelical seminaries who tout as their main argument that annihilationism supposedly matches the *literal* meaning of the text better and thus should be adopted. However, as I will illustrate, even this claim is said on false grounds.

Not-So Destruction

> Matthew 10:28 (NKJV): "And do not fear those who kill the body but cannot kill the soul. But rather fear Him who is able to destroy both soul and body in Gehenna."

Annihilationists view this as a plain indication that damned souls will be destroyed and not merely remain in torment for all eternity. For Edward Fudge, Jesus in this line equates "kill" [*apokteinai*] and "destroy" [*apolesai*]. If these terms are synonymous, then if humans can kill each other's body, and they can, then God can destroy both the soul and body. Hence, the damned will cease to exist as God will eventually destroy their soul and body.[3]

This interpretation has a fatal flaw. Fudge seems to be applying an eschatological literalist hermeneutic where not only is it unfounded, but the context decries this. Donald Hagner notes how the language of Matthew 10:28 is very similar to that of 4 *Maccabees* 13:14: "Let us not fear him who thinks he kills."[4] The context of the relevant section of 4

1. DBH, *That All Shall Be Saved*, 87.
2. See the commentary on Matthew 10:28 in Ehrman, *Heaven and Hell*.
3. Fudge, *Fire that Consumes*, 155–70.
4. See the entry for Matthew 10:28 in Hanger, *Matthew 1–13*.

A BRIEF CRITIQUE OF BIBLICAL ANNIHILATIONISM

Maccabees is martyrdom. *4 Maccabees* 13:9 reads, "Brothers, may we die brotherly for the Law. Let us imitate the three young men in Assyria who despised the equally afflicting furnace." This context of martyrdom (4 Macc 12–13) tracks with the borrowed language in Matthew. The worst event that can happen to a martyr is death after a long period of torture. But still, the persecutors can only kill the body. God, on the other hand, is so powerful and mighty that he can "destroy the soul and body." Hence, this language is not intended as a cogent eschatological vision but a metaphor for how much more powerful God is over those, like Roman officials, who persecute the Jews. This is again confirmed with further context surrounding *4 Maccabees* 13. Verse 16 reads, "Let us therefore arm ourselves in the self-control, which is divine reasoning." The importance of reason and self-control is a common theme of *4 Maccabees*. For our purpose, the mention of self-control can tie into Matthew 10:28. We should fear God and practice self-control because he is so mighty and powerful that we don't even know the extent of his power. In a metaphorical sense, it is *like* God can destroy the soul and the body. He does not *literally* destroy the soul and the body. As R. Culpepper notes, Matthew was not concerned with spelling out the details of hell. He certainly didn't think of eschatological annihilation. The message of this verse is that we should behave properly in all instances because God is so powerful and can do anything.[5]

Moreover, the exact phrase "soul and body" appears only one other time in the Bible. Isaiah 10:17–18 in the NKJV reads, "So the Light of Israel will be for a fire, and his Holy One for a flame, it will burn and devour his thorns and his briers in one day. And it will consume the glory of his forest, and of his fruitful field, both soul and body, and they will be as when a sick man wastes away." In this case, the "soul and body" is not referring to any particular person or people in general. It is a metaphor meant to be synonymous with "entirely." All of Israel will be *entirely* destroyed and burned. But did Israel cease to exist after this? No, of course not. We see in Isaiah 19, under an eschatological context, that Israel will be one of three nations (Egypt, Assyria, Israel), and these will be a blessing in the land. Israel clearly has not ceased to exist even though the "soul and body" of Israel were said to be destroyed. On the contrary, Israel is now blessed! In Isaiah 27:13, we see another eschatological overtone when the prophet says that all the outcasts in the land of Egypt will come

---

5. See the entry for Matthew 10:28 in Culpepper, *Matthew*.

PART 2: UNIVERSALISM IN HOLY TRADITION

to worship God in Jerusalem. Once again, if Israel's soul and body were destroyed, why is it possible for Israel to not only be blessed but possess inhabitants? Even if we do not believe the use in Isaiah completely informs the use in Matthew 10:28, and I grant that this alone is not sufficient evidence, there is still a pretty high level of credence to admit that there has to be some sort of related reason why Jesus would reference this verse. Margaret Davies notes, "This warning to fear God [in Matthew 10:28] is immediately followed by a depiction of God's care for his creation."[6] The message of redemption certainly plays some part in why Jesus would reference this phrase. Fudge and other annihilationists completely omit this factor in their exegesis.

We may also briefly respond to the assumption from annihilationists that "can" is synonymous with "will" in Matthew 10:28. If there is an argument with strong credence that "can" does not indicate an action that God "will" do, as in, that he will destroy the damned in hell, then the justification for the annihilationist interpretation diminishes substantively. The Greek *dunamenōn* most commonly refers to "being able." To my knowledge, it is very rare (practically unheard of) for this verb to be used to mean "will" in any definitive case. As such, it is very reasonable to argue that the text does not teach that God *will* destroy some souls.

If the annihilationist wants to claim that their argument is not that "can" equates with "will" but rather that "can" means the option is very well left open, they have a few difficult tensions to square away. John 3:17 in the NKJV reads, "For God did not send His Son into the world to condemn the world, but that the world through Him might be saved." Is the annihilationist fine with leaving the option open that the entire created order will be saved? Romans 11:32 in the NKJV reads, "For God has committed them all to disobedience, that He might have mercy on all." Is the annihilationist fine with leaving the option open that God will have mercy on all people? First Timothy 2:3 in the NKJV reads, "For this is good and acceptable in the sight of God our Savior, who desires all men to be saved and to come to the knowledge of the truth." I wouldn't argue these alone are sufficient to prove universal salvation, yet is the annihilationist fine with leaving open the option that all people will be saved here as well? I cannot say with certainty that many annihilationists would accept this. More possible tensions arise for the annihilationist who argues that Matthew 10:28 leaves open the option for God to annihilate souls,

6. Davies, *Matthew*, 90.

and this somehow constitutes enough justification for their argument that certain souls will be destroyed.

Doesn't this fly back in the face of the universalist? If the universalist grants subjunctive language can be employed in their exegesis, they must grant it can be employed by the annihilationist as well. The difference between the former and the latter is that many universalists grant that God is capable of destroying the body and soul. He is all-powerful and all-mighty. We just argue that God would never do this. Hence, the universalist can grant that God is ontologically capable of bringing about the annihilation of the damned; this just doesn't happen because of his love, goodness, and so on. On the other hand, many annihilationists do not grant that God is able to save all people. Some say this is because God cannot violate the free will of humans. Others say this is because it goes against God's divine justice. Regardless of the reasons—many of which I respond to in Chapter 15—annihilationists tend to hold that, in the ontological sense, God is fundamentally unable to save all people. They have reasons for getting around how this avoids obvious tensions with standard motifs of transcendence, but those do not concern us here. The point is that for many annihilationists, but not all, mind you, the argument that God could save all people is simply an impossible assertion. Hence, many universalists can skirt this issue, but many annihilationists cannot. If annihilationists altered their stance, they could skirt this issue, and then they would be fine. However, if annihilationists altered their stance on free will or justice in opposition to universalism, I get the feeling many would just become universalists. The position of annihilationism would then, forgive the pun, be annihilated.

9

An Extensive Critique of Biblical Infernalism

WHETHER YOU ALIGN MORE with St John Chrysostom or John Calvin, infernalism is the most widely held position in the history of Christian eschatology. Some have argued, to varying degrees of success, that universalism was just as widely held in the first five hundred years of Christianity, but unlike infernalism, it dwindled in prominence over time. This argument has aspects of truth—the Origin-influenced eschatologies of the patristic period were universalist—but such a general statement lacks nuance. See my Introduction for more on this. Whatever the case, it is true that infernalism gained steam over time and soon became the dominant position in Christian eschatology. Due to it holding such a monopoly on the hearts and minds of God-fearing Christians around the world, a further critique of its scriptural basis is necessary before I expect anyone to jump ship.

The "Eternal" Controversy

Many assume without much warrant that hell is undoubtedly taught in the NT, and its eternality or everlasting nature is explicitly emphasized. A verse that seems to prove this is Matthew 25:46. The NKJV reads, "And these will go away into everlasting punishment, but the righteous into

AN EXTENSIVE CRITIQUE OF BIBLICAL INFERNALISM

eternal life." Other prominent translations like the New International Version and the New American Standard Bible follow in suit. Jesus says this statement at the end of his famous parable about the sheep and goats. For many, the biblical defense of eternal hell centers on this verse. After all, we get the pop-eschatology of some people experiencing eternal punishment and others, the righteous, experiencing an eternal blissful life. The Greek that underlies the translation of "everlasting" or "eternal" is *aiōnios*. This is one of the adjectival forms of the noun *aiōn*, which translates to age or era.

Several popular New Testament lexicons have no problem translating *aiōnios* as "everlasting" or "never-ending." A 2009 lexicon identifies three common meanings of *aiōnios*: (1) Relates to a period of time extending far into the past. (2) Relates to a time without boundaries or interruption. (3) Relates to a period of unending duration.[1] Seemingly, Matthew 25:46 falls under the connotation of the second and third definitions. Punishment will be undergone by the non-righteous for a period of unending duration that lacks interruption. However, this translation of Matthew 25:46 as "eternal punishment" is much more debatable than you may think. A brief background on the function of language is beneficial before I begin, just so those not used to linguistics can be prepared before diving into the pool.

Language is a system where a source communicates their intentions to a respondent through the means of signs and the proper arrangement of those signs. According to linguistic scholars Eugene Nida and Johannes Louw, language has strict limitations on four key points: (a) The number and sequences of sounds; (b) The way that words are formed by compounding and affixation; (c) The ways in which phrases and clauses are arranged; (d) The thematic structure of discourse that unfolds through various scenarios.[2] These are respectively shortened to phonology, morphology, syntax, and poetics. Language is living and is shaped by the people using it. Concerning Greek-English translation, these considerations lead us to the point that a word in one language, such as Greek, is by no means equivalent to a word in another language. Greek and English certainly share some commonalities (such as incorporating prefixes and suffixes as a similar two-tiered structure), but how,

---

1. Danker and Krug, *Greek-English Lexicon of the New Testament*, 12.
2. Nida and Louw, *Lexical Semantics*, 21–23.

for just one example, nouns become affixed to adjectives (and their connotation) is quite different.

The reason why the translation of "eternal punishment" may be disagreed with is that the word *aiōnios* does not literally mean "eternal," nor was it ever only used to mean "eternal." The most relevant literal translation is something like "of the Age to come." Indeed, this fits the second definition of the lexicon above. DBH emphasizes this in the extended postscript at the end of his NT translation.

> "The adjective *aiōnios*, unlike the adjective ἀΐδιος [*aïdios*] or adverb ἀεί [*aei*], never clearly means "eternal" or "everlasting" in any incontrovertible sense, nor does the noun *aiōn* simply mean "eternity" in the way that the noun ἀϊδιότης [*aïdiotēs*] does; neither does *aiōnios* mean "endless," as ἀτέλευτος [*atelevtos*] or ἀτελεύτητος [*atelevtētos*] does; and, in fact, there are enough instances in the New Testament where the adjective or the noun obviously does not mean "eternal" or "eternity" that it seems to me unwise simply to presume such meanings in any instances at all."[3]

He makes a few good points here. Presuming that the gospel authors wrote down accounts of Jesus that at least roughly correspond to what he said (see Chapter 3 for more on this), Jesus in his ministry never once employed terms that undoubtedly meant "eternality." Fr Aidan Kimel notes how it would be very odd for the Greek authors of the gospels, if they believed Jesus thought punishment was eternal, to employ *aiōnios* here. They could have gone for terms that more properly express eternality as an unceasing duration, like *aïdios, aperantos,* or *adialeiptos*.[4] These terms are never employed in the gospels. However, these are employed by another first-century Jew, Josephus Flavius. The historian Josephus described the teachings of the Pharisees as involving "eternal retribution" (αἰδίῳ τιμωρίᾳ) and "eternal imprisonment" (εἱργμὸν ἀίδιον).[5] First-century Jews were using *aïdios* and other terms to express eschatological teachings. If Jesus so clearly believed in eternal punishment, why were his words rendered as *aiōnios*? I take it that if the former were true, they probably wouldn't have been.

---

3. DBH, *The New Testament*, 445.
4. Kimel, *Destined for Joy*, 138.
5. Josephus, *War*, 2:154.

More likely, since Jesus spoke Aramaic, could at least read Hebrew, and probably had a slight command over Greek,[6] then the Greek rendering of *aiōnios* was probably written from a saying where Jesus employed the Hebrew *'olām* or the Aramaic *alma*.[7] Both of these can mean a time of long duration, a time hidden from view of the present, a time in a far-away future, or even an eternal time that does not end. When made definite as *le-'olām*, the Hebrew begins to read as "unto the Age." When made definite as *ad-alma*, the Aramaic begins to read as "unto the Age" or perhaps "until the Age" or even "until the [start] of the Age." Since the NT authors translated the relevant connotation into Greek as *aiōnios*, it would make sense that Jesus was preaching to his disciples and the people of Israel with the term *le-'olām* or *ad-alma*. This would track with the ambiguous correspondence of eternity that *aiōnios* has. Simply put, Jesus expressed that an indefinitely long punishment would begin in the next Age. This is emphasized in DBH's translation of Matthew 25:46. "And these will go to the chastening of the Age, but the just to the life of that Age."[8] This has a very different connotation from what we saw earlier in the NKJV. "Eternal punishment" has become "the chastening of the Age." After this chastening, the wicked are then given life. The Age is not said to be eternal; it is just an Age that corresponds to some indefinite time. The duration of this Age is not specified.

By translating *aiōnios* this way, I and others do not deny that the Age to come is everlasting, but we do deny that the punishment is everlasting.

6. The second-century *Infancy Gospel of Thomas* records a legendary tradition that as a young child, Jesus knew the Greek alphabet so well that his teacher made Joseph take him back home because he was unsure what to teach him. This is very probably not historical, but it is not improbable that Jesus could have learned to read and speak Greek in a Hellenistic Jewish setting. Although it is a minority position in NT scholarship today, there is suitable archeological evidence that points to Greek being known by both elite and non-elite Palestinian Jews and non-Jewish Palestinians in the centuries surrounding the time of Jesus. This could indicate that Jesus knew at least some Greek. See Porter, "Did Jesus Ever Teach in Greek?," 218–22. To my knowledge, the only text in the last ten years that likewise takes an affirmative stance on this is Gleaves, *Did Jesus Speak Greek?* One of the most convincing pieces of evidence they both put forth is the existence of the "'Theodotus Inscription," which dates from the first half of the first century. The existence of this and other Greek inscriptions should lead one to conclude that many Jewish synagogue leaders in Palestine both knew of and were accommodated to Greek, such that they would employ it here to discuss the rebuilding of a synagogue.

7. A Hebrew word that shares a semantic affinity with *'olām* is *nētsach*, which finds forty-two uses in other parts of the OT, but it does not occur in the classical Torah. See Keizer, *Life Time Eternity*, 120.

8. DBH, *New Testament*, 68.

St Augustine of Hippo famously argued that if you translate *aeternus* punishment as anything but everlasting/eternal, then you lose the ability to say that *aeternus* life is everlasting.[9] That is, you lose the ability to say that heaven is everlasting. Many non-universalists concur on this point without much thought. After all, *aeternus* is used here in context to the punishment for the unrighteous and the life for the righteous.

However, this is a very problematic argument. First, Augustine did not know Greek. In Latin, there is no distinction made between *aïdios* and *aiōnios*. In the Latin manuscripts, both are translated to *aeternus*. This makes it difficult to say that Augustine could have even known about the distinction made throughout the NT between *aïdios* and *aiōnios*. Namely, that *aïdios* and similar words are never once used in reference to punishment in the world to come for humans. There is no reason to think he knew this, which should lead to the safe assumption that he did not since such recognition is neither explicitly nor implicitly seen in his writings. Second, one cannot logically deduce the conclusion that since punishment in the Age to come is not everlasting, this entails that blissful life in the Age to come is not everlasting. The reference to the Age is the same for both, but nothing is said about the duration of such Age. The punishment in the Age to come can be thought of without much trouble as coming to an end; all the while, life in the Age does not come to an end. Origen of Alexandria came to a similar conclusion in his response to the verse. "Since it is certain that death is the opposite of life: therefore it is certain that if life is eternal, death cannot be eternal."[10] Since eternal death and eternal life are opposites, if one is true, the other cannot be. Since Scripture never identifies eternal death with *aïdios*, only *aiōnios*, but life is often identified with *aiōnios*, then eternal life must be true, and eternal death must be false. There must, then, be an implicit distinction between the duration of eternal life and eternal punishment.

Thomas Talbott argues that Augustine's argument also fails because it assumes that an adjective functions the same regardless of the noun it qualifies.[11] If I refer to a child as smart and an adult as smart, these obviously have different connotations depending on the respective noun, even if both are used in the same sentence. A smart adult is far smarter than a smart child. When considering the English word "everlasting," the connotation of this also depends on the noun with which I qualify it. Suppose

9. Augustine, *City of God*, 387.
10. Origen, *Commentary on Romans*, 5.4.
11. Talbott, *Inescapable Love*, 80.

I reference an "everlasting struggle." This would be a struggle that does not have a temporal end. Many pagan myths and the early Christian heresy of Manichaeism posited such an everlasting struggle between good and evil. Suppose I reference an "everlasting transformation." This signifies a transformation that need not involve an unending temporal process but rather one of a limited duration that comes to an end. The effects of the transformation last forever. For a universalist, the result of everlasting punishment is a completed act of purification, of correction, whose effects last forever. Put back in the context of Matthew 25:46, everlasting life is the result of such punishment that eventually is given to all people when they are purified. Those who cite this parallel without further justification would do well to review the strength of their argument.

Another topic to discuss in our examination of Matthew 25:46 is that "punishment" as an English translation of *kolasis* is also not without controversy. In Plato, Aristotle, Antiphon, Plutarch, and many other Greek works, this term properly meant a punishment done for the sake of correction. Aristotle in *Rhetorics* specifically distinguishes *kolasis* from *timōria*, the latter of which has a remedial connotation with a linguistic origin in horticulture.[12] To subject a person to a punishment of *kolasis*, in at least the widespread Greek understanding, would be to remove what is diseased in a person (just like you would a plant) to put them back on the road of virtue (or in the case of a plant, for it to grow again).

If the NT authors believed that Jesus taught about how punishment will be undergone by sinners in the next world for the sake of God's satisfaction and they wanted to employ the most precise term to indicate this, they would have employed *timōria* rather than *kolasis*. This is, however, not the only meaning of it. Non-universalists are right to point out that it very well could mean "punishment" in a more remedial sense. Some argue that by the time of Jesus, the term was just used as punishment in general; one that does not take a sharp stance of correction or remediation. If we look at the Septuagint, *kolasis* indeed seems to take a more generic meaning (2 Macc 4:38; 3 Macc 1:3; Wis 11:3; 19:4; Jer 18:20; Ezek 18:30; 43:11). Perhaps the translators of the Hebrew Scriptures into the Septuagint did not feel a need to specify when punishment was *timōria* because all punishments by this time were grouped under *kolasis*. On the other hand, the only other use of this word in the NT is in 1 John 4:18, which does not refer to remedial punishment but to suffering

---

12. See Artman, "Hell," for some helpful points on this debate.

experienced by someone who is fearful. The verbal form, *kolazō*, is mentioned in two verses. The book of Acts, in 4:21, uses it in reference to disciplinary punishment, and 2 Peter 2:9 uses it in reference to the fact that fallen angels are being held until the day of judgment. Since none of these reference a remedial punishment without end, those who argue this as straightforward seem to have misplaced confidence. Also, a tangentially relevant point is that the teaching of *kolasis* as a corrective punishment fits more with the central messages of Jesus' ministry rather than if there was no distinction between *kolasis* and *timōria*. Jesus taught us to love our enemies so that we can be like our Father in heaven, and he explicitly rejected the principle of equal retaliation (Matt 5:38–42, 47). When we put this together with Paul's statements in Romans 11 that revolve around the fact that even God's severity is an expression of his mercy (see later in the chapter), the argument that *kolasis* is used purposefully here grows in evidence.

A more decisive consideration that should increase our credence that *kolasis* was distinguished from *timōria* in the NT is that early Christians recognized such a linguistic distinction. St Clement of Alexandria adopts the Aristotelian definition for *kolasis* and *timōria*. In *Stromateis*, he defines *kolasis* as "absolute discipline" and *timōria* as the "return of evil done for evil." St Basil the Great, in one text, refers to otherworldly fire as *pur kolastikon*, an adjective which derives from *kolasis*; while he does not explicitly juxtapose this to *timōria* like Clement does, he employs this term purposefully to stress the correctional function of otherworldly fire. St Gregory the Theologian, like his good friend Basil, uses a variant of *kolasis* (for him, the verb *kolazein*) to say that he is persuaded that God punishes for the correction of sinners in the future age.[13] St Gregory of Nyssa expectedly makes a very similar point several times in his writings.

Considering all this and more, I favor (though not *strongly* favor) the view that *kolasis* was purposefully used to indicate a correctional process in the NT. While I do not land as dogmatically on one side of the coin as some scholars, I will not fall as hard on the sword if the position is shown to be untenable at some future point.

Before closing our discussion of Matthew 25:46, I want to move away from Scripture and the early Church for a moment. The case has been made and will continue to be made that *aiōnios* does not necessarily mean eternity and, most of the time, does not in the context of the NT.

---

13. Ramelli, "Patristic Readings."

AN EXTENSIVE CRITIQUE OF BIBLICAL INFERNALISM

Here, I want to touch upon a part of Holy Tradition related to this verse that goes unmentioned in secular scholarly discussions of how *aiōnios* is used in Matthew 25:46. Many are aware that this parable is known, somewhat in an anachronistic way, as the "Final Judgment" in many Christian circles. In Orthodox iconography, this event is often shown with luscious detail. Jesus is in the middle, surrounded by angels, and on both sides is the heavenly council, populated by all the great saints and martyrs. Below him, usually on the right side (symbolizing the sheep), are the Theotokos and St John the Forerunner, among others. Below him, usually on the left side (symbolizing the goats) is the lake of fire that is pouring from his figure and has many men and women in it whom Leviathan is devouring. This is a pretty sordid picture.

While this may be a common image of the Final Judgment in iconography today, it was not always. One of the most beautiful iconographical works on the Final Judgment was completed by Andrei Rublev and Daniil Cherny at Vladimir's Assumption Cathedral in 1408.[14] The pious artists sought to engage with the Final Judgment from a hesychast theology. The image of Christ coming back into the world is at the center. Jesus is adorned with golden garments against a background of blue circles. His whole figure is in motion towards those waiting to be judged. Angels are behind him, and they are playing a glorious composition outfitted with instruments and joy. All the wisdom of the apostles and saints is pouring out towards the people waiting to be judged. But there is no fear on any of the waiting faces. They are encountering perfect love which casts out all fear (1 Jn 4:18). All they can see is the Light of Christ descending towards them. The mural has no darkness. There is no lake of fire. There is no Leviathan gobbling up unfortunate souls. The mural exudes pure and utter light. All souls are brought into this light.

What Fr Sergius Bulgakov writes about this verse is also worth mentioning. The separation of the sheep and goats is a representation of the aeons and aeons of torture that will befall the wicked, though as we know from many other verses, these aeons will eventually pass away into the fullness of universal salvation.[15] Perhaps this is what Rublev and Cherny sought to illustrate in their icon of the Final Judgment. I recognize that this example moves us a bit away from the Scriptures, which is the focus of this section. Still, I found this image edifying and perhaps convincing

---

14. I am indebted to Jesse Hake for this example.
15. Bulgakov, "Redemption and Apocatastasis."

to those who wonder if there are universalist images of what this parable could look like if we dispose of associating "eternal" with punishment. We can now move on from Matthew 25:46.

Ilaria Ramelli and David Konstan are famous for producing a detailed study of *aiōnios* as it was used in Greek literary works, the Septuagint, and the New Testament.[16] In the Septuagint, *aiōnios* and *aiōn* are often the rendered adjective and noun forms of the Hebrew *'olām*. In Genesis 9:16, the covenant made with humans after the flood is modified as *aiōnios*. In Esther 4:1, Israel is chosen as God's possession, and this is modified with *aiōnios*. In these cases, and others that Ramelli and Konstan study, they argue that none possess absolute certainty of eternity but relate to something that lasts over the centuries.[17] There is, however, a case where absolute certainty may be entailed. In Genesis 21:33, God is modified by *aiōnios*. This seems to entail that God's nature, what he is, is not merely long-lasting or lasting for an indefinite period of time, but is itself a never-ending duration—eternality. The first eschatological use of *aiōnios* is likely found in Tobit 3:6. This describes the afterlife as *aiōnios*. Another key eschatological use of *aiōnios* is *4 Maccabees* 13:15, which explicitly says that those who are evil will suffer torment in the Age to come. In fact, this exact rendering of *aiōnios* fire and *aiōnios* life is mirrored in Matthew 25:46. When we look at uses of *aïdios* in the Septuagint, the adjective that strictly signifies "eternality," this is only found twice: Once in Wisdom and once in *4 Maccabees*.[18] Both of these were also late compositions. This goes to show that *aiōnios* and *aïdios* only took on an eschatological connotation very late in Jewish history. Marvin Vincent argues that *aiōnios* occurs one hundred and fifty times in the Septuagint, and in four-fifths of those cases, the term implies limited duration.[19]

---

16. Despite the great applause they have received in the field, their study is not without its flaws. The critical review by Heleen Keizer illustrates this. Indeed, the authors should have spent more time examining the use of *aiōnios* in Johannine literature. Also, the study is limited because the authors do not consider perhaps as many cases as they should have in Scripture. There are seventy occurrences of *aiōnios* in the NT; when put with the Septuagint, there are two hundred and twenty-two. Granted, if a proper study was to be conducted on 222 uses, this would require time that most scholars simply do not have. Still, Keizer is right that the study is limited, and this may be potentially misleading; she explicitly says the lack of "numerical data" is surprising and unfortunate. See Keizer, "Review of I. Ramelli and D. Konstan," 205–6.

17. Ramelli and Konstan, *Terms for Eternity*, 38–39.

18. Ramelli and Konstan, *Terms for Eternity*, 48.

19. Vincent, *Word Studies in the New Testament*, 59.

In the NT, we see *aiōnios* employed in several contexts. At times, we see what cannot possibly mean eternal, such as in Romans 16:25–26. The expression *chronois aioniois* is said in context to the revealed mystery of Christ. For many ages, it was kept hidden, but it has now been revealed. If the mystery is revealed, it is not eternal. Then, in Jude 7, it says that the fires that consumed Sodom and Gomorrah burned *aiōnion*. The fire that destroyed these cities is obviously not still burning to this day. What this means to say, drawing from several verses in the Septuagint, is that the fire is divine and is not from this world. The fire that destroyed these cities is divine, that is, from God. It is not just a random fire started by some human. Since God is divine, and his divinity is eternal, *aiōnios* is used as a somewhat obtuse shorthand to denote this. Other times, *aiōnios* modifies an aspect of God and may entail eternality (1 Tim 6:16; 2 Pet 1:11; 1 Jn 1:2). In any case, there is eschatological relevance given to *aiōnios* throughout the NT. Matthew 19:16 records a person asking Jesus what they have to do to live a life that is *aiōnios*. Jesus responds that they must keep the commandments. Mark 3:29 has that famous line about how the person who sins against the Holy Spirit will fail to have forgiveness in the world to come and will be guilty of a sin *aiōnios*. Although the meaning of this verse has remained a mystery and is often prone to very serious theological abuse, it seems fair to say that if Jesus wished to phrase the punishment of this sin with the most force possible, the gospel writers would have rendered this *aïdios*.

Ramelli and Konstan argue the eschatological connotation of *aiōnios* is clearest in Mark 10:30.[20] The followers of Christ are promised goods a hundredfold in the present time, and in the time to come, they are promised a life *aiōnios*. Then in John 6:47, it is said that the faithful have guaranteed life *aiōnios* because Jesus is the bread of life. Those who eat the bread will live unto the *aiōn*. The *only* clear eschatological indication where *aïdios* is used in the NT is Jude 6. Romans 1:20 is the only other place in the NT where *aïdios* is used, and it (presumably) means to say that God's power is eternal. Jude 6 records that the evil angels are cast into Tartarus and imprisoned with eternal chains. However, even here, there is a stipulation because these angels will only be chained until the judgment of the great day. For our purpose, what is important to note is that the only undisputable connotation of eternality in an eschatological context in the NT is referenced towards non-humans and is shortly followed up with a

20. Ramelli and Konstan, *Terms for Eternity*, 61.

limiting qualification. The text does not specify or say what happens to these angels after the great day, but it seems to indicate that this state of being in chains will end. Ramelli and Konstan close their study on the NT with the following remark:

> "On the other hand, [aiōnios] is also applied to punishment in the world to come, particularly in the expression [pur aiōnios]: [aïdios] is never employed either for fire or for other forms of future punishment or harm of human beings, and on one occasion (in 4 Macc) [olethros] [aiōnios] is contrasted specifically with [bios aïdio]."[21]

No matter how often *aiōnios* is applied to eschatological fire, *aïdios* is never once applied to describe the duration of eschatological fire.

One cannot claim with certainty or even high credence that the NT means "eternality" when it employs *aiōnios*. It very well, as with many times in the Septuagint, likely means "unto the Age." Second and third-century apocryphal texts picked up this theme. There too, *aïdios* is never used in the context of eschatological fire or punishment in the next life for humans. Eschatological fire and punishment in the world to come are modified by *aiōnios*. For example, the *Apocalypse of Peter* states emphatically that those who need saving after death will be purified *aiōnios* in the "river of fire" before they can pass unto Paradise. Granted, this explicit statement is out of the ordinary even in apocrypha (as it is openly universalist), but all other apocryphal texts from this period still omit any connection between *aïdios* and eschatological punishment. Hence, apocryphal texts more or less maintain lexical continuity on this point. This may tell us that the authors of these texts also believed that punishment in the next life will eventually cease. In the case of *Apocalypse of Peter*, this is explicit. If the authors of these texts sought to parrot the lexical similarities and theology from the NT, perhaps this tells us that they, too, believed the NT never once spoke of everlasting punishment.

Many early Christian figures understood what the NT and apocrypha meant by *aiōn*. Expectedly, the most explicit on this is Origen of Alexandria.[22] "Whenever Scripture says, 'from aeon to aeon,' the refer-

---

21. Ramelli and Konstan, *Terms for Eternity*, 69–70. I transliterated the Greek for the sake of the reader. This more ambiguous conclusion that Ramelli takes in her earlier co-authored text, differs from her very unambiguous conclusion in *Christian Doctrine*. I prefer the earlier one, as I find it to be more defendable. See Pedersen, "Critical Assessment," 5.

22. However, there is reason to be careful with how we understand this. This

AN EXTENSIVE CRITIQUE OF BIBLICAL INFERNALISM

ence is to an interval of time, and it is clear that it will have an end. And if Scripture says, 'in another aeon,' what is indicated is clearly a longer time, and yet an end is still fixed. And when the 'aeons of the aeons' are mentioned, a certain limit is again posited, perhaps unknown to us, but surely established by God."[23] This means that all expressions such as *aiōnios* fire or *aiōnios* punishment cannot be thought of as eternal because there will someday come an end to all aeons. These terms, then, *only* have reference to periods constituted by space and time. P. Tzamalikos concurs. "[In Origen], whenever 'aeon' is regarded with respect to the 'horizontal' perspectives of historical agents, it has a predominantly temporal meaning."[24] This end to all aeons will be signified by the perfection of God in all things. Aeons as we know them will cease to be as God is all in all (1 Cor 15:28). There will be a leap into the perfect eternity of the divine life. There will be an unceasing presence of blissful divinity for all beings as they share in the life of the Trinity. The final state will not be the same as the beginning. It will be infinitely greater because all beings will express voluntary orientation to God after some complete necessary spiritual development. God subjects some to spiritual development, even in this world, because they are not properly prepared to receive correction. Take Pharaoh. His heart was hardened in Exodus not because God hated him, but rather because God showed him mercy and gave him time to develop spiritually. This same theme will continue in the Age to come. God gives time, an indefinitely long time, an *aiōn* that depends on each creature, before eventually, the eternal consequences of universal salvation or *apokatastasis* will take root.[25]

Origen's position is not novel. His own teacher, St Clement of Alexandria, seemed to have come to a similar position, but it was perhaps less clear than Origen; I don't doubt Origen's own exposition was inspired by him. Clement seems to only refer to the *apokatastasis* as itself *aïdios*, while the sufferings experienced by the damned are *aiōn*.[26] As well, an Alexandrian Platonist who Origen was very probably familiar with

---

statement is only preserved in Latin and so we lose out on some of the intricacies associated with the Greek.

23. Quoted in Ramelli, *Christian Doctrine*, 161.

24. Tzamalikos, *Philosophy of History and Eschatology*, 203.

25. Ramelli, *Christian Doctrine*, 177.

26. Seijas, "La Apocatatasis O Restauración Universal," 436. This is the first Hispanic/Spanish work that engages directly with Ramelli's scholarship. Also, this present book is the only English text so far that addresses Hispanic/Spanish scholarship on universalism.

PART 2: UNIVERSALISM IN HOLY TRADITION

due to having been taught Greek philosophy by Ammonius Saccas and sharing several distinct thematic and linguistic relationships—Alexander of Aphrodisias—was clearly aware of the distinction between *aïdios* and similar adjectives, seen especially in his commentary on Aristotle's *Meteorologia*, as he, seeking to differentiate himself from Platonists who said that the universe isn't eternal, employs *aïdion* to qualify the existence of the universe. He then juxtaposes this to large rivers and seas, which, while longstanding and ancient [*aenaōn*], are not *aïdioi* like the universe. St Athanasius of Alexandria—the Father of Orthodoxy, a disciple of Origen, and a universalist—does not provide an explicit statement on how to read *aiōn*, but we do find a very conservative use of *aïdios*. This was almost always used in reference to God's eternality or the eternality of the Persons in the Trinity. This is never once used in connection to punishment in the Age to come or eschatological fire. A prime example of his usage pattern is in *Three Speeches Against the Arians*. Athanasius refers to God as the *aïdios* source of his wisdom and explicitly denies *aïdios* having context to anything created.[27] In an eschatological statement about punishment like that found in *Exegeses of the Psalms*, Athanasius affirms that while some will experience *aiōnios* enjoyment, others will experience *aiōnios* punishment for "interminable ages."[28]

Here, we find a dilemma similar to that in Matthew 25:46. The adjective must be understood in light of the noun it modifies. In this case, however, it is even clearer that the reference is to temporal ages and not to eternity. The Cappadocians continue the pattern of using *aïdios* and *aiōnios* in these respective contexts. Unsurprisingly, St Gregory of Nyssa takes the cake here. Gregory concurs with Origen about the meaning of *aiōn*. "Aeon designates temporality, that which occurs within time."[29] Many later Fathers in the first millennium share this understanding.[30] St John Chrysostom, although an infernalist, explicitly uses *aiōnios* to describe the reign of Satan's kingdom over this world for the purpose of emphasizing its transience. While long-lasting, Satan's kingdom is not *aïdios* like God's kingdom and will only last until the end of the Age. Likewise, St John of Damascus was an infernalist, though he spoke honestly about the meaning of *aiōnios*.

27. Ramelli and Konstan, *Terms for Eternity*, 157–58.
28. Ramelli and Konstan, *Terms for Eternity*, 163.
29. Quoted in Keizer, *Life Time Entirety*, 252–53.
30. See Ramelli, "Patristic Readings," for more examples from the patristic period and later.

AN EXTENSIVE CRITIQUE OF BIBLICAL INFERNALISM

By no means does this study prove definitively that *aiōnios* in the context of NT eschatology means "unto the Age" and cannot in any way mean "eternal." A claim like this not only lacks a shred of humility but also is entirely unjust, considering how short this study was. Most of what I sought to accomplish here is an overview of relevant texts from early Christianity and secondary literature on *aiōnios* to show how the translation of this is much more debatable than most English translations of the Bible make it seem. By briefly examining other texts surrounding the NT and early Christian employments of *aiōnios*, it seems safe to say that many early Fathers (and learned pagans) followed suit from the lexical employment in Scripture when writing their own commentaries and philosophical explorations. This is not because the Greek in the Scriptures was unique for the time, but seemingly because this was simply acknowledged by Greek speakers to be a word with a polysemic meaning that presented the speaker with a far less absolute connotation of "eternality" than other words of the time.

Going forward, I shall assume that my arguments in favor of rendering *aiōnios* as "unto the Age" are justified. By translating *aiōnios* as "unto the Age," some may argue that we have stripped away the shred of evidence remaining to believe that the teaching of ECT can be found in the NT. In 1877, the Anglican archdeacon Frederic Farrar preached a series of universalist sermons where he argued precisely this. While Farrar's universalist stripes were personally denied, many have assumed that his disagreement with this translation stemmed from his belief in a punishment of contingent length. Since this chapter argues against ECT (or infernalism), I believe it is only logical to utterly lampoon the "eternal" part of ECT before an exegesis of other verses even takes place. Have my arguments in this section laid waste to the infernalist paradigm altogether? The *aiōnios* controversy is surely what led several notable theologians to be wary about pursuing anything further than a "hope" for universalism. However, I still would not go so far as to say this. A good deal of the infernalist position rests on a misinterpretation of *aiōnios*, but there is much more to cover. I cannot end the chapter here.

The Unquenchable Fire

Matthew 3:12 (NKJV): "His winnowing fan is in His hand, and He will thoroughly clean out His threshing floor, and gather

PART 2: UNIVERSALISM IN HOLY TRADITION

His wheat into the barn; but He will burn up the chaff with unquenchable [*asbestō*] fire."

This statement comes at the end of St John the Forerunner's announcement that soon someone will come, Jesus, who baptizes with the Holy Spirit. For many infernalists, the meaning is obvious: Jesus will separate the righteous (wheat) from the unrighteous (chaff), and the unrighteous will endure ECT. However, a reading like this completely disregards what we know about mentions of fire in the Scriptures. Fire is depicted in roughly three ways: (1) God's presence; (2) God's punishment; (3) God's purification. A reading like this may also disregard what we know about God's punishment having a restorative purpose (Ps 66:10–12; Hab 1:12; Job 5:17–18; Rom 11:32). These are tentative examples but may show at least in some way that God's punishment is restorative.

(1) Fire is a symbol of God's presence in numerous passages in the OT (Gen 15:17; Ex 3; 14:24; Deut 4:11), and perhaps the most famous depiction in the NT is Acts 2. This symbol of God should not be taken lightly. In all these instances, God's presence acts as a sort of guide to those it appears to. In Exodus 3, Jesus appears as a burning bush to speak to Moses. Jesus informs Moses that he must go to Egypt and rescue his people. As we see later in Exodus and told to us in Jude 5, Jesus is the Angel of the Lord who saves the people from Egypt. The presence of God in the burning bush was not a one-time event for Moses, but that presence remained with him during the Exodus. A presence that guided the Israelites out of Egypt. In Acts 2, the Holy Spirit acts as a guide to the apostles at Pentecost. This presence, which in Orthodox iconography is symbolized by flames atop the heads of the apostles, is the same presence that guided all future ecumenical councils.

(2) Closely aligned with fire as a symbol of God's presence is fire as a symbol of God's punishment. Probably the earliest sighting of this is when Sodom and Gomorrah were destroyed due to practicing the Nephilim ritual and turning away foreigners who sought help (Gen 19:24). There are texts such as Matthew 3:12; Mark 9:43, as well as many other texts that speak to the hereafter with the connotation of fire. Then there is the dreadful statement in Hebrews 12:28–29, which quotes Deuteronomy 4:24 to say that God is a "consuming fire." When fire is used to symbolize God's punishment, it cannot be thought of as separation from God's presence itself. The existential separation that classifies hell (Matt 8:12) is in tandem with an ever-too-present experience of God.

(3) Infernalists often like to take (1-2) and forget altogether about the last one, but for a cogent and biblical eschatology, this, too, cannot be left out. Fire also, at least a few times in Scripture, is a symbol for testing and purification. Isaiah 1:25 in the NKJV reads, "I will turn My hand against you, And thoroughly refine away your dross, And take away all your alloy." It is confirmed later in 48:10 that this indeed occurs. "Behold, I have refined you, but not as silver; I have tested you in the furnace of affliction." Second, there is 1 Corinthians 3:12-15, which reads in the NKJV, ". . .If anyone's work which he has built on *it* endures, he will receive a reward. If anyone's work is burned, he will suffer loss; but he himself will be saved, yet so as through fire." Finally, there is the mysterious statement in 1 Peter 4:12, which reads in the NKJV, "Beloved, do not think it strange concerning the fiery trial which is to try you, as though some strange thing happened to you." Fire burns away that which is impure and leaves only that which is pure. All people will be tested by God's fiery judgment and will either burn until the fire purifies them, or they will pass through the fire without harm, having already purified themselves of sin in life.

Let's now look at three cases where "unquenchable" [*kabah*] is used in the Hebrew Scriptures. Take Ezekiel 20:47. This word is said in context to God's analogy that every green and dry tree will be devoured by the flame. It is then said that the fire is *kabah*. Every green tree is a symbol of the righteous. Every dry tree is a symbol of the unrighteous. All people, whether they are righteous or unrighteous, will meet the flame of God. For this reason, *kabah* is not meant to indicate that the fire itself will never end but rather to highlight the power and strength of the fire. This is to say that God's judgment will never be put out because he is forever judging creation. His judgment, then, is all-consuming, as God judges all things. Then take Amos 5:6. God says that he will sweep through Bethel, and no one will be able to quench his devouring fire. When considering the context of Amos, this verse makes a great deal of sense. Amos is filled with statements about God displaying his wrath towards those who have turned away from him towards the material decadence in life. This is because Amos was presumably written about a point at which Israel was living the high life and this distracted them from putting God above all else. Bethel, which was once a "House of God" especially, had become consumed by idolatry. As such, God expresses a great condemnation towards the people for doing such a thing. While condemnation, however, this fire is also directed at all "tribes of Joseph." This seems to refer to all people in Bethel. Like in Ezekiel 20:47, *kabah* is used to indicate that God's judgment will be expressed towards all people. God's work is never done and all people who meet this fire will be purified by it. Finally, take Jeremiah 17:27. God commands the Judeans to keep the Sabbath holy when they come to Jerusalem, or else he will create an unquenchable fire in the gates of Jerusalem that will consume the fortress. The fire that may be brought to Jerusalem will not literally be without end. The word *kabah* is meant to emphasize that the fire will be very strong and God's judgment is ever-enduring over the people.

When examining the NT, "unquenchable" [*asbestō*] is found only one other time in the Synoptic gospels besides Matthew 3:12's parallel in Luke 3:17. In Mark 9:43, Jesus likewise puts the concept of eschatological fire in reference to Gehenna. This is in context to a very extreme statement where he says that one should cut off their hand and foot if it causes them to sin, lest they be thrown into *asbestō* fire. This verse has caused a lot of trouble for NT scholars in recent years. It has been widely assumed this is meant to be taken figuratively and starkly punitively. *Prima facie*, this makes sense from a modern perspective, and at the very least, as far as we know from extant literary materials, from St Clement of Rome onwards, it was interpreted figuratively; however, Origen does recognize some naysayers of his day who read it literally. Obviously, Jesus wouldn't be commanding his followers to cut off their appendages to avoid sin, right? Several prominent scholars today aren't so sure.

Candida Moss has especially begun to turn the tide on this assumption. She argues that the command, as understood by Jesus' earliest hearers, would be taken literally because amputation was seen as a highly therapeutic action in the ancient world.[31] Amputation was not a punishment, contra the modern cultural consensus, it was seen to prevent the onset of many diseases—almost all were assumed to be caused by evil invisible forces—gangrene being a clear case that even called for amputation by doctors in World War I, but less clear cases as well, such as those that we would now classify as spiritual illnesses involving the eye, hand, and foot, i.e., lust, gluttony, and other forms of debauchery. In our post-Cartesian world, it is hard to conceptualize spirit as more substantial than materiality but this was the way that the ancients understood it. Spirit was not some sort of "woo-woo" matter-less abstraction to our ancient forebears like it was to René Descartes. Cutting off the

---

31. Moss, *Divine Bodies*, 52–55.

appendage that was leading them to sin was a healing action in that the sin was now thought to be quite literally "cut off" with the respective appendage. The spiritual power affecting the person that had attached itself to the person's material body was cut off at this moment as well, rendering it null. This is a shock to many, that is, unless they actually know the extremist culture that ancient Jews lived in—that touted beliefs in the "evil eye" (Tob 4:7; Wis 4:12; Matt 6:22; Mk 7:22; Gal 1:3) and other medical superstitions—which then it is part-and-parcel for the course. DBH puts the issue best:

> "The New Testament knows very little of common sense. The Gospels, the epistles, Acts, Revelation—all of them are relentless torrents of exorbitance and extremism: commands to become as perfect as God in his heaven and to live as insouciantly as the lilies in their field [. . .] This extremism is not merely an occasional hyperbolic presence in the texts or an infrequent intonation sounded only in their most urgent moments; it is their entire cultural and spiritual atmosphere."[32]

The extremist rhetoric seen in Mark 9 is not hyperbolic but genuinely a command from Jesus that his followers should amputate the part of their body that is causing them to sin. Still, I must contend against Moss that she does not show the literal connotation as necessarily true. She just notes it would make sense in light of the textual and archeological evidence from the ancient world. As Meghan Henning also notes, for Jesus' ancient listeners, it would be considered honorable to remove one's own appendage if that is what is needed to prevent them from sinning.[33] I concur with Moss and Henning, but I think it very plausible to argue, along with practically all NT scholars, that the command in Mark 9 also had a figurative meaning to the earliest hearers as well: Gehenna is so bad that it would be better to live life as an amputee then end up there. Read figuratively, then, Mark 9:43 repeats the motif established well throughout the gospels of how a life lived justly is a life of order and honor. You avoid Gehenna if you live justly with order and honor.

This importance is noted by St Paul as well (1 Cor 14:40). Paul wrote his letter to the church of Corinth because he perceived they were being consumed by idolatry and pagan worship.[34] A key tenant of pagan wor-

32. DBH, *New Testament*, 22.
33. Henning, *Educating Early Christians*, 115–17.
34. See Campbell, *Pauline Dogmatics*, 93 for a list of the fifteen distinguishable problems that Paul identifies with the church at Corinth.

PART 2: UNIVERSALISM IN HOLY TRADITION

ship, according to Jewish tradition, involved overturning societal norms. In the Jewish historical consciousness, pagan worship often devolved into public orgiastic frenzies (Ex 32:6; Num 25). Paul understood the tendency of pagan worship, and in a world still so dominated by idolatry, it is expected that he would make very extreme statements like this. Pagan worship was against holy order, and sin is metaphysically the degradation of holy order. Extreme statements were the norm because only by hearing extreme statements would people turn away from their evil doings towards the Lord. Turning towards the Lord would bring, in the case of the now-amputee ex-sinner, an eschatological healing in the next Age. Disabled on earth and exalted in Paradise.

Moreover, even if we want to frame Mark 9:43 as an eschatological reality meant to be taken seriously today by Christians today who now know there are more humane and less brutal ways to stop sin that don't require you to remove an appendage, it is said a few verses later, in the context of Gehenna, "For all will be salted with fire." The idea then, in this grossly literal understanding, is that if someone is a really terrible sinner, then they have a choice: Endure the fiery punishment now, which is employed as a therapeutic action of one cutting their appendages off, or endure the fiery punishment in Gehenna once you are dead. Both cases still have the connotation of purification. You may be purified in this life by cutting off what causes you to sin or you may be purified in the next by enduring the fiery punishment of Gehenna. Either way you look at it, this indicates purification, and both routes will eventually lead you to Paradise. Before moving on, let's briefly recall our study of Gehenna from Chapter 6.

The primary connotation of Gehenna in the NT seems to be eschatological. There is also a clear case where the connotation is figurative (James 3:6). There also may be some cases where the connotation is both figurative but also points to an eschatological reality (Matt 5:22). If I were to categorize Mark 9:43 into one of these three (rough) categories, I argue it points to a connotation that is highly eschatological and also figurative. But there is no sense in which the eschatological connotation can be argued to denote eternality. Again, in both cases, whether you are purified in life or death, the purification is thoroughly *therapeutic*. The purpose is to be raised back to good spiritual health.

Turning back to Matthew 3:12, how can we understand this in a universalist framework? The *asbestō* fire does not refer to the never-ending nature of the fire but rather the strength and power of God's judgment. When the chaff are burned up in the *asbestō* fire, they do not cease to exist or keep burning forever. They burn until their purpose of purification is complete. As St Gregory of Nyssa tells us, "In the same way when evil is consumed by the purifying fire, the soul which is united to evil must necessarily also be in the fire until the base adulterant material is removed, consumed by the fire."[35] As his sister St Macrina the Younger tells us—Gregory reassuringly reminds us of her theological authority by referring to her as a teacher (masculine) with a feminine article beforehand—the wheat must be separated from the chaff just as the unwanted proclivities in our soul must be separated so that we can "attain the Beautiful." The torments of hell will endure so long as the chaff remains and the soul pays back what it owes.[36] Thus, all the evil material in a person that separates them from God, from their pursuit of the Good, must be consumed in the fire before they are cleansed to enter Paradise. Paradise is given to all, but no evil is permitted there. There is only the Good since Paradise is a perfect union with the Good, God himself. If you still have evil in you, you are not ready for Paradise. You will someday be ready, but you must endure purification; the chaff must be separated. Let us purify our minds and bodies in this life to hopefully avoid purification in the next.

The Election Scandal

In Chapter 5, I argued, among many things, that several verses in Romans 5 teach universalism. Is the Book of Romans altogether universalist? Some think not due to what may seem like an infernalist paradigm that stretches from Romans 9–11. The use of language like "vessels of wrath" and "vessels of mercy" struck some, like John Calvin, as even indicating an ontological predestination enshrined in the fabric of reality, whereby some souls are predestined as "vessels of wrath" and others as "vessels of mercy." The former being the non-elect, the latter being the elect. Even in early Western Christianity, these chapters were already used by St Augustine of Hippo in his late writings to form a semi-predestination doctrine. One cannot

---

35. Gregory, *On the Soul and Resurrection*, 84.
36. Gregory, *On the Soul and Resurrection*, 86. English translations do not display the radicality of Gregory's move to refer to his sister with the masculine noun and a feminine article. In a world where the intelligence of women was systematically downplayed by Church hierarchs, for Gregory to refer to his sister this way is to say that her theological voice is just as valid as any male theological teacher.

PART 2: UNIVERSALISM IN HOLY TRADITION

overstate the theological abuse done to St Paul's writings in general, but these three chapters may be the most abused of all. We are forced to recall the statement that Paul's epistles are difficult, and those who are theologically unstable are bound to misunderstand them (2 Pet 3:16).

Unlike some universalists, I don't consider Paul's argument in Romans 9–11 easy to follow. I think the level of debate surrounding these verses and Paul's somewhat complicated (if not idiosyncratic at times) use of OT prophecy is reason enough to recognize that this is not a walk in the park. Still, however, I believe there is an argumentative trajectory that can be noticed. Much of this resembles a Socratic dialogue, a rhetorical style of dialectic that Paul undoubtedly was familiar with either formally or informally. Paul is trying to figure out, by means of examining various hypotheses, why so few Jews around him have accepted the coming of Jesus as the Messiah, but many who were once pagans and did not believe in the OT prophecies have recognized Jesus as the Messiah.

Paul begins by first noting how not all who descended from Abraham receive the promise of Israel (9:6). This is something well established in the Scriptures. To become a part of Israel had less to do with your biological family tree but rather your initiation into the rituals of the Jewish people. An example of this is Caleb, who, although not biologically related to Abraham, became a founding member of Israel and took possession of the Promised Land along with Joshua (Num 13). This is why Israel, contra replacement theology, does not *become* the Church but has always been the Church.[37] Paul illustrates this by naming Esau, who was a descendant of Abraham but did not inherit the promise of God (9:13). He sets this in contrast to Jacob, who became the father of Israel. We will come back to this shortly. Paul then laments the rejection that Israel has of God's purpose (9:10–13). God's purpose was to send his Son so the world would be cleansed of sin and those in the world could take part in the divine life. Those whom God saves, however, are determined by divine election. Salvation is in God's hands since he decides who he shows mercy to and who he hardens (9:17–18). This is like how a potter has power over clay and could very well make one piece of clay for dishonor and another for honor (9:20–21). By using the analogy of a potter here, Paul employs a

---

37. I argue identifying Israel as the Church is theologically valid so long as the identification is not taken to mean "replacement." The Church does not replace Israel. Israel (the believers in fidelity to God) is simply the Church. Or rather, to be more precise, the historical-living institution of the Church is the continuance of Israel in its forever redeemed form after the Incarnation of the Son.

well-known image from Jeremiah 18. In the story, God leads the prophet to a potter's house and shows how a vessel that was thought to be spoiled can be worked into something better. This holds out hope for Israel's repentance; as we will see, this shall come to fruition.[38]

But before that, Paul must offer a central "what if" question. What if God created two fundamentally different pots of people in Israel? The first comprises Christian Jews and Gentiles who follow the Lord Jesus. The other pot comprises Jews who did not follow Jesus and still reject the Word of the Lord (9:22). What if the former is elected to be a vessel of mercy and the latter is elected to be a vessel of wrath that makes God's power known (9:22–24)? All the riches of his glory would go to the blessed vessels of mercy, and longsuffering and destruction would be put on the vessels of wrath. He closes Romans 9 by reiterating the astonishing observation, laid out at the start, that the people of Israel who claim to follow God's righteousness are precisely those who have rejected God, yet the Gentiles, the once pagan-worshiping nations, have found righteousness in Christ (9:30).

Paul is not satisfied with such a conclusion. After all, this sounds like a terrible end to the story. We have two groups who are forever irreconcilable. The next two chapters are spent rejecting this dreadful "vessels of wrath" hypothesis. Paul's desire is that all people will be saved through Christ (10:1–2). Christ is the end of the law, and all those who claim to be righteous but fail to follow him are merely deluding themselves (10:4). This must be understood in two ways: Jesus has fulfilled the law and is himself the end of the law. This is why all those who now follow Jesus will obtain righteousness. The distinction between Jew and Gentile has been cast aside, and all prior restrictions that burdened the Israelites are no longer a concern (10:10–11). Throughout the OT, God would stretch his hand out to his people, and they would continuously turn away from him and turn towards idolatry (10:20–21). Israel has continued its disobedience, and this is why the Gentiles will inherit their blessings, whether or not they are biological descendants of Abraham. This pattern of election, laid out so far, follows that of Genesis almost to a T.

God's process of election in Genesis is repeatedly antinomian. The elder to whom the birthright properly belongs is continually overtaken by their younger sibling whom God has chosen as elect.[39] This is seen

---

38. Sumney, *Reading Paul's Letter to the Romans*, 119.
39. DBH, *That All Shall Be Saved*, 135.

PART 2: UNIVERSALISM IN HOLY TRADITION

in the story of Cain and Abel, among others. Paul understands this motif and uses it precisely in the case of Esau and Jacob, as mentioned above. Although Esau is originally rejected earlier in the Genesis story and becomes the symbol for Edom (in Malachi's verse that Paul draws from), he and Jacob meet in Genesis 33. When they are reunited, Jacob remarks, "I have seen your face like I was seeing God's" (Gen 33:10; NKJV). This story illustrates how the brother who was once rejected has now been brought into a wider scope of election than what was first believed. Up to this point in Genesis, Jacob and Esau were split into two groups: Elect and non-elect. Now, these groups have reconciled to the benefit of both. Paul sees this as an archetypal story of how to paint the relationship between Israel and outsiders. Where once Israel was heralded as the firstborn (Gen 17) and thus the one who in ancient culture would "naturally" receive the glory of the Father, the Gentiles have continually usurped this and will ultimately usurp this entirely. Israel has indeed become a light to all nations (Isa 49:6) because all will be brought into it.

This culminates in Romans 11. Paul begins the chapter by noting how God has not rejected his people (11:1). There is a believing remnant who is elected by grace (11:5). Paul includes himself in this remnant to say that he will be chosen at this present time. Then there are the non-believing Jews who, at this point, are still blind to the truth (11:7). We have once again returned to that duality: Elect vs. non-elect. Here, all hope seems lost. Was Augustine right? Was Calvin right? Does Romans 9–11 really teach unconditional election or (for more sober infernalists) does Romans 9–11 teach that some will be damned because they will never confess belief in Christ? I suppose that if you stop reading the text at this point or let everything so far inform precisely how you interpret the statements to come, then yes. However, this is not how Paul wrote the letter. As stated in the beginning, he employs a hypothesis to see how it pans out. This is part-and-parcel with a Socratic dialectic. So, has it panned out?

Paul goes on to say that although Israel has stumbled, they will never fall (11:11). The non-believing Jews stumbled because they failed to heed the gospel of Jesus, but they are not beyond recovery. In fact, their fullness is coming and the failure of all to heed to Christ's words has been part of God's plan all along (11:12). Paul then explains how Israel is like an olive tree, and the Jews who have turned away from Jesus are broken off, but God still has not rejected them (11:15–18). As Terence Donaldson notes, Paul in vv. 11–15 seems to hint that future blessings are in store for all of Israel.[40] Indeed, God has not rejected them because all will be saved (11:26). Those who were once thought of as a believing remnant have become the remnant who will ensure the salvation of all (11:16). This idea that the believing remnant will ensure the salvation of all fulfills several prophecies (Gen 7:23; Mic 2:12; 4:7; Zech 8:12). The olive tree, even if some branches have refused to believe and were consequently ripped off (11:22), is made holy in total through the firstfruit, the believing remnant, being holy. The holiness of the believing remnant is paramount for the holiness of the entire olive tree. All the rejected vessels, Esau and other vessels of wrath will become vessels of mercy (11:31–32) when Jesus returns and takes away all sins (11:26–28). This is because God's gifts to Israel are irrevocable (11:28). His wisdom, knowledge, beauty, and love surpass anything that we can imagine (11:33). Why do so many try to understand the purpose of his judgments? Why do so many limit his greatness and justice to what they personally can understand?

Everyone has been bound to disobedience so that God can show mercy to all people. The fullness [*plērōma*] of people will enter God's kingdom. Paul's desire that all will be saved in Christ (10:1–2) has been brought to fruition. The image from Jeremiah and many other prophecies have also been brought to fruition. The theological belief that everyone is bound to disobedience to later be redeemed also has a history in later periods of Second Temple Judaism. In the *Community Hymns* from the Essenes, for instance, God's present work in humans cleanses them from their "spirit of corruption" so that they can join the "sons of heaven." Paul likely knew of these traditions and took them to heart; just as we explicitly see in his use of the title "Belial" in 2 Corinthians 6:15, the name of a satanic entity only mentioned in several Qumran texts. Thus, God created all as vessels of wrath for the purpose of them being "reworked" into vessels of mercy. This is the way in which all will be saved (11:26). The leading Pauline scholar Douglas Campbell, who does not consider Paul an *explicit* universalist at all times, notes that Paul was *implicitly* a universalist when it came to his conclusions about the unbelieving Israel. He writes, "In the contest between divine benevolence and human recalcitrance fought out in the space that is the human race, God will win. All humanity will be saved."[41] Thus, the hardening of the hearts

---

40. Donaldson, *Paul Within Judaism*, 289–90.
41. Campbell, *Pauline Dogmatics*, 435.

PART 2: UNIVERSALISM IN HOLY TRADITION

was necessary (9:17–18) but only temporary. This conclusion is not close to the infernalist message in the slightest. Romans 11 preaches the glorious conclusion that God will show to all when all are brought into Israel, that is, (or rather, which coincides with)[42] the Church.

Gomorrah or Grace?

We have spent an ample amount of time on Paul's letters and the gospels but there has yet to be a response to alleged infernalism in the book of Jude. Jude is often overlooked by many due to its short length and striking subject matter. A lot of Jewish theology is summarized in just a single chapter. A lost narrative from the Jewish text *Assumption of Moses* that discusses the debate between Satan and the Angel Gabriel over who owns the body of Moses is referenced as presumably authoritative. There is a mysterious reference to the "Glories," which was a name used for a particular subclass of angels that was perhaps synonymous with the stars in *2 Enoch* 22. Most famously, there is a tradition from *1 Enoch* that references the Nephilim. The author of Jude was probably a Jewish-Christian who wrote between 70 and 90 CE. This short text caused much controversy in the early Church as debates raged over its canonicity. It still leads to controversy today. In this section, I shall briefly respond to a verse that catches the eye of some.

> Jude 7 (NKJV): "As Sodom and Gomorrah, and the cities around them in a similar manner to these, having given themselves over to sexual immorality and gone after strange flesh, are set forth as an example, suffering the vengeance of eternal fire."

This verse brings us back to that fateful day recalled in Genesis 19:24–29 and Deuteronomy 29:22. Fire reigned from the heavens as the cities of Sodom and Gomorrah were destroyed for engaging in human-god sexual relations; this became seen as the Nephilim ritual in later Jewish history.[43] Jude 7 alludes to this event to say that those in the Age to come who likewise are wicked and false teachers will endure eternal

---

42. John Milbank uses the language of "coincides with" in reference to the relationship between Israel and the Church in Romans 11. Referring to the earlier olive tree analogy, he agrees that the ultimate reconciliation here must necessarily involve the Gentile branch and the Jew branch of Israel. See Milbank, "Paul against Biopolitics," 52.

43. See Jersak, "Lake of Fire," for a summary of how the destruction of Sodom and Gomorrah was interpreted by Jewish commentators up to Josephus.

fire [*puros aiōniou*]. Throughout the Scriptures, Sodom and Gomorrah are the models for what happens to those who endure divine wrath (Isa 1:10; 3:9; Jer 24:14; 3 Macc 2:5; Matt 10:15; 2 Pet 2:6). 3 Maccabees 2:5 explicitly refers to how the cities are an example for "later generations." Jude 7 is a puzzling verse because the fire of Sodom and Gomorrah, if there indeed was such a historical event, obviously did not burn forever. Moreover, recall the argument that *aiōnios* and other words in this family do not indicate "unending" but rather "unto the Age." The idea, then, is not that the fire in the world to come will burn literally forever but rather that the fire was other-worldly.⁴⁴ The fire comes from God, not from a random human who lit a piece of wood on fire or something like that. This is how the destruction was set forth as an example [*deigma*]. Just as the destruction that consumed Sodom and Gomorrah was otherworldly in that it was sent by God, the fire in the Age to come will also be other-worldly since it will be sent by God; more specifically, the fire in both cases is the presence of God's judgment.⁴⁵ What about the necessary aspect of purification that must be included in a universalist eschatology? We do not find this in Jude, but we do find this in Ezekiel 16:53–55. Here, God says that he will restore the fortunes of Sodom to what they were before he destroyed them. Whatever the case may be regarding the historical truth of Sodom and Gomorrah, there are inklings in the OT that God will indeed restore these cities to the glory they held before their destruction. Perhaps this should be taken into account when discussing Jude 7. The fire that destroyed Sodom and Gomorrah is both not unending and has with it, if we tentatively apply the extension given in Ezekiel, an element of purification/restoration. Even the lowest of sinners are given the opportunity for restoration. I can only assume that sinners who commit far less egregious transgressions will be given this opportunity.

I close this brief section on a relatively high note. Looking solely at the use of language alone and removing the context altogether, Jude 7 seems to be a difficult passage to square away with universalism. However, those who argue that *aiōniou* genuinely entails a never-ending span of time have to reconcile with the obvious fact that the fires of Sodom and Gomorrah did not burn eternally, supposing there even was a historical Sodom and Gomorrah. There are also issues with the infernalist argument because, in all honesty, the author may not have in mind a cogent

---

44. Ramelli, *Christian Doctrine*, 32.
45. Seijas, "La Apocatastasis O Restauración Universal," 433.

eschatological reality at all. This may just be one of many instances where an author overstates the case for following God, juxtaposing this to terrible suffering so that their audience picks up on this basic notion: Follow God's law or else you will be like *this* wicked group. When writing to an audience, you seek to make your point known. If you believe that your audience will overlook what you say if you do not hyperbolize, then it is natural to drum up their emotions and get their blood pumping while they sit on the edge of their seats. In addition, it is worth mentioning that never once in Jude is the punishment of "fire *aiōniou*" said to be the consequence of not following Jesus. This makes Jude 7 stand out from many (all?) other allegedly infernalist NT texts, which see this punishment as the specific consequence for those who do not follow Jesus. In the end, this verse causes very few problems from a scriptural point of view for a universalist. Does Gomorrah lead to grace? It certainly isn't off the table.

Apocalypse or *Apokatastasis*?

One should not publish a response to infernalism without at least mentioning the Apocalypse of St John, better known in English today as the Book of Revelation. Many argue that certain components of this text contain knockdown "proof texts" in favor of ECT. But what precisely is the Apocalypse getting at? This has been subject to heated theological discussion since the book was written between 75 and 100 CE. One can use the Apocalypse to justify practically any theological position. Sure, many other books can be used the same way, but no book in the Bible is more prone to theological abuse regarding eschatology than the Apocalypse.

We would be utterly deluding ourselves to think we can even grasp a central message from a text like this. Many have tried but with little success. Martin Luther was utterly baffled by the text and wrote in his Preface that he would bind "no man to opinion" from what they garnered out of it. There was probably no Greek commentary written on the Apocalypse before the sixth century. If there was one, it was from St Didymus the Blind, who was a universalist. In general, the Eastern Fathers who discussed this text before and after the sixth century came away from it with a multitude of messages that, if taken all together, would result in a total contradiction. Eusebius of Caesarea reported in the fourth century that the Apocalypse is universally recognized as canonical, but he thinks it lacks apostolic origins. He likely did this to express that while he recognized its theological significance and value, as a historian dealing with facts, he did not feel comfortable claiming it stemmed from an apostolic source.[46] St Cyril of Jerusalem in the fourth century was less fluid with his negative stance toward the Apocalypse. Even the Cappadocian Fathers did not include the Apocalypse in their respective canons. Indeed, the lack of commentaries on the Apocalypse may explain why Eastern debates about the canonicity of this text extended far beyond the compilation of the NT canon at the Council of Hippo in 393 and the Council of Carthage in 397. Fr Sergius Bulgakov writes that the Church "has not established any definitive and conclusive dogmatic or exegetical response" to the Apocalypse.[47] Indeed, Orthodoxy still does not consider the text liturgically canonical because it wasn't read in most churches during the time when liturgical texts were being compiled.

Determining the author's background of the Apocalypse is difficult, but a few characteristics of the text stick out. The author likely did not have access to any of the Synoptics, he probably had access to John's gospel and some Pauline letters, but he mainly worked off inherited tradition from the Jesus movement as well as the heavenly visions that he experienced, which lay behind the text. Also, the text displays a very poor use of grammar that exceeds even the awkward writing of a text like 2 Thessalonians. This indicates to some that Greek was either his second language, perhaps he spoke a Semitic language, or it indicates that, frankly, the author just wasn't that skilled at writing. I tend to think of the author, supposedly John of Patmos, as likely a Jewish-Christian, not a recently converted Gentile, who was struggling to synthesize his prized Second-Temple Jewish beliefs with his belief that Jesus was the Messiah and would return to rule. This gave way to an Angel-Christology, likely expressed by identifying Jesus as the Archangel Michael, as it was a common motif to identify the coming Messiah with various well-known angels in Second Temple texts; though, there are some proto-trinitarian statements in the text as well, seen especially with the Alpha and Omega statements made by Jesus (Rev 1:8; 22:13). This conflict also manifested in bizarre symbols and allegories (a lamb with seven horns, locusts with human teeth, and so on) pointing to the destruction of Rome and the restoration of Jerusalem, which John and the Christian communities receiving this would have understood.

---

46. Koperski, "Eusebius," 89–91.
47. Bulgakov, *Apocalypse of John*, 177.

PART 2: UNIVERSALISM IN HOLY TRADITION

This basic summary of the Apocalypse leads me to think of it as something like a (very bizarre) proto-Marxist tirade against the ruling powers. Friedrich Engels went so far as to write that it was "The simplest and clearest book of the whole New Testament."[48] For Engels, the entire NT is the story of people abandoning the ruling ideology and accepting a newer, more dangerous one that threatens the existence of social hierarchies and maybe even the state itself. This is certainly an aspect of the NT, just look at the social teachings of Christ and the communistic lifestyle lived by the apostles in Acts. However, as an overall theme, this is a bit reductive. When it comes to the Apocalypse, however, this reading may have some basis. The plot certainly involves the notion that a worldly authority (Rome) that persecutes an oppressed class (Christians) will become usurped by a truly unifying authority (God) who shall rule with perfect justice. One can see the roots of communist intelligentsia in this. At any rate, we, as twenty-first-century Christians, are blind to whatever John was trying to communicate. This book is a puzzle and will likely always remain so.

Take just one brief example of a clearly historical figure, the Whore of Babylon. The Whore is referred to as "Babylon" because she is the archetype for those that destroy Jerusalem, just as Babylon did in 586 BCE. All future cities that destroy Jerusalem and the temples thereof (this harkens back to Rome's destruction of the Second Temple in 70 CE) take part in the archetype of the Whore. This is why the Whore is said to be "drunk with the blood" of martyrs (Rev 17:6). Under Nero, Christians were heavily persecuted, as attested to by several ancient historians like Tacitus and Josephus. John seems to draw this back to how Christians were heavily persecuted at the time of the Babylonian onslaught as well. Interestingly, there was also a pretty common belief among people at this time that although Nero was reportedly dead by suicide in 68 CE, he was hiding out in secret (perhaps in a cave in a far away land) and one day would return to conquer the lands his successors lost. This was a palpable fear to many early Christians and could easily explain why Babylon and Rome were connected through symbolic language (Rev 17:11 might identify Nero with the "Eighth Beast").[49] There is a final reason why we know of the clear connection between Babylon and Rome. 1 Peter, on a fair estimate, was written between 60 and 80 CE and indirectly identifies

---

48. Engels, "Book of Revelation," 206.
49. DBH, *New Testament*, 439.

AN EXTENSIVE CRITIQUE OF BIBLICAL INFERNALISM

Rome with Babylon in 5:13. The author does so again at the end of the letter. This indicates that Christian communities around this time used Babylon as a cryptic and disheveling term for Rome.

With all this said, I do consider there to be a few scriptural images toward the beginning and middle of the Apocalypse that, genuinely, on a sober reading, can be understood as portraying a final eternal separation of the damned and the saved. Still, even these are often overblown by infernalists and endorsed as somehow straightforward declarations of eschatological reality (for instance, Rev 14:11). And as Origen argued, maybe these verses are put as stumbling blocks in Scripture by the Holy Spirit to test us.[50] The use of the noun *skandala* here by Origen, which etymologically can be traced up to our English verb "scandalize," and which in the verb form meant "to cause to stumble" in Greek, is to say that some things in Scripture should truly scandalize the reader and cause them to stumble while they are blissfully concentrating on Scripture. The reader should be taken aback and feel a justified intuitive recoil at some of the events supposedly ordained by God in the Scriptures. When we encounter *skandala* in Scripture, we must turn to a deeper spiritual meaning of the text that is sublime and overflowing with divine knowledge because we certainly do not encounter the divine in *skandala*. Perhaps this is like how God allows evil spirits to attack us so that we can be tested and turn towards repentance. If *Jubilees* 10 is to be believed along with the theology underpinning 1 Samuel 16:14; 18:10, there is a plausible case for this. Whatever the case may or may not be, it is simply odd for the infernalist to draw on such verses: Are you seriously going to put a ton of stock into the argument that, for example, a book that mentions legendary figures like Hades, Beast(s), and Satan could plausibly be read to entail anything like a doctrinal statement? I would hope not. This section does not respond to such claims but rather shows how, even if we accept that an eschatological reading of the Apocalypse is justified, a universalist conclusion cannot be dismissed altogether. Some even confidently argue that this is what the Apocalypse teaches.[51]

Chapter 21 begins with the vision of a "New Jerusalem," a refurbished holy city that was ordained by God to come like a bridegroom

---

50. Origen, *On First Principles*, 515.

51. Fr Robin Parry/Gregory McDonald provides a detailed exegetical argument for universalism in the Apocalypse. See Chapter 5 of his *Evangelical Universalist*. His argument accepts all the common Evangelical presuppositions about the Apocalypse and engages with the text in what I consider an unnecessary but sometimes fruitful way.

PART 2: UNIVERSALISM IN HOLY TRADITION

ordains his bride (21:2–3). This informs us that the text discusses the "Age to come." It also fulfills several prophecies in other parts of the NT that discuss how God seeks to sum up all things in Christ by bringing heaven to earth. An eschatological duality is then organized: Those who submit to God will inherit the grace of God, but those who are wicked, cowardly, liars, and unbelievers will endure the lake of fire (21:7–8). The next passages explain the reason why the holy city has walls. The walls are understood as protection from those outside. For instance, the Romans set up walls against the barbarians. This served as a physical identification of "our group" vs. "their group." The use of walls here indicates that those in the lake of fire are barred from the holy city. The walls protect everyone in the holy city and repel those in the lake of fire. All hope for universalism seems lost at this point, right? Not at all. We see in vv. 22–27 a very different story. One must leap over *skandala*.

Verse 22 begins with the statement that there is no more need for a temple because God is himself the temple. This stands as a perfect inversion to YHWH in the OT, who was worshiped at temples in particular places. When God himself is there, the structure that points to his presence is no longer needed. It is then said that even the sun and moon are unneeded at this point because God's glory lights up New Jerusalem. Then we have the kicker verse that can be quoted from the NKJV. "And the nations shall walk in its light, and the kings of the earth bring their glory and honor into it." The nations were said to be cast into the lake of fire (21:8; 21:27), but now they are allowed into the city. In fact, the next verse tells us precisely that the gates will *never* be shut (the Greek is emphatic here) because there is no night. There is no night because all in the New Jerusalem are forever glorified by the light of God. The language and theme here parallels precisely to Isaiah 60. In Isaiah, the gates were said to be left open to allow the nations to enter. The parallel here indicates the same idea: The gates are left open so that all the rebellious nations, unbelievers, and whoever else was in the lake of fire can be admitted back in. How exactly the rebellious nations and others in the lake of fire will be admitted back in is not said. Regardless, this has a clear universalist sentiment. Chapter 21 closes by saying that nothing impure will enter the city because it would cause defilement (21:27). For some, this statement means that universal salvation is completely off the table at this point. But a universalist should have no problem accepting that only one cleansed in fire—either in this life or the lake of fire—can be admitted into the city and added to the Book of Life. Thus, the sentiment

AN EXTENSIVE CRITIQUE OF BIBLICAL INFERNALISM

in this chapter should lead us to recall the sentiment in numerous other universalist texts we examined. Reconciliation is open to all.

The Apocalypse ends with a few relevant verses for our purpose here. Chapter 22 begins with an allegorical representation of the River of Life. It is said that near the River is the Tree of Life that yields apples which are for healing the nations (22:1-2). The Tree may be an inverse to the tree in Eden, which brought forth the finitude of the human race. The Tree may also be an inverse to the cross where Christ was hung. The Tree was once an instrument of death but now is the saving grace for life. St Jerome the Great offers yet another way to look at this. He views the fruit as that which bears the meaning of Scripture, while the leaves only bear the words. If we are left with the leaves alone, we lose the spiritual insight in Scripture. The most relevant aspect of this verse is that it emphasizes the notion of "healing." The Greek is *therapeian*. This exact verb is only found here, but another verb in the family is found two times in Luke, and iterations of this verb are used quite a lot in John's gospel, and around twenty-five times overall in the NT. Most reference Jesus healing or caring for those who come to him. Since the nations are mentioned here and the last chapter (along with earlier verses) established that the nations are in the lake of fire, this verse does not make sense unless one expresses that reconciliation is possible for the nations. St Primasius of Hadrumetum, a sixth-century North African bishop who participated in Constantinople II (see Chapter 10), is a rare outlier in Church history because he recognized this. (It's important to remember that few read the Apocalypse in any theological depth before the sixth century, which may explain why he's such an outlier.) The nations will become the sons and daughters of God, and his name shall be on their foreheads to mark them as so (22:5).

This furthers the point made at the end of chapter 21. There is now a rough schema for reconciliation for those not currently written in the Book of Life: They are admitted into the holy city only when healed through the love and life that Christ pours out onto those who accept him. Towards the end of the chapter, we read, "But outside are dogs and sorcerers and sexually immoral and murderers and idolaters, and whoever loves and practices a lie" (22:15). Like 21:27, this verse is not a stumbling block for universalism because the universalist accepts that there are those outside of the city walls in the lake of fire. However, the universalist believes that those outside the city walls *can* enter the holy city. The infernalist cannot accept this, and so they must engage in special pleading by trying to derail the identification of nations [*ethnōn*] as somehow not meaning those who reject Christ.

John's vision closes with an allegory that may reference the story of Jesus and the Samaritan woman at the well (Jn 4). The story goes that Jesus asked for a drink from a Samaritan woman. She is surprised that a Jew, a sworn enemy of the Samaritan people, would ask for a drink from her. Jesus then explains that although the water she gives him will only quench his thirst for a period, the water of life he brings will quench her thirst forever. In Revelation 22:17, Jesus says that those who desire may drink the water of life.[52] Since we know that those already in the city are taking part in the Tree of Life, this verse *only* makes sense in an eschatological reading if Jesus is speaking to those outside of the city. Those outside the city (Samaritans) are seen as sworn enemies of the righteous (Jews), but Jesus doesn't care. Jesus' love transcends all these divisions. Jesus calls to those in the lake of fire that if they so choose, and they are properly cleansed, they can be fulfilled by the water of life he offers to all.

The Apocalypse began with an affirmation of grace [*charis*] and invited the readers to engage with it as a bountiful expression of grace (1:4). The text now ends with the expression of grace (22:21). "Grace" is only mentioned in these two verses and does not appear at any other point in the Apocalypse. This seems to show that whether we realize it or not, grace is a constant theme throughout the Apocalypse. Even those difficult and confrontational verses, the *skandala* we may stumble on, still have the reality of grace as their backdrop. We can easily forget this due to the sheer complexity of the book at times, but we must not. Finally, it is notable that John addresses grace to all, not just those receiving the letter. Did John seek to indicate that grace is given not only to those in the present but, in an eschatological reading, quite literally *all*? Perhaps he did.

Thus, the universalist interpretation is left open but does not seem to be delivered with certainty. It is not said whether all people will eventually enter the open gates and accept the life-giving water that flows from New Jerusalem. At the same time, it is certainly not said that the gates are closed and an eternal separation is enshrined in the ontological constitution of the Age to come. Several universalist commentators overemphasize the universalist sentiment that can be drawn from the Apocalypse.

---

52. Whether or not this has its basis in John is debated. The author could have drawn on similar motifs present in Isaiah and Joel. Regardless, I argue that this is mentioned because the author knows Johannine traditions; this is too much of a conceptual cross-over for there not to be a shared heritage.

AN EXTENSIVE CRITIQUE OF BIBLICAL INFERNALISM

By my lights, universal salvation is not taught in the Apocalypse, but the hypothesis is left open. What we can say, with relative certainty, is that the Apocalypse does not claim there to be an eternal separation between the saved and damned. The Apocalypse should lead us to accept that salvation is open for all in the Age to come, but one cannot speculate from this book alone if everyone will accept it.

Frankly, I don't think the universalist interpretation is all that likely, but neither is any other eschatological interpretation of the Apocalypse. I accept that my thoroughly critical-historical interpretation is boring, and maybe I could even tentatively accept both instead of embracing one side. However, the puzzling nature of this entire book leaves me to turn away from a more fun and mystical interpretation. While I am not dogmatically opposed to such an eschatological reading, I just genuinely don't think that's the purpose of why the text was written, so any meaning we wish to impute into it is based on our own theological prerogatives. This is not to say that my exegesis is utterly pointless, as I wouldn't have written it if I believed that. But hey, if you really wish to draw out an eschatological commitment in the Apocalypse, universal salvation is indeed not out of the question. Maybe, just maybe, Apocalypse is *Apokatastasis* after all.

10

Constantinople II and its Discontents

HAVING REACHED THE END of Part Two, there are likely still some who remain unconvinced of universalism. For Orthodox and Catholics, this may be due to the alleged condemnation of *apokatastasis* at the Fifth Ecumenical Council. I have even seen Evangelicals in recent years mention this, as if a condemnation at an ecumenical council has any relevance to their theology; does the Evangelical now accept the validity of icon veneration enshrined dogmatically at Nicaea II? Of course not. Indeed, however, if universalism as a doctrine was truly anathematized, then any Christian who holds to this would be in profound heresy. As I said in the Introduction, the question of where we will end up after death is fundamental in Christianity. But what if universalism was never condemned by Constantinople II? What if universalism was never condemned at any ecumenical council? What if there is much more to the story? I have glorious news: All of these are true!

Historical Background on Constantinople II

Emperor Justinian I convened the Fifth Ecumenical Council (Constantinople II) in 553 CE. In Byzantine times, the emperor had the duty to call an ecumenical council if he and leading members of the state and

Church saw it as necessary.[1] Justinian called the council for the explicit purpose of condemning the Three Chapters.[2] The Three Chapters refers to the person and writings of Theodore of Mopuestia, specific writings of Theodoret of Cyrrhus, and the letter to Mari the Persian that allegedly was written by Ibas of Edessa; the *persons* Theodoret and Ibas were not condemned.[3]

The above were accused of peddling Nestorianism.[4] This is a christological doctrine that taught that Jesus was two independent persons, one divine and one human, who were loosely united together in the Incarnation. Since Jesus was two persons united together, Mary, the Mother of Jesus, could not be considered the Mother of God (as the Church desired at the time) since she only birthed the human person Jesus and not the divine person Jesus. God did not have a mother, according to Nestorianism. This doctrine was condemned by Ephesus I and Chalcedon in the prior century. In response to this doctrine, Ephesus I, and definitively Chalcedon, dogmatically imposed on the Church that Jesus was one person with two natures, one divine and one human. This allowed the Church to maintain that Mary was both the Mother of Jesus and the Mother of God. This also allowed the Church to maintain that Jesus united all of human nature to his divine nature so that the sin of Adam—which had been passed down to every human in the form of a finite life and propensity towards spiritual weakness (see Chapter 5)—has been ameliorated by the coming of Christ in the Incarnation. All can now participate in the divine life.

The Fifteen Origenist Anathemas of 553

Origen and Origenism were not mentioned in Justinian's letter announcing the council or in Justinian's letter read at the start of the council. Despite not being mentioned in either letter, Origen was condemned alongside several others in Canon 11 of the conciliar documents. "If anyone does not anathematize Arius, Eunomius, Macedonius, Apollinarius, Nestorius, Eutyches and Origen, as well as their heretical books, and also

1. McGuckin, *Eastern Orthodox Church*, 125.
2. Price, *Acts of the Council of Constantinople of 553*, 17.
3. Price, *Acts of the Council of Chalcedon*, 54.
4. This is a serious charge and one that many historians believe was an over-exaggeration on Justinian's part. See Wessel, *Cyril of Alexandria and the Nestorian Controversy* for a detailed examination of the history and reception of Nestorianism.

all other heretics who have already been condemned and anathematized by the holy, catholic and apostolic Church and by the four holy synods which have already been mentioned, and also all those who have thought or now think in the same way as the aforesaid heretics and who persist in their error even to death: let him be anathema."[5]

There are a few oddities about the mention of Origen here. First, Origen is a new name on this list. Every other name was denounced at a prior ecumenical council. Second, Origen's name is the only one out of chronological order on this list. He is the most recent name condemned yet is chronologically last on the list. Third, Origen's name is only found on this list but not on Justinian's earlier sketch list, which had all the other names. Ilaria Ramelli argues these observations "strongly" indicate that Origen's name is a later interpolation and was not originally in Canon 11.[6] Ramelli is in the minority of scholarship here.[7] I will explain later why I personally find her hypothesis unlikely. Whatever the case, the canon does not specify what teachings of Origen's are condemned, nor do the extant acts in Latin record any discussion from the councilmen about what teachings are condemned.

Around the time the council convened, fifteen anathemas were produced and directed at Origenist doctrine. The nature of these anathemas and their status in connection with the council is debated. Today, there is consensus among scholars that the anathemas were in some way connected to Constantinople II, but they were not from the proceedings of Constantinople II itself. Brian Daley goes so far as to say that it "seems certain" the anathemas were not from Constantinople II.[8] In the eighteenth and nineteenth centuries, it was common for scholars to embrace one of two extreme views: The fifteen anathemas were from the council's proceedings; the fifteen anathemas are entirely disconnected and may even be forgeries.[9]

Indeed, the former was the position of Cyril of Scythopolis, who, in 558, just five years after Constantinople II, attributed the anathemas to

---

5. Price, *Acts of Constantinople of 553*, 123.

6. Ramelli, *Christian Doctrine*, 737.

7. See an examination of this argument in Daley, "Discovery of the True Origen," 546–62.

8. Daley, *Hope of the Early Church*, 190.

9. See a summary of eighteenth and nineteenth-century scholarship in Kimel, *Destined for Joy*, 240.

Constantinople II itself.[10] Yet much work has been done to show how unreliable and often biased of a commentator he was on Origen's theology and the proceedings of Constantinople II.[11] Despite the latter certainly being a minority position in both historical and contemporary scholarship, some still support it today.[12] And some like Fr Richard Price, the leading scholar on the ecumenical councils, are agnostic about the nature and origin of the anathemas. Although he used to unequivocally agree with the consensus, in 2020, he altered his position. He began to hold that since the extant published acts were *specifically* sent for dispatch to Rome and Origenism was not much of a worry in the West since its most grotesque mutations were already banished, the anti-Origenist sentiment may have been omitted. He leaves open the possibility that the fifteen anathemas were indeed approved at Constantinople II itself but does not explicitly argue they were or were not.[13] This brief survey of the state of

10. Price, *Acts of the Council of Constantinople of 553*, 270.

11. See Hombergen, *Second Origenist Controversy*. Samuel Rubenson considers the use of Cyril of Scythopolis to require a "prudent call for caution." See Rubenson, "Asceticism," 655. In private correspondence, Fr Richard Price said that Cyril's knowledge of Constantinople II is "too general" to suggest direct knowledge of the proceedings. (Email received on 7/27/24).

12. Tanner, *Decrees of the Ecumenical* Councils, 106

13. Price, *Acts of the Second Council of Nicaea (787)*, 535–36. In private correspondence with Price, he has adjusted his position again after I brought up to him what he wrote in his 2020 text. At the time he was writing the above, he had not yet studied in detail the extent to which the various acts of ecumenical councils were disseminated and known. There are questions that remain regarding this, such as whether private persons had much access to them (he claims this is unlikely), but it is clear that the documents of 553 were known and presented by Bishop Macribius of Seleucia at Constantinople III (Sixth Ecumenical Council). This is to say that the extant Latin acts we have today were not composed specifically for dispatch to Rome. By updating his position on this, he is now moved to believe the reception of the fifteen anathemas was carried out formally at Constantinople II and thus was included in the original Greek acts we no longer have. He considers it to have been *sui generis*: The fifteen anathemas were presented to the bishops at the council and there was no conciliar debate, rather all the bishops consented verbally ("possibly") as a collective. The relevance of it being *sui generis* to his original position is that since there was uncontested agreement among the bishops, this gives reason to think either that the Latin acts did not include the fifteen anathemas because Origenism was a bygone worry in the West *or* that the Latin acts did not include the fifteen anathemas because there was no disagreement among the bishops when they were formally received. He is, at this point, leaving both options open. (Email received on 7/27/24).

I consider the *sui generis* hypothesis unlikely for several reasons. It does not seem like any other document or topic was approached like this at Constantinople II (to our knowledge). If this was indeed the way that several other documents or topics were approached at Constantinople II, we would have to take the fifteen anathemas seriously

present scholarship shows that both the extreme positions—the anathemas are from the council itself or the anathemas are entirely disconnected—do not find wide support.

This is because the tides had turned in scholarship on Constantinople II by the end of the nineteenth century. The extreme positions were no longer seen as attractive due to the synthesized and well-evidenced alternative hypothesis that first became popular through the work of the German scholar Franz Diekamp.[14] The hypothesis goes that, early in the Spring of 553, before the council began on May 5th, Justinian and his advisors composed the fifteen anathemas and ordered the patriarch to present them to the bishops and then present them in Constantinople.[15]

Some questions remain with this that unfortunately cannot be answered. We don't know when the anathemas were compiled or when the meeting occurred. The accepted period is anywhere between February and April. We also do not know who attended or where it took place in Constantinople. This last one is very important because we know, due to extraneous political reasons, that this pre-synod, which condemned Origen and produced the anathemas, could not have been attended by all

---

into account as being another case of this. Indeed, it does not seem like any other document or topic regarding Origen was *ever* broached this way at any ecumenical or local council prior (to our knowledge). If this was indeed the way that conciliar decisions at several of the anti-Origenist local councils in the fifth century were approached (and it was clearly not, as I implicitly explain later), then this argument might have solid probabilistic reason in favor of it; alas, it does not. Moreover, when we couple these reasons with the fact that Origen had *never* been condemned at *any* ecumenical council in name (or in context to a series of anti-Origenist anathemas) prior to Constantinople II, it seems unlikely that Justinian (and the Church) would assume the presentation of the fifteen anathemas would result in an uncontested agreement in favor of condemnation. This seems like a very unnecessary risk to take. We would much rather expect this to have been in the minutes of the council to avoid embarrassment if there was a failure to reach a complete agreement among the bishops. Doing this in the traditional way would have strongly increased the likelihood that the bishops reached a majority vote in accepting these fifteen anathemas; after all, a majority vote is far easier to reach than a complete agreement among peoples with different theological and political proclivities. As such, Price's updated position is not convincing. I continue to argue that the fifteen anathemas were accepted at a council prior to the opening of Constantinople II and *not* formally (dogmatically) received at Constantinople II. The anathemas are not in our Latin acts because they were not in the original Greek acts that recorded the proceedings of Constantinople II.

14. Diekamp, *Origenstischen Streitigkeiten*, 81–84. Diekamp's work has some flaws due to how old it is, but it has strengths as well. Diekamp was one of the first scholars to fluently lay out the Prochrists vs. Isochrists dispute, which I will explain later.

15. For a detailed list of twentieth-century scholars who held this position, see the footnote in Hombergen, *Second Origenist Controversy*, 21.

CONSTANTINOPLE II AND ITS DISCONTENTS

five patriarchs. In Justinian's time, a council was only deemed ecumenical if the five patriarchs from Constantinople, Rome, Alexandria, Antioch, and Jerusalem were in attendance. Even if all five approved the anathemas afterward, and this must be left open as a historical possibility, this pre-synod cannot in any way be deemed an ecumenical council due to there having been only (at most) three patriarchs present.[16] Notably, Pope Vigilius was not in attendance because of the bad blood that remained between Rome and Constantinople. As such, we do not know when this meeting happened, where it happened, or who exactly was present. All we know with certainty is that it occurred before May 5th. If we are serious about trying to establish what constitutes conciliar dogma as Orthodox Christians, our basis should not be a one-off mention in a canon that does not even explain what is being condemned and a document from a mysterious meeting convened at least a month before an ecumenical council. I shall return to both of these points later in the chapter.

Moreover, there is debate if the fifteen anathemas were actually directed at Origen himself, a certain group of his followers, or a misunderstanding of one or both. When examining the anathemas, some do seem to be directed at Origen, but others are towards positions that we know Origen did not hold. The fifteen anathemas are as follows:

> 1. *If anyone advocates the mythical pre-existence of souls and the monstrous restoration that follows from this, let him be anathema.*
>
> 2. *If anyone says that the origin of all rational beings was incorporeal and material minds without any number or name, with the result that there was a henad of them all through identity of substance, power and operation and through their union with and knowledge of God the Word, but that they reached satiety with divine contemplation and turned to what is worse, according to what the drive to this in each one corresponded to, and that they took more subtle or denser bodies and were allotted names such that the powers above have different names just as they have different bodies, as a result of which they became and were named some cherubim, some seraphim, and others principalities, powers, dominations, thrones, angels, and whatever heavenly orders there are, let him be anathema.*

---

16. Hombergen, *Second Origenist Controversy*, 313. Mitigating factors can come into play and make a synod attended by all five patriarchs still not an ecumenical council. These councils then become retroactively what are known as "robber councils."

3. If anyone says that the sun, the moon and the stars, belonging themselves to the same henad of rational beings, became what they are through turning to what is worse, let him be anathema.

4. If anyone says that the rational beings who grew cold in divine love were bound to our more dense bodies and were named human beings, while those who had reached the acme of evil were bound to cold and dark bodies and are and are called demons and spirits of wickedness, let him be anathema.

5. If anyone says that from the state of the angels and archangels originates that of the soul, and from that of the soul that of demons and human beings, and from that of human beings angels and demons originate again, and that each order of the heavenly powers is constituted either entirely from those below or those above or from both those above and those below, let him be anathema.

6. If anyone says that the genus of demons had a double origin, being compounded both from human souls and from more powerful spirits that descend to this, but that from the whole henad of rational beings one mind alone remained constant in divine love and contemplation, and that it became Christ and king of all rational beings and created the whole of corporeal nature, both heaven and earth, and what is intermediate, and that the universe came into being containing real elements that are older than its own existence, that is, the dry, the liquid, heat and cold, and also the form according to which it was fashioned, and that the all-holy and consubstantial Trinity did not fashion the universe as the cause of its creation but that mind, as they assert, existing before the universe as creator, gave being to the universe itself and made it created, let him be anathema.

7. If anyone says that Christ, described as existing in the form of God, united to God the Word even before all the ages, and as having emptied himself in the last days into what is human, took pity, as they assert, upon the multifarious fall of the beings in the same henad and, wishing to restore them, passed through everything and took on various bodies and received various names, becoming all things to all, among angels an angel, among powers a power, and among the other orders or genera of rational beings took on appropriately the form of each, and then like us partook of flesh and blood and became for human beings a human being, [if anyone says this] and

does not profess that God the Word emptied himself and became a human being, let him be anathema.

8. *If anyone says that God the Word, consubstantial with God the Father and the Holy Spirit, who was incarnate and became man, one of the holy Trinity, is not truly Christ but only catachrestically, on account of the mind which, as they assert, emptied itself, because it is united to God the Word and is truly called Christ, while the Word is called Christ because of this mind and this mind is called God because of the Word, let him be anathema.*

9. *If anyone says that it was not the Word of God, incarnate in flesh ensouled by a rational and intelligent soul, who descended into hell and the same ascended back to heaven, but rather the mind they mention, whom impiously they assert to have truly been made Christ through knowledge of the monad, let him be anathema.*

10. *If anyone says that the Lord's body after the resurrection was ethereal and spherical in form, and that the same will be true of the other bodies after the resurrection, and that, with first the Lord himself shedding his own body and [then] all likewise, the nature of bodies will pass into non-existence, let him be anathema.*

11. *If anyone says that the coming judgment means the total destruction of bodies and that the end of the story will be an immaterial nature, and that thereafter nothing that is material will exist but only pure mind, let him be anathema.*

12. *If anyone says that the heavenly powers, all human beings, the devil, and the spirits of wickedness will be united to God the Word in just the same way as the mind they call Christ, which is in the form of God and emptied itself, as they assert, and that the kingdom of Christ will have an end, let him be anathema.*

13. *If anyone says that there will not be a single difference at all between Christ and other rational beings, neither in substance nor in knowledge nor in power over everything nor in operation, but that all will be at the right hand of God as Christ beside them will be, as indeed they were also in their mythical pre-existence, let him be anathema.*

14. *If anyone says that there will be one henad of all rational beings, when the hypostases and numbers are annihilated together with bodies, and that knowledge about rational beings will be*

> accompanied by the destruction of the universes, the shedding of bodies, and the abolition of names, and there will be identity of knowledge as of hypostases, and that in this mythical restoration there will be only pure spirits, as there were in their nonsensical notion of pre-existence, let him be anathema.
>
> 15. If anyone says that the mode of life of the minds will be identical to that earlier one when they had not yet descended or fallen, with the result that the beginning is identical to the end and the end is the measure of the beginning, let him be anathema.[17]

Many of these are outrageous positions and Origen believed very few of them. He did not believe that demons have a double origin, that the state of angels originates from the soul, that Jesus had a spherical body after his resurrection, that there wouldn't be a difference between Jesus and all beings, and so on. Although he did, at least in his early writings after his conversion to Christianity, believe in a heretical doctrine of the Trinity. However, the extent to which his doctrine is heretical is debated. He may have put the Father ontologically above the Son, the Son ontologically above the Holy Spirit, and the Holy Spirit ontologically above all creation but ontologically below the former two.[18] He may have gone further than this and believed that only the Father as the Primary Person of the Trinity has domain over all things; the Son has dominion over all rational beings, and the Holy Spirit has dominion over the saints. This is a hierarchical view of the Trinity that is sorely against Nicene dogmatics, which uniformly asserts the consubstantiality and co-eternality of the Persons in the Trinity.

On the other hand, Origen may not have held such stringent views of subordinationism because several of his statements seem to teach a trinitarian theology that, although still ante-Nicene, is not dogmatically opposed to Nicene teaching.[19] Generally, it's best not to paint Origen as a systematic thinker who held the same beliefs throughout his life after his conversion to Christianity; like St Paul, his greatest inspiration, his beliefs likely evolved. On this note, I must also remind the reader that Origen's corpus was undeniably corrupted within a few generations after his death. This corruption was so wide-scale, impacting many extant and non-extant works, that St Pamphilus of Caesarea was led to write a text

17. Price, *Acts of the Council of Constantinople of 553*, 284–86.
18. Lee, *Origen and the Holy Spirit*, 144–45.
19. Lee, *Origen and the Holy Spirit*, 154–56.

titled *On the Falsification of the Books of Origen* around the start of the fourth century. This corruption could very well have led to the interpolation of heretical views into Origen's otherwise largely "orthodox" writings. Putting aside the possibility of corruption, by the time of Origen's late writings, notably *Contra Celsum* and *Commentary on Matthew*, he was certainly not a subordinationist. Rather, he believed in what would later be termed, more than a century later, the Nicene Trinity.[20] The faithful should also remember the cautious reminder from St Jerome the Great on Origen. "If someone [...] points to me his mistakes, he will have to answer in Horace's words: 'The fault is venial, for his work is long.' Let us not imitate the faults of one whose virtues we cannot equal."[21] Discussing this in any more depth is outside the scope of this present study.

Contemporary scholarship considers the concept of "Origenism" to be almost meaningless when used to describe a particular person, group, or belief that existed in the sixth century.[22] Elizabeth Clark writes, "At times, [the charge of Origenism] was so malleable that Origen's theology was often obscured in the clamor of contemporary debate."[23] It was a buzzword thrown around to either authorize or condemn those who threatened ecclesial and sometimes political control. The term not only involves the theological system of Origen but also his legacy, his followers (some living three hundred years after him) and was used in broad strokes to cover any transgression against orthodox theology. An absurd example of how polemical the term became is seen in a statement from Pseudo-Caesarius. He tries to equate the epithet ἐπωνύμου with Origen's name [Ὠριγένης] and then argues that the noun for wrath [ὀργή] is a cognate of this. This is to say that Origen operates "under the name" of wrath. In general, when the term "Origenist" was thrown at a group, person, or belief, this by no means tells us how much they share with Origen's theology. We are left with a few questions here. Who is being condemned if not Origen? Why was Origen roped into this? Most importantly, was universalism anathematized? To answer these questions sufficiently, we must go back in time by a few years.

20. Again, see Ramelli, "Origen, Greek Philosophy," 302–50; Ramelli, "Origen's Anti-Subordinationism," 21–49.

21. Quoted in Ramelli, "Patristic Readings."

22. For a summary of twentieth-century scholarship on this, see Hombergen, *Second Origenist Controversy*, 29–30.

23. Clark, *Origenist Controversy*, 86.

PART 2: UNIVERSALISM IN HOLY TRADITION

Justinian's Nine Anathemas of 543

The year was 543, ten years before Constantinople II. Palestinian monks had been in a theological debate over Origenism for more than thirty years by this point.[24] Origenist doctrine began to make headway in Palestinian monastic communities after the arrival of a prolific Syrian Origenist named Stephen bar Sudayle in the region around 512. There were two large monastic communities there at the time: the Lavra Monastery, located between Jerusalem and the Dead Sea, and the New Lavra Monastery, located south of Jerusalem. The latter became the hotbed of Origenism since it is where Sudalye began to develop followers.[25] By 543, tensions had risen enough for the patriarchs of Jerusalem and Antioch to write to Justinian and argue for a condemnation of Origen.[26] The decisive factor came when Patriarch Mina of Constantinople also wrote to Justinian with the same request.

Despite several Origenist voices in Constantinople, Justinian heeded Mina's call and wrote a treatise against Origen (humbly) entitled *The Treatise of the Most Pious Emperor Justinian*, often cited in Latin as *Liber adversus Origenem*.[27] This was a long treatise that responded to Origenism using Scripture, the Fathers, and philosophy. The document closed with a dramatic line that claimed Origen to be a Manichean, an Arian, and a pagan who is wicked and insane. Out of all these claims, Origen's early theology, as discussed, could possibly be labeled "Arian," but this would be an anachronistic move. The claim that Origen was a "pagan," despite its clear polemic tone without much care for substance, does have a basis in truth since Origen likely converted from paganism and continued to be revered by famous Hellenistic pagans after his conversion.[28] Regardless, the most relevant part of the document for our purpose is its inclusion of nine anathemas that condemn what was thought to be Origen's theology:

---

24. Origenists were present in Palestine by the early fifth century. This was largely due to immigration from Alexandrian monasteries after the condemnations delivered to Origenism in 400 at several local councils led to the banishment of Origenist monks (discussed later in the chapter). See Rubenson, "Asceticism," 653.
25. Telea. "Origenism," 37.
26. Price, *Acts of the Council of Constantinople of 553*, 274.
27. Telea, "Origenism," 41.
28. Ramelli, "Origen, Patristic Philosophy," 217–63.

1. If anyone says or holds that the souls of human beings pre-exist, as previously minds and holy powers, but that they reached satiety with divine contemplation and turned to what is worse and for this reason grew cold in the love of God and are therefore called souls, and were made to descend into bodies as a punishment, let him be anathema.

2. If anyone says or holds that the Lord's soul pre-existed and came into being united to God the Word before the incarnation and birth from a virgin, let him be anathema.

3. If anyone holds or says that the body of our Lord Jesus Christ was first formed in the womb of the holy Virgin and that afterwards both God the Word and the soul, being pre-existent, were united to it, let him be anathema.

4. If anyone says or holds that the Word of God became like all the heavenly orders, becoming cherubim for the cherubim, seraphim for the seraphim, and becoming (in a word) like all the powers above, let him be anathema.

5. If anyone says or holds that at the resurrection the bodies of human beings will be raised spherical and does not profess that we shall be raised upright, let him be anathema.

6. If anyone says or holds that heaven, sun, moon, stars, and the waters above the heavens are ensouled and rational powers, let him be anathema.

7. If anyone says or holds that in the age to come Christ the Master will be crucified on behalf of demons as well as on behalf of human beings, let him be anathema.

8. If anyone says or holds that God's power is finite and that he created [only] what he could grasp and comprehend, or that creation is coeternal with God, let him be anathema.

9. If anyone says or holds that the punishment of demons and impious human beings is temporary and that it will have an end at some time, and that there will be a restoration of demons and impious human beings, let him be anathema.[29]

Once again, however, very few of these condemnations apply to Origen. Many apply to figures such as fourth-century Evagrius Ponticus and fourth-century Didymus the Blind. Others only apply to sixth-century Leonitus of Byzantium, the most influential disciple of Sadayle in Palestine. Origen certainly did not believe that Jesus became like angels after

---

29. Price, *Acts of the Council of Constantinople of 553*, 281.

his death on earth, that human bodies after the resurrection would be spherical, that the stars have rational powers, that God's power is finite, etc. Shown to agree with Elizabeth Clark, who mentioned a similar point earlier, P. Tzamalikos notes, "False attributions to Origen were the rule rather than the exception."[30] By the sixth century, the concept of "Origenism" had become so broad that it was practically vacuous and could be used to condemn figures who did not even like Origen, such as Theodore of Mopuestia, who received this treatment from Justinian.[31] Some argue that Justinian's decision to consider these anathemas "anti-Origenist" stemmed from his disinterest in faithfully representing Origen. It is more likely that Justinian was oblivious to Origen's theology, and what his advisors knew about it was learned from anti-Origenist texts of the time.[32] Many of these anti-Origenist texts, such as the treatise by Antipatrus of Bostra that grew to become the "black book of Origenism," failed to even consider that what they were critiquing was not Origen's theology but later innovations by followers centuries removed from him. Whatever Justinian's advisors thought they knew about Origen mostly came from this book and others like it that were available at the time.[33]

Still, Anathema 9 may be relevant to our purpose. To some, it reads like a blanket condemnation of all forms of universalism. However, like the other anathemas, this was written to respond to specific Palestinian monks (discussed below) who posited the obscene theological conclusions that earlier anathemas on the list condemn. Perhaps when we abstract away this single anathema, universalism in all forms does seem to be condemned. This, however, is simply *not* the way that Orthodox Christians are asked to approach Holy Tradition. We are asked to engage with Holy Tradition with a recognition that it is divinely inspired but also with the recognition that the persons who formed such tradition, participated in such councils, and wrote such decrees come from a particular time in a particular place and responded to particular needs and worries of such a particular time and place. This is obvious when it comes to Scripture. I can only assume that Orthodox Christians alive today do

---

30. Tzamalikos, *Real Cassian Revisited*, 283.

31. One can be a universalist without being an Origenist like Theodore. However, it is very hard to be an Origenist without being a universalist. Seijas, "La Apocatatasis O Restauración Universal," 439.

32. Tzamalikos, *Real Cassian Revisited*, 259. Also, McGuckin, *Origen of Alexandria*, 88.

33. Tzamalikos, *Anaxagoras, Origen, and Neoplatonism*, 905–7.

not believe that the sun revolves around the earth or that there is a firmament above the earth that holds off the heavenly waters from flooding the earth. Yet when it comes to other aspects of Holy Tradition, many pious believers flounder and adopt ahistorical conclusions. Moreover, this is just the opinion of one emperor and his advisors. This does not in any way constitute a dogmatic statement. To twist this into anything more serious than a decree made by an emperor is unsound. Emperor Justinian was a very strict ruler. When he wanted something done, it was done, and few questions were asked. Failure to heed Justinian's call may have been grounds for treason, especially in a case like this, where political pressure was very high. Fr Aidan Kimel asks the right kind of question here. "Did either Justinian or the synodical bishops believe they were condemning the universalist views of St Gregory of Nyssa?"[34] There is no reason to think they did or intended to.

Constantinople II and the Origenist Controversy

This leaves us enough room to answer the questions posed at the end of the section before the last and pose a major new one at the close of this section. Many overlapping themes exist between the nine anathemas of 543 and the fifteen anathemas of 553. If indeed these were directed at Origen this would naturally follow. However, we have shown that both could not have been seriously directed at Origen himself. Efforts must also be taken not to overstate the notable differences between the two sets of anathemas. The descriptions in each anathema of the fifteen anathemas are longer than those in each anathema of the nine anathemas. This is especially relevant to how they address Origenist Christology. The anathemas of 543 condemn the belief that Christ had a pre-existent human soul before the Incarnation, that the Word of God took an angelic form, and that in the next Age, Christ will be crucified anew to redeem the demons.[35] The anathemas of 553 explain the above with much more detail and seem to purposefully tie it to positions associated with Nestorianism. Nestorianism is not a prominent theme in the anathemas of 543. Hence, we are left wondering how and why Nestorianism became associated with Origenism in the 553 anathemas. I argue below that both sets of anathemas were directed at the beliefs of a sixth-century Palestinian

---

34. Kimel, *Destined for Joy*, 232.
35. Price, *Acts of the Council of Constantinople of 553*, 278.

PART 2: UNIVERSALISM IN HOLY TRADITION

Origenist monastic group known as the Isochrists. There was a conscious attempt made by their opponents to link Origenism to Nestorianism so that they would be politically condemned, and their opponents could control Palestinian monastic communities without pushback.

Theological disputes in the Palestinian monastic community led to a split in the Origenists a few years after the nine anathemas of 543. Many Origenist monks were forced out of both the New and Old Lavra monasteries due to the Imperial decree from Justinian.[36] By 547, there were two main Origenist factions.[37] There were the Protochrists who believed that the saints and all the believers would forever be surpassed in holiness by Christ because he is God and has the status of the firstborn. Then there were the Isochrists who believed that the saints and Christ attained equality with holiness and divinity. The main theological dispute was over christological matters concerning soteriology, but there was also a dispute over intellectual freedom and its place in monastic life.[38] Despite the presence of two Origenist factions at the time of the pre-synodal meeting in 553, only one was targeted. This may be for a few reasons. Patriarch Peter of Jerusalem died in 544, and the Protochrists were able to place Marcarius II on the throne, who was more amenable to their political positions and would push against the positions of the Isochrists.[39] This, coupled with oppressive policies in favor of the Isochrists in the years following the split of 547, further convinced the Protochrists to take sides with Marcarius and orthodoxy over the Isochrists.[40] Although Marcarius was removed from the throne by Justinian in 552 due to his earlier relationship with the Protochrists and for holding some unorthodox positions, the Protochrists found themselves no longer on the outskirts of orthodoxy in Palestine. In the years before 553, a coalition was thus formed between the Protochrists and the ecclesial orthodoxy against the Isochrists.

In fall 552 or early winter 553, the Palestinians and bishops under other patriarchs arrived in Constantinople, all prepped for the upcoming ecumenical council. In Justinian's official letter read at the opening of the council, he references that a letter written to Pope Vigilius on January 6

36. Telea, "Origenism," 43.
37. Hombergen, *Second Origenist Controversy*, 199–200.
38. See Perrone, "Palestinian Monasticism," 245–61. See especially his conclusion to the essay. Also, Baghos, "Conflicting Portrayals," 74.
39. Seijas, "La Apocatatasis O Restauración Universal," 450.
40. Hombergen, *Second Origenist Controversy*, 86.

was written after the bishops arrived in Constantinople. This places their arrival anywhere from late fall to early winter. The Palestinians had likely known about the council for at least a year before this because Justinian began taking steps to call the ecumenical council as early as 550 due to the increased tension with Vigilius over the Three Chapters. The Palestinian bishops recognized that the council was primarily called to condemn the Three Chapters but sought to make their voice heard against Origenism. They came up with a plan to tie "Origenism" as such to the specific Origenist Isochrists.[41] This manifested in the condemnation of Origenism in the fifteen anathemas without care for a distinction separating Origen from the Origenists or the Isochrists from the Protochrists. There was no desire to separate Origen from the Origenists or the Isochrists from the Protochrists because the Protochrists had been accepted as orthodox. All of Origenism was subsumed under Nestorianism, and Origen was heralded as the long-dead ringleader of the circus.

Therefore, the only group targeted and condemned by these fifteen anathemas were the Origenist Isochrists. The theology of the Isochrists was thought to be similar to Evagrian Origenism. This was the theology that the compilers of the anathemas *believed* they were condemning, but mistakenly, they attributed their condemnation to Origen himself. Fr John Behr comments, "It has also become universally accepted that the anathemas of the sixth century and the reports of Justinian were directed primarily against Evagrius and sixth century 'Origenism' rather than Origen himself."[42] This position stems from Antoine Guillaumont who wrote in his famous study, "Evagrian Christology is absolutely that of the Isochrists."[43] Yet Guillaumont's language is far too exaggerated.[44] The Isochrists did not solely follow Evagrian Christology and theology but took elements of it, like they took elements of Origen's actual theology, and derived a synthesis between them. They also incorporated the beliefs of others, such as beliefs from the Neoplatonic Christianity of St Dionysius the Areopagite that was growing in popularity across the East.[45] Regardless, I must concur with Behr that Evagrian Christology

---

41. Tzamalikos, *Anaxagoras, Origen, and Neoplatonism*, 1441.

42. Behr, "Introduction."

43. Evagrius, *Kephalaia Gnostica*, 156. My translation.

44. See Casiday, *Reconstructing the Theology*, 194–204 for a detailed critique of Guillaumont's position. The central thesis is that Evagrian Christology differs in stark ways from what was condemned in the fifteen anathemas.

45. A further study into whether the Isochrists held to Evagrian Origenism is seen

was relevant to why the Isochrists were condemned, if only because their opponents falsely believed they held to it. After all, several anathemas cite and paraphrase sections directly from Evagrius.[46] Perhaps this was done because it was believed these sections adequately express the views of the Isochrists. Whatever the case, the Protochrists made a clear and successful attempt to connect Evagrius to the Isochrists.

Before I close this section, I must answer a lingering question. Anathema 12, in the fifteen anathemas, seems to condemn not only what Origen believed but also universalism overall. The anathema reads:

> "If anyone says that the heavenly powers, all human beings, the devil, and the spirits of wickedness will be united to God the Word in just the same way as the mind they call Christ, which is in the form of God and emptied itself, as they assert, and that the kingdom of Christ will have an end, let him be anathema."[47]

If this can be shown to condemn the theology of Origen, then isn't the "traditional" view from Cyril of Scythopolis that Origen himself was condemned in 553 true?

There are three major issues with this argument. First, Origen did not wholeheartedly believe that the devil would be reconciled. He seems to go back and forth on this. In a well-attested letter to his friends in Alexandria, Origen fiercely denied that the devil would be granted salvation even in the universal restoration.[48] This was likely written after those around him accused him of holding this due to a few controversial passages in his *First Principles*. We do not know whether he denied this out of genuine conviction or to save face. Second, the specific language of "united to God the Word in just the same way..." is a denial of Christ's sole consubstantiality with the Father, and hence refers to a *very* specific construal of universalism. One that Origen did not teach. Third, Origen did not believe the phrase, "the kingdom of Christ will have an end."[49] Origen sometimes spoke about an "after" eternal life where the

---

in Perczel, "Pseudo-Dionysius and Palestinian Origenism" 261–83. Perczel is clear that there are stark differences.

46. Clark, *Origenist Controversy*, 249.

47. Price, *Acts of the Council of Constantinople of 553*, 281.

48. Hombergen, *Second Origenist Controversy*, 278.

49. To our modern ears, this is a very odd statement. However, it followed from the axiom of perishability known to all Middle Platonists: What had a beginning in time must also have an end in time. Despite a very peculiar statement in Plato's *Timaeus* that the world "came into being" [*gegonen*], which seems to say that the world is *not*

Son would deliver the Kingdom to the Father, but this does not mean the Kingdom will come to an end. That is to say, he did not believe in "eternal recurrence" in the way that St Augustine of Hippo wrongly attributed to him. He did, however, believe that the temporality of eternal life as a never-ending duration will come to an end as all the saved will share in the divine life.[50] Yet this is not a heterodox position. St Gregory of Nyssa held to this, as did St Dumitru Stăniloae of blessed memory; the latter was an infernalist, for him, the saved would all enter the divine life, but the damned would not. This indeed points us, once again, to the conclusion that the fifteen anathemas were directed at the Isochrists and not Origen himself. Origen's name may have been tacked on for good measure, but the positions this anathema condemns are both not Origen's own and are not positions held by universalists today.

But suppose that believing "united to God the Word in just the same way. . ." and that "the kingdom of Christ will have an end" is not a necessary and sufficient condition for one to be condemned under Anathema 12. In other words, is a person who holds to other aspects of this Isochristic universalism still condemned? First, this would be a very odd way to read the anathema. Anathemas seem to be all or nothing. You can't just pick what part of an anathema you think matters for the pious today and disregard the context it is in. Second, we must remember that these fifteen anathemas were not from Constantinople II but rather a pre-synodal meeting that convened at least a month before the council. This makes the meeting not an ecumenical council by the ecclesial standards of the time, nor by the present standards, and thus not a binding affirmation of faith for the pious today. Hence, even if we grant that only following certain aspects of Anathema 12 should lead to condemnation (and we should not),[51] the severity of this condemnation must be considered in light of the fact it was produced at a non-ecumenical council and no mention of it was made in the extant Latin acts of Constantinople II.

---

eternal, many Middle Platonists continued to believe it was. Some Christians seem to have brought this cosmological attitude with them and applied it to the eschatological "kingdom of Christ." Origen himself quite liked this perishability axiom because of its usefulness in proving universal salvation: Evil had a beginning in time and so it must have an end in time. However, he did not apply it to what this anathema is claiming.

50. Tzamalikos, *Philosophy of History and Eschatology*, 271–74.

51. In private correspondence, Fr Richard Price wrote that in his scholarly opinion, Anathema 12 "doesn't constitute a condemnation of saner and more sober varieties of universalism." (Email received 7/27/24).

PART 2: UNIVERSALISM IN HOLY TRADITION

Having examined the relevant canon of Constantinople II, the presynodal fifteen anathemas in 553, and the nine anathemas sent by Justinian's decree in 543, the argument that all species of universalism were *explicitly* anathematized or even *implicitly* anathematized seems weak. This leaves us with a new question: Did earlier local synods influence the decrees in these cases? If so, does this open the door to the argument that Constantinople II at least *implicitly* anathematized all forms of universalism?

The Reception of Origen and *Apokatastasis* at Local Synods in the Fourth Century

Once one rejects the position that Constantinople II *explicitly* anathematized universalism, their argument tends to go as follows:

P1: At least one local council before Constantinople II *explicitly* condemned Origen's universalism (P);

P2: If at least one local council before Constantinople II *explicitly* condemned Origen's universalism, this entails that Origen's universalism was *implicitly* condemned at Constantinople II (P → Q);

C1: Origen's universalism was *implicitly* condemned at Constantinople II (Q).

P3: If Origen's universalism was *implicitly* condemned at Constantinople II, this entails that all species of universalism were *implicitly* condemned at Constantinople II (Q → S);

C2: All species of universalism were *implicitly* condemned at Constantinople II (S).

I provide this syllogism as a show of goodwill to my opponents. Despite the many falsehoods, there are nuggets of truth here.

The most noteworthy local synod that condemned Origen is often called the Synod of Alexandria (399–400), but this may be a misleading title. During these two years, there were likely two synods: One held in Alexandria and the other in Nitria.[52] The one held in Alexandria was not related to the Origenist condemnations, although it is often the only one mentioned by scholars. The synod in Nitria, held in 400, is the one that probably oversaw the condemnation of Origenist monks. Patriarch

---

52. Banev, *Theophilus of Alexandria*, 40.

Theophilus of Alexandria convened both. Although there is still a debate in scholarship regarding the status of these two councils due to somewhat ambiguous evidence on both sides, I think it is fair to go with the stance that there were two synods. One which was unrelated to the condemnations of Origen and the other, later, which issued them. While holding to this, due to the overabundance of scholars who title their studies on the "Synod of Alexandria," I shall do the same. Do keep in mind that references to the "Synod of Alexandria" in this section are really about the synod that issued the Origenist condemnations, whether that occurred in Alexandria or Nitria. This is one of the few early local synods with well-attested evidence of what was condemned.

An extant *Synodal Letter* of Theophilus to the bishops of Palestine and Cyprus identifies six "chief errors" of Origen. Condemnations are given to those who believe that we should only pray to the Father, that Christ's kingdom will come to an end, that the stars are conscious, and so on. Similar to the later anathemas of 543 and 553, these are not beliefs that Origen held. Once again, Evagrian Origenism seems to be the target of these anathemas. Putting these aside, once again, there is a condemnation that seems to refer to Origen's doctrine of *apokatastasis*. It reads, "Christ will also save the demons[. . .] he will come to suffer again, becoming a demon." But this, too, is not something Origen believed. While there is a reference to a type of *apokatastasis* doctrine here in the phrase "Christ will also save the demons," one cannot even reasonably misconstrue Origen to think he taught that Christ would suffer again and become a demon. And certainly, no contemporary universalist believes this either.

We are left with roughly two options for what to make of this. (a) The synod led by Theophilus was unaware of Origen's eschatology, and hence, even if they were against universalism, they did not know it stemmed from Origen. (b) The synod led by Theophilus frankly didn't see universalism as important enough to mention it among Origen's "chief errors" because it wasn't considered an error worthy of condemnation.

The first option is unlikely since Origen's theology was known throughout much of the East at this point, especially in his home turf of Egypt, and especially in Egyptian (Coptic) monastic settings, where he inspired many students who then had their own students.[53] Indeed,

---

53. Recent scholarship has largely put to rest the argument that a large number of Coptic monks in the fourth century were theologically illiterate. See Rubenson, "Origenist Controversy," 329–35; Lundhaug and Jenott, *Monastic Origins*.

PART 2: UNIVERSALISM IN HOLY TRADITION

Theophilus demonstrates his knowledge of Origen's eschatology in one extant text by mentioning that Origen believed in the universal reconciliation of all humans. We also know that Theophilus himself drafted this list based on his knowledge rather than relying on prior conciliar papers. Unlike Justinian, Theophilus was not ignorant of Origen, nor the theology circulating in monastic communities of his respective time, nor was he unequivocally abrasive in combating Origen.[54] He saw himself as a fair judge of Origen due to his knowledge of his theology and because he once (like all Alexandrian Christians) shared admiration for him to an extent.[55] While Theophilus still had a bias against Origen, compared to fellow anti-Origenists of his time and later Justinian I, he operated in much better faith, even if he still misunderstood Origen's theology in some ways, as will be examined later.

The second option is more likely. Ilaria Ramelli concurs, "If Theophilus, who was well aware that the core of Origen's doctrine (philosophy of history, anthropology, eschatology, theodicy) was the doctrine of *apokatastasis*, nevertheless decided not to include it in his official accusations against Origen, this is very probably due to the fact that he knew that many Christians still upheld that theory."[56] Her statement may track well with what we know about the number of universalists in the fourth century. St Basil the Great recorded that the "great majority" of his fellow Christians assumed that punishment in the Age to come would only be temporary and not eternal. St Augustine of Hippo was also keen to note that a "great many" of Christians were universalists. These two attestations add further credence to Ramelli's argument that many Christians in the East and West held to this doctrine. (And it's worth remembering that neither writer stated this explicitly as a negative but rather as merely a neutral observation.) Thus, not wanting to upset any universalists he knew of and respected, Theophilus felt no need to step in and turn Christians away from believing in the Greater Hope. Universalism was likely allowed to remain a *theologoumenon* or respected private opinion of the pious. Unfortunately, the same cannot be said today.

This is not to say that the synod approved of *apokatastasis*, which would be mere conjecture, but it is to say that the synod did not consider the doctrine worthy of condemnation at a formal junction. No matter

---

54. Rubenson, "Origenist Controversy," 326.
55. Banev, *Theophilus of Alexandria*, 129.
56. Ramelli, *Christian Doctrine*, 587.

how much they disliked the doctrine, their dislike did not seem grave enough to usher in a condemnation. If one wants to argue that perhaps there was originally more heinous language directed towards a belief in the universal reconciliation of humans, this is an argument from silence, one that has at least some evidence against it. It is true that we do not have the original *Synodal Letter*. What we have is the Latin translation preserved by St Jerome the Great.

As I will discuss later, Jerome was an avowed anti-Origenist later in life who, years before, had petitioned other local synods to address and condemn Origen. It would be unlikely for an opponent of Origen to forget to specify the clear condemnation attached to his belief in *apokatastasis* if there ever was such. Perhaps some universalists would argue that Jerome may have even added in the prior information, which offhandedly mentions the universal reconciliation of all humans. I am not one to accuse an esteemed Father of the Church of an action like this on mere conjecture. Though at least this would be an argument that makes a modicum of sense in light of Jerome's expressed bias. Regardless, it is still a very unlikely hypothesis. Jerome was an accurate translator of later documents from Theophilus—such as the *Festal Letter* of 404—which we still have in the original Greek and Jerome's Latin translation.[57] While circumstantial, as historians, we must operate off a view of credential likelihood, especially when it comes to allegations of edited documents from late antiquity. The credence that Jerome substantially altered the *Synodal Letter* to offhandedly mention a belief in the universal reconciliation of all humans is very low. It's safe to say that the *Synodal Letter* offhandedly mentions that Origen believed in the universal reconciliation of all humans, but it is clear that this position was not condemned.

Soon following the condemnation of Origen at the Synod of Alexandria, local synods in Jerusalem and Cyprus were held to condemn Origen under the leadership of Epiphanius of Salamis. Following Theophilus's *Synodal Letter*, they condemned many of the same Origenist positions that stemmed from his later followers but likewise attributed them to Origen himself. The next year, Pope Anastasius wrote a letter to St John of Jerusalem that condemned Origen.[58] He did not specify what doctrines were condemned, but he mentioned the Synod in Alexandria, which points to the fact that he agreed with the condemnation

---

57. Banev, *Theophilus of Alexandria*, 76.
58. Anastasius, "Letter of Anastasius."

that Theophilus issued. It is remarkable that the non-universalist (to our knowledge) Anastasius did not feel the need to mention that Theophilus forgot to condemn *apokatastasis*. You would think that if it ever truly was such a grave heresy, enshrined dogmatically as hellbound, the good pope would make sure to remind everyone that Theophilus implicitly meant that *apokatastasis* was condemned in his *Synodal Letter*, or he would have corrected Theophilus altogether. And yet, not a word. However, what Anastasius did say about Origen in this letter was quite comedic. He criticized Origen for his "complicated" arguments that betray the apostolic faith. If logic isn't your strong suit and you struggle to understand the implications of St Paul's eschatological claims (see Chapters 5 and 9), then Anastasius is right: Universalism doesn't make much sense to you.

Since Origen, at least in name, was condemned in Alexandria, Jerusalem, and Cyprus, and even by a sitting pope, it's fair to argue this condemnation was quasi-authoritative for the Church in later councils. Canon 1 of the Council of Chalcedon, held in 451, specified that all canons decided in prior ecumenical and local councils remain in force.[59] A prior condemnation of a figure and/or their writings in a local council may not indicate that a later ecumenical council will subscribe to all the decisions involved in their condemnation, but it indicates that there is an expectation that the later council will examine the decrees of the local council, and this may influence their own decisions to some degree. This is a reasonable explanation for why Origen was condemned in Canon 11 of Constantinople II. The councilmen who compiled the canons examined prior condemnations of Origen from local councils. This strongly influenced their decision to add Origen's name to Canon 11.

Thus, I can harden my disagreement with Ramelli's hypothesis mentioned at the start of the chapter, that Origen's name was a later interpolation. Despite the granted irregularities associated with it, I argue it makes sense that a condemnation of Origen *in name* was originally included in Canon 11 and was *not* an interpolation. While satisfying from a secular historical perspective, from a theological perspective, that is, a spiritual one, this should not deter us in the *slightest* from celebrating and even venerating Origen. As St Paul says, the letter of the law kills, but the spirit gives life (2 Cor 3:6). The spirit or purpose or intention of Canon 11 was to condemn certain teachings associated with the Isochrists. It is those teachings and persons, not Origen, who, from a theological perspective,

---

59. Price and Gaddis, *Acts of the Council of Chalcedon*, 94.

were condemned on that fateful day when Canon 11 was read aloud in 553. It is those teachings and persons who, in the definition of "anathema" from St Theopan the Recluse, were excluded and separated from the midst of the Church because they did not "fulfill the conditions of unity and thought of what was established in the Church."[60] As Fr John McGuckin writes, regardless of whether Origen's name is included in Canon 11, because the positions condemned were not his, the posthumous condemnation issued to Origen "fails in force" regarding its implications for Orthodox and Catholics today.[61] Just like the Scriptures, we cannot stop at the word itself on the page, the *skandala*; rather, we must dig deeper, and only then do we find the truth.

Returning to the point at hand, in the years following the Synod of Alexandria, Theophilus continued his anti-Origenist screed with several *Festal Letters*. These repeated many charges against Origen from the *Synodal Letter* but added some new ones to the mix. Sometimes he argued against Origen's theology, and sometimes he argued against Origen's stance on social issues. Perhaps the most interesting theological argument is found in the *Festal Letter* of 401, where Theophilus critiques Origen's *apokatastasis* based on orthodox sacramentology. He argued that demons cannot share in the blood and body of Christ and are thus impervious to salvation.[62] Few commentators who mention this critique note that Origen probably didn't believe in the reconciliation of demons. Few commentators also note that Theophilus never once in this letter nor any other criticizes Origen's belief in the salvation of all humans; hence, I am led to think Theophilus was *likely* a universalist, as the Introduction states. In another letter a few years later, he argued against Origen's doctrine of the Fall, which, to his credit, responsibly engaged with what Origen said in *First Principles*. It even has some genuinely well-written arguments, probably due to the training that Theophilus received in Aristotelian philosophy in his youth.[63] When it came to Origen's views on social issues, his denounced status as an alleged eunuch (although this was very likely false propaganda)[64] was often caught in the crossfire, and

60. Theopan, "What is an Anathema?"
61. McGuckin, *Origen of Alexandria*, 88–89.
62. Baghos, "Conflicting Portrayals," 81.
63. Banev, *Theophilus of* Alexandria, 136–37.
64. The fourth-century historian Eusebius of Caesarea is one of the first to comment on this. As a universalist disciple of Origen himself, it is unlikely he made this up out of the blue to discredit Origen; the same goes for Pamphilus who wryly said the

so marriage was a hot-button issue. But although his arguments in the years after the Synod of Alexandria were very critical of Origen, Theophilus sought to fairly engage with him and only rarely, that is, at least in comparison to other anti-Origenists, do we see him severely misunderstand a doctrine that Origen taught or identify later Origenist doctrines with Origen himself. It happens several times over, yet when compared to his contemporaries and, most notoriously, Justinian I a hundred or so years later, Theophilus is much better off.[65] Elizabeth Clark is right to conclude that Theophilus's engagement with Origen's writings often involved substantial theological critique instead of the more polemical statements you see in St Jerome the Great's engagement with Origen.[66]

The dutiful engagement that Theophilus had with Origen's writings made him one of the most charitable anti-Origenist interlocutors in the first five hundred years of the Church.[67] However, it's worth noting that once Jerome claimed to have abandoned Origen and then began to write long polemical treatises against his once-beloved spiritual teacher, his charitability towards Origen did increasingly grow in later years. It never reached the level of Theophilus, but it substantially improved. This was likely because Jerome's anti-Origenism was less dogmatic than other "heresiologists" of his time, like Epiphanius of Salamis. It was rather grounded in his admiration for Epiphanius as an ecclesial leader and because of his personal quarrels with other admirers of Origen like St John of Jerusalem and Rufinus of Aquilea.[68]

In 409, Jerome began a deep study of *First Principles*, which probably lasted a year or two. Lo and behold, Jerome realized that much of what he had attributed to Origen before this time was false and it solely applied to Origen's later followers. In the famous *Letter to Avitus*, he apologized for

---

same. It is much more likely, I concur with several, that Eusebius accepted this as gospel since it was a common hagiographic rumor spun up by pagans (and perhaps other Christians) about Origen after his death to discredit him. For a long while, scholars accepted this tale of voluntary self-castration, if only to explain how it would be possible for a man to write thousands of books as we know Origen to have done.

65. Several contemporary Orthodox theologians, while not definitionally anti-Origen, accept too much of Theophilius's gloss on Origen's doctrine of the Fall. For instance, Alfeyev, *History and Canonical Structure*, 37–40; Baghos, "Conflicting Portrayals," 95–96.

66. Clark, *Origenist Controversy*, 121.

67. Despite the disagreements that both Theophilus and Jerome had with Origen, they continued to use his theories and writings "extensively." McGuckin, *Eastern Orthodox Church*, 55–56.

68. Rubenson, "Origenist Controversy," 324.

certain misunderstandings, and with his newfound knowledge of Origen, he summarized the false teachings of Origen as he saw them. Many but not all of these accurately corresponded to what Origen taught. While some claim he denounced *apokatastasis* in this document, I strongly disagree. He does denounce the belief that the devil will be saved but nowhere in this letter nor in any letter before or after does Jerome denounce the belief that all humans will be saved. There is not even a hint that this is alluded to, which leads me to think that Jerome may have remained a universalist until the day he died, as I state in the Introduction. Overall, this letter is probably the most comprehensive summary of Origen's teachings written by an anti-Origenist in the first millennium. If only contemporary opponents to Origen, especially his Orthodox opponents, would undertake a two-year study of his work, think about how much more insight could be drawn from responsibly engaging with him rather than rampaging about doctrines he most certainly did not hold.

At this point, we can answer the question posed at the end of the last section: Earlier local synods did not influence the alleged condemnation of universalism at Constantinople II because universalism was never *explicitly* nor *implicitly* condemned at any local synods. Since this is true, universalism was not condemned at Constantinople II.

The Reception of Origen and *Apokatastasis* at Constantinople III and Nicaea II

Like all ecumenical councils, the Sixth Ecumenical Council (Constantinople III) held in 680–681 announced the decrees of prior ecumenical councils. Concerning Constantinople II, they said, "In addition to these, with the fifth holy synod, the latest of them, which was gathered here against Theodore of Mopuestia, Origen, Didymus and Evagrius, and the writings of Theodoret against the twelve chapters of the renowned Cyril, and the letter said to have been written by Ibas to Mari the Persian."[69] The councilmen are already off to a poor start. We know that Constantinople II was not called for the purpose of condemning Origen or Origenism. We also know it was not called to condemn Didymus or Evagrius, who did not even make an appearance in the council proceedings. The prior council was called to condemn the Three Chapters, which included Theodore of Mopuestia, certain writings of Theodoret, and the letter by

---

69. Quoted in Kimel, *Destined for Joy*, 250.

Ibas. This shows us that Origen's denunciation had already risen to a sort of legendary status even by the next ecumenical council. Constantinople III did not promulgate any new canons, but we do have records of its eighteen sessions.[70] Many of these sessions were spent condemning and addressing the heresies of Nestorianism, Monothelitism (the belief that Jesus had one will in the Incarnation), and others. There is no mention of Origen in the eighteen sessions of the council, nor is there any historical evidence that leads us to conclude the bishops were at all focused on discussing Origen or Origenism. Most importantly, there is no mention that *apokatastasis* was condemned.

When it comes to the Seventh Ecumenical Council (Nicaea II) in 787, the story becomes a bit more complicated. Nicaea II was primarily called to address the issue of iconoclasm and ensure the dogmatic status of icon veneration. Origen's name was brought up more than six times throughout the eight sessions. I shall examine a few mentions since many of them just repeat that he is condemned. Session One reviewed what took place at Constantinople II. "Origen and Theodore Mopuestia, together with the speculations of Evagrius and Didymus, concerning the pre-existence and restitution of all things, were subject to one common and Catholic anathema."[71] Once again, the good councilmen are not off to the best start. Evagrius and Didymus were not anathematized at Constantinople II. Also, the Three Chapters Controversy is not mentioned here. Only Theodore is mentioned, but not the writings of Theodoret or Ibas's alleged letter to Mari the Persian. As we know from Justinian's letter and other attestations, the council was explicitly called to condemn the Three Chapters. For there to not even be a mention of Theodoret's writings nor Ibas's letter and instead for this to be substituted with two names—Evagrius and Didymus—who were neither condemned nor mentioned in the council is odd and ahistorical, to say the least. Oxenham offers a fascinating hypothesis that may explain this.

> "Is it not much more reasonable to suppose that Tarasius had in mind the act of that Synod [of 543] which was exclusively with Origen and his followers, and that—having no special reason to inquire what was or was not done by the Fifth Council—he took these acts to belong to the Fifth Council, as others had done

---

70. Price and Whitby, *Chalcedon in Context*, 158.
71. Medham, *Seventh General Council*, 36.

before, though in reality they were not the acts of that Council, but of another held a few years previously?"[72]

However, we should be wary about accepting this hypothesis too early. Let's see how the evidence stacks up before making any declarations.

Origen's name is mentioned twice in Session Three. "With the fifth, I also agree, which, as a sword of the Spirit, cut off the lawless heresies which prevailed from ancient times, and openly exposed those who originated them, as Origen, Didymus, and Evagrius—which heresies I also reject as strange and deceitful babblings."[73] This may lend more credence to Oxenham's hypothesis since, as we know by now, Evagrius and Didymus were neither mentioned nor condemned at Constantinople II. The second mention of Origen here reads as follows.

> "[Constantinople II] anathematised Nestorius, Eutyches and Theodore of Mopuestia with his blasphemies; and moreover, it anathematized Origen, Evagrius, and Didymus, and their fabulous and heathen mystifications, together with the epistle said to be sent from Ibas to Mari the Persian, and the writings of Theodoret against the twelve orthodox chapters of St Cyril."[74]

In this review of Constantinople II, we have all the common suspects of heresy, but once again, Evagrius and Didymus are included. This is strikingly similar to the cases above, and it may lend even more credence to the position that Tarasius had unfortunately grouped Constantinople II with the synod in 543. The "fabulous and heathen mystifications" are not indirectly referring to universal restoration but referring to the belief in pre-existing souls, circular bodies after the resurrection, conscious stars, and so on. Whatever the case, *apokatastasis* is not condemned in either of these two mentions.

In Session Six, several names are read off a list as anathematized prior. "We have declared our consent to the recorded decisions of the sixth councils [. . .] We anathematize the madness of Arius, the frenzy of Macedonius [. . .] the trifling confabulations of Origen, Didymus, and Evagrius. . ."[75] Origen is grouped together with Didymus and Evagrius, two Origenists. However, earlier, we have seen that the beliefs of Origen are very distinct from those of Didymus and Evagrius. Evagrius and

72. Oxenham, *Catholic Eschatology and Universalism*, 68.
73. Medham, *Seventh General Council*, 95.
74. Medham, *Seventh General Council*, 112.
75. Medham, *Seventh General Council*, 445.

PART 2: UNIVERSALISM IN HOLY TRADITION

Didymus were the darling figures that the councilmen at Constantinople II believed the Isochrists were very influenced by. The cosmology attributed to them was bizarre, and they held heretical positions on the nature of Christ, eschatology, etc. Yet Didymus and Evagrius were never even condemned at a prior ecumenical council. As in the case of Constantinople III, a historical mistake was committed by the good councilmen here. This gives even more credence to Oxenham's hypothesis that Tarsaius threw together decrees of the 543 synod with Canon 11 of Constantinople II.

Having examined the mentions of Origen and his compatriot Origenists in Nicaea II, I shall leave the credence of Oxenham's hypothesis to the reader's discretion. It is certainly plausible that Tarasius was misinformed about what happened at Constantinople II and equated synodal declarations made ten years prior with it. Is there enough evidence to be certain of this, or even relatively in favor of it? I tentatively lean towards this conclusion but hope to see further evidence come to light that supports it.

Now that the cakewalk is over, there is one difficult position for an Orthodox universalist to square away in relation to Nicaea II: Definition 18 in Session Six. Gregory says, "If any one confess not the resurrection of the dead, the judgment to come, the retribution of each one according to his merits in the righteous balance of the Lord, *that neither will there be any end of punishment,* nor indeed of the kingdom of heaven—that is, the full enjoyment of God [. . .] let him be anathema."[76] Epiphanius then concurs, "This is the confession of the patrons of our true faith the holy Apostles, the divinely inspired Fathers—this is the confession of the Catholic Church and not of heretics."[77] Here, there seems to be a focus on those who deny that there will be an end to punishment. There is no mention of Origen or Origenism in this context. By the lights of some, this is a blanket statement anathema to all species of universal salvation. Is universalism condemned? Is the Greater Hope absolved, and we must capitulate to the belief that some humans will be tortured for eternity? There are a few problems with this statement that deserve to be fleshed out.

First, it is not issued in any canon or even decrees, which means it does not represent the dogmatic univocal voice of the council. This is a conversation between councilmen. The language "this is the confession. . ." has led many to presume this constitutes univocal dogma, but we

---

76. Medham, *Seventh General Council,* 423.
77. Medham, *Seventh General Council,* 423.

must remember the context of this statement. It is given in the Sixth Session during the minute-by-minute discussion. This allows it to represent what was believed, but it does not come to a dogmatic status with simply this language alone. Second, St Gregory of Nyssa was heralded as the "Father of Fathers" in the same session as this statement. Fr Richard Price notes this was an unexpected title because Gregory's status was often less than that of the other Cappadocian Fathers.[78] Nonetheless, it was indeed the title given to him, and he is still the *only* Father ever to have been given this title by a council. It is also worth noting that the Council of Ephesus in 431 referred to Gregory as the "bulwark" against heresy.

Let's briefly recall Gregroy's avowed universalism with just one example I gave in Chapter 5. Psalm 150 in the NKJV reads, "All will become one body, and one spirit, through one hope to which they were called." For Gregory, the psalms form a coherent whole, and this final psalm serves as the perfect recapitulation of the universalist promise. There is one hope for salvation that all are called to receive and all shall indeed receive it at some point; as we know from his commentary in other places, this is received freely. It would be very contradictory for Gregory to be referred to as the Father of Fathers in the same exact session where an alleged blanket condemnation of universalism was given.

Is the Father of Fathers a universalist, yet universalism is condemned forever and ever? Is the Father of Fathers a bulwark against heresy and yet follows the heretical doctrine of universalism? I think few would make this argument, and in that case, they would have to adopt the alternative position: The minute-by-minute acts cannot be taken as dogmatic because there are contradictions at times. Instead, we must turn to the decrees and, to a lesser extent, the canons. But this is *exactly* the same position that infernalists criticize universalists for taking. So, which is it? Is every minute-by-minute statement as authoritative and dogmatically binding as the decrees and canons, or can we make a rational distinction between the two's respective dogmatic statuses? The latter being given dogmatic authority and the former being useful for establishing the context of the relevant debate. You cannot hold both of these positions.

There is a third issue with the argument that universalism as a whole is condemned in Definition 18. The language used is "retribution of each one. . ." This is not language employed by even Orthodox infernalists to describe eternal punishment. Eternal punishment, according to the

78. Price, *Acts of the Second Council of Nicaea*, 498.

LM, is not constituted by punishment from God but punishment from the person on themselves. The person rejected God in this life, so their hatred and wrath towards God becomes reflected back onto them in the Age to come. The person is "burning" in their own wrath and hatred of God. This is the common Orthodox way to think about eternal damnation. What is not a common way for Orthodox Christians to think about eternal damnation is the language of "retribution." This matters when determining the dogmatic status of a statement like this. If universalism is condemned in this statement, then so is any model of eternal hell that rejects the retributive aspect of punishment. If universalism is condemned because of this statement, this entails that most Orthodox infernalists today, be they saints, clergymen, or laypeople, are also heretics. Nobody wants to accept this extreme conclusion.

In a 2020 article, Fr Aidan Kimel cites a passage from St Sophronius of Jerusalem's *Synodal Letter* written in 680 that confirms this reading. "From thence he will come again to make judgment of the living and the dead, and to repay each one according to the actions which each has performed, whether someone has performed good and beautiful deeds, or foul and blameworthy."[79] It is not taught in the Orthodox Church that punishment will be retributive and determined by what each has performed. This is not even taught in Catholicism. Since I can only assume that the Orthodox members of my audience do not think that the majority of Orthodox infernalists, including saints, are heretics, then they cannot accept that Definition 18 is a condemnation of universalism. It's all or nothing.

These three issues cause a lot of problems for the argument that universalism was condemned as a blanket statement in Definition 18. The first issue attacks the dogmatic status of the minute-by-minute proceedings. The second issue shows how even if we accept these proceedings as dogmatic, then the infernalist must admit there is a contradiction not only in a single council but in a single session. The third issue illustrates that the exact language used in Definition 18 would entail that the majority of Orthodox saints and laypeople are heretics if universalism is believed to be dogmatically outlawed by this statement. Thus, while addressing these concerns was not as simple as putting to rest the Origen-related condemnations, I close this section with the conclusion that universalism was neither *explicitly* nor *implicitly* dogmatically condemned at the

---

79. Kimel, "Divine Retribution, Hell, and the Development of Dogma."

Sixth or Seventh Ecumenical Council. There is not a single ecumenical council where universalism was blanketly condemned.

The 1672 Synod of Jerusalem and Universalism

The Orthodox Church accepts seven Church councils as ecumenical. Some prominent voices have argued for one or two other councils to be accepted, but as of writing this book, there are only seven ecumenical councils.[80] Some argue this is because a council can only be deemed ecumenical if and when it was called by the emperor. Since we do not have an emperor anymore, a council that is held can no longer be deemed an ecumenical council. Whatever the case, the Orthodox Church does not consider any other council to have the same dogmatic status as the ecumenical councils. Most of the time, this even includes the Pan-Orthodox Synods. Knowing this, however, has not stopped some from claiming that since later councils have taught the doctrine of eternal damnation, this means universalism has received blanket dogmatic condemnation. The council often mentioned in this argument is the 1672 Pan-Orthodox Synod of Jerusalem.

The 1672 Pan-Orthodox Synod of Jerusalem was held during a very contentious period in the East. It had been almost two hundred years since Martin Luther decided on that fateful day to post his ninety-five theses to the door of a Catholic church. Since then, Protestantism had spread like wildfire in the West, and the Latin Church was frantically trying to contain the flames. The 1672 synod was held for the primary purpose of addressing the rise of Protestantism, specifically Calvinism. Hence, this synod for Orthodoxy is somewhat akin to the Council of Trent for Catholicism. Like Trent, but across a larger time frame (as all decisions go in Orthodoxy), the council was accepted by the consensus of the Orthodox hierarchs of the time. In 1723, at the Council of Constantinople, the Orthodox Churches of Constantinople, Alexandria, Antioch, Bulgaria, and Romania officially signed off the decisions before sending

---

80. The Pan-Orthodox Council of Crete in 2016 numbered the "Palamite Councils" of the fourteenth century as ecumenical councils, but Crete itself was not an ecumenical council, at least, if we go by the requirement laid out at Nicaea II which states that all Patriarchs must be in attendance. Since several did not show (including Russia) this council cannot be deemed an ecumenical council on the basis of Nicaea II and thus cannot declare other councils as "ecumenical." The standards given at Nicaea II are debatable of course, but it would be odd for the Palamite Councils to be given the same status as ecumenical after all this time.

PART 2: UNIVERSALISM IN HOLY TRADITION

it to the Russians, who then began to republish versions of it throughout the eighteenth and nineteenth centuries. From this wide acceptance, one can see how dire of a fear Protestant teachings were to the holy hierarchs of Orthodoxy. Our focus here is on the conciliar statements related to eternal punishment.

One statement stands out from the rest. "They convey the pious and worthy remission of sins and life eternal; but to the impious and unworthy involve condemnation and *eternal punishment*."[81] This has all the tell-tale signs of an infernalist statement. A duality is set up between those who inherit eternal life and those who inherit a condemnation that never ends. It seems like the infernalists were right. The statement clearly affirms the existence of eternal punishment, which means that universalism is wrong and thus indirectly condemned for false teachings. Not so fast. The statement *does* teach eternal punishment, I freely admit this, but we must put it in context with other statements in the acts before we declare anything as dogmatically decided.

The debate immediately becomes more complex than what first meets the eye. Take the sentence, "[Baptism] delivers him from the *eternal punishment*, to which he was liable, as well as for original sin, as for mortal sins he may have individually committed."[82] This is a very odd statement to be found in an Orthodox synod. Orthodox infernalists do not usually believe that unbaptized infants will undergo eternal punishment. The Antiochian Archdiocese puts this in no uncertain terms:

> "The Orthodox Church does not believe that children are born guilty of Adam's sin and that unless freed of that guilt through baptism and communion they will die without God's mercy. Such a notion is pernicious both for its barbarism and for its distortion of God."[83]

Indeed, there are some naysayers in Orthodoxy, those who in the online Orthodox world are known disparagingly by its more respectable figures as "Orthobros," who quote mine from several notable Fathers to paint the picture that non-baptized infants will suffer the same fate as all the unrighteous (or at the very least, not experience salvation at some point in the future). Nonetheless, I agree with the Antiochian estimation on this point, even if only because I recognize how morally abhorrent

---

81. Overbeck, *Acts and Decrees of the Synod of Jerusalem*, 146. My emphasis.
82. Overbeck, *Acts and Decrees of the Synod of Jerusalem*, 141. My emphasis.
83. Hainsworth, "Infant Baptism."

and demonic the other belief is. There is also an issue with the language of "mortal sins" which is entirely foreign to Orthodox theology. Further, there seems to be the acceptance of the Augustinian theological point that "original sin entails original guilt which every human being inherits," which, as discussed in Chapter 5, and which will be discussed in Chapter 14 in the context of Fr Pavel Florensky, is not something Orthodoxy holds to be true. Hence, this statement was indeed uttered in the council but cannot have *any* dogmatic bearing on Orthodox theology because we know that unbaptized infants are not condemned to hell, that "mortal sin" does not exist as an ontological categorization of certain sins as it does (or at least, historically did) in Catholicism, and that original sin does not equal original guilt.

This poses problems for those who argue that the earlier statement, which teaches ECT, is binding for the faithful. Claiming that the former statement is binding yet the latter is not is simply cherry-picking to fit your preconceived ideology. A rational person cannot hold one as binding and the other as irrelevant. Once again, it's all or nothing. This issue alone has shown that not every single statement uttered in the acts of the 1672 synod is dogmatic, but let us humor the infernalist with another example, one that is far more destructive to the position than the above.

Recall the second issue I pointed out with the alleged condemnation of universalism in Definition 18 of Nicaea II. The statement there entails that punishment for the wicked is retributive and eternal. In the 1672 synod, however, there is a *clear* rejection of retributive punishment. "But of eternal punishment, of cruelty, of pitilessness, and of inhumanity, we never, never say God is the author, who tells us that there is joy in heaven over one sinner who repents."[84] Once again, this poses an issue for Orthodox infernalists. Definition 18 of Nicaea II is flatly in contradiction with this statement in the 1672 synod. You can try to squirm around this contradiction as much as you want, as fundamentalists of all stripes try to do when it comes to other mediums of the Holy Spirit, like the Scriptures, but more than anything, your avoidance just illustrates your deep cognitive dissonance.

By my lights, the Orthodox infernalist has to pick from two options to avoid accepting a contradiction. (a) They can appeal to Definition 18 in Nicaea II since it is an ecumenical council and hence, they admit, it has more dogmatic relevance than a non-ecumenical council. (b) They

---

84. Overbeck, *Acts and Decrees of the Synod of Jerusalem*, 116.

can argue that since Definition 18's acceptance of retributive punishment flatly contradicts Orthodox tradition, then the 1672 synod issued a corrective action to this by clearing up theological confusion. If the infernalist accepts (a), they have to say that all those who believe punishment is not retributive are heretics. Earlier, I explained why this is a poor response. If the infernalist accepts (b), they have to say that a specific statement in a synod should be valued more than a specific statement in an ecumenical council. As such, the acceptance of (a) is patently absurd while the acceptance of (b) leads to a very unpopular argumentative grant where the infernalist must admit that an ecumenical council was completely wrong about a statement they made and it took Holy Tradition almost a thousand years to correct such a statement. Everyone agrees that later councils correct earlier councils on theological matters and enshrine what they missed, but it would certainly set a precedent—one that few are willing to accept—if one of the seven ecumenical councils was corrected by a Pan-Orthodox synod and it took almost a thousand years for this to occur. Seemingly, both of these options are untenable. Therefore, the infernalist should abandon their position that the minute-by-minute acts of the 1672 Jerusalem Synod, which profess eternal punishment, indirectly dogmatically condemn all forms of universalism.

Before I close this section, I have to criticize some of my fellow universalists. Some take the dogmatic issues with this synod too far. In English translations of the acts, there is a misleading way that a certain word has been translated. It is mentioned five times as "transubstantiation," the Catholic doctrine about the Eucharist. For example, in the passive verb form, "And the wine is converted and transubstantiated into the true Blood Itself of the Lord."[85] Some have argued that the acts of this synod cannot be dogmatic because they use the word "transubstantiation," but this argument fails because the council itself does not use these words. The English translations often render it this way because, if taken literally, the Greek does translate to Latin as *transubstantiatio*. However, this is a fallacy that arises when we believe that the meaning of one language can perfectly correspond to the meaning of another language. Transubstantiation, at least historically, involved the presupposition of Scholastic metaphysics, which was never something the East wholly bought into.

When the acts use "transubstantiation," they do not mean to presume Scholastic categories of being but rather simply express that the

---

85. Overbeck, *Acts and Decrees of the Synod of Jerusalem*, 145.

Eucharist is the "truly truly" "real presence" of Jesus. *The Catechism of St Philaret of Moscow*, written soon after the 1672 synod, expresses this in no uncertain terms.

> "In the exposition of the faith by the Eastern Patriarchs [at the 1672 synod], it is said that the word transubstantiation is not to be taken to define the manner in which the bread and wine are changed into the Body and Blood of the Lord; for this none can understand but God; but only thus much is signified, that the bread truly, really, and substantially becomes the very true Body of the Lord, and the wine the very Blood of the Lord."[86]

While this is *a* catechism and not *the* official binding catechism for every single Orthodox Christian, this is a resource that points us to the fact that the Eastern Patriarchs at the synod did not buy into the Scholastic ontological presumptions associated with transubstantiation. So, there are dogmatic issues with this synod, and every single word uttered in the acts cannot be taken as binding, but we must not overstate the extent of the issues. This synod is very important to the Orthodox Church today, and if we neglect it, we neglect substantial portions of the faith.

On a brief and final note, I recognize my partial dismissal of Philaret's catechism may come off as irresponsible to some. If we really want to play the "cite your favorite catechism" game, I implore the reader to read the chapter on eschatology in the French catechism from 1979 *Dieu est Vivant: Catéchisme pour les familles*, also known in English as *God is Alive: Catechism for Families*.[87] This catechism was popular across Europe, was released as a second edition in 1987, and states that ECT is no longer an acceptable teaching for Orthodox Christians. "Let us state outright: the idea of eternal hades and eternal torment for some, and eternal blessedness, indifferent to suffering for others, can no longer remain in a living and renewed Christian consciousness the way it was once depicted in our catechisms." It goes on to say, "It is high time to put an end to all these monstrous assertions of the past centuries." The book with this statement received a blessing from Met Meleitos of Greece and Met Anthony of Surozh. Interestingly, the chapter on eschatology was edited out when the text was prepared for English readers. Although this text is rarely mentioned today, and few English speakers even know of its original universalist contents, I cannot in good conscience leave it

---

86. Philaret, "Catechism of St Philaret."
87. I thank Jesse Hake for informing me about the existence of this catechism.

unmentioned when claiming that St Philaret's catechism is only *a* catechism. Like Philaret's, this, too, is only *a* catechism. Neither should be seen as dogmatic. There is no single official binding catechism for the Orthodox Church; this is a totalitarian move that strikes against the conciliatory process of the Orthodox Church, which arises naturally through the work of the Holy Spirit. Hence, one should not be in any controversy with the Orthodox Church whether they affirm or deny ECT. While I can say this freely, the infernalist who cites other catechisms is less willing to grant this.

Conciliatory Fundamentalism and the Problem of Dogma

While well-intentioned Evangelical Christians struggle against biblical fundamentalists, Orthodox Christians are often in a struggle of their own against conciliatory fundamentalists. Historically, biblical fundamentalism was not so much of a worry in Orthodoxy, though this is starting to change due to the onramp of Evangelical Protestants who become Orthodox and bring with them all their ideological baggage. Often, when a convert brings with them a fundamentalist view of the Bible, they are poised to accept conciliatory fundamentalism as well. But even many Orthodox Christians who will criticize biblical fundamentalism in one breath are itching to preach conciliatory fundamentalism in the next. Fr Richard Price defines conciliatory fundamentalism as when "Acts and not just the decrees were treated with exaggerated respect."[88] He goes on to cite Ferrandus of Carthage's letter in defense of the Three Chapters as an example of this. Ferrandus argued that every single word uttered in the Council of Chalcedon is confirmed by the Holy Spirit and no part is open to criticism. By the sixth century, the councils came to be viewed by some as equal to the Scriptures and sometimes were treated even better than them.

There are many problems with this doctrine from a theological perspective, let alone a historical one. The decrees made by the councils were not decided by *deus ex machina* robots who mechanically function as the embodiment of the Holy Spirit, nor were the Scriptures written in this way, for that matter. The councilmen, just like the authors of the Scriptures, came to their respective mediums with personal biases and even ideological grudges against certain viewpoints. This is only to be

---

88. Price, *Acts of the Council of Constantinople of 553*, 98.

expected because even when we are dealing with saints, they are not perfect people, nor do they claim to be. Those who like to paint the saints as flawless would be ridiculed by that same saint who considers themselves unworthy to be brought into sainthood. Humility is a stringent condition that the saints embody each and every day, and such humility allows them to recognize the flaws that stain their souls and make them susceptible to worldly corruption. This is not to say that the Holy Spirit did not inspire the councils. It is a dogmatic statement of faith that the councils were divinely inspired, but it is to say that, like when it comes to the Scriptures, divine inspiration is a very ambiguous word and is often exaggerated by those who have certain heinous ideological proclivities.[89]

Justinian I, the emperor who called for Constantinople II, summarizes the historical problem with conciliatory fundamentalism in the following statement:

> "However, those in search of the truth ought also to attend to the fact that often at councils some things are said by some of those found at them out of partiality or disagreement or ignorance, but no one attends to what is said individually by a few, but only to what is decreed by all by common consent; for if one were to choose to attend to such a disagreement in the way they do, each council will be found refuting itself."[90]

As I have shown with several examples, if the infernalist framework is to be believed, the councils contradict themselves in the acts of the same council, sometimes even in the same session, and contradict each other at times too.[91] This is why when we are considering what is and is not dogma, we should not turn to the acts of any given council, but rather the decrees and, in some cases, the canons of the ecumenical councils which mark what has been decided by "common consent" (which, by

---

89. I highly recommend Met Hilarion Alfeyev's article on how the early Church interpreted ecumenical councils. The article rejects conciliar fundamentalism and explains why all Christians should reject it. See Alfeyev, "Reception," 413–30.

90. Price, *Acts of the Council of Constantinople of 553*, 150–51.

91. A famous contradiction between two ecumenical councils I didn't mention earlier is that the Letter of Ibas to Mari was accepted at the Council of Chalcedon (Third Ecumenical Council) yet condemned at Constantinople II (Fifth Ecumenical Council). One cannot believe that a document is both theologically condemned and accepted without granting a clear logical contradiction. See Price, *Acts of the Council of Chalcedon*, 270–73. To avoid this contradiction, some claim that the letter was not written by Ibas; yet this is not taken seriously by scholars because of the several witnesses at Ephesus II who testified that Ibas admitted authorship.

the way, *apokatastasis* has never been condemned in). This allows us to avoid viewing historical errors as binding for the faith. By doing this, the Orthodox Christian, be they infernalist or universalist, can safely uphold ecclesial infallibility on matters of faith as they so desire.

Let's now briefly turn to the problem of dogma. I do not seek to develop a complete heuristic for what constitutes a dogmatic statement and how to interpret dogmatic development in the Church, but I hope to have some fruitful thoughts on these issues.

Dogmas are truths of Christian teachings. They are what has been enshrined in Holy Tradition through the Scriptures and other mediums like the decrees of the ecumenical councils. Over the years of Christian history, many teachings have been thrown out, but others have been accepted. The ones that are accepted form what we call dogma, but the ones that are thrown out—heresies—still often play a fundamental role in forming such dogma, as F. W. J. Schelling was so keen to note (in a very dialectical fashion).[92] As St Dumitru Stăniloae says, the purpose of dogma is to preserve the development of a human's spiritual capacity for union with God.[93] The purpose of dogma is not to restrict freedom for the sake of limiting freedom but rather to edify the believer. All dogmas are based on the hope for the believer to commune with God. Communion with God takes many different shapes, sizes, and forms. Orthodoxy does not have many dogmas for this reason. To bolster a stringent and mechanistic framework for communion with God is anachronistic and Pharisaical. Dogmas are meant to form a system of unity where each dogma supports the other one through mutual communion, just as we are supported by each other when we engage in communion through the Eucharist. The Eucharist is never received by an individual alone for this reason. Like the Persons in the Trinity, to understand a single dogma in abstraction is incoherent. The dogmas are always-already with one another, even when one was historically not revealed by the time that another had been accepted. The dogmas were, in a sense, pre-ordained to be developed because they are moments on the timeline of God's self-revelation to creation. A self-revelation that never ends, and never has a limit, as we infinitely pass from "glory to glory" in becoming more like God.

Fr Sergius Bulgakov nicely sums up the dogmatic commitments in Orthodoxy. "The teaching on the Holy Trinity (as found in the

---

92. Schelling, *Philosophie der Offenbarung*, 201–2.
93. Stăniloae, *Experience of God*, 65.

CONSTANTINOPLE II AND ITS DISCONTENTS

Nicene-Constantinopolitan Creed), and mainly those about the God-man (as found in the definitions of the seven ecumenical councils)."[94] However, a list like this may make it seem like there are fewer commitments than there really are. There are a host of sub-commitments that follow from this list such as Mary's title of Theotokos. Yet even with these sub-commitments, in the grand scheme of things, there are not many dogmatic statements of faith. Again, this is because the idea of dogma and why we have the dogma we have, all relate back to the Trinity, the Person of Jesus, and communion with God or *theosis*. As expected, DBH puts the issue even more bluntly. "There are essential doctrines in every creed, which are few in number and obvious, and then there are accidental excrescences on those doctrines, which are legion and ponderous, stifling and stupefying."[95] While I have to disagree some with where DBH takes this assertion, namely into his hardened syncretic approach that openly draws from Vedantic and Indigenous spirituality (which, granted, I am not wholly opposed to), the core of what he says here is true.

All the dogmas we have are essential to the faith. This has been proven time and time again. And then, as much as we hate to admit it, there are many accretions; perhaps one may go so far as to say, lies from the evil one, that trick us into dividing ourselves as Christians and produce, to use DBH's words, "stupefying results." The idea of eternal hell, limited atonement, forensic imputation, and predestination all fit under this category. Not to rely on the rhetoric of Counter-Reformation propaganda or anything, but really, these lies of the evil one do seem to manifest most abrasively in Protestantism. Make of that what you will.

Do we know how many dogmatic statements there are in Orthodoxy? No, because that isn't the point. Any Catholic or otherwise who asks this question seriously needs to take a look in the mirror because there is not a numerical list of dogmas in their tradition (however much some like to pretend there is) nor in any other tradition. The purpose of dogma is to be brought closer to God. For this reason, Orthodox dogma cannot be simplified or properly quantified. The lack of simplification in dogma is a fear of some. A specific piece of dogma can become privy to a cookie-cutter set of conditions and be defined so stringently that it loses the mystery that is supposed to be heeded towards dogmatic expressions of faith. Orthodoxy has been better about not falling prey to these types

---

94. Bulgakov, "Dogma and Dogmatic Theology."
95. DBH, *Roland in Moonlight*.

of rationalist mechanizations. Yet, in the case of eschatology, our focus here, some still try to draw out dogmatic commitments in relation to this. Those who do this are aware that certain catechisms say this while others say that, certain councils say this while others say that, and certain Fathers say this while others say that. Nevertheless, they seek to draw out a "mind of the Fathers," or "mind of the councils," or "mind of the catechisms." This is a fruitless exercise, the last being the most ridiculous, and I find that it manifests especially in discussions over eschatology. What this causes, rather than any sort of clarity or simplification, is even more dysfunction and confusion in the Orthodox Church over the genuine dogmatic definitions of the faith. Let us avoid simplifying dogma and understand it for what it is.

The Discontents

Since I have reached the close of my study, I should explain the title of this chapter: "Constantinople II and its Discontents." The way I view Constantinople II, or the Fifth Ecumenical Council, is similar to the way that Sigmund Freud views civilization in his 1929 text *Civilization and its Discontents*. For Freud, civilization began from a terrible crime, that is, a primordial patricide, and has never been able to rid itself of psychic guilt from that crime. Each successive generation inherits the discontents of this crime. This does not lead him to morally judge civilization but rather to inquire about the alleged beginnings of civilization and how this affects our daily lives. I view Constantinople II in a similar way. The historical mishaps that stem from this council, the pre-synodal meeting, and the anathemas of 543 have led to a tirade against universalism that continues to this day. Each successive generation of Orthodox Christians inherits these historical misunderstandings. This first manifested in later ecumenical councils ratifying mistaken judgments about what went down at Constantinople II. Then this manifested in such a simulacra—in the sense of a created representation that does not have an original reality it mimics—becoming manifest in the writings of later Fathers, catechisms, and most notoriously, the anathemas read out during the Sunday before Holy Week, known as Sunday of the Last Judgment. Thus, in the present, having inherited all these discontents, this manifests in the near-unanimous belief that universalism was condemned and any universalist is caught in deep if not damnable heresy.

With twilights in our eyes, let us sing together in a solemn tone and pray for the Truth to come to light and for the gods to hear our message of hope.

Part 3

A Philosophical Defense
of Universalism

11

Free Will and Universalism

Two Views of Free Will

FREE WILL IS A contentious issue in contemporary philosophy. According to the "2020 PhilPapers Survey," 60 percent of philosophers lean towards compatibilism, 18 percent towards libertarian free will, 13 percent reject free will altogether, and then there are others who hold to an array of alternative positions.[1] In the philosophy of religion, the percentages are quite inverted. Thirty percent of philosophers lean towards compatibilism, 54 percent of philosophers accept libertarian free will, and 6 percent reject free will altogether. For our purpose, I shall focus on two relevant free will camps in this debate. These include a wide swath of universalist and non-universalist positions. The first camp is libertarian free will (LFW). LFW is defined as the power of contrary choice. A person chooses freely in the libertarian sense if and only if the person is psychologically able to choose otherwise. The second camp will be called classical free will (CFW). DBH provides a rough definition of what I call CFW: Freedom is the power to choose the good that is in our nature to choose.[2] CFW entails a teleological basis for free will, but LFW does not necessarily have a teleological basis. When it comes to compatibilism or a denial of free will altogether, frankly, these positions are of little concern

1. Editors, "Survey Results."
2. DBH, *That All Shall Be Saved*, 172–73.

PART 3: A PHILOSOPHICAL DEFENSE OF UNIVERSALISM

to me. Compatibilism can roughly be defined as the stance that human free will and responsibility are compatible with determinism because the person feels free and acts as if they are free. Determinism is the denial of free will altogether and the attribution of the happening of every event to prior causes that necessitated the event's happening. CFW may be similar to compatibilism in the sense that it does not deny human freedom but, at the same time, tries to mingle with a deterministic view by recognizing that there is a *real* value to the basic human intuition that our actions are (largely) decided freely. On the other hand, CFW cannot be grouped into this camp and remains external to this classification. Determinism at the transcendental level is a necessary attribute of CFW but not a necessary attribute of any sort of basic compatibilism that a non-theist philosopher could hold to.[3]

The argument that our will is shaped by determinism on the transcendental level harkens back to Plato: Humans are oriented towards the Good. This stance was then developed in Eastern patristics over the centuries. My focus will be on the classification from St Maximus the Confessor.

The gnomic will is the choosy will or will of deliberation. It is the will that we have as a result of our fallen nature as humans. Since it is the will that we have due to our fallen nature, the gnomic will involves the pull towards evil that we can feel. Since the gnomic will involves the pull towards evil and evil does not exist as a self-subsistent essence, then the gnomic will likewise does not exist as a self-subsistent essence. Even if we perform an objectively evil action—say, murder an innocent person—at the transcendental level, our personhood is still directed at the Good. In a sense, an evil action requires us to pass through the Good, reject it, and then come out on the other side in an illusory attempt to separate ourselves from God. No matter what we do or do not do, we must pass through the Good in order to determine a proper mode of action. The gnomic will is in contrast to the natural will.

The natural will is the will that is always directed at the Good and retains that grace-filled nature that always undercuts, whether or not we realize it, our fallen nature. There is not a duality present: grace-filled nature vs. fallen nature. As said, the gnomic will is not self-subsistent since it only has bearing in virtue of the natural will. Since the natural

---

3. Theologians sometimes refer to what I have termed CFW as roughly "*source* incompatibilism" and juxtapose it to "*leeway* compatibilism." Another term theologians may use for CFW is "*transcendental* determinism" and juxtapose it to "*particular* indeterminism."

will is perfectly self-subsistent and the gnomic will is not, the natural will can exist and will exist without the gnomic will; it would be clearer to speak of fallen nature as a pseudo-nature. It is not the essence of humanity to be in this fallen nature, nor is it the *telos*/pre-determined end goal. Our fallen pseudo-nature, as the harbinger of gnomic will, will pass. Fallen nature is a blip in time compared to the eternal reality in which the ideal human hypostasis is forever present. Spiritual warfare shall cease as God's glory will permeate every inch of creation. For now, we persist in a mode of being that is caught up in spiritual warfare: How do we orient our person to be in this world but not of this world? This is where worldly freedom—the freedom that both LFW and CFW take a stance on—becomes relevant.

Action and Intentionality

Since antiquity, it has been understood that an action is freely chosen if and only if the action is done with intentionality. I take it that any cogent theory of free will must have it as a necessity that intentionality is involved in what constitutes a free action. If a contrary choice were the only condition that constitutes a free action, as LFW claims, then no distinction could be made between actions made by personal agency and actions made by pure impulse or even pure chance. If an act is free despite lacking motives and a rational disposition of will, I would not want to have this freedom. This freedom is not much better than slavery for all intents and purposes.

With this in mind, consider the following short schema that lays out a rough *telos* of action. When one freely acts, they see action (a) as achieving a purpose (p) that corresponds to a disposition (d); (a) is done for (p) because of (d). If one acts from a standpoint where they are not free, they do (a), but (a) does not correspond to (p) or (d) because of the lack of (p) or (d). If there is a lack of (p) or (d) in the process of (a), an action is not free. This schema, while lacking to account for certain situations, as we will see later, is based on the axiom of intentionality that I want to develop here briefly. In my view, intentionality is essential to what makes an action free and this is a systematic element that CFW necessarily provides, but LFW does not necessarily provide. Intentionality is not contradictory to what constitutes a free action under LFW, but it is not included as necessary in what constitutes a free action. I see this

PART 3: A PHILOSOPHICAL DEFENSE OF UNIVERSALISM

as one of the fatal flaws of LFW, and it is one of the reasons why I claim CFW should be adopted.

The twentieth-century economist Ludwig Von Mises took great delight in the fact that human action was teleological and intentional. He defined the study of "human action" as praxeology. In short, a person acts because they are dissatisfied with the state of affairs they are in and believe the action to be one that will take them to a more desired state of affairs. Mises considered the proposition above to be synthetic *a priori*, as it does not rely on empirical confirmation but is a truth that underlies all action as such. All human action is about one transitioning from a less desired state of affairs to a more desired state of affairs because of the fact that they themselves cannot bring about the more desired state of affairs without acting. Actions are done with an end in mind, and then means are taken to reach that end. While the libertarian economic conclusions that Mises drew from this were absurdly diabolical, and the neo-Kantian underpinning to much of his epistemology was surely anachronistic even for its time, the proposition itself has a lot going for it both philosophically and scientifically.[4]

The proposition centers on the role of intentionality in action and the importance of corresponding to the disposition of a person. For Mises, all action fell under this category (or at least the action he somewhat tautologically claimed to be "human action"), but for our purpose, I think this explains what a free action is. Because not all actions are free, as we know. An action is not free if it is not done for a purpose and/or does not correspond to my cognitive disposition. A contrary choice alone does not merely indicate that an action is free, there must be further conditions met. Moreover, a *truly* free action can itself never be accessed in this life since we maintain partial ignorance of God; this will be discussed later in the chapter. Since LFW does not necessitate an account of the relevance of intentionality and teleology in action, it is in a very dubious position.

Is Faith a Free Choice?

To have faith is not chosen in the same way as other contrary options. To take the first step towards faith, whatever that may look like, cannot be thought along the same lines as deciding to eat a cheeseburger over

   4. For an innovative scientific approach to this subject, see Ball, "Agency."

a hotdog. Song of Songs 1:4–5 in the NKJV reads, "Bring me into the house of wine, set love in order upon me, strengthen me with perfumes, encompass me with apples, for I have been lovesick."[5] Many English translations, including the NKJV, render the most proper translation of "wounded by love" into "lovesick" or another term along that order. We must not do this. The Hebrew poet is very clear that this is a wound caused by love itself. St Gregory of Nyssa provides commentary on this. "O sweet and happy wound, by which life slips through to the inward parts, opening the arrow's cut to make itself a door and an entrance! As soon as she has taken love's arrow, archery is straightway changed into the joy of marriage."[6] Since God is love, the archer who shoots the arrow is God. The arrow shot by God is none other than the Son who was made incarnate by the Holy Spirit. Who does the archer shoot the arrow at? Humankind. In Christ we are made objects of God's love.

The concept of falling in love can illustrate how we might approach the choice of faith in CFW. When we say that we "fall" in love, we mean it in a way where the apprehension of difficulties suddenly disappears as we are enthralled with our beloved, and they are (hopefully) enthralled with us. We cannot control or have any say in falling in love with our beloved, it just happens. In psychoanalytic terms, love is approached by both the lover and loved wielding unconscious knowledge. The lover believes the beloved loves them back, and the way the beloved receives the love of the lover is determined by their unconscious desire. Whether the beloved responds, "I love you too!" or if the beloved turns away from the pouring of love by the lover is determined by the unconscious of the beloved. The beloved becomes the sole focus of our world when we fall in love, and there is not much else we can do to rationalize this. Hence, love is like an infinite yearning that rejects every object in front of it because of the singular object it holds as the harbinger of its subjectivity. Since love necessitates partiality in the object of love, love must be distinguished from desire. As the character Diatima highlights in the *Symposium*, to love someone entails knowledge that you will possess them forever. Desire can be flipped on and off at a moment's notice, but love guarantees eternal possession of the loved object.

When we notice the arrow of Christ has pierced us with his eternal love, the veil on our hearts is lifted, and we can clearly see that the

---

5. My emphasis.
6. Gregory, *Homilies on the Song of Songs*, 141.

blood pouring from this wound is the Holy Spirit. The arrow has the same sharpness in all cases, but the wound that forms in us depends on our response to the piercing blow. Do we shout, "I love you too, Lord! Have mercy on me, a sinner!" Or do we try to heal this wound? Many try to heal this wound with worldly passions. The passions only put a band-aid over the wound, but the blood, that is, the Holy Spirit, continues to pour out without the person knowing. The person may believe that their descent into the world has healed the wound, but in the eyes of God, the wound never disappears. The wound persists because we are his image. The wound grows, and more blood pours out when we become like him through divinization. Hence, the entrance into faith is decisively not a free choice in the LFW sense. Freedom cannot be mechanized like proponents of LFW so often do.

The Dilemma of Faith and Ignorance

In the following statement, Thomas Talbott adequately expresses the dilemma of faith with a focus on the role that ignorance plays in whether or not we affirm Christ in this life:

> "Either I am fully informed concerning who God is and the consequences of rejecting him, or I am not. If I am not fully informed, then I am in no position to reject the true God, as we have just seen; and if I am fully informed, then (as Craig himself insists) I am incapable of rejecting the true God freely. So in neither case am I free to reject the true God."[7]

Talbott says this towards the end of his response to William Lane Craig's argument against universal salvation. I concur with Talbott here that Craig and many like him who posit this "freely choose Christ or burn" argument fall into a two-horned dilemma. If I am ignorant or deceived of (say, by a demon) the consequences of what would follow from my actions, then I am in no position to freely embrace the consequences that follow. I cannot reject God in any fundamental sense. Moreover, as Craig recognizes, suppose that God is the ultimate end of rationality; such that if a person were maximally rational, they would follow God. If I am not ignorant of the consequences of my actions, as in, I am fully informed, then I would be displaying irrationality to reject God. If I display irrationality, this is incompatible with any cogent idea of free choice.

7. Talbott, *Inescapable Love*, 175.

An example can serve to explicate this. If a person does an action that seems to lack a motive and in the presence of a very strong motive for not doing so, the person displays irrationality that is incompatible with free choice.[8] Suppose I light my hair on fire in a crowded mall. Suppose I have a fire extinguisher that is guaranteed to work next to me. Suppose my action isn't for a religious ritual, a protest, or any matters of that nature. All the people around me are yelling for me to use the fire extinguisher, but I simply plug my ears with my fingers and wait until I eventually burn to a crisp. All the while, I am obviously in a great amount of pain (and I don't have any medical condition that would prevent me from feeling such pain). Few would remark that I acted rationally in this situation. I seemingly acted without a motive and did so with a very strong motive for not doing so. While I burned to a crisp, I screamed in pain, and I even had an accessible tool to end the pain—the fire extinguisher—that I did not use. Since this was an irrational action, I did not act freely. Hence, irrationality is incompatible with free choice. LFW does not take this into consideration.

By any reasonable measure, if a person who is fully informed rejects God knowing that (1) God exists and (2) rejection of God will lead to eternal punishment, then a rejection of God would have to constitute an exemplary case of a choice made irrationally. Could I freely reject God from a position of being "fully informed" of what will occur? If we accept that irrationality is incompatible with free choice, then I cannot.

However, consider a counterargument from the annihilationist James Spiegel. Spiegel claims this argument contradicts the established fact of moral weakness. Moral weakness is the empirically proven and philosophically cogent stance that while a person knows x is the right option, a person does not always choose x; they very well may choose y.[9] Indeed, as anyone familiar with psychoanalysis knows, we do not always choose the right option, even when we know it is right, because we may have an unconscious desire to choose the other option for whatever reason. However, Spiegel seems to assume that "knowing the right option" is on the same level of knowledge as what would constitute being "fully informed" of God. Surely, a person who is fully informed of God has

---

8. From the perspective of CFW, this is granted. Here, I am performing an internal critique of the LFW position to show why there must be more stipulations to free will than just having a contrary choice available.

9. Spiegel, *Hell and Divine Goodness*, 93.

PART 3: A PHILOSOPHICAL DEFENSE OF UNIVERSALISM

some sort of information that is richer than "knowing the right option" to take in a finite situation.

Suppose I am standing in front of two buttons. If the left button is pressed, it will cause the random death of a person in my city. If the right button is pressed, nothing will happen. Assume I know what both buttons cause. In light of moral weakness, even though I know the morally good option is to press the right button for any number of reasons, I may still press the left button because I am angry, I am hoping for the button to cause the death of my enemy, and so on. Whatever the exact reason is, I may choose the left button, and there is no way to foretell with certainty that I will press the right button. This seems to constitute "knowing the right option" in a finite situation. Surely, whatever being "fully informed" of God means, involves far richer knowledge than what is present in this situation. Moreover, in all documented cases of moral weakness, be they philosophical or scientific, the person with moral weakness *never* knows the outcome of their action when they take the action. I suppose that if "full information" could be obtained in reference to epistemic access to God's existence, then that information would constitute a person knowing the consequences to be endured if they do not follow God. Since there is no documented case of moral weakness that deals with a person having foreknowledge of what could happen if they do not choose the right action that they know is right, this response fails to procure a justification for doubting (at least) part of Talbott's response to Craig. We have shown that one cannot ever truly reject God if they were able to act from a fully informed position. This would constitute irrationality, which, as shown, is incompatible with free choice.

Can a person reject God when acting from a position of partial ignorance? This is probably the more relevant question because we are all partially ignorant about God. None of us have the full picture because, in actuality, there is no full picture for us to have. St Paul says in 2 Corinthians 3:18 that we go from glory to glory, and he is keen to leave this as an open-ended process. The process of learning about God is not a philosophical exercise. Rather, it is a personal path marked by humility, long-suffering, and love towards others (1 Cor 13). All of us remain somewhere along this path, but our position is by no means static and constantly fluctuates depending on our observance to the likeness of him.

Suppose I hand a Bible to my good friend Jake, who has never read or heard the Scriptures and wants to learn what they are all about.

FREE WILL AND UNIVERSALISM

However, Jake does not realize that the Bible I handed him only contains the books of Joshua and Judges. As Jake is reading, he seems puzzled by the depictions of God. He turns to ask me why God sent Joshua and the Israelites to slaughter so many people, seemingly without much reason. Having read both books, Jake sets the Bible down in utter dismay. These depictions in Joshua and Judges have defined his information about God's actions in this world. Jake cannot understand why anyone would ever want to follow the God depicted in these texts. He then decides from that point onwards that the God depicted in Joshua and Judges is an entity that he completely rejects. He now looks down on those who accept the existence of and worship this God.

Do we seriously think that Jake's disavowal of God could plausibly constitute anything like "total" or "complete" rejection?

Suppose now that on the way home from my house, Jake veers off the road due to no fault of his own and, unfortunately, dies at the scene of the crash. Does it follow that Jake deserves ECT? Jake clearly reacted poorly due to his partial ignorance of God, but even he was better off than many others who never even got to read the Scriptures for whatever reason. Regardless, the depiction of God that Jake received from his brief reading of the Bible is a depiction that cannot be "true" in a vacuum. Consciously, he did not reject the God that is described as loving throughout the Bible and the God who brought Christ to earth with the gift of salvation. He rejected a certain caricature of God. To be clear, I am not claiming that, necessarily, the God depicted in these books is a different god or is not an accurate portrayal of the one true God (though it is obviously a less theologically developed concept of God). The point is that the depiction of God that Jake received is not the depiction of God that includes all the other things we are told about God through the Scriptures and other outpourings of Holy Tradition. So, we come back to the question: Did Jake truly and completely reject God even though he acted from a position of partial ignorance? As well, does Jake deserve ECT for his rejection? Frankly, I don't see how anyone could rationally agree to either of these. The only thing we should agree on is that I am a terrible friend for putting Jake in that situation!

I recognize this example is very specific, but I do this so readers who are not amenable to CFW can get acclimated first by noticing how the role that ignorance plays in our lives is fundamental and should be taken into account by any eschatology. A broader example can now follow.

PART 3: A PHILOSOPHICAL DEFENSE OF UNIVERSALISM

In our everyday lives, we operate from a position of partial ignorance in relation to our knowledge of divine revelations received through the Scriptures and Holy Tradition. All people have the law written on their hearts (Rom 2:15), but not all people receive this law with the Holy Spirit (2 Cor 3:3). There is no clear distinction between grace and nature, as grace is inseparable from nature due to the unconditional promise of the resurrection. But while all people begin from the same starting point in a transcendental sense, the way this pragmatically unfolds is not so egalitarian. Where you were born impacts your access to the gospel, making a free choice in the LFW sense very complex. You have access, in the most fundamental sense, to the gospel because the law is written on your heart, but if you are unable to experience the full presence of the Holy Spirit through the Scriptures and the sacraments, then the ability for you to choose becomes severely distorted. This discrepancy makes it difficult (if not pragmatically impossible) for LFW proponents to argue that *all* people have the same level of free choice towards affirming faith and then following this with deeds that develop their likeness to Christ.

Atheists often employ the above as the argument from "divine hiddenness." While the conclusion of their argument—that since God doesn't reveal himself equally to everyone, he does not exist—is flawed, the foundation of their argument can certainly be utilized by universalists who are skeptical of LFW. Atheists often employ the argument as if it only applies to a certain group of humans; such as an uncontacted native tribe. In reality, divine hiddenness applies to all people. Even those who have gazed upon the uncreated light of God, like Moses, St James, St Peter, St John, and others, do not then receive perfect knowledge of God. Their experience is still tainted by partial ignorance because God's ineffable presence is forever outside the limits of human cognition. Divine hiddenness is not a problem to solve or an issue for Christianity. Rather, the argument is the perfect encapsulation of why those who do not "choose" to follow Christ, as if he is some sort of thing you can pick from a range of options, do not deserve to endure eternal punishment. Partial ignorance is necessitated by the essence/energy distinction, and even if you reject this as a "real" distinction in God (which is such a minutia debate that I find no desire to take part in), partial ignorance is still necessitated by the ever-increasing glory and knowledge of God that we pass into by deepening our relationship with him.

In summation, a person who rejects God could only do so because they persist in delusions and falsities in relation to how they approach

FREE WILL AND UNIVERSALISM

him. And if a person persists in delusions and falsities, it seems behooved of us to suppose they rejected God as he truly is. For Jake, his rejection was a rejection of God as depicted in Joshua and Judges; two books that are notoriously controversial for their violent imagery that displays God as a wrathful and genocidal maniac who destroys large-scale populations subjecting men, women, and children to the power of the sword. For anyone who has ever existed, if they reject God, their rejection still stems from falsities and delusions concerning their knowledge of God. As David Artman says, "Our wills only become truly free once they are finally liberated from all falsehood and evil and sin."[10] Nobody here deserves eternal punishment due to their "choice" not to affirm faith.

The framework of LFW has trouble accounting for the ever-present problem of partial ignorance. The framework of CFW has less of a problem accounting for this. In LFW, a choice is free if and only if contrary options are available to choose. In CFW, a choice is free when the choice made is intentional and in service of the Good that is in our nature to develop and grow in. LFW cannot rationally account for partial ignorance because choices can be made in partial ignorance, and the person who made those choices, since they were chosen from an array of contrary options, bears responsibility for all consequences that follow. CFW can account for partial ignorance because it is based on an epistemic foundation that prides itself on the fact that all people are partially ignorant. The fact that they do not choose what is the Good at all times, need not necessitate responsibility for all consequences that arise from this. LFW also cannot rationally account for a hypothetical in which an allegedly fully informed person rejects God. Under LFW, the fully informed person's choice may be irrational, but this does not mean it contradicts what constitutes a free choice. Under CFW, an irrational choice contradicts what constitutes a free choice. For these reasons, CFW is the more rational and proper way to view freedom than LFW.

On a brief and final note, I should, for the sake of goodwill to my opponents, make a case for the justification of eternal punishment on behalf of free will. If ECT could be justified, it would only be justified for an entity that meets two necessary and sufficient conditions: (1) The rational entity must have acted with foreknowledge of the consequences that would arise from their choices to not act in service of the Good; (2) The rational entity must have perfect knowledge of God. There may be

---

10. Artman, "Mystery and Free Will."

PART 3: A PHILOSOPHICAL DEFENSE OF UNIVERSALISM

some rational entities that fit the first condition, certainly not humans, but there are no rational entities who could ever fit the second condition. The second condition could only be met by an abolishment of the essence/energy distinction and/or an abolishment of the dynamic state of glory (and knowledge) that we experience by strengthening our relationship with God. Either way, the second condition cannot be met. For this reason, eternal punishment is never justified by allegedly free choice.

The Fundamental Error with LFW

The above errors with LFW are all sound but DBH really hits the nail on the head and strikes to the core of why LFW is incoherent. He writes:

> "If God really is 'God' in the classical acceptation of the word—the transcendent plenitude of all reality, as well as an infinite act of consciousness and love—then all these concerns about discrete personal agency and autonomy of the will must vanish as just so many category errors."[11]

Those who worry about free will in relation to universalism often just admit category errors when they assume God to be some sort of external agent who remains in distinction to the normal everyday cognition that humans experience. God is obviously not distinct from our everyday cognition, acting as some sort of third party. His omnipresence itself entails an ever-present action upon our minds so that we naturally will the Good. If we adopt LFW, this seems to entail that God is an agent of ultimate coercion who keeps us in perpetual bondage. Are humans merely slaves chained to the sovereignty of God? A Calvinist may nod their head, but most Christians certainly do not think of God in this frightful of a way. However, if LFW is true, it seems that any influence of God on our minds would have to be regarded as an infinitely detrimental act of coercion.

In response, the LFW proponent may argue that God's influence on our minds in the normal everyday sense is distinct from the influence he would play in a hypothetical coercion scenario. Maybe God's influence in the transcendental sense is an influence in an ontological way, i.e., his presence pervades all of creation, but his influence never leads us to deliberate thought. Such that if we were going to choose x option from the array of x, y, z options, God's presence would not in any way inform

11. DBH, *That All Shall Be Saved*, 182.

us of selecting a different option than the one that we freely deliberated upon and chose. Yet this does not solve the problem because the LFW proponent is once again presupposing God to be a discrete cause that acts on our free will. When really, God is the Plentitude of reality. Everything has its being in him and through him (Acts 17:28). He knows all the events in our lives, the events that could have happened in our lives, and all our desires, both conscious and unconscious. Reality is crafted by him in every way imaginable. There does not exist a single thing, person or otherwise, that does not interact with God *directly* at all times. (I emphasize *directly* because of that very pernicious tendency among certain Thomists to claim that God could "indirectly" influence creation. This is plainly incoherent from an Orthodox perspective, the patristic understanding of God, and frankly, common sense too.)

The proponent of LFW has an untenable bullet to bite at this point. If God's influence on free will is deemed coercive, then all of God's actions are coercive. If God's influence on free will is not deemed coercive, then all of God's actions are not coercive. It's either all or nothing. If you accept the former, I question why you would worship a God who is always coercing you. If you accept that coercion is not an action a God who is the Good itself would take (and this is unquestionable), then by your own logic, you would be worshiping an evil entity (since a being that is coercing you at all times would be evil). Since it is obviously not morally good to worship an entity that you believe is evil and is evil, you are committing a morally bad action by doing this. The first position cannot be cogently held. The second position is the only cogent response to the controversy of divine coercion. God cannot coerce because the accusation itself arises from a category error.

Hence, God is both immanent and transcendent to creation. As the psalter says in 139:7, "Where can I go from your Spirit, where can I flee from your presence?" Since no created being can flee from God's presence, no created being should construct a heuristic that somehow legislates and relegates God's presence and action. This is the highest manifestation of the Babelian tendency in cataphatic theology. Go build your tower to the heavens but leave us be. Those who attempt to apply a heuristic to qualify what exactly "God's presence" constitutes and when this does or does not have a coercive nature are chasing their own tail. It is a fruitless exercise excluded from the life-giving spirit of Holy Tradition. This does nothing to build a house for faith and only serves to

PART 3: A PHILOSOPHICAL DEFENSE OF UNIVERSALISM

cause confusion and an atomized attitude among Christians in how they conceptualize their relationship to the Creator.

Hear the Angelic Hymn

The last section introduced us to the fundamental error that erodes away almost all arguments for LFW. There, we saw the claim that if God were to influence our free will, God would commit a coercive action. I argued this is incoherent and struggles from a cataphatic tendency to regulate and legislate God's presence. This short section puts the concept of divine coercion to the test in another way.

Suppose you are listening to your favorite song. Suddenly, you begin to tear up because the song is so beautiful and strikes you in such a way that cannot be put into words. I am sure many have experienced this at least once, if not a number of times. I know I have. The striking lyric or chord of a certain song, along with the environment you are listening to the song in, certainly can bring one to tears. But was I brought to tears in a way that stripped me of freedom? Was I brought to tears in a way that involved coercion? To answer this, briefly consider my schema of action from earlier but strip away the transcendental commitment to CFW that involves an orientation towards the Good: When a person freely acts, they see action (a) as achieving a purpose (p) that corresponds to a mental disposition (d) they have. I sought to listen to music by performing an action like turning on my phone and putting headphones on, but I did not act for the purpose of crying. Since crying eventually happened, but it was not for the purpose that corresponded to my disposition, it would seem that my crying was not a free action.

I hope the reader can tell that all this logical overhaul has clouded how we admonish our experience of the world. When someone is brought to tears due to the beauty of a song, they certainly do not feel like they have been violated in any way. The feeling is often one of bliss. A bliss that surprises the person because they did not intend for it, but this altogether makes the presence of bliss even stronger. Moreover, it is not only the feeling of bliss that accompanies this context of crying, but often a continuance to keep listening to the song that caused this. If this truly was an action that was not free and caused by a violation of my personal agency, why would I continue to listen to the song? That's exactly it. Assuming I was a rational being, I wouldn't keep listening to the song. The choice to keep listening tells us something.

If we adopt LFW, the beauty of the song has overrun my personal agency. I just wanted to listen to my favorite song and had no intention of crying. However, I think it's clear the LFW framework does not correspond to my experience of the situation. I do not feel like my personal agency has been overrun in any way. In fact, I feel that my experience has increased in its level of preference because I am deriving such joy and bliss from the song! This everyday scenario can perhaps inform us of the general experience of God. God is like the beautiful song we hear and cannot help but cry. The psalter writes, "He put a new song in my mouth. Praise to our God" (Ps 40:3; NKJV). His love flows into us like the soundwaves from our headphones. Some of us will enter a state of being, say post-mortem purification, without any intention of responding to God. Yet, like in the case when that specific lyric or tune hits our ears, we cannot help but cry and beg for mercy and forgiveness.

The Anglo-Catholic theologian John Milbank writes, "If forgiveness is a reality, then it seems that it is somehow not subordinate to ontology, or rather that being is now shown in time as forgiveness and finality and as revisable via narrative. Here, therefore, finite ontology does not yield to, but nonetheless coincides with, eschatology."[12] Forgiveness exists, this is not questioned by any Christian. Still, the infernalist cannot help but view forgiveness in the context of finite ontology; forgiveness exists insofar as we exist in a finite mode of temporality, a fallen temporality, but once we exit this and enter into a redeemed temporality, forgiveness must fall by the wayside like so many other things—this is far from the truth. Forgiveness will be the final state of being for all things. God does not need to involve any sort of forced subjectification for this to occur. As we saw in Chapter 5, this subjectification involves an eventual joyful response (Phil 2:10–11). All people who were once forgotten in the realm of Gehenna will cry out and confess that "Jesus is Lord." The concept of coercion is utterly absent here. All shall hear and sing the angelic hymn.

The Divine Checkmate

The last section operated off a rough analogy between beautiful music and the beauty of God to illustrate why divine coercion is incoherent as a

12. Milbank, *Being Reconciled*, 71.

concept. This brief section will explicate a scenario related to God's presence and the issue of divine coercion. Thomas Talbott offers an analogy to illustrate how God's omnipresence and foreknowledge entail a consequence similar to one that occurs when a grandmaster faces a beginner in chess.[13] I expand his analogy with what I take to be crucial details.

When a grandmaster in chess plays a beginner in chess, the end is already known by everyone watching the game and the two players involved. The grandmaster will win not because he determines the beginner's move in a coercive manner, but because the grandmaster knows that no matter how many resourceful plays the beginner makes, he has the skill and experience to counter every move. A similar point can be made about God. He is the ultimate Grandmaster. Suppose, for the time being, that God can indeed coerce us in a way that is cogent with what LFW tries to argue. Even if we suppose this is possible, God would never do so, and yet, the same outcome would be obtained. The grandmaster knows he will win, his opponent knows he will win, and the crowd knows he will win.

Once the grandmaster declares "checkmate," nobody is surprised. Of course, the grandmaster won. He is the grandmaster. The beginner can make all the moves they want leading up to this point. They can castle their king and make a queen trade, but none of this will matter in the end. The grandmaster will win and declare victory. Like the grandmaster who doesn't need to coerce, God also doesn't need to coerce. The sinner will twist and turn, they may even repel themselves to the outer darkness of Matthew 22:13 to escape God, but they will never succeed in ridding themselves of God. After all, he is the Grandmaster of the world. He is the Grandmaster of everything that has ever existed and will ever exist. The damned who freely choose to cast themselves out of his grasp will see their resistance melt away like wax before a flame. The angelic hymn will sound, and all resistance will be proven futile.

LFW and Universalism: Mutual Exclusion or Synthesis?

I understand that some may still be unconvinced that CFW (or another alternative) is preferable to LFW. I recognize that the last two sections are pretty rudimentary and employ analogies that can be picked apart. God is obviously not a song, nor is he a chess grandmaster. The purpose

13. Talbott, *Inescapable Love*, 170.

of these sections was to provide a break for the audience that would separate the more "intense," shall we say, philosophy found in earlier sections and this one. The thesis here is as follows: LFW is not necessarily incompatible with universal salvation. In fact, Eric Reitan and John Kronen argue that universal salvation can be obtained under LFW.[14] By my lights, the key proposition of their syllogism, Proposition (3), will give us almost *mathematical certainty* of universal salvation in LFW and CFW. Reitan and Kronen argue that for the conditions of universal salvation to be obtained under their syllogism, there have to be a few things ensured for the person in hell. Before I explain these conditions, a precautionary warning must follow.

I recognize that for many, the following conditions that God must ensure seem beyond what God does ensure. But I must question why they assume this. There is not a single biblical text that says that worldly death is the point at which repentance is closed off. Hebrews 9:27, which is the closest to teaching this, only says that once we die in this world we will all face judgment.[15] All sides agree on this. At the same time, I can admit that for Orthodox Christians, there is a suitable reason ingrained in tradition (or so some think) to deny that repentance is wholesale available after death. Prayers for the dead may only do so much. Suppose that is true. Even if this argument only applies to Protestants and those with similar foundations, I still consider it worthwhile to mention since this text is meant to be relatively ecumenical. The conditions are as follows.

(a) Remove all inhibitors that exist to salvation before salvation; (b) Sustain all people in a temporal existence, at least until they choose communion with God; (c) Leave communion with God as an open choice whereby every person is free to choose communion with God at any given time. Condition (c) is particularly relevant to LFW. Supposing LFW, then, (c) is coterminous with the stance of LFW that communion with God *is* an option that can be chosen instead of a contrary option. The option seems to be: Remain in hell or accept communion with God. Again, this argument assumes LFW and does not in any way entail the transcendental orientation towards the Good like CFW does. This does not mean that a proponent of CFW should be opposed to this argument in favor of universalism, far from it, but it does mean that the argument need not

---

14. Kronen and Reitan, *God's Final Victory*, 160–62; Kimel, *Destined for Joy*, 347–48.
15. See Artman, "Hell," for a universalist response to this verse.

PART 3: A PHILOSOPHICAL DEFENSE OF UNIVERSALISM

necessitate a non-LFW framework. I argue that a proponent of LFW is justified in accepting (a–c) in virtue of Reitan and Kronen's syllogism:

1. It is in God's power to bring about (a) to (c).
2. In bringing about (a) to (c), God would not be doing anything morally impermissible.
3. If God brings about (a) to (c), then all persons will freely choose salvation.
4. Therefore, it is in God's power to bring about that all persons will freely choose salvation without doing anything morally impermissible (follows from 1,2,3).

Proposition (1) is not controversial and follows from God's established omnipotence. If God is omnipotent, it is in his modal power to bring about (a–c). Since he is omnipotent, it is in his modal power to bring about (a–c). You may deny that God would bring about (a–c) for several reasons, but you cannot plausibly deny, if adhering to basic traditional theistic commitments, that God *can* bring about (a–c).

Proposition (2) is more controversial, but I believe it can be justified. If God's love is universal (1 John 4:9–10) and he desires all people to be saved (1 Tim 2:4), God would remove all inhibitors to salvation. Any inhibitor to salvation that is external to the LFW of the person would be removed so that the person, if they so choose, can unite with God. Also, following this, God would sustain all people in a temporal existence where they have the capability to choose to be united with him. If they are not sustained in some sort of temporal existence (though 2 Peter 3:8 is a warning for us not to assume much about this), they cannot choose to unite with him. From (a–b), we reach (c). If God's love is universal, he desires us to be saved, and he puts us in a temporal existence after death so that we can choose to be united with him, then he also would leave open the option for a soul to choose communion with him. To posit that he would put a temporal limit on when the union with him can be obtained for a soul in hell is arbitrary and lacks sufficient reason. His everlasting love (Jer 31:3; 1 Cor 13:8) and everlasting mercy (Lam 3:23) cancel out this possibility. For these reasons, it does not seem God would be doing anything morally impermissible by meeting the conditions (a–c). He is not violating anyone's LFW, nor is he performing any other actions that would presumably entail moral impermissibility if a finite creature were to do it.

Proposition (3) is also controversial but can be justified as follows. I employ inspiration from Reitan and Kronen to defend this. Imagine a penny that starts heads-up in a box and has glue on the heads-side of the penny. Suppose there is an even chance, a 50 percent chance, that when the box is shaken, the penny will either be heads-side up or tails-side up. The 50 percent chance of this follows from the nature of a penny. After shaking the box a few times, we expect the penny will eventually be "stuck" with the heads-side down. Suppose we were to rattle the box indefinitely; by this, I mean suppose we were to rattle the box from time $(t_1)-(t_n)$. We are guaranteed that the penny will eventually stick heads-side down. The percentage of "possible worlds" in which the penny does not stick heads-side down approaches zero as the timeline of $(t_1)-(t_n)$ approaches infinity.

A definition is necessary at this moment before moving forward. A possible world, in the simplest of terms, is a possibility that, for every possibility x, entails either an affirmation of x or a denial of x; there is a possible world in which instead of typing this book at this moment on my computer I am typing up a paper about the existence of fairies.[16] And there is a possible world in which I am typing up a book about my childhood. And there is a possible world where I'm not even typing at this moment, but rather, I'm sailing the seven seas as a pirate. You get the point; the possibilities are endless so long as one remains within the bounds of the laws of logic. This is all in contrast to the actual world, where the only possibility that is true is that I am indeed typing up this book at this moment.

Returning to the argument, the number of pennies in this box makes no difference because this same analysis can be applied to every penny. Hence, the same outcome will be obtained whether there are one hundred billion pennies in this box or two pennies in this box. Now, replace "box" with "hell" and "pennies" with "souls of the damned." This scenario has demonstrated that universal salvation is mathematically guaranteed. As we narrow down the percentage of possible worlds where the damned do not eventually "stick heads-side down" or, rather, where the damned do not choose to unite with God, the percentage becomes infinitesimal. An infinitesimal number is any quantity closer to zero than any real number but is not zero. An infinitesimal percentage is the closest one can possibly get to mathematical certainty that an event will probabilistically

---

16. I have done just this before. See Coates, "Fairies Exist."

not obtain. Therefore, the probability that a possible world will have a single soul in eternal damnation if conditions (a–c) are accepted is next to none and, practically speaking, guaranteed.[17]

The conclusion to the syllogism nicely ties up what has been established in (1–3). God's omnipotence ensures that it is in his power to ensure that all souls eventually choose salvation, and he can do this without violating their LFW. The syllogism from Reitan and Kronen provides a handy proof for why a proponent of LFW can be a universalist if they so choose.

I close this chapter with a few words. The arguments levied against LFW are devastating in ways that strike to the core of the doctrine. CFW offers a far more cogent understanding of free will. One that aligns with ancient ontology (Plato, Proclus) along with patristic ontology (St Gregory of Nyssa, St Maximus the Confessor, St Dionysius the Areopagite, and others). I grant that the arguments for CFW are quite underdeveloped in this chapter, but that isn't my central focus. I am not worried about developing a completely new system but rather critiquing one I see as utterly flawed. You can reject LFW and adopt tens of other ways to think about free will; CFW is certainly not the only one available. I will assume going forward that my arguments against free will are justified and refer back to this chapter when the topic comes up in later responses.

---

17. The mathematical guarantee under universalism that all beings will be saved is in direct opposition to the inability to mathematically guarantee, under the LM of infernalism, that all beings in hell will remain in hell forever. See Chapter 13 for a formulation of a similar, though I humbly believe, stronger argument.

12

An Interlude on Love

GOD'S LOVE IS DISCUSSED throughout the Old and New Testaments. His love is said to be everlasting, unconditional, universal, and without limits. A few examples can follow. Jeremiah 31:3 in the NKJV reads, "I have loved you with an everlasting love." Sirach 25:11 in the KVJAAE reads, "The love of the Lord passeth all things for illumination." 1 John 4:8 in the NKJV reads, "He who does not love does not know God, for God is love." Look at any period in Christian history, and you will see, metaphorically and literally, the phrase "God is love" or "God is loving" being shouted from the rooftops. As Christians, we are drawn to this description of God for a few reasons in no particular order. (1) We experience God's love in our life all the time; (2) God is the perfect Father and a perfect Father is loving; (3) Scripture tells us that God is loving many times and the liturgical texts remind us of this every Sunday. This short chapter of several meditations explores what it means for God to *be* Love.

The Love Chapter

It was established in Chapter 1 that the Divine Names from St Dionysius the Areopagite are the most accurate linguistic terms we can employ to understand God. One of those Divine Names stood out from all the rest: Love. Love is interwoven with the Divine Names, but there is something

PART 3: A PHILOSOPHICAL DEFENSE OF UNIVERSALISM

distinct about Love. St Paul offers a very exquisite and poetic explanation of love in 1 Corinthians 13 (NKJV):

> "Love is patient, love is kind; love does not envy; love does not parade itself, is not puffed up; does not behave rudely, does not seek its own, is not provoked, thinks no evil; does not rejoice in iniquity but rejoices in the truth; bears all things, believes all things, hopes all things, endures all things. Love never fails."

St John Chrysostom offers the most extensive patristic commentary on 1 Corinthians 13 that will serve us for this chapter. By love, Paul means God. God suffers for us, he does not envy, does not parade himself, is not rude, does not seek his own, is not provoked, is not evil, rejoices in his truth, bears all things, and never fails. As John writes, "Love brings in virtue as well as eliminates vice—in fact, she makes it so that vice will not spring up at all in the first place."[1] The source of love's excellence is patience, and the source of patience is self-denial. This is why a patient person cannot be moved in their disposition by irrationality. You can insult and bash them, yet they have no wound. If love is patient, love must be kind for it to be love. As John explains, a patient person is not always a kind person. If a person is not kind, then love can become a vice since they are only patient. Since love is kind and patient, that is, since the one who loves is kind and patient, love does not become a vice. But sometimes kind and patient people have big egos and puff themselves up. This is why love corrects that vice. Love renders those people not to puff themselves up. Instead of being puffed up, they are kind, patient, and without envy. When we see those achieve a high status in society because they do evil, we should not envy their status. We see their status, but instead of envying it and believing that we deserve it because all we do is good, we must put these thoughts aside. (In quite a Nietzschean fashion, I would argue that the failure to do this is the downfall of a revolutionary mindset.)

Love cannot insist in its own way. When you have a beloved, that beloved becomes the sole focus of your world. Your love for them cannot insist on your own will but on their will. Their love for you, likewise, cannot insist on their own will but on your will. What we should try to do for our beloved on earth, and what God always does for us, is follow the will of the beloved. God loves us and he follows our will because our will of what we want for ourselves is inseparable from his will of what he wants for us. If God is the underlying motor to all desire, conscious

---

1. John Chrysostom, *Love Chapter*, 30.

AN INTERLUDE ON LOVE

or unconscious, we cannot understand our will separate from God in the metaphysical sense. What God wills for us is always what we will for ourselves. On the flip side, what we will for ourselves is what God wills for us. This is because of the transcendental orientation underlying all action (see Chapter 11).

Paul and John have offered us a very Stoic understanding of love. This theme continues when we understand that love does not rejoice in wrongdoing. When love sees someone who suffers, love reaches out to help them. Think of the dogs in the story of Lazarus who, although they could not increase Lazarus's material sustenance, nonetheless came over to lick his wounds.

We can understand why love rejoices in the truth in three different ways. None of which John explores. When we love others in the proper way with virtue and without vice, we follow the message of the gospel that is the truth. Jesus says to love others and treat others the way you want to be treated. So, when we love others and treat others the way we want to be treated, we rejoice in the truth of the gospel. When we love God in the proper way with virtue and without vice, we rejoice in his truth. By this, I mean that God is the Truth, and thus, when we love him in the proper way, this leads us to rejoice in his truth. Finally, when God loves us, he rejoices in the Truth. Since God is Love and he is the Truth, his love for us is a rejoice in Truth. The inner life of the Trinity can be mentioned here. God loves the Son because the Holy Spirit is Love and displays the Son to the Father. Such that when God loves us, he loves the image of humanity eternally in the hypostasis of the Son, and thus, he loves humanity in the plural, which, in essence, is the Son. He loves us through loving the Son because all that we are is the Son. Jesus is the "New Adam," as the old Adam has come and gone. All is fulfilled in Jesus, all is made spotless in Jesus, and all is rendered beautiful in Jesus.

When Paul says that love bears all things, he means that love can truly deal with the horrible undertakings that humanity puts it through and still come out on top. Love prevails. John asks us to consider the story of David and Absalom from 2 Samuel 15.[2] When King David heard that one of his most revered captains, Absalom, killed his son, he was truly devastated. This devastation, however, did not lead him to exact revenge on Absalom. The devastation did not lead him to put Absalom to death. No, King David showed love to Absalom. His love remained even after

---

2. John Chrysostom, *Love Chapter*, 41.

the death of his son. For love to hope and believe all things, a similar point follows. Love hopes and believes in all things because love is a type of faith. In context to our love for God, it is faith. In context to our love for other humans, it is a type of faith as well, even if we don't qualify it in this way. When we tell another person we love them, be it *philia* or otherwise, we imply there is a level of faith in this love. We are telling the person that we trust them, we care for them, and we hope they trust and care for us.

The psychoanalyst Jacques Lacan once said that love is giving to the other what one does not have.[3] Love opens us up to the void of our own self because we need another subject or person in our lives. When we love, we give what we don't have, and the beloved gives what they don't have. Love is an exchange of lack. A mutual exchange, one hopes, but in order for it to be mutual, the lover must take the first step and declare the lack. "I love you!" They shout. The beloved then has the onus to respond. Do they say, "I love you" back, or ignore this declaration of lack? If they say, "I love you back," the lover and beloved rejoice as one soul. If they ignore this declaration of lack or, in some other way, attempt to thwart the situation, the lover is left in shambles. The lover has put the void of themselves on display for the beloved, and the beloved has rejected it. The lover has distilled a deep truth to the lover, namely, that they require another person to complete them, and the beloved has rejected this.

When we declare our love for God and he declares his love for us, a perfect union of rejoicing erupts. In the words of St Dionysius the Areopagite, divine love is like an infinite and absolutely eternal circle "for the Good, from the Good, in the Good, and towards the Good."[4] God loves us not because we deserve it in any way but because he is Love. Even though God deserves more love than we could ever give him, he accepts the love that we give because he knows it is enough. He knows that it is meaningful and heartfelt. He knows that the love we give rises from the very bottom of our hearts and overflows in the form of joy. It is a love that hopes and believes all things. His love is a love that hopes and believes all things. When we love, it is a love that hopes and believes all things. God's love is the only love that can overcome the lack implicit in the concept of love because he is the fullness of Being and the fullness of Life. God's love is the only love that can fill us and make us whole.

---

3. Lacan, *Seminar VIII*, 34.
4. Quoted in Ramelli, "Apophaticism, Mysticism," 569.

AN INTERLUDE ON LOVE

Love never fails because it does not end. Paul sums up everything about love in this one line. Love never ends, in the sense of finite love between humans, because love is universal. First Thessalonians 5:14 reads in the NKJV reads, "Warn those who are unruly, comfort the fainthearted, uphold the weak, be patient with all." Here, Paul speaks to the universality of love persisting even when confronted with difficulty. More relevant, love never fails and never ends because love is God. God never fails and God never ends because he is Love. The two go hand-in-hand. A philosopher disenchanted with religion would call this a "circular argument" or something along those lines, but they struggle to see the beauty in this. Love never fails because God never fails, and God never fails because Love never fails. The entirety of 1 Corinthians 13 leading up to this point has explained why love never fails. We know why God never fails because he is God. For if God were to fail, this would impart imperfection into his nature. Since his nature is perfect, God never fails. As such, Paul's statement that love never fails acts like the cherry on top to the whole poem. Did it really need to be said? Perhaps, but it is implied in all that has been said up to this line. Paul is reiterating himself in order to come to a close in a way where there would be few questions left as to what he means. This is why the verses following this speak to the difference between love, prophecies, and knowledge. The latter two will end. We know that Jesus fulfilled many of the Old Testament prophecies; more were fulfilled at the destruction of the Second Temple, and some still lie in wait to be fulfilled. The fulfillment of these prophecies signifies to Paul the end of all prophecies.

John writes, "Signs and wonders may make them jealous of you, but if you love them, they will both admire you and love you back. And if they love, they will also lay hold of the truth in Jesus Christ in due time."[5] Knowledge will come to an end as well. The worldly wisdom of philosophy only takes you so far in life until you realize how much time you lost by pursuing worldly ventures and not godly ways. Ultimately, worldly knowledge will end in death. Yet love overcomes the faults of both. Love does not end in death. Love extends into eternal life and is, in fact, the essence of eternal life.

---

5. John Chrysostom, *Love Chapter*, 46.

PART 3: A PHILOSOPHICAL DEFENSE OF UNIVERSALISM

The Fullness of Love

Love is an active disposition of the mind. To love requires some sort of action or pressingness that a person or God feels. Since God always acts in some sort of way, be it just between the Persons of the inner-trinitarian life or his interactions with creation overall, God's love is an action. A perfect action. God's love is perfect, and our love can also be perfect. Perfect, not in virtue of our fallen human nature, but perfect in light of undergoing the process of deification as we go from "glory to glory" (2 Cor 3:18). Deification does not strip us out of fallen nature as we do not rise into our spiritual bodies in this world at any point of living. Deification causes the ontological inner change in the constitution of our individual personhood.

Perfect love, the love of God and what can be the love for us to obtain, is not partial. St Maximus the Confessor writes, "Perfect love does not split up the single human nature, common to all, according to the diverse characteristics of individuals; but, fixing attention always on this single nature, it loves all men equally."[6] God loves all men equally and if we want to be brought into his love, into his glory, we must love all men equally. Partiality is a sign of weakness. Partiality is a sign that one does not have the strength to love the other. Most devastatingly, partiality in love leads to spiritual partiality. To have spiritual partiality is to have a lack of understanding of God. Deification is the process in which our Lord seeks for us to overcome this lack. Not entirely, mind you, as who he is in himself, is unknowable in this Age and in the Age to come. The lack of understanding in terms of his presentation to creation—or, in Palamite terms, his energies—will subside. This can only be obtained by advocating against the partiality of love and thus spiritual partiality.

We persist in a moment now, a world for that matter, where the light of understanding available to us is very dim due to the world's fallen nature. The light grows dimmer as we continue a path where the virtues of deification are avoided. The light will never entirely fade as God is the light of the world. Yet as the Church incurs crisis, the light grows dimmer. St Paul writes, "For we know in part and we prophesy in part" (1 Cor 13:9; NKJV). The partiality present in this world is stark. Maximus then writes, "When these things are revealed, what is partial will cease to exist."[7] When all is revealed through the love of the Father dragging all to Christ,

---

6. Palmer et al., *Philokalia*, 60
7. Palmer et al., *Philokalia*, 160.

partiality as a concept will cease to exist. Love will be all-encompassing, and all things will be united in love with God who is Love.

13

All is Fair in Love and Hell

IN THE LAST CHAPTER, I delivered a few meditations on what it means for God to *be* Love. We will now apply those implications to eschatology. Would a God who is Love send billions of people to ECT? Or would a God who is Love eventually reconcile all the damned to be in union with him? In this chapter, I examine a few texts that center on the love of God and respond to their belief in the necessity of ECT. In doing so, I address some of the most prevalent contemporary arguments concerning ECT and some less prevalent arguments concerning ECT.

The chapter is split into levels of assumed philosophical difficulty for the reader's sake. Level 1 is a casual conversation that provides some hypotheticals that might lead the reader to think twice before adopting a position like ECT. Level 2 responds primarily to what is known as the "status argument" in favor of ECT. I develop two detailed arguments against this. Level 3 responds primarily to what is known as the "perpetual sin hypothesis" in favor of ECT. I develop three detailed arguments against this. The chapter ends with addressing some practical concerns for universalism and why these practical concerns are either misplaced or irrelevant.

Level 1: Gentle, But Not to The Damned

The Protestant theologian Dane Ortlund, in his 2020 text *Gentle and Lowly*, offers a compelling response to those who feel they are suffering in sin and do not see a way out. Sin and suffering seem to be all around in our world. Where is the light of Jesus Christ in all of this destruction? Ortlund pushes against the message of Voltaire's *Candide*. Even in the wake of suffering, the light of Christ is there, and we must reach out to it. As you would expect from a topic like this, Ortlund has a lot of wonderful insights into the love of God. "God's love is as expansive as God himself."[1] God is all-powerful and all over the universe, and if God's love is as expansive as God, his love must be all-powerful and all over the universe as well. As Ephesians 3:18 reads, "the width and length and depth and height" of God's love is immeasurable. Earlier, he writes how the heart of Jesus upends those who need to be upended in a way that is appropriate but embraces those who are penitent with more openness than is imaginable to feel.[2] The death of Christ instructs us with this love more than we could ever know, from Ortlund's view, because Christ died for all those who believe in him, so that we will never be extinguished. When we have communion with God, as Ortlund writes, it is like the oxygen and meat and drink that sustains us for our whole life.[3] Ortlund certainly offers an exquisite account of God's love, mercy, and grace, as any decent theologian can do well. Yet, there is an undercurrent to this entire text: The dogma of eternal hell.

Ortlund writes, "Left to our own natural intuitions about God, we will conclude that mercy is his strange work and judgment his natural work."[4] He says this in context to defending the Wesleyan theologians Johnathan Edwards and Thomas Goodwin. Edwards and Goodwin were all-in on the notion of ECT and believed whole-heartedly in the literalist interpretation of eternal hell as a physical place with fire and whatnot. It is unclear if Ortlund concurs with them on the physicality of hell, but he certainly seeks to defend them in this context. This is because he dislikes what some have termed the "mushy gushy" side of theological discussion about God's love. You see this a lot from contemporary Protestants in the more Evangelical camp. He seeks to ensure that the reader is aware he and the two men he mentions do not let the mushy-gushy of God's love deter them from affirming the existence of eternal hell. Yet why must we be so against the "mushy gushy" side of God's love?

1. Ortlund, *Gentle and Lowly*, 192.
2. Ortlund, *Gentle and Lowly*, 99.
3. Ortlund, *Gentle and Lowly*, 201.
4. Ortlund, *Gentle and Lowly*, 144.

Indeed, love is not always easy. Love is often challenging. Imagine your best friend is addicted to heroin. Suppose that every time you visit her, you continually affirm the point that she should stop heroin. All she wants to do in life is receive that shoot-up of heroin, and she bemoans you for trying to stop her from taking it. Eventually, she gets tired of your nagging and decides to drop you as a friend. You two stop talking, and everything goes quiet in terms of your regular communications. But you do not stop loving her. She has left you in the dust, but you do not stop loving her and wishing her the best. You certainly do not support her drug addiction, but you hope she gets the help she needs. You hope she finds a good influence in life that she will listen to. You hope she eventually sorts out her life and realizes how much she was in the wrong. But your love for her does not end. Is this mushy-gushy love? I am unsure how Ortlund would respond. It seems that this love is never failing, but at the same time, it does not simply give in to the whims of the beloved. It seems this love cannot be extinguished, but that does not mean the love will become less or respond in a completely different way to the beloved than we think it should respond.

Likewise, God's love does not extinguish nor respond in an opposite way to how we think it should respond. Suppose our ex-best friend suddenly comes to her senses and seeks our help. We would be behooved to completely reject her if we can assume that we still love her. On the other hand, however, it would be irresponsible to pretend that nothing has gone down between us. We can neither accept her back immediately nor cast her out forever. She has sought our help, and she wants to change her ways. Suppose we give it a month or two in order to verify that our ex-best friend really wants to change her ways. Suppose she bought a new apartment, has a job now, and is back in the dating market. It would seem these all point to the fact that our ex-best friend truly wants to change her ways. Can we accept her back now? Maybe we should wait a few more months. A few months pass, and our ex-best friend is now maintaining mortgage payments on time, she has a steady relationship, and her career path is panning out. It seems at this point that our ex-best friend truly has changed. She does want to reconnect with us. Do we just deny her request at connection until we both die? Colossians 3:13 teaches us not to hold grudges against others, so we should slowly and gradually let our ex-best friend back into our life. Perhaps she will once again become our best friend.

This hypothetical seeks to demonstrate what should happen when we lose a friend we still want to love and keep dear to us. We do not immediately let them back in, lest they have tricked us or fall back into their old ways due to temptation. But we do not completely cast them out, never to be seen or experience what our love feels like again. We give them time just as God gives all of us time, even if we find ourselves in that nasty condition we call hell. Ortlund writes, "Christ is a lion to the impenitent, he is a lamb to the penitent."[5] Like a lion, Christ is brave, courageous, and fierce to those who do not believe in him. Like a lamb, Christ is gentle, pure, and innocent to those who do not believe in him. More or less, Scripture tells us these are the two faces of Christ. He appears one way to those who trust him and another to those who do not. But like a lamb and a lion, Christ does not abandon his pack or flock either way. A lion is fierce and brave, but a lion is also dignified. A lamb is gentle and pure, but a lamb is also sacrificial. Christ died for all of us. Indeed, every single one of us. So that we, ourselves, would be dignified and sacrificial in fulfilling the Kingdom.

The hypothesis of universalism seemingly does not enter Ortlund's mind throughout this entire text. He knows two things are true: God is Love; hell is eternal. He must now try to bind these two contradictory stances together to form a cogent story. He never directly addresses the arguments in favor of or against eternal hell. ECT is assumed to be an obvious, though unconsciously recognized, fact of reality. Some might chalk this up to the fact that, like many Christian authors, Ortlund writes for a relatively lay audience who would rather not get into the nitty-gritty of eschatology. Or he simply might be unaware of the position. Or maybe he felt that addressing the possibility of universal salvation, even giving a voice to the argument, could bring some of his readers over. After all, St Augustine of Hippo referred to *apokatastasis* as the position of the tender-hearted. Whatever the reason he did not address universalism, I have shown that it reasonably follows what he discusses in this text.

Level 2: The Calvinist Curse

The renowned Calvinist theologian R. C. Sproul's 2012 text *God's Love* is another drop-in-the-bucket of Reformed theological work from Sproul. Sproul begins by offering what it means to say that God is Love.

---

5. Ortlund, *Gentle and Lowly*, 111.

PART 3: A PHILOSOPHICAL DEFENSE OF UNIVERSALISM

Compared to the secular use of love, which often denotes a passive variation, God's love is always active.[6] He compares it to influenza as it comes over us unexpectedly. Few deny that God is sovereign, but what Sproul seeks to do as a Calvinist is hammer home what he takes to be the obvious consequences of this thesis (even though they most certainly were not seen to be by most Christians living before the sixteenth century). (1) God is sovereign in authority over all his creatures. (2) God is sovereign over the universe and history. (3) God is sovereign in the distribution of his grace that saves. More or less, Acts 17:28 sums up all three postulations that Sproul makes.[7] "For in Him we live and move and have our being. . ." If we have our being in God, he is sovereign over us, and this seems to imply he is sovereign in the distribution of his grace. If his domain of sovereignty only covered (1–2), it would seem that we would encounter a weird roadblock. Such that we live and have our being in him, but he cannot guarantee where our being is? It would seem that denying (3) would lead us to say that he has no guarantee about whether we experience the conditions of Paradise or hell. Suppose we accept all three postulations just for hypothetical purposes. I argue that universal salvation can be obtained even in this case.

Universalism *can* follow from accepting (1–3) if the universalist accepts that God is love. Since universalism by and large accepts that God is love, universalism *can* follow from the acceptance of (1–3).[8] (1) God is sovereign in authority over all his creatures. I agree. So, what does this entail if we accept that God is sovereign in authority over all his creatures? Well, it entails that we can once again skirt the issue of free will that keeps popping its head up even though we keep hitting it with a mallet (though, granted, Calvinism is too far in the opposite direction of libertarian free will). It also seems to entail that God has judgment over all creatures. (2) What does this entail if we accept that God is sovereign over the universe and history? Imagine I am typing a book. As I type, I mess up and make what seem to be mistakes. I might forget punctuation or spell "Jerusalem" wrong (speaking from experience), forget an accent on a Greek transliterated word (again, speaking from experience), and so on. However, in God's view, these mistakes are necessary because they serve his will. What seems to me to be mistakes are, to God, a success.

6. Sproul, *God's Love*, 22.
7. Sproul,.*God's Love*, 108.
8. I don't accept (1–3) as I reject (2) and (3). My point is that universalism can follow from this. A Calvinist who believes all this *can* still be a universalist.

Nothing in the objective sense makes a mistake. Every happening goes according to God's plan...

I have to pump the brakes here. This is not something I endorse. There is no "grand plan" that all evil falls into, as if God is a finite utilitarian subject who must allow and permit evil because it eventually leads to a greater good. Frankly, it is vile to think that all the horrors that have taken place in this world served God's will. These events did not serve his will. These events were dredges on the creation that God set out to ordain with grace. What the Christian must recognize, rather than this, is that there are two realities: There is our world, with all the horror and tragedy that evil has beset upon it. And there is another world, the primordial state of creation, creation in its purest state, that was effervescent in glory and clothed in a spectacular robe of loving communion. Unfortunately, as explained in the Introduction, the latter is not the world we live in.[9] We should not be cosmically optimistic, as Sproul and others are, thinking that all evil is just "according to God's plan." This is not what the NT teaches in the slightest. From the gospels alone, we get the idea that this world [*kosmos*] hates Jesus and that Jesus has come to raise us out of the world (Jn 15:18–19) because Jesus has overcome the world (Jn 16:33). What is the "world" in question? As we know from Paul's very detailed cosmology, this Age, this world, is ruled by spiritual powers and principalities (Col 1:16), the elemental spirits of the world (Gal 4:3), the prince of the power of air (Eph 2:2). While God does have power over all of these beings such that they can never separate us from his love (Rom 8:38), their presence and their dictation of world history cannot be overlooked.

Evil arises then, not from some Manichean battle between "good" and "evil," but from one turning their will away from God and toward that which is fleeting and not static like the love of God. Evil is a turn toward oneself, an attempt at achieving a subjectivity of self-relation, but such a subjectivity, such a state of personal existence, is impossible because of the triune nature of reality that our existence presents itself in. There is the self/subject/person, there is the other to which we relate to and yet differ from in the constitution of our individual soul, and there is God. Evil comes about when we (or a spiritual being) forget such a triune structure of reality, and instead see ourselves as the source of reality, the only entity in the triune relationship, thereby negating the triune

---

9. DBH, *Doors of the Sea*, 60.

PART 3: A PHILOSOPHICAL DEFENSE OF UNIVERSALISM

structure. Evil is totally illusory in a teleological context, and its presence is fundamentally against the essence of being. With all that extraneously said, we can move on to the third postulation.

Since Sproul is a Calvinist, he believes in predestination. Since Sproul is an infernalist and a Calvinist, he believes in double predestination: There is an elect group of the saved that has been determined by God before that group was ever born. Those who are not in that elect group of the saved will go to eternal hell. There is nothing the non-elect can do so that they won't go to eternal hell because by nature of not being the elect, they will go to eternal hell. In the past five centuries, much ink has been spilled, combatting and challenging this core position, so I need not go through those critiques. What I will say is that (3) from Sproul does not entail this. As a reminder, I accept that God is sovereign over the deliberation of his grace. God's grace is a gift that is given to humanity not because we deserve it but because he loves us. In the Orthodox view of the Incarnation, the Godman primarily brought forth the process of cosmic deification, which will eventually lead to the conclusion of creation's *telos* (see Chapter 3). The *telos* of creation is for God to be all in all. But this does not entail that God must deliberate grace to all, as some Orthodox infernalists have duly noted. I argue that God *will* deliberate grace to all because he is the Good Father. As such, I do not postulate any metaphysical necessitarianism in relation to God's deliberation of his grace. To do so would be incoherent because God is above all categories of necessity and dependence.[10]

In older texts, Sproul is, in my view, more honest about the consequence of Calvinist predestination in relation to God's allegedly universal love:

> "If some people are not elected unto salvation, then it would seem that God is not all that loving toward them. For them, it seems that it would have been more loving of God not to have allowed them to be born. That may indeed be the case."[11]

Quite a different picture than what he paints later in life. If God does not offer his love to those who are not already elected into salvation (which is out of their control), then a display of God's love would be greater if he never had them born in the first place. The conclusion of this then leads to

---

10. See David Artman's response to a similar objection about God's sovereignty and the scriptural evidence in favor of the universalist response in Artman, "Bible."
11. Sproul, *Chosen by God*, 51.

a logical follow-up question: If God did not create them to be loved, why did he create them? It is here where the truly vile and grotesque response of Calvinism comes in: God created the non-elect to glorify himself.[12] I don't fault Friedrich Nietzsche for crying out, "Heaven and Hell and humanity are thus supposed to exist so as to—gratify the vanity of God! What a cruel and insatiable vanity must have flickered in the soul of him who first conceived or first appropriated such a thing!"[13] Sproul doesn't really believe in God's love. God isn't the ultimate being of love and bliss who extends this love universally. God is just a being that "may indeed" only love those who are not the elect. I don't worship whoever this deity is.

Before we close our discussion, let's engage with Sproul's argument for hell. This is known as the status argument (SA). SA's main goal is to justify the necessity of ECT as the only condition where divine justice prevails. The rationale that divine justice must prevail is justified in almost every Christian framework. The universalist does not disagree with this in the slightest. The universalist, however, believes that what constitutes divine justice prevailing necessarily involves a universal reconciliation to obtain; that is a topic for Level Three. For now, I will recreate SA below.

Suppose an entity exists that has infinite value. This can be referred to as G. Suppose an entity of finite value exists. This can be referred to as H. Suppose that H offends G in some way. By nature of the infinite value of G and the finite value of H, H has an infinitely great debt. An infinitely great debt can only be justly repaid by a punishment of infinite length that corresponds to the infinite value of the offended entity. A punishment of infinite length, in virtue of its infinite length, will never end. Thus, in order for God to procure justice, H must be subject to a punishment of infinite length. Let's now rephrase this with some more familiar terms. If a human offends God, because of a human's finite value and God's infinite value, the human must undergo an infinitely long punishment. In Christianity, we call this ECT.

Before my response, I should note SA's *prima facie* credence. SA is a traditional argument in favor of ECT. You can find SA in the writings of some early Fathers, and you can especially find it in the writings of the

---

12. It is worth briefly mentioning that this tenet of Calvinism actually does have Gnostic roots, unlike universalism as Michael McClymond and others claim. The Greek philosopher Plotinus criticizes Gnostics for believing that the demiurge created humans in order to be honored [ἵνα τιμῷτο] on the basis that this reason is absurdly anthropocentric. See Plotinus, *Enneads* 2.9.

13. Nietzsche, *Human, All Too Human*, 331.

PART 3: A PHILOSOPHICAL DEFENSE OF UNIVERSALISM

Reformers. John Calvin is not the only Reformer who supported an argument like this. Traces can be found in Martin Luther as well. Later Protestants like Johnathan Edwards especially liked SA. Another credence that SA may have is that proponents of it are found in faiths outside of Christianity, like Islam. Since Islamic infernalists borrow images of God's fiery wrath from Christianity, SA seems to enjoy a non-exclusivist appeal; see the Appendix. A final credence that SA may have is that it attempts to maintain the absolute distinction between humanity and God. Any mix-up of this valuation could lead to a "pantheism" of some sort. Much of Western Christianity shudders at this possibility.

However, this argument has many problems despite the credence it may have at the offset. I have chosen two that illustrate how SA entails absurd conclusions that cannot be rationally justified. (1) The (problem) of original sin (OS).[14] (2) The (problem) of value-correspondence (VC).

(1) OS begins on the basis that all humans are born with a guilt that has been passed down from Adam, the forefather of humanity. Since all humans are born with this guilt that derives from Adam's transgression, all humans at their conception are already sinful. And if a being dies without being baptized into Christianity, this being will likely end up in hell. Suppose we now consider all the babies ever conceived in Christian families (and non-Christian families, for that matter)[15] who have died before they were born into the world or baptized in an official way. If we assume that the soul and the body come into being at the same moment in time (as Holy Tradition teaches), then any baby that dies during miscarriage, stillbirth, or from one of the hundreds of diseases that claim the death of a child before or soon after it is born, that baby is very likely going to suffer for all eternity.

Many contemporary infernalists seek to disregard this entailment because it is obviously a very uncomfortable conclusion. Perhaps our medieval predecessors like Anselm of Canterbury took this whole

---

14. Many Orthodox infernalists escape (1) because they reject a particular iteration of how many in the West have historically viewed "original sin." For Orthodoxy, as I have said before, original sin pertains to the finite lifespan of all creatures. Every infernalist who adopts some sort of the Augustinian original sin approach (most Protestants and some traditional Catholics) must contend with this critique.

15. Christian orthodoxy is sometimes up in arms about the entailments of OS leading to the babies of Christian families enduring ECT, but I have not seen as much outcry for the babies of families with other faiths. Does a stillborn baby that was birthed by a Muslim or Jewish woman deserve to endure ECT? I don't see how a clinically sane person could answer yes to this.

approach too far. At a lecture given in a Dominican monastery, Albert Camus once said, "I was not the one to invent the misery of the human being or the terrifying formulas of divine malediction. I was not the one to shout *Nemo bonus* or the damnation of unbaptized children."[16] It is rare for me to sympathize with a writer like Camus, but even he has his moments. Regardless of whether this personally makes you feel bad, the stance is entailed by the infernalist's acceptance of this argument.[17] This alone should make you adjust the argument's claims to exclude the offense of OS while preserving the conclusion—the justification of ECT. Or the easy option is to discard the argument altogether.

(2) If sinning before God constitutes an infinite level of offense towards God, then after committing my first sin as a child, I am now viewed in his eyes to be just as infinitely wicked and guilty as a serial killer. The offense made by a being with finite value towards a being with infinite value is the same in both cases. Sure, one may *seem* much worse of an offense, but you shouldn't let emotions cloud your judgment! If we base the reason for ECT on the fact that a being of finite value has offended a being of infinite value, the argument entails this conclusion. But, like (1), this is atrocious. This violates all grounds of intuition and violates our basic moral sensibilities to the extent that it causes what philosophers call "moral outrage." The seriousness of the sin cannot be determined along the lines only of *who* the sin offends; hence, the VC. The seriousness of the sin should take into account the nature of the sin itself (intent, character of the person, effects on self and others).[18] A finite creature simply does not deserve an infinite punishment because they are finite, and the victim is infinite. Suppose we even bite the bullet on the moral outrage caused by this. This is still an untenable conclusion from a scriptural point of view. Romans 3:23 reads, "For all have sinned and fallen short of the glory of God." Indeed, we are all guilty before God because we are all sinners. But there is no scriptural ground to argue that we all have infinite guilt before God. To argue we are all of infinite guilt before God,

---

16. Camus, *Christian Metaphysics*, 123.

17. I should also add that dead unbaptized infants being sentenced to ECT is supported in chapter 9 of the *Westminster Confession of 1647*. It is entailed by Article VII of the *United Methodist Confession* (updated in 2016). It is entailed by chapter 6 of the *Baptist Confession of 1689*. All three of these are respectively held by some of the largest Protestant denominations.

18. A few of these are suggested by Fr Robin Parry in Parry, *Four Views on Hell*, 53.

lacks scriptural proof; and as said, is utterly unintuitive to the highest degree. Since SA entails this absurd conclusion, SA should be rejected.

Due diligence has been paid to give SA a fair shake. We determined that SA entails two absurd conclusions. Problems (1–2) specifically respond to SA but may have far-reaching implications for other arguments for ECT. Sproul and others like him who adopt ECT should look for alternative arguments that avoid absurd conclusions like these. Or Sproul and others like him should look at an alternative eschatology altogether. Might I suggest universalism?

Level 3: A Hellish Love

The Anglican theologian Gerald Bray's 2012 text *God is Love* is a systematic *tour de force* that arrived on the scene with bustling reviews and many awards. Bray writes, "Even in the face of evil, God is love. He reaches out to people he cannot naturally like and enters into fellowship with them, although they have done nothing to deserve it."[19] God's love is universal, and the most sinful person is always just a few steps away from being in God's grace. Evil has no match for God because evil is created. Evil is not co-eternal like the Good that is God, and thus, evil will always and forever be lesser than God, who is the Good. He later says, "But however hard it may be to understand or accept, everything that God does he does in his love and in his goodness. Even his wrath and punishment must be understood in that context."[20] Indeed, God's wrath is always a loving wrath.

Take the example of a good parent. A good parent loves their child, and when they exert wrath upon their child, this wrath is always enacted from the position of a loving authority. A good parent enacts wrath in order for the child to learn the right way to live, to learn the correct behavior that is asked of them. A good parent does not enact wrath for the sheer purpose of wrath. In the United States, depending on how bad this wrath is, we would want that parent to be visited by Child Protection Services or at least have some sort of mediator to stop them from enacting such sheer wrath. Wrath is always enacted by the good parent in the backdrop of love. Since God is the Parent, or rather the Father of all, his wrath would especially be enacted with the backdrop of love. His punishment

19. Bray, *God Is Love*, 71.
20. Bray, *God Is Love*, 140.

and his wrath are all varied expressions of his love and do not have an existence on their own. They rely on the existence of God's love for them to be expressed. Accordingly, we can call his wrath and punishment a mode of his love. They are an expression of his love because, like a good parent would exert wrath on a child who continually disobeys them, our Heavenly Father likewise does this. He always distributes it mercifully and justly.

Bray puts the issue in a paradoxical way further down the same page. He says that God hates sinners because God loves them. Since sinners rebel against God, he hates them, but this hate is distinct from the possibility of him being indifferent to sinners. If God was indifferent to sinners, he could destroy them without thinking twice. Since God is not indifferent to sinners, he does not destroy them, rather he allows them to fester in their sin because he loves them. To apply a parental analogy, a good parent allows the kid to fester in their punishment rather than, as an analogy for destruction, kick them out of the house. The punishment is given because the good parent loves the child and wants the best for the child. I concur. God punishes us because he loves us and as a good parent, the Good parent, that is, he desires us to change our ways. He eternally wants his creation to embrace his love. But a bizarre jump will be made after this. Bray goes from the analogy of a good parent issuing corrective punishment to the need for ECT and existential separation from God for the damned. I struggle to see how he makes this jump, considering how he repeatedly harps on how important it is to view God as the most perfect Parent over humanity.[21]

If God is the perfect Heavenly Father, wouldn't we expect him to know precisely how to reach us humans? One of the most important roles of a parent in a child's life is to figure out what makes them tick, that is, what leads them to make their life decisions. The parent tries to figure this out so that they can always be there for the child even when the child has gone astray. If their child has gone astray, the parent seeks to figure out what precisely they can do, perhaps even leading to a change of their attitude towards the child and/or their actions, which would lead the child back to them. The goal of a good parent is to remain in good conscience with the child but to do so without sacrificing too much on their part.

---

21. Bray, *God Is Love*, 170; 219; 334; 381; 516.

PART 3: A PHILOSOPHICAL DEFENSE OF UNIVERSALISM

This is why I am lost with how Bray thinks the most good parent of all, our perfect Heavenly Father, would not know exactly what makes his sons and daughters "tick." Since God is the Heavenly Father and at all times knows everything we will ever do or could ever do, it does not make sense to think that he is oblivious to the path to our hearts. God knows the path to our heart better than even the greatest parent on earth, and he knows what must be done for us to accept him; that is, for us to enter back into good conscience with him. He does not force this, just as a good parent does not force their rebellious child to enter back into good conscience with them. Like a good parent, God searches out for what it is that makes the rebellious child tick. But unlike a good parent, God does not need to sacrifice anything to bring the child back into a positive relationship with him. He is on an ever-present search for how the path to all our hearts can be opened towards him. Since God is the perfect parent, he will achieve this search. No matter how rebellious any of his sons or daughters are, they will all find themselves in good conscience with the Father, who knows precisely the right medicine needed to mend their relationship—the right medicine for the right wound.

Bray's overall argument for ECT is not provided in-depth anywhere in the text, but he adopts many aspects of the LM. In Chapter 4, I referred to this as the dominant model among contemporary proponents of infernalism. This is true as a generalized statement, but reality often does not mesh with this generalization. When an infernalist argues for ECT, they do not always section off their arguments into organized categories like this. Multiple justifications for ECT often run together.

In any case, the argument for adopting the LM can be referred to as the perpetual sin hypothesis (PSH). My recreation goes as follows. Suppose there is a wicked person (WP) on earth. Wickedness is constituted by a rebellion against God (RAG). RAG is a consistent mental disposition of rejecting God that extends from a given temporal moment (t_1) to an undefined temporal moment (t_n); (t_1)–(t_n). Wickedness is the character trait that RAG corresponds to. Due to the WP's wickedness, which corresponds to their RAG, they will endure ECT when they die. They will remain in hell due to wickedness being an essential character trait of their personhood. This means that they will likewise continue their RAG while in hell. If they continue their RAG in hell and hell is eternal, this means their RAG must likewise be eternal. The RAG of the WP will be consistent from (t_1)–(t_n). Since the WP maintains an eternal

RAG, the eternally long sentence of hell is necessary for God to obtain symmetrical justice.

PSH has *prima facie* appeal, and this is why it enjoys many proponents. It overcomes the scrupulous issue of basing the eternal temporal length of hell on the need for God to satisfy his anger toward sinners. PSH also overcomes the absurd entailments of VC that we identified earlier in the case of SA. The infinite sentence of hell is not based on a correspondence with the infinite value of the entity offended, it is based on the soul perpetually committing sin. Finally, PSH seems to overcome the issue of God's love being cut off at any point from the person in hell. This maintains that God's love is eternal and universally extended to all.

However, there are still many problems with PSH. Since this is the most favored argument by contemporary infernalists, especially Orthodox infernalists, I feel it is my due diligence to examine three responses. (1) The (problem) of guaranteed certainty (GC); (2) The (problem) of eternal sin (ES); (3) The (problem) of necessary divine justice (NDJ). Problems (1–2) directly respond to PSH, and their entailments *may* impact *other* arguments for ECT. Problem (3) directly responds to PSH, and the entailments of this *will* impact *every* argument for ECT.

(1) Suppose there is a WP in hell due to their RAG on earth carrying over into the next life. Suppose we grant that the WP in hell has libertarian free will (LFW). The assumption of LFW is justified in virtue of the fact that most infernalists accept LFW and thus presume it to apply to an entity in hell. This is why the LM refers to hell as "trapped from the inside." The damned have LFW to remain in hell and orchestrate their LFW to remain in hell for whatever reason. But if the damned have LFW and are only in hell because they orchestrate their LFW to remain in hell, this does not guarantee that *all* the damned will undergo ECT. This undermines the traditional argument for hell in such a way that the damned, if by virtue of their own LFW decide to exit hell, they can exit. The possible temporal moment of the WP exiting hell can be denoted as (t^). Hence, the infernalist does not have GC that the WP will undergo ECT. They could very well undergo conscious torment for a long while and, after a number of successive temporal states, decide to obtain (t^) for whatever reason. This critique alone does not require me to provide any specific reason *why* the WP might suddenly decide to obtain (t^). It just remains true that they very well could decide to obtain (t^) for whatever reason. If the WP can decide to obtain (t^) then the fundamental framework of

PART 3: A PHILOSOPHICAL DEFENSE OF UNIVERSALISM

ECT is undermined as it is no longer eternal. Hell may just exist for a really long time, which is precisely the position of a universalist.

Suppose now we populate hell with more than one WP. We have been dealing with a single WP in a vacuum, but since more than one WP is undergoing ECT, we should consider the set of all wicked persons in hell (SAWP). At an extremely conservative estimate, assuming infernalism is true, we can estimate that at least thirty billion people have been subject to ECT since the beginning of human history.[22] Thirty billion people is synonymous with the SAWP. Suppose there is, on a purely hypothetical whim, a .000000000000000000001 percent chance that a single WP, considered in a vacuum, will reach (t^). This leaves an extremely small likelihood that if there is just one WP in hell, they will obtain (t^). But, even then, it is not impossible.

If the SAWP is taken into account, the minuscule chance that (t^) is obtained would be maximized to a great extent. Suppose now there are thirty billion possible worlds with the same number of SAWP in each hell. That is to say, there are thirty billion possible worlds, and in each possible world, there are thirty billion people in hell. (Assume for simplicity purposes that these possible worlds are all extremely similar to our own—such as having similar laws of physics—and that God treats sin the same way in all of them.) The total SAWP in all possible worlds can then be referred to as TSAWP. In every possible world, every WP has a .000000000000000000001 percent of obtaining (t^). Hence, it is very unlikely that not a single WP out of the TSAWP will obtain (t^). Even if you disagree with these numbers as they are, *admittingly*, a complete shot-in-the-dark, under PSH, the infernalist cannot guarantee that the TSAWP will stay in hell for all eternity. Even excluding all talk of possible worlds, the infernalist cannot claim certainty that a single WP out of the SAWP will not obtain (t^). Let alone that many WPs in the SAWP will not obtain (t^). PSH inherently suffers from an inability to claim GC.

---

22. According to most statistics, although we do not have accurate population numbers for the majority of human history, more than one hundred and ten billion people are estimated to have died. If ECT is for all those who do not come to Christ in this life, the number could probably be around thirty billion. This is even assuming that the Harrowing of Hades implies that every single person who died before Christ was brought to Paradise. If, as most infernalists, you qualify the Harrowing to only having freed the righteous or even just the prophets of the Old Testament, this number must be upwards of seventy billion or higher. Even when taking into account the many souls that could have been freed due to postpartum prayers for the dead, it is unlikely this number would decrease in any meaningful way. But this is all speculation of course.

Consider a counterargument. The following argument implicitly assumes there is a reasonable claim for GC, and it questions if, in a sense, God even desires a WP to choose to follow him. The Orthodox philosopher Richard Swinburne writes,

> "If a man did not seek such a life on earth, why should he seek it if he comes to learn that it can go on forever and provide deep happiness? Either because he wants to live forever or because he wants the happiness. But while someone is seeking to live the good life for those reasons, he will not find the happiness of heaven."[23]

Suppose that a WP could exit hell (as I have shown, PSH entails this). Unlike humans on earth, the WP does not show faith by turning to God. Unlike humans on earth, they decide to follow God to procure that blissful state of being that we call heaven. They seek the "good life," but not for good reasons. These reasons are incompatibly selfish, and since selfishness is against the nature of what would constitute the bliss of heaven, then even if the WP could exit the conditions of hell, God might simply turn them away. They do not seek God as their rational *telos* as humans in this life do, they just seek him because he is a tool that will end their suffering. In short, the happiness of heaven should only be happiness given to those who do not seek it. Swinburne makes a compelling argument often not found in the Evangelical philosophical literature on infernalism, but it fails to hold up under scrutiny.

I struggle to see why the WP's choice to exit hell *must* constitute a selfishly chosen act. I will begin with a very extreme case and then ground this response more to the general population of WPs. Suppose there is a WP who falls under the broad category of erotic masochism. An erotic masochist is a person who derives sexual satisfaction out of suffering and pain. This person can be referred to as a masochistic wicked person (MWP). Throughout the temporal successive moments $(t_1)-(t_n)$ of the MWP's stay in hell, they have been procuring sexual pleasure. Though improbable, it is not impossible that such a person could exist. Erotic masochism comes in all degrees of tolerance. Most masochists probably do not find pleasure through a painful torture-like experience such as one could only imagine would constitute the condition of hell; they much rather prefer experiences where the pain is less intense and

---

23. Swinburne, "Theodicy," 50. Swinburne's leading justification for ECT is based on a libertarian concept of individual choice. I dealt adequately with this in Chapter 11.

PART 3: A PHILOSOPHICAL DEFENSE OF UNIVERSALISM

continuous, but there very probably could still be some who would find pleasure in this. Hence, let us say that the searing pain from the fires causes great sexual delight for the MWP.

Supposing PSH is true, the entailment is that the MWP could exit hell by virtue of their own LFW. If they choose to exit hell even though hell is procuring such a high degree of pleasure, then they may be choosing this for a non-selfish reason. They are seeking the good life for a good reason. Since they enjoy the torment, they are not seeking God as a tool that will cease the torment. Seemingly, they are seeking God because he is the rational end to their *telos*. Even in the fiery conditions of hell, a pervert like this can still choose God for a non-selfish purpose. We can never know the MWP's purpose for choosing God. Only God knows. Swinburne's argument does not hold up.

Moving away from this more extreme case, a non-masochistic WP could likewise choose God for a non-selfish purpose. Many WPs have families that may or may not be subjected to ECT. Some, a vast majority that is, may very well be in Paradise. Unless Swinburne argues there is a complete loss of memory for WPs undergoing ECT (which I respond to in Chapter 14), then we can assume that a large number of them still have family ties of some sort that they are holding onto from earthly life. If WPs have family ties, they may seek to reunite with their family one day (see Chapter 16's response to annihilationism's denial of this). The desire to reunite with one's family is not necessarily a selfish act. If a WP desires to reunite with their family because a reunion would satisfy some sort of basic pleasure for them, this seems to be a selfish act. However, if the WP desires to reunite with their family because they believe this reunion would ensure some sort of mutual pleasure, this does not seem to be a selfish act. Following the entailments of PSH, a WP could exit hell in virtue of LFW since they themselves are the ones "trapped from the inside." If they could exit hell and exiting hell for the purpose of reuniting with their family is not a selfish act, then they *are* seeking the "good life" for good reasons. Swinburne's objection does not seem to hold up even under this much less extreme case.

But suppose that, for whatever reason, this still does not qualify as a non-selfish act. The infernalist might counter that the WP is not choosing God for God's sake. This may be a valid response. In the hypothetical above, the WP is choosing to follow God to reunite with their family. While a familial reunion is not selfish per se, it does not seem that they are viewing God as an end in himself: God is still a means to an end.

Suppose I grant this. The WP could still choose God for a non-selfish purpose if choosing God is due to their deep desire for the divine, which finally manifests itself concretely in the person's conscious psychological disposition. To argue this would require the infernalist to grant the rejection of total depravity, the doctrine made popular in Reformed circles that assumes original sin has made humans completely alien to grace. The claim goes that we do not seek grace; it is forensically imputed into us by an exterior source, and we either accept it or deny it. This is utterly foreign to Eastern patristics and most Western patristics. If total depravity is accepted, this response seems to fall flat, but since I don't really take seriously the opinions of anyone who holds this doctrine, I shall *a priori* dismiss their retorts, if any are given.

There is a divine light in all people that shines through whether or not they allow it to. All people have an intrinsic thirst for God. In John 4, this is symbolized by the spiritual water that Jesus offers to the Samaritan woman at the well. Even the Samaritans, an enemy of the Jews, have the desire to drink from the wellspring of life. Likewise, all WPs, no matter how wicked, have a desire to know God and to meet his love. As such, Swinburne's objection still falls flat because it does not entail that a damned soul will only follow God for selfish reasons. Swinburne lacks GC that none of the damned will exit hell.

(2) Suppose a WP is in hell due to their RAG on earth carrying over into their sentence of ECT. Suppose that (t_1) is the first temporal moment when they begin ECT, and (t_n) indicates the undefined eternality of the sentence. Any temporal moment in their sentence is somewhere between $(t_1)-(t_n)$. If there is not an end to eternal RAG by nature of what eternity entails, then the sin of the damned, their RAG, becomes ES. If ES obtains, God never conquers sin. If God never conquers sin, then God's justice does not prevail. The entailment is that sin is such a terrible moral offense to God, yet he wills it to continue eternally $(t_1)-(t_n)$. This means that for all time, there will be a divine dualism: God vs. sin. The silly Miltonian notion that God and the Devil stand opposed to each other on equal grounds, like some sort of cosmic chess match, is entailed by the acceptance of ES. This surely borders on incoherence. Hence, the philosophical entailment of ES seems to fall flat on its face. What about a biblical argument for ES? There is very little support here as well.[24]

---

24. See several biblical objections to this in Blocher, "Everlasting Punishment," 301–3.

PART 3: A PHILOSOPHICAL DEFENSE OF UNIVERSALISM

Some contemporary proponents of PSH argue Mark 3:29 supports ES. This is where Jesus states that the one who blasphemes against the Holy Spirit "does not have forgiveness unto the Age and has the guilt of a sin unto the Age." (The common phrase *eis ton aiōna* is used here in the first part and the adjective *aiōniou* is used in the second; see Chapter 9 for a review of these terms.) Matthew's account adds that the one who blasphemes against Jesus can be pardoned but not the one who blasphemes against the Holy Spirit. As any theologian can tell you, these verses are fundamentally a mystery. We have many theories on what they could or could not mean from the Fathers and beyond. My personal interpretation is largely in agreement with St Ephrem the Syrian and others in the Syrian tradition. In a somewhat obvious way, he states that this verse means that sin against the Holy Spirit cannot be forgiven outright; rather, the believer must undergo purification in Gehenna.[25] Ephrem does not state what he believes constitutes "sin against the Holy Spirit," but he says that whatever it may be is so devastating to the soul of the offender that they must undergo purification in Gehenna and cannot be forgiven before this. Such a sentiment, I believe, may be due to the East Syrian emphasis on the importance of teaching and how every stage of the world brings with it a teaching that must be passed down. God taught Adam, the patriarchs, Moses, and so on unto the New Covenant where God, in the Person of Jesus, taught the disciples who taught their successors, who taught their successors, and so on. The relevance here is that just as a teacher would punish their students for not abiding by their teaching, if we are all said students of God, yet some of us do not abide by God's teaching (handed down through traditions), then we are meant to be punished. If some of us go so far as to rebuke the teacher in some extreme way (sin against the Holy Spirit), then our punishment must certainly be far more serious than if we were just to not abide by the commands or words of the teacher. Hence, we must undergo purification in Gehenna. Forgiveness is no longer an impossibility in the eschatological future but rather an impossibility until the believer undergoes a necessary punishment. This is in line with universalism.

Compared to the lack of biblical evidence in favor of ES, there is at least *some* biblical evidence against ES. Isaiah 57:16 in the NKJV reads, "For I will not contend forever; Nor will I be angry." Christians can agree that God is angry towards sin. If God is angry towards sin, but his anger

---

25. Biesen, "Syrian Church Fathers," 441.

will cease at some point, then sin must cease as well. RAG cannot be eternal. Psalm 103:9 in the NKJV reads, "He will not always strive with us, Nor will He keep His anger forever." Again, if sin leads God to anger and his anger will someday cease, then sin cannot be eternally perpetuated. As Andrew Hronich also notes, Jesus in Luke 12:47–48 affirms the notion of differentiation in punishment but not an unceasing punishment.[26] Some receive more of a beating than others in terms of numerical count, but none receive an endless beating. Certainly, none of them receive an endless beating they cause to themselves, which, as shown in (1), PSH claims. Not only is the philosophical justification of ES weak, but the biblical justification is as well.

(3) Suppose a WP is in hell. Suppose (t*) is the temporal moment in which the conditions of NDJ are obtained. At any temporal point during the WP's stay in hell, there is always more of the sentence to be carried out. This is by nature of hell's infinite temporal length. If NDJ is obtained by the WP serving their sentence, but their sentence is infinitely long, then NDJ is *never* obtained. That is, (t*) is never reached. No matter how many successive temporal moments $(t_1)-(t_n)$ have passed since they arrived in hell, there is never an infinite number of successive temporal moments. One million years can pass, and there is still never a sentence served that is of infinite length. Ten million years can pass, and there is still never a sentence served that is of infinite length. One quintillion years can pass, and there is still never a sentence served that is of an infinite length. The length of a sentence served by the WP will always and will forever be of a finite length. The desired actual infinite always and will forever remain a potential infinite. Since an actual infinite length of a sentence served is never obtained, NDJ is likewise never obtained. Consequently, the ECT model, adopted by those like Bray and many others, never achieves NDJ. If the purpose of the model is to ensure NDJ, the model has absolutely failed. If the infernalist really desired to ensure NDJ, they would adopt one of two approaches: Universal reconciliation or annihilation; however, see Chapter 16 for why the latter does not achieve NDJ either. There must be an end to punishment that ends either in a reconciliation that constitutes NDJ or an annihilation of the damned that constitutes NDJ. That is, the WP must reach (t*). From this argument alone, we cannot arrive at the position of universalism, but we certainly can overturn any model that justifies an infinite sentence of conscious torment in order to

---

26. Hronich, *Once Loved Always Loved*, 152.

PART 3: A PHILOSOPHICAL DEFENSE OF UNIVERSALISM

obtain NDJ. This argument is a silver bullet to any position that adopts ECT. ECT cannot obtain NDJ by nature of what ECT entails.

Suppose we adjust the argument a bit. We can keep the supposition of VC but dismiss the absurd entailments for whatever reason (maybe it was divinely revealed the argument was incorrect). What if we address the sneaky presumption that (t*) must be a stand-alone temporal moment when NDJ is obtained. The argument can be rephrased as follows. The necessary conditions that ensure the entailment of NDJ is that a WP must be subject to a sentence in hell of a *potentially* infinite length. Since NDJ is obtained when the WP is sentenced to a *potentially* infinite length, this skirts any issue of (t*) failing to correspond to an *actually* infinite number of successive temporal moments $(t_1)-(t_n)$. But this runs into an immediate problem. If (t*) corresponds to the *potential* infinite length itself, rather than a moment where the sentence ends, then when *exactly* is NDJ obtained? It seems to just kick the can down the road if the opponent argues that NDJ is obtained by the *potential* infinite length of the sentence itself. Suppose we qualify (t_1) to be the moment at which a WP enters hell. This is literally the first moment of their sentence. At (t_1), the length of the sentence is *potentially* infinite. The WP has already crossed the Rubicon. There is supposedly no turning back for God's grace, yet (t*) has already been obtained. This is again because, from the onset of (t_1), their sentence becomes of a *potentially* infinite length. So, if NDJ is obtained by the WP serving a sentence of a *potentially* infinite length, then NDJ is *immediately* obtained at (t_1). And if the acquisition of NDJ is argued as the necessary reason why they must be subject to ECT, then this counterargument fails. The entailment of this argument would be that at the first moment in which the WP enters hell, NDJ is immediately fulfilled. This is an absurd entailment not only for the infernalist but likewise for the universalist and annihilationist. This would mean that hell ceases to exist altogether because, at the moment when the WP enters hell, they immediately exit hell.

Suppose once more that we briefly adjust the argument. Suppose the infernalist claims that there is a temporal moment at some point in the range of $(t_1)-(t_n)$ where (t*) is obtained; say, (t_8). The simplest and most conclusive response would just be: Why at (t_8)? What is so special about (t_8) that (t*) is obtained at this point? Why not (t_7) or even (t_9)? In other words, this objection fails because it posits a completely arbitrary moment that NDJ is obtained in the infinitely long punishment. There can never be a non-arbitrary cut-off point for NDJ to be obtained under ECT. NDJ is forever out of reach under ECT.

After examining the arguments for the general PSH framework adopted in part by Bray, it seems clear that PSH not only fails to justify ECT but is utterly incoherent altogether. PSH fails from the start because it cannot guarantee certainty that those who are in hell will remain eternally in hell. PSH then fails because it adopts a completely non-scriptural and theologically incoherent stance that sin can be propagated eternally. PSH then ultimately fails to bring about necessary divine justice. For these and other reasons, I ask all infernalists to stop using this argument. Genuinely, it is terrible. If you want to remain an infernalist (God help you), at least adopt something more cogent like SA. Sure, as illustrated, SA has at least two absurd entailments; still, it guarantees certainty of your stance, and it is duly represented in the infernalist tradition along with a few *prima facie* proof texts in Scripture. PSH is not represented in the infernalist tradition outside of the last few hundred years, and it has very little evidence for itself in Scripture. But even if one adopts a non-Lewisian model, even if one adopts SA, the inability to procure NDJ has far-reaching entailments that stretch to every single model of ECT. Adopting SA, too, is just kicking the can further down the road. There is no escaping this argument short of renouncing the concept of ECT altogether. Let us now continue our examination of Bray's text.

He writes, "If the God of love we want to believe in is incapable of sending anyone to hell, then we have created an image of God that goes against what we find in Scripture and is false, however much we might want to believe it."[27] I am unsure how much universalist literature Bray has read, but this statement displays his sheer ignorance of the scriptural defenses of universalism. He also displays a deep ignorance of the historical accounts of universal salvation from the early Fathers as he blames this tendency to not believe in eternal hell as a tendency of the "modern man." His argument mainly focuses on a straw man that he concocts and then responds to. According to him, the hope for all to be saved relies on creating a deity that reflects our current value system. By doing this, the person who hopes for all to be saved rejects the value system of Scripture and past ages. Maybe it tells us something about his lack of care in this discussion since it was placed within three pages of an equally poor understanding of Mary's role in Catholic theology.

27. Bray, *God Is Love*, 398.

PART 3: A PHILOSOPHICAL DEFENSE OF UNIVERSALISM

In the text, he also approaches the question of whether Christians should support annihilationism or ECT.[28] Universalism is completely off the table at this point. I not only disagree with Bray that the annihilationist case cannot be made from a holistic use of Scripture, but I also disagree with his haphazard dealings with the question. He believes the primary verse in favor of annihilationism is Revelation 20:10, which reads in the NKJV, "The devil, who deceived them, was cast into the lake of fire and brimstone where the best and the false prophets are. And they will be tormented day and night forever and ever." He rightly notes that if the annihilationist uses this as a proof text, they seem to forget the part where it allegedly says they are tormented forever. He then follows this up with an analogy about life imprisonment vs. execution for a crime. Since Bray says that annihilationism mainly relies on this verse as a proof text, I must assume, and I don't like to claim these things, that he has not read much annihilationist literature as well. Annihilationists love to cite Matthew 10:28; see Chapter 8. A simple purview of a blog post on annihilationism could tell you this, much less studying the published literature. Perhaps Bray does not cite this verse because *prima facie* it offers a far better proof text for annihilationism than Revelation 20:10. I do not mean to accuse him of downplaying his opponent's position without evidence here, but I am bewildered how this was not his go-to verse to show an example of what annihilationists might say.

Towards the end of the text, while discussing the Final Judgment, he writes, "Those who have done what is right will go to eternal bliss, and those who have not will go to eternal punishment."[29] At least we can thank him for being so forward with his infernalism. A few pages later, he offers more unsound responses to what he says is the view of hell as "mythological," which some liberal Christians adopt. This is idiosyncratically often partitioned as the view of universalism. Whether or not Bray is under the impression that universalists believe hell is mythological, it may still be fruitful to explain why, from a universalist view, hell *does* and *should* exist. I shall approach this through the soul-making theodicy.

The soul-making theodicy is a widely endorsed but also widely criticized response to the problem of evil. The rudimentary problem of evil is as follows. God is wholly good; God has the power to do anything (omnipotence); Evil exists. Since God is wholly good and omnipotent,

28. Bray, *God Is Love*, 371.
29. Bray, *God Is Love*, 732.

why does he permit (or allow) evil to exist instead of preserving a perfectly good creation? (This is not meant to be a formulation of the so-called *logical* problem of evil—God's existence and the existence of evil are logically or formally or even just nomologically incompatible—rather, this is a rough formulation of the *evidential* problem of evil: The existence of evil is itself the *strongest evidence* against the proposition that a wholly good and omnipotent God exists; most philosophers today do not presume there to be logically inconsistent relationship between the propositions that God exists and evil exists, so they prefer the *evidential* problem of evil.)

The soul-making theodicy can be explained in context to the above as follows: The overarching goodness of soul-making is why God permits the existence of evil. Soul-making is the process where a person develops second-order virtues like courage, forgiveness, and perseverance. The logic goes that if evil did not exist, then these virtues could not develop because they arise only in the face of evil. Since these virtues should be valued, evil is thus permitted by God to exist; it is, then, as a consequence of this view, expected that evil exists, and such a condition where there is no evil is unexpected from this view. Hence, there is, supposedly, no difference in expectation between the actual and expected condition of the world. Under the expectation of the soul-making theodicy, evil exists in the world; and evil does exist in the world.

Much has been debated in the literature from atheists and theists on this; namely, whether it can account for *gratuitous* types of evils like starvation and genocide, which seemingly, do not balance out in the increase of second-order virtues which arise from them. And whether it can account for *gratuitous* specific events of evils, like the Stalinist purges and the Rwandan genocide, which likewise seemingly do not balance out in the increase of second-order virtues that arise from them. At the very least, the theodicy utterly fails in the context of evils that occur naturally (destruction by earthquakes and tsunamis) to non-human animals who cannot develop such second-order virtues like courage, perseverance, and so on. Putting aside these and other problems with the theodicy, I would rather employ it to justify the process of justice under a universalist eschatology. The philosopher John Hick famously argued this but certainly with non-orthodox commitments.[30] Suppose we briefly adapt this type of framework to an Orthodox universalist eschatology. It seems

---

30. Hick, *Death and Eternal Life*, 371–72.

PART 3: A PHILOSOPHICAL DEFENSE OF UNIVERSALISM

that if character/soul can be built through suffering in hell, the options are (1) for the damned or (2) for those still alive.

For (1), hell could easily serve the function of repentance, and through repentance, continued repentance of some sort, the damned shall even come to inherit the kingdom of God. This function of repentance would not solely, perhaps like in a Protestant framework, be thought of with a moral entailment. This function of repentance would ensure some sort of ontological change in the being of the damned soul. Through this process of repentance-*theosis*, the damned begin to develop second-order virtues that they would be unable to develop without undergoing some sort of post-mortem punishment. The damned may learn courage in some sort of way. The damned may learn forgiveness in some sort of way. How this is obtained is a mystery. Maybe, as the annihilationist James Spiegel remarks, the damned experience the psychological effects of the sin and suffering they caused to others while on earth.[31] This might lead them to develop forgiveness and humility. Whatever way this obtains, the soul-making theodicy seems to be a fine philosophical justification as to why there must be hell before the damned are allowed into Paradise.

For (2), the lack of knowledge by living humans regarding the nature of hell may enhance some soul-making benefits but could limit other soul-making benefits. If we could be confident that universalism is true, this would likely inspire confidence in the hearts and minds of our family and friends. If I know that no matter what my family members do in this life that causes suffering or sin to another person, they will still eventually be reunited with me, this could bring with it many benefits. This may also have positive effects in terms of uniting those sheep who left the flock to Christ. If, as it seems to be true from many I have talked to, the looming doctrine of eternal hell stifles people's desire to adopt Christianity, then we better start promoting a view of universal salvation.

Charles Darwin and Bertrand Russell are famous examples of this, but many everyday ones exist.[32] I am certainly one of these. I dramatically fell away from Christianity at the ripe age of ten after struggling

---

31. Spiegel, *Hell and Divine Goodness*, 77.

32. Darwin is known for saying that he does not wish Christianity to be true, much less think it is because of the doctrine of eternal hell. Russell went back and forth on whether a belief in eternal hell is necessary to be a Christian (or, more accurately, an Anglican Christian). However, he was clear in his belief that Christ in the gospels taught eternal hell. This alone was enough for him to reject Christianity. See Russell, *Why I Am Not a Christian*, 13.

ALL IS FAIR IN LOVE AND HELL

with some truly existential questions that no ten-year-old should be dealing with. To make a long story short, after learning that Santa Claus did not exist despite my loving parents reinforcing the belief that he did exist for my entire childhood up to that point, which is usually nothing out of the ordinary for Christian families, this sent me on a Cartesian-esque quest to question everything I believed. Naturally, the existence of God came into question. I distinctly remember asking my father whether Jesus existed one night. (Coincidently enough, Bart Ehrman released a book that same year arguing against some of his fellow atheists that Jesus did, in fact, exist. If only I was reading biblical scholarship instead of *Harry Potter*!) Despite having grown up and, let's say, "persuaded" by my parents to attend Sunday service in a "high-church" Methodist liturgical tradition, that exposure was not enough, and my questions were not satisfactorily answered by those around me. So, I hit the high road and didn't look back until nearly a decade later. I shall not disclose what precisely occurred in the experience that led me back to Christianity and to what I later realized was the true Church, as the experience of the third heaven is unspeakable. However, suffice it to say that if I had been unwilling or unable to push past the doctrine of eternal hell (something that, before becoming Christian again, I assumed was an *a priori* truth of the faith), I would not be where I am today. (I would no doubt be religious, but in a different home.) Indeed, the loss of church attendance in recent years could perhaps be reversed if only this unconscious symptom that lingers on could be done away with once and for all. The consequences of promoting a confident belief in universalism may stretch so far and wide that there could even be downstream effects on national birth rates. If I know that no matter what my child does, be they the dastardliest individual in the world, they will still inherit the kingdom of God eventually, I may be more likely to have a child and less likely to force religion onto that child. Certainly, I would like my future child to be religious, and I would always want to encourage them to adopt Christianity, but even if they die in an unfaithful state, I know that I will eventually reunite with them.[33] If more people have children, this could bring a lot of benefits

---

33. On a side note, a universalist could even make a "devil's advocate" argument against natalism on the conditional proposition of ECT being true: If ECT is true and I still have children, I would be committing an extremely evil act because I would be bringing a life into the world knowing that it statistically has a far greater chance of being sentenced to ECT than being exalted in Paradise. Childbirth under the condition of ECT being true is an extremely evil act and, in a just world, would seemingly deserve a harsh jail sentence (if not death). Now comes a tinge of epistemic intuitionism (an

PART 3: A PHILOSOPHICAL DEFENSE OF UNIVERSALISM

to the world; especially the West, where natural birth rates are declining, and we continue to see the negative consequences. These are only a few of the many positive results that could be obtained from promoting universalism.[34]

On the other hand, maintaining a confident belief in universalism could lead to a lack of moral seriousness that develops among the general populace and even Christians. As mentioned in the Introduction of this book, St Basil the Great wrote that a great number of Christians in his region were developing sympathies for universalism. Basil's biggest worry about this was not related to a perceived lack of biblical warrant. His biggest worry was that if a large portion of the population adopts universalism, then it seems the main reason for not adopting a sinful lifestyle flies out the window. What is stopping Christians from adopting a sinful lifestyle if not the looming fear of ECT? This is a question posed by many infernalists but also some who may be classified as "hopeful universalists."[35] See Chapter 16 for more on "hopeful universalism."

Now, to state the obvious, I would hope that people are not adopting Christianity out of fear. Perfect love casts out fear (1 Jn 4:18). Furthermore, if I want to get empirical for a moment, a life lived in fear of the eternal torment to come will cause downstream psychological effects. These effects not only cause unneeded suffering in the individual's life, but they also have material impacts on the way they live their life with others around them. This conclusion is reached in a notable analysis of three studies. Azim F. Shariff's and Lara B. Aknin's 2014 analysis "The Emotional Toll of Hell" came to a few conclusions that, I would argue, are practically *a priori* true.[36] When hundreds of thousands of participants (450,000 in one of

---

obviously justified epistemic framework): Since it *strongly* seems like childbirth is not an extremely evil act deserving of a harsh jail sentence and/or death, ECT is probably not true.

34. I do not mean to say that we should teach every single person the universalist message. There are many other topics privy to pastoral discourse that would be more beneficial for some souls. My main point here is that universalist sentiment should not be confined to an elite special class of theologians who are "in the know." A famous scene in all the Synoptics records that Jesus told his disciples not to tell anyone he was the Messiah because it was not the right time (Mk 8:27–30; Matt 16:20; Lk 9:18–22). Perhaps the same could be true with universalism. It is not time *yet* for everyone to know the truth about universalism. The time will come, just as it did in the former case.

35. Moltmann, *Coming of God*, 239. For Moltmann, this is a defeating blow to universalism. He does not consider any counterarguments.

36. Shariff and Aknin, "Emotional Toll of Hell." Note that they assumed the only model of hell is ECT and did not prime participants with annihilationism or universalism.

the studies) from over 150 nations were primed for belief in eternal hell, those who believed in eternal hell had higher levels of negative emotion day-to-day and lower well-being altogether when compared to those who just believed in eternal heaven. Those who believed in an eternal hell also had lower life satisfaction, corresponding to a higher likelihood of daily negative emotions and lower well-being. All three studies found similar results. Not a single one reported that participants who believe in eternal hell had an overall higher well-being, higher life satisfaction, or more of a positive day-to-day attitude. From an empirical psychological view, this seems like a terrible doctrine to promote.

Suppose these poor psychological effects can be overshadowed by a greater good. Maybe the moral seriousness outweighs the negative psychological effects of broader society. Let's say I grant this. If people are truly just disregarding morality because eternal hell is no longer thought to exist, this is indeed a sad state of the world. But why presume that eternal hell leads people to adopt a strong morality in the first place? This fear has unfortunately been an assumption since early Christianity, and even many universalists bought into this. Origen writes, "But the remarks which might be made on [universalism] are neither to be made to all, nor to be uttered on the present occasion [. . .] for the sake of those [not] plunging into any degree of wickedness, and into the flood of evils which result from sin."[37] St Maximus the Confessor's honorable silence on universalism was probably stoked by similar fears. Modern fears about this persist to this day. I argue this fear is misguided. If we look at the Middle Ages, when ECT in the West was perhaps at its most prominent support, we see a level of lust and vice that is only just now starting to be on the rise again. Sure, there were some very pious individuals, but even those individuals, as we have now come to learn, were often up to no good in private.[38]

Hence, the threat of ECT rarely leads people away from sin. G. K. Chesterton was perhaps right when he said that Christianity's outer ring of piety is just the frame for "pagan freedom."[39] The Anglican Fr Rudolph Suffield can be mentioned as well. He writes:

37. Origen, *Contra Celsum*, 9.26.

38. It is no surprise that when sexual repression is common, expressing that repression often takes forms that are frowned upon in society. Seeking out prostitutes, both male and female presenting, was not uncommon for clergy and laymen in the Middle Ages. See *Fires of Lust*, 164–87.

39. Chesterton, *Orthodoxy*, 292.

PART 3: A PHILOSOPHICAL DEFENSE OF UNIVERSALISM

> "The dogma of hell, except in the rarest cases, did no moral good. It never affected the right persons. It tortured innocent young women and virtuous boys. It appealed to the lowest motives and the lowest characters. It never, except in the rarest instances, deterred from the commission of sin. It caused infidelity to some, temptations to others, and misery without virtue to most."[40]

Suffield puts the issue of pragmatic arguments against universalism better than anyone: They rely on a false premise that the dogma of hell leads people away from sin. This is why St Paul writes in Romans 13:8 that "love is the fulfillment of the law." People are truly led away from sin by their love for God. The law of God, that is, morality, is only enacted when we have love for the God who creates the law. The law is only fulfilled when we love following God's law for the sake of following God's law. This does not come about through promulgating the doctrine of ECT.

Finally, the negative pragmatic effects of eternal hell become even worse when we consider the power of division. Over here are the soon-to-be-damned, and over there are the soon-to-be-saved. There are some Christians who genuinely adopt this sort of attitude. Everyone has heard of the Westboro Baptist Church and their psychotic tirades against gays and lesbians; they use a certain f-word for these folks. For most Christians, the grouping is probably not so distinct. The grouping is more of an unconscious division. Regardless of how extreme, this is still a refurbished us vs. them formula. And if you know anything about human history, you are aware that these types of attitudes never really pan out well for the "them" side. The Holocaust is an obvious but extreme example. Other examples that are probably more relevant to a case like this might be shootings and bomb threats on mosques and abortion clinics by Christian radicals.

These distinctions may even manifest as impediments to compassion for others. We cannot know the hearts of our neighbors in the world and whether they are truly in Christ. For this reason, we might be led to base our judgment of our neighbors on surface-level characteristics. Sexuality can be mentioned, but a more surface-level judgment would be something like tattoos or piercings. I, myself, fall into this judgment at times when I see a characteristic of my neighbor that strikes me as non-Christian or with some other sort of "them-ness." All of us must learn to resist this and the promotion of universalism may aid in this mission

40. Quoted in Allin, *Christ Triumphant*, 26.

of unraveling the us vs. them mindset. Unraveling this mindset is not kowtowing to the sins in our world, as this is a silly "liberal" position that is against our ancient faith, but it is recognizing that such a mindset does not bring over sinners to Christ. Nobody wants to hear the gospel if they are told they are hated for who they are. Sin should be repelled, and the governance it has over a person's life should be overcome, but the person themselves should not be repelled. There is no Jew or Greek in Christ (Gal 3:28). All these worldly identifications, which today often manifest as one's pride in their sexuality and gender identity, fall away at the foot of the cross. The healing blood of Christ that pours out from the spear wound caused by St Longinus replenishes and fulfills sinners more than pride in their worldly identities ever could (Jn 19).

The final argument that Bray levies against universal salvation is that it not only diminishes the death of Christ but denies its exclusivity altogether.[41] He seems to think that if God eternally guaranteed universal salvation, then this throws away the reason that Christ came to the earth to die for us. Bray buys into the Reform story of the Incarnation and atonement, where the primary reason Christ was sent was so that he could save the sins of the world from the world by sacrificing himself as God incarnate to bear them. See Chapter 3 for my retort to this. The argument would seem to be that if universalism is true, there does not seem to exist a good reason that Christ died for our sins and thus a good reason for why Christ became incarnate if our sins would be saved no matter what. This is a popular argument against universalism in Reformed circles, and even the atheist philosopher Slavoj Žižek expresses sentiment in this direction. "But are our debts [due to the death of Christ] already paid? For a Christian, of course not: If we take this statement literally, then the notion of Hell becomes meaningless."[42] I admit that under the Reformed view, universalism *does* diminish the Incarnation in a way that it does not under the Orthodox view. Having admitted the inferiority of the Reform view, I argue we can still salvage the great significance of salvation even under the preconceptions associated with this view.

Adopting a Reform view, how can we get out of this bind? We might say that the sheer *number* of people being saved does not diminish the degree of saving-ness. Think about the COVID vaccine. The vaccine is meant to be distributed to the most people possible so that they will

---

41. Bray, *God Is Love*, 525–26.
42. Žižek, *Christian Atheism*, 37.

hopefully not catch COVID. When the vaccine is distributed to more people, its efficacy and significance do not diminish depending on how many it is given to. Even if the vaccine were guaranteed to every single person on earth, this would not diminish the purpose and function of the COVID vaccine. Perhaps this can allow us to see how the significance of Christ's death, if we are universally saved, is not diminished. Salvation can be given to all people through his death on the cross and this does not change the efficacy or the significance of salvation. If anything, it magnifies it! Granted that you are a sane individual, wouldn't you want the COVID vaccine to be given to the most people possible?

We could also directly respond to the issue about how if the work of being saved is guaranteed in advance, then the Incarnation becomes irrelevant. In this case, the purpose of the Incarnation as a means of God forgiving the sins of the world has not changed. God forgives the sins of the world, and we love him for this reason. Our love of God increases by means of the Incarnation because we see him, for the first time ever, as truly one-to-one with his creation. We see him as not a transcendent Oneness that exists in some far-off realm. He is here, with us, and for us, for all eternity. Since we see God as a fellow man, we connect with him like a fellow man, but in a more exalted sense, of course. We connect with him as we connect to our earthly biological father. We connect to him as we connect to our loved ones. We speak to God like we are talking with a friend. This is what the Incarnation of Christ set out for us—a paradigm change in the relationship between man and God.

I see no reason why Bray would deny the Incarnation as involving a paradigm change, and I see no reason why it would combat the Reform view of the Incarnation. Note that I have entirely omitted any statement about cosmic deification. Moreover, believing that we love God not for his being but out of fear of some sort blatantly defies what the author of 1 John asks of us. The Incarnation brought forth a forgiveness of sins and this forgiveness of sins has brought us to love God in an even deeper way than we have before. Now, imagine if we believe that God will save everyone. Just how much more abundant could his love seemingly grow!

I believe that my responses to Bray about how universal salvation does not diminish the death of Christ are justified. Here, I want to show how even if we assume his framework for what constitutes the maximization of significance for Christ's death, then his eschatology could be diminishing the death of Christ in a way that he could never know. Suppose there exists a possible world w_2 where if you do not affirm the

Christian faith by age thirty-five, you immediately die in some way and endure ECT. Since the beginning of human history, this has been a consistent truth.[43] When every single person reaches the age of thirty-five, if they have not affirmed the Christian faith at this point, they die with no exceptions. Suppose we now grant in our world w_1 that ECT does obtain and those who do not come to Christ in this life before they die, by and large, endure this punishment. Still, the significance of Christ's death on the cross in w_2 is greater than the significance of Christ's death in w_1. In both worlds, ECT obtains, but in w_2, many more people die at a much younger age in causal connection to their lack of faith.

This hypothetical is meant to illustrate that the significance of Christ's death is only diminished under universal salvation if and only if you presuppose that ECT for the damned is the alternative. As shown, w_2 increases the significance of Christ's death on the cross compared to w_1 because it extends your earthly life. In w_1, the significance of Christ's death on the cross (assuming Bray is right) would only save you from ECT. Hence, if we accept the parameters that Bray has laid out for what would maximize the significance of Christ's death, and he believes ECT is just that, then it seems w_2 would satisfy these parameters to a greater extent than w_1 does. Therefore, Bray's position, according to his own parameters, diminishes the death of Christ in a way that an infinite number of other possible worlds would not. Moreover, Bray's parameters would indicate that w_2 seems more desirable to obtain rather than w_1 since it further maximizes the significance of Christ's death. This entailment seems plainly untenable. I don't think anyone wants to live in w_2. Sure, Bray might say that universalism is the most desired outcome, *ceteris paribus*, as many infernalists do for good-boy or good-girl points, but if he makes the argument that it diminishes the death of Christ, then this runs into a two-horned dilemma.

If universalism is the most desired outcome, but it diminishes the death of Christ, is Bray accepting that diminishing the death of Christ is the most desired outcome? Or, if universalism does not diminish the death of Christ, then why isn't Bray just a universalist? On the other hand, suppose that Bray rejects the response that universalism is, in

---

43. For those who lived before Christ, the idea would be that those who did not align themselves with the Jewish faith endured ECT. For those who lived before the beginning of Judaism, such as proto-Israelite religions, and even before that, the idea could perhaps be that those who did not live justly and with righteousness were condemned to ECT.

PART 3: A PHILOSOPHICAL DEFENSE OF UNIVERSALISM

fact, the most desired outcome *ceteris paribus*. Suppose instead he argues that w_1 with ECT is the most desired outcome because, unlike w_2, it does not diminish the length of lifespans that could be put towards evangelizing the gospel or some other holy purpose. Well, if we remember back to the hypothetical, once you accept Christ, you don't die at thirty-five. The only ones who die at this age are the ones who did not accept Christ. In that case, suppose he revises his argument that if we have shorter lifespans until we do or do not accept Christ, then this diminishes the number of chances a person has to come to God. And a world that diminishes the number of chances a person has to come to Christ is undesirable; w_2 is undesirable.

If Bray or any other infernalist argues this against the desirability of w_2, they have fallen into a trap. Indeed, the finite life of a person does extraordinarily diminish how many times a person has the chance to come to God. Good thing there are positions that overcome this! Sure, universalism is not the only position that believes in post-mortem repentance. But still, what Bray would be getting at here is broaching a universalist commitment. Why do we cut off the chances for a person to come to God at the age of seventy-five (which is roughly the average age of death in developed countries)? Thirty-five is only forty years less than seventy-five. Most humans in history have not even lived that long. What is another forty or so odd years of time to repent if you do not leap on the chance to repent in the first thirty-five years of your life? As you can see, if Bray or any infernalist argues that w_2 is not desirable because it cuts off time to repent, then the onus is on the universalist to flip this around and provide an internal critique of their framework.

Bray's *God is Love* served as a valiant resource to expand on a few common arguments while developing some original ones of my own in favor of universalism. Like Ortlund and Sproul, Bray believes that the love of God is total, inviting, and inextinguishable. At the same time, he believes that ECT is a necessary sacrifice that Christians must make, all the while maintaining a God of love. In this chapter, I have shown how these two stances are utterly in conflict, and one of them must be abandoned. I assume that none of these authors, or any Christian for that matter, wants to abandon the stance that God is loving. In that case, these authors should abandon the stance of ECT and adopt the gospel of universal salvation. All Christians, be they Orthodox, Catholic, or Protestant, should come to see the truth and beauty found in universalism. I shall close with some edifying words from Origen of Alexandria:

I want to be called a man of the church. I do not want to be called by the name of some founder of a heresy but by the name of Christ, and to bear that name which is blessed on the earth. It is my desire, in deed as in Spirit, both to be and to be called a Christian.[44]

44. Quoted in Banev, *Theophilus of Alexandria and the First Origenist Controversy*, 2.

14

Pavel Florensky's Damning Doctrine

FIRST RELEASED IN 1914, Fr Pavel Florensky's series of letters addressed to a hypothetical "brother" that became *The Pillar and Ground of Truth* form what is probably the greatest systematic work of Orthodox Christian philosophy. Quite a high praise, right? Well, it certainly deserves it. Florensky offers what many believe are very compelling arguments against *apokatastasis* in his "Gehenna" chapter. Few have addressed his arguments in much detail. This could be because he is still not very well known outside of Orthodox circles. This could also be because the book is over six hundred pages of continental philosophical prose that rhetorically, and perhaps conceptually, goes over the heads of many who solely specialize in the analytic strand of the philosophy of religion. Whatever the reason is, Florensky's arguments deserve the light of day in a universalist text like this. Don't get me wrong, I have a strong reverence for Florensky. I admire him for his spiritual and philosophical aptitude. Everything I write should be taken with this remembrance. But this reverence, as in the case of other holy men like St Augustine of Hippo, does not exempt him from critique. This chapter will examine what Florensky says about love, human freedom, and eternal damnation. For some, this is a two-premise syllogism and eternal damnation is the obvious conclusion. I hope to change that.

An Ontology of Love

Florensky writes, "Love is God's essence, His own nature, and not only His providential relationship, which is proper to Him."[1] Florensky recognizes the essence/energy distinction, so when he says that love is God's essence, he means that in the essence of God, i.e., the trinitarian inner life, there is an abundance of love eternally occurring. The Father loves the Son, and Love is the Holy Spirit itself. This love then abounds onto creation in the form of God's energies. Love is what reveals truth. Only in love is truth realized as truth. As he says, the metaphysical triad of Truth, Good, and Beauty is one principle.[2] It is a person's spiritual life seen from different points of view. Manifested truth is love, realized love is beauty, and the action of loving is good. Florensky offers what he calls an "ontologism" of love. He sets this in opposition to the modern view where love becomes a mere psychological phenomenon. In the modern understanding of love, since philosophers like Gottfried Leibniz and Baruch Spinoza, it has become more or less synonymous with desire. Some might stipulate that desire is more about immediate happiness and love is more about long-term happiness, but the presupposition of psychologism remains. Christian love, the love we have for God, the love he has for himself in the Trinity, and the love he has for us, must take back its ontological foundation. Even love that is expressed towards the neighbor, for that matter, cannot be true love if one has not learned to love God. The act of loving God is a necessity for all true forms of love. A true form of love is not merely psychological but has an ontological underpinning to its action. As we grow in the knowledge of God, our love for him increases as well. These are inseparably linked if the following is understood in a rich metaphysical sense. 1 John 2:9 reads, in the NKJV, "He who says he is in the light, and hates his brother, is in darkness until now." Light is truth. Hatred is the failure to transmit love. Darkness is ignorance. The one who fails to transmit love, even if they claim to be a beacon of God's grace, lives in ignorance of his glory. Love cannot just be for God; otherwise, it is not love. Love must extend to others in creation as well.

Florensky does not argue this, but it seems this is why Jesus in the gospels tied together the commandments to love the neighbor and God. Mark 12:30–31 in the NKJV reads, "And you shall love the Lord your God with all your heart, with all your soul, with all your mind, and with

1. Florensky, *Pillar and Ground*, 54.
2. Florensky, *Pillar and Ground*, 57.

PART 3: A PHILOSOPHICAL DEFENSE OF UNIVERSALISM

all your strength. This is the first commandment. And the second, like it, is this: You shall love your neighbor as yourself." Jesus ties these commandments together because they must go together. They are not simply listed as "do this" and "do that." They are listed as a conditional statement: "If you do not do this, you will not do that." They cannot be separated, and neither can be diminished. Some may believe it is possible to follow the first without the second or the second without the first, but they are sorely mistaken. You cannot love your God if you do not love your neighbor, and you cannot love your neighbor if you do not love God. 1 John 4:12 tells us why: Us loving each other, in turn, is loving God. The ontological understanding that Florensky has of love puts him duly opposed to any solipsistic postulation on the self. Love, in its concrete expression, involves the operation of *kenosis*, an emptying. Love requires us to go beyond the boundaries of our selfhood, the boundaries of what seems to be the "I," in order that we become another, a non-I. We dissolve the set-in-stone boundaries by emptying our love into another person and God. Love, as the psychoanalyst Jacques Lacan understands it, involves that ontological process of *kenosis* and can almost be seen as a Plotinian emanation from the One.[3] The lover is a One, emanating itself into the beloved, and the beloved is a One, emanating itself into the lover. This mutual emanation must be viewed on the ontological level when it comes to understanding love not only between people but between humanity and God as well.

However, where Lacan sees love as an emptying of nothing into nothing, this must be inverted in a dialectical fashion to mean the emptying of fullness into fullness. By this, I mean to echo G. W. F. Hegel, who described pure being as synonymous with nothingness itself. A fullness of being, if there are no further predicates to it, is synonymous with nothing itself because there are no predicates to nothing itself. Hegel writes, "Pure being should mean nothing but being in general; being, and nothing else, without further determination and filling."[4] If you try to cognize being itself without any predicates, what Hegel calls "determination and filling," you are unable to complete this task. This is why pure being and nothing are ineffable, that is, beyond the realms of thought. Instead of successfully conceptualizing pure being and/or nothing, in both cases, you derive the concept of a something. A something is a being with

---

3. Coates, *Conspiracy and the Subject*, 49–50.
4. Hegel, *Science of Logic*, 47.

properties/predicates/determination. What we should take from this exquisite ontological contribution from Hegel is that if we think of love as an emptying of nothing into nothing, what we have dialectically stated is that love is an emptying of a fullness of being into a fullness of being. Since God so loved the world, he emptied and continues to empty the fullness of his being (which is itself the fulcrum of Being) into creation. Love abounds through the cosmos.

Those very familiar with Hegel may also find interest in the schema: Universality-Particularity-Singularity. The Universality is to say that love is an emptying of nothing into nothing. This negates itself because nothing into nothing is dialectically a fullness into fullness. By self-negating the Universal into the Particular and then the Particular into itself, we have sublated the Universal and the Particular into Singularity. The Singularity is the Florenskian theory of love as it typifies this dialectic and preserves the moments of Universality and Particularity in itself.

The Issue with Libertarian Free Will (Again)

Florensky begins the "Gehenna" chapter with what I take to be the following thesis, "If human freedom is a genuine freedom of self-determination, then the forgiveness of an evil will is impossible, for this will is a creative product of this freedom."[5] There is nowhere in the text where he defines "human freedom," but it seems that his view of self-determination would constitute human freedom as more or less congruent with the libertarian model of free will (LFW) examined earlier. This is a likely interpretation, considering he then writes that if we do not recognize evil will as evil, we do not recognize freedom as genuine. Although the text is a bit unclear here, Florensky does not mean to say that there is an evil will inherent to humanity. By "evil will," he means the will that pursues sinful actions; what we have referred to in other places as a tendency of the gnomic will. The faculty of gnomic will is not evil itself, the gnomic will takes on the modicum of evil when it pursues sinful actions. For this reason, if a person does a sinful action, this is a genuine expression of that person's mental fortitude of self-determination. Florensky believes we must establish the above for the following reason: If we do not postulate human freedom as freely genuine in this way, it would seem to follow that God's love of creation is also not freely genuine. Once again,

5. Florensky, *Pillar and Ground*, 154.

PART 3: A PHILOSOPHICAL DEFENSE OF UNIVERSALISM

the textual argument is a bit unclear, but I believe the following principle is a presupposition that Florensky accepts: If love is genuine, it must be an act freely chosen. Assuming this is sound, Florensky then offers his defeating blow: If God does not have love, he does not have forgiveness.

This is in contrast to the fact that if there is divine forgiveness, there is also divine love. He concludes, "Therefore, creation has genuine freedom. If there is genuine freedom, its consequence—the possibility of evil will—is inevitable, as is, therefore, the impossibility of forgiveness." Florenky's argument so far is interesting but unconvincing. The lack of clarity in what he constitutes as "genuine freedom" really makes it difficult to approach the argument altogether. I do not mean to say that Florensky should have a fully constructed definition of freedom (I do not have this by any means), but it would be nice if he had something more substantial we could work off of. Still, in light of the presented textual evidence, it is fair to claim that Florensky operates off the LFW model. LFW postulates that a freely chosen act is an act that is deliberated and determined in light of the practical alternatives that are available. Since this is the model Florensky works with, my counterarguments from Chapter 11 apply here. To avoid taking up unnecessary space, the onus is on the reader to turn back if they wish to refresh their mind on these.

Later in the chapter, Florensky's stance on freedom is fleshed out a bit more but still lacks a clear definition. Humans are free because (1) we are epistemically conscious of ourselves and (2) because we are conscious of ourselves as the cause of our own acts.[6] A lot can be said about this, but I shall limit myself to two responses. (a) The postulation of an unconscious mind would seriously wreck the cogency of both claims. (b) There is a presupposition in both claims that we can know the nature of our own self. Consider (a). If we presume there exists an unconscious mind (that is perhaps structured like a system of signifiers that signify one another and, through their signification, produce semantical meaning) that functions without conscious recognition by the person, then both claims cannot hold.[7] The first cannot hold because the postulation of an unconscious mind entails that we are not conscious of it. The second cannot hold because the postulation of an unconscious mind entails that we are not the cause of our own acts in the sense that Florensky would

---

6. Florensky, *Pillar and Ground*, 159.

7. There is certainly a recognition of the unconscious in Paul's letters, particularly in Romans 7:15, where he decries that he does what he does not want to do; Paul does the "involuntary." See Badiou, *Saint Paul*, 79.

like us to be. Rather, unconscious influence is always part and parcel of every desire. Consider (b). Suppose we grant the existence of an immaterial self or soul, meaning that cognitive faculties cannot be reduced to the physical brain alone. I believe we must; if we do not, we cannot cogently account for continuous conscious experience over intervals of time, multiple conscious experiences being co-present at one time (thinking about moving one's arm and smelling a flower), long-term memory, and so on. Still, granting this does not entail that we know the nature of ourselves.

St Gregory of Nyssa makes an argument against this assumption.[8] If we do not know the nature of God's self and we are made in the image of God, why do we presume we know the nature of our own self? If an image is understood to be reliant on an archetype for what constitutes it as an image, we would assume that a seemingly fundamental aspect of the archetype—that we cannot know the nature of the archetype—would likewise be considered in constituting what it means for the image to be an image. St John of Damascus makes a similar point. "Every image is a revelation of knowledge concerning what lies hidden."[9] John wrote this in the context of arguing for the validity of icon veneration, but the same principle holds true in the case of human anthropology. Judith 8:14 even says that since one *cannot* find the depths [LXX: *bathos*] of a man's heart, they should not expect to comprehend the mind or purpose of God. Because of this, I am unsure as to why Florensky assumes we know the nature of ourselves. If we do not know the nature of ourselves, this renders the first claim dubious. If we do not know the nature of our actions because we don't know the nature of ourselves, the second claim is dubious because the second claim is a conditional statement and can only be true if the first is true. Both of Florensky's claims that pertain to his grounding of the libertarian doctrine are dubious and can be rejected until further justification is provided (and it isn't).[10]

To close this section, DBH offers a fascinating christological argument against LFW that we can examine. "Could Christ have freely rejected the will of the Father, or rejected the divine Good as the proper end of

---

8. Gregory, *On the Making of Man*, 150.

9. John, *In Defense of the Holy Icons*, III, XVII.

10. The German philosopher Immanuel Kant seems to make a similar case here, albeit from a quasi-deist viewpoint. He elaborates on a three-fold understanding of the self in the 1771 edition of *Critique of Pure Reason*. See Coates, *Conspiracy and the Subject*, 168–69 for a summary of this very difficult concept.

PART 3: A PHILOSOPHICAL DEFENSE OF UNIVERSALISM

his rational intentionality?"[11] Florensky and any pious Christian would immediately respond, "No!" Christ could not have rejected the Father because, in the onto-epistemic sense, he did not have the capacity to do so. If we understand the inner life of the Trinity as the Father procuring the command/will, the Son accepting it, and the Holy Spirit revealing the Son to the Father and being the command/will itself; then the Son cannot have any capacity to reject the will of the Father. On earth as it is in heaven. In the Incarnation, if Christ had the capacity to reject the will of the Father, that is, to sin, this would demonstrate a blemish on his will, and he would not be the Christ that we know and worship.

Moreover, if Christ is two natures in the one hypostasis, then he has the human will and the divine will. Both the human will and the divine will are perfect and without confusion. All the properties of what constitutes a human will are in the one person of Christ, and all the properties of what constitutes a divine will are in the one person of Christ. If we accept this, which every Chalcedonian Christology must, and we also accept that Christ did not have any capacity to reject the Father's will on earth, which also every Chalcedonian Christology must, then we have the following confusion: If only humanity has the capacity to reject God freely, and Christ does not have this capacity in his humanness, then Christ was not fully human. This is a difficult argument for proponents of LFW to escape. They do not want to deny Christ was two natures in one person without contradiction. They do not want to deny that Christ did not have the capacity to reject the Father's will on earth. However, they deny the logical conclusion of this: No human can entirely reject God. Therefore, if no human can entirely reject God, then no human deserves eternal damnation because, in light of this conclusion, they did not reject God.

Some might quibble with DBH's conclusion. Perhaps it is too haphazard in what constitutes a rejection of God. Maybe, instead, you could have degrees of rejection. Suppose the proposition: Humanness has the capacity to reject God to *n* degree. What is *n* degree? I don't think we can explain this in any non-arbitrary way. It seems that any quantification we suppose onto *n* could be questioned, resulting in us extending the quantification to a higher or lower degree. In order to remain consistent, we must say that rejection is totalizing. Humanity cannot reject God just as Christ in the Incarnation cannot reject God. The capacity does not exist

11. DBH, *That All Shall Be Saved*, 189.

in human nature. On the other hand, maybe DBH does not adequately account for the reality of sin. It seems that if humanness cannot reject God, then humanness cannot sin. Since we know that humanness can sin as we are humans and are all sinners (Rom 3:23), DBH's argument is rendered null. I would counter the latter with the fact that sin, in a sense, does not exist as a substantive being. Sin, since it is evil, exists as a privation of being and only persists as a succubus upon the Good. So, humans can sin, but sin has a limit. This is for two reasons: (1) The capacity of a person to sin has a limit. (2) What constitutes the concept of sin has a limit. Moreover, all created things have a limit in the respective potentialities available for them to actualize. We will come back to these lucrative points later in the next section.

101 Damnations

Florensky's argument for ECT relies on the postulation of a distinction in the hypostasis or personhood of an individual rational being: in-itself; for-itself. The in-itself is the postulation of a holy seed in man's nature. Following Orthodox tradition, God created humanity to be potentially immortal. Then, Adam screwed this all up, and we inherited the original sin, which is the condemnation to a finite life. Hence, humans in this life are not immortal. Although we inherited original sin and thus will all die someday, we also retain the fact that humanity was created in the image of God. Since humanity was created in the image of God, there is a holy aspect to man's fallen nature. This holy aspect is indestructible in this life and the life to come. In line with *theosis*, the growth of this holy seed through worship and participation in the body of Christ is the process of the Orthodox spiritual journey. Hence, the in-itself is the foundation to all salvation, but like a house that is left merely as a foundation, salvation will not be given for those who do not build from this foundation. The for-itself is the postulation of the worldly aspect of man's nature. The core of all sin is pride. Pride is defined as the bolstering of the self or the "I" over and against God and neighbor. Pride, in its most extreme form, is self-worship. If the worldly aspect, the fallen aspect of man's nature, is determined by pride, then the for-itself postulation is the prideful self. The for-itself seeks to bolster the "I," the individual, above and against God and neighbor. This is detrimental to salvation, and ultimately, when this becomes out of control, salvation may become entirely impossible

PART 3: A PHILOSOPHICAL DEFENSE OF UNIVERSALISM

for the person. We will return to this crucial distinction between the in-itself and for-itself in a moment.

Florensky probably believes that some individuals will reject God for eternity.[12] They cannot contemplate the possibility of God's existence without hate in their hearts. They demand that they would rather have no God in their life, even if this leads to eternal damnation. Their wish is duly granted. God does not give them annihilation, and he does not give them a moment of peace. Their existence from worldly death onwards is marked by eternally burning in the wake of their own wrath towards God. God offered forgiveness, and they rejected it and kept rejecting it.

Those who endure this eternal self-perpetuated wrath are those who have what Florensky calls an "evil character." In light of the in-itself/for-itself distinction, those with confusion between the in-itself and for-itself have an evil character. Those without confusion between the in-itself and for-itself have a good character. Since an evil character prevents a person from being saved, there is a separation between a person's character and that person themselves. Personhood itself is the totality of the in-itself and for-itself. The character of a person is determined by how they act in life. The confusion between the in-itself and for-itself thus arises when a person is overbearing with pride and bolsters their "I" over God and neighbor. The lack of confusion between the in-itself and for-itself thus arises when the person is not overbearing with pride and does not bolster their "I" over God and neighbor.

Suppose a person dies in this life with confusion between the in-itself and for-itself. They have been overly prideful and have not taken the due diligence to repent. How is the damning process, per se, undergone? The "I" splits apart, all the while remaining one "I." Think of the Trinity. The Trinity is Three-in-One. God is the Father, the Son, and the Holy Spirit, all the while remaining one God. Hence, if the person is evil, their evil will, which manifests in the for-itself, is psychologically split off from the in-itself. The for-itself, since it does not have anything that it is "for," then becomes thrust into the outer darkness of Gehenna. The for-itself, since it is psychologically disconnected from God and God is the grounding of all that objectively exists, becomes "naked subjectivity."[13] It freely exists in eternal agony because it is nothing but the empty

---

12. Florensky, *Pillar and Ground*, 155. There is some debate if this was a genuine belief of Florensky's or an attempt to appease infernalists who wholeheartedly denied that all people will eventually be saved. See Gavrilyuk, "Divine Judgement," 16.

13. Florensky, *Pillar and Ground*, 157.

assertion of the prideful "I." In the case of the in-itself, it becomes forever out of reach for the damned since they have been psychologically partitioned into the for-itself. Florensky offers an intricate argument here—synthesizing the dogma of the Trinity with eschatology—to explain the process of damnation. However, this argument has a few major flaws. Namely, the presupposition that a finite being can reject God for eternity. This was addressed in Chapter 13, so we can move on.

I ended the last section with the argument that sin has an ontological limit. Since sin has an ontological limit, the sinful person likewise has an ontological limit whereby they are unable to sin past a certain point. Florensky would concur here and add that this ontological limit is satisfied by the Final Judgment. He writes, "Sin becomes an independent act separated from the sinner and directed at itself."[14] Indeed, after the Final Judgment, sin does not exist in the personal sense. An eternally damned person who continues to reject God is not sinning in the way that a person who rejects God in this life would be sinning. But sin is not the only created thing with a limit. All created things have a limit. Since all created things have a limit, a person cannot eternally reject God. This is because an eternal rejection of God, which is not bound to a temporal end, would entail that some created things do not have a limit.

Suppose we tentatively grant Florensky's outline of freedom critiqued in the last section. The damned for-itself exists in perfect freedom to burn up in their own wrath and hatred against God. The perpetuation of their hatred and wrath, if they are free, cannot be forced by God. The perpetuation of their hatred and wrath must be a psychological act in some sort of way. To repeat Florensky, humans are free because they are epistemically conscious of themselves and of themselves doing actions. The psychological state of perpetual hatred and wrath is thus a freely willed action that the for-itself imposes upon itself. It does not seem cogent to claim that a psychological state of perpetually willing hatred and wrath upon oneself could be eternally obtained. This is because a perpetual psychological state requires the perpetual freely willed obtainment of that psychological state. Since psychological states are created things, there cannot be an eternal and perpetual psychological state of hate and wrath. Hopefully, the reader can tell that I am specific with what I classify as a created thing. If heaven is not a created thing, hell is not a

14. Florensky, *Pillar and Ground*, 161.

created thing either. Hence, I argue that the perpetual psychological state is the created thing, but I do not make any indication that hell is created.

Some might counter what I have said with the following: If all created things have a limit, then the Kingdom of God has a limit since it is a created thing. But this relies on a shotty understanding of the Kingdom. The Kingdom, as both infernalists and universalists recognize, is not some faraway land in the sky. We must interpret the immaculate descriptions of New Jerusalem in Revelation 21 as nothing more than a picturesque attempt by the author to express how alien our final destination is from the ugliness of finite life. Following the LM, the Kingdom of God is the blissful and Paradise-like experience of God for the saved. In the Orthodox iteration, this Kingdom is the deified union of the saved with God through his energies. Either way, our experience of God is not due to any created thing. The experience we have of God is due to the nature of God himself. Or for Orthodoxy, for those who like the dualist opposition, his energies. Still, either way, the cause of this experience is not anything created. Hence, we can dismiss this retort.

Let us now briefly, perhaps too briefly, combat the hypothesis from Florensky that an "evil character" prevents a person from being saved. There are two ways this argument seems plausible. First, all actions play into developing and maintaining a person's character. Second, original sin has led to infinite guilt and, thus, evil in all humans that can never be repaid. Most Orthodox Christians reject the second proposition, so Florensky's argument relies only on the first. Regardless, this argument is untenable for a number of reasons. First, there is no such thing as an infinitely evil character. A person's life is finite, and the number of actions a person takes in life is finite. Adding up all the finite actions taken from a person's life does not constitute an infinitely evil character. It would seem that if eternal hell is of an infinitely potential length of time but that a person in this hell is not infinitely evil, then that person does not deserve to endure this. Since no person has an infinitely evil character, it stands to reason that no person deserves to endure an infinitely long punishment.

Suppose we now bring in the earlier critique. If all created things have a limit, and a person's character is a created thing, it likewise has a limit. We can speak of a person as maximally virtuous or maximally vicious, but an infinitely virtuous or infinitely vicious person does not make sense. Satan, for instance, would be a maximally vicious person.

Jesus, for instance, would be a maximally virtuous person.[15] Every action that Satan (some sort of grandiose demonic entity) has committed in this Age is vicious.[16] Every action that Jesus has committed in this Age is virtuous. Their respective viciousness and virtuousness are maximized in that they are the greatest extent to which the properties of viciousness or virtuousness could be obtained. Since every human is neither as virtuous as Jesus nor as vicious as Satan, it stands to reason that every person is a mixed bag of virtuousness and viciousness. Even a person who is very vicious is not infinitely vicious, and they aren't even maximally vicious because only Satan is. And even Satan's maximal amount of viciousness is still infinitely less than the maximal amount of virtuousness that Jesus has. Hence, the appeal to a person's evil character to justify ECT does not seem justified because an infinitely evil character does not exist. A finite character can never do anything to deserve an everlasting punishment. (See also Chapter 13's response to the status argument.)

We can close this section with a few thoughts that will not be expanded upon much but should instruct further research in the universalist camp. How can a universalist, or should a universalist, even want to apply the in-itself/for-itself distinction to our approach to temporal damnation? I recognize that not much has been said in this book about what will happen to those who do not come to Christ in this life. To restate my position, I strongly believe that hell, as some sort of divine purifying restorative punishment, exists for those who are far enough away from the path of *theosis* at death. There will be "biting and gnashing of teeth," as the Scriptures say. Suffice it to say that hell will not be pleasant in any way, and everyone should seek to avoid this experience.

Florensky offers a fascinating argument as to how we can schematize the process of damnation. The argument is Orthodox to the utmost degree, as this aspect of his eschatological vision is justified by the dogma of the Trinity. Something not found in any prevalent Protestant or Catholic iterations of ECT. But his process of damnation does not, in any way, necessitate *eternal* damnation. Much to his dismay, I would assume. His language that the for-itself becomes split off and becomes

---

15. I borrow this language from Spiegel, *Hell and Divine Goodness*, 37.

16. I specify "in this Age" to be clear that I am excluding any notion of the angelic or pre-angelic age that is discussed in apocryphal literature and is supported by some early Fathers. We can only assume that this satanic entity at some temporal moment before this Age did an action that was not particularly vicious. After all, he was once an angel himself, according to much of Christian tradition.

stuck in self-relating negativity of wrath and torment is not far from an eschatological position I would accept. Likewise, his language that the in-itself remains holy and pure because it is that seed of godliness in us is something I don't have an issue with accepting either. If I were to inquire more into the nature of what will happen to those who are not immediately saved at death, I would assume some sort of splitting process occurs. How it occurs and how long it occurs are answers unknown to humans. Perhaps it is best they remain unknown.

Scripture and the Eschatological Split

In what I consider a somewhat surprising start, Florensky begins his exegetical argument for his psychological partitioning of hell by examining 1 Corinthians 3:10–15 (NKJV). This can be quoted to the extent needed to grasp the context:

> "According to the grace of God which was given to me, as a wise master builder I have laid the foundation, and another builds on it. [. . .] For no other foundation can anyone lay than that which is laid, which is Jesus Christ. Now if anyone builds on this foundation with gold [. . .] each one's work will become clear [. . .] it will be revealed by fire [. . .] and tested [. . .] If anyone's work [. . .] endures, he will receive a reward. If anyone's work is burned, he will suffer loss [. . .] but he himself will be saved, yet so as through fire."

A summary of Florensky's interpretation goes as follows. Through the awakening of our souls in virtue of the sermon of God, he has made a house for himself in us. The works of everyone, as collected in their soul, are the building materials. There is no firm foundation other than Christ, as we are told in Matthew 7. All people begin with this firm foundation, as we are all made in the image of God. So we must take care when choosing our building materials. If we build a house, i.e., a constitution of the soul made from gold and other fire-resistant materials, this house will shine in the presence of the divine image of God.[17] If we build a house made from straw and other non-fire-resistant materials, they will burn in the presence of the divine image. When the Day comes about, the material used in building the foundation of Christ will once and for all be tested. The real value of the works in life shall come to fruition. The only work

17. Florensky, *Pillar and Ground*, 164.

that will withstand the test is valuable work built on faith, hope, and love. Those who have not created a contradiction between their in-itself and for-itself shall be saved and given the reward of eternal life. Those who have created a contradiction between their in-itself and for-itself shall burn for eternity in the wake of their illusory work that was not set on fastening a building for Christ but through partaking in illusory being, i.e., sin.[18] This is because their selfhood is devoid of true work. They have fastened themselves to sin, and so now, in their separated for-itself, they spend eternity in a perishing state. A perishing state that is existentially forever experienced by the damned for-itself as an abiding "now" that never becomes the past or future.[19]

I accept the eschatological interpretation of these verses in 1 Corinthians 3, but this is not a clear connotation of the text. Some commentators, almost all Protestant, argue this text is about the scrutiny of God's work in building up various priests and leaders. But I believe Florensky is right to assume it has an eschatological overtone. Ephesians 6:13 mentions "the evil day," referencing the Final Judgment. Hebrews 3:8 mentions "the day of temptation," which Paul likewise speaks about in 1 Corinthians 1:8. First Peter 2:12 mentions "the day of visitation," and of course, there is Revelation 3:10 with "the hour of trial." I don't deny that 1 Corinthians 3:10–15 could mean something else in tandem with an eschatological connotation, but I certainly hold to the position that it has a primary eschatological overtone.

I want to center on the focus that Florensky pays to v. 15. I have not seen this exegesis anywhere else. He underscores "despite" to indicate that the subject will undergo fire, but despite this, they themselves will be saved.[20] In this sense, the whole makeup of the human will not be saved (in-itself and for-itself) only the in-itself, the God-created part of the human, is saved. The for-itself is damned, and the in-itself is saved. Scripture does seem to support in places the notion that there is a sundering after death. Take the parable of the unprofitable servant in Matthew 24. When the servant returns, the lord will give him the position he deserves along with hypocrites and "cut him in two" [*dichotomesei*]. The lord of the house, the Lord himself, will cut the human who does not bear good fruits in half. This is repeated in Luke 12:46. Florensky cites Origen, who concurs that the Luke verse involves the separation of the human into

18. Florensky, *Pillar and Ground*, 171.
19. Florensky, *Pillar and Ground*, 180.
20. Florensky, *Pillar and Ground*, 170.

PART 3: A PHILOSOPHICAL DEFENSE OF UNIVERSALISM

"he himself" and the works of the human.[21] The works, if they are bad, become like the lust described in Matthew 5:29 because they are cut off. Once again, the "cut" motion, a severing in two, appears in Scripture. In both cases, he seems to indicate, though it is not clear, that this cut is made voluntarily. The servants were unprofitable because of their own free choices, so they were cut by the lord. Christ calls us to voluntarily cut off our lust as well. Florensky does not note the following Old Testament verses, but I believe they can support his argument: Proverbs 10:31 and Psalm 129:4. The latter is especially pertinent as it indicates a "cut in two," once again, to the wicked. More could be said, but I consider Florensky's argument plausible from the grounds of Scripture.

What I don't consider plausible is that those who are saved and not in Gehenna feel no sorrow about those who are eternally burning. He writes, "[They] exist just as little [. . .] as the unknown thoughts of other people exist."[22] This is a very philosophically loaded statement as it hopes to escape what I view to be one of the numerous philosophical downfalls of ECT that has not been touched on yet: The infernalist does not take into account that people have memories of others, and if those others they have memories of are in hell, they would know this or at least have a relative credence of this fact. In turn, this would presumably decrease their enjoyment of the bliss that Paradise promises. And if there was a decrease in the bliss that Paradise promises, it should then not be considered Paradise. This weakens the idea of salvation to an extraordinarily substantial degree that slaps historical Christianity in the face.

Florensky seems to dodge the above bullet, but he still inevitably bites the bullet on what I shall call a fundamental epistemic block (FEB) for those who are saved. An epistemic block is a supposed limit on knowledge created by an entity and imposed on another entity. For those with an epistemic block, their knowledge is always limited. As such, there must be an epistemic block, created and maintained eternally by God, that prevents the saved from knowing about the torment of the damned. FEB involves a type of ignorance that differs from what we commonly call ignorance. We might say, "I was ignorant about that," while watching the news and learning about a migrant crisis at the Southern border. We might say, "I was ignorant about that," while hearing from our friend about how someone we know is getting married. The ignorance in FEB is *qualitatively* distinct. In these two examples, there is a way for us to

21. Florensky, *Pillar and Ground*, 173.
22. Florensky, *Pillar and Ground*, 176.

lose our ignorance on the subject. Regarding FEB, God has eliminated any ability for us to lose our ignorance. The saved are perpetually and unshakably ignorant of the state of the damned.

I understand why Florensky grants FEB. Like many other infernalists, he truly cares for those around him. A relevant conversation between St Silouan the Athonite and a fellow monk is worth mentioning here.

> "I remember a conversation between [Silouan] and a certain hermit, who declared with evident satisfaction, 'God will punish all atheists. They will burn in an everlasting fire.' Obviously upset, Silouan said, 'Tell me, suppose you went to Paradise and there looked down and saw somebody burning in hell-fire—would you feel happy?' The hermit said, 'It can't be helped. It would be their own fault.' Silouan answered him with a sorrowful countenance: 'Love could not bear that,' he said. "We must pray for all."[23]

Suppose we even put aside atheists and those who Florensky does not know. I can only assume that Florensky has great care for his loved ones. For him to know that some of his loved ones were not saved and are now burning in their own wrath is quite heartbreaking. Could we experience the bliss of Paradise with the knowledge that the ones we love are in eternal torment (be it in virtue of their own "free" making or not?) I would like to think we could not.[24] St Augustine of Hippo famously asked this but came up short. Eric Reitan and John Kronen propose a syllogism to illustrate this argument that we can briefly mention.[25]

1. Anyone in a state of eternal blessedness possesses both perfect bliss and universal love for all persons.

2. Anyone who possesses universal love for all persons and who is aware that some persons are eternally damned cannot possess perfect bliss.

23. Sophrony, *Saint Silouan*, 48

24. Though I doubt the critique would be made, this could be turned back around at the universalist. The universalist believes that some will be in hell. So what if their family member is experiencing a hellish torment and they are experiencing Paradise? Wouldn't this make their Paradise, not Paradise? Since the universalist does not believe hell is eternal, they have an easier time answering this. That is to say, the conceptual tools a universalist could use to respond to this solely belong to the universalist position and not the infernalist one. Such that even if this is a problem for the universalist (and I don't think it is), the universalist is still in a better position to come up with a response than the infernalist.

25. Reitan and Kronen, *God's Final Victory*, 80.

PART 3: A PHILOSOPHICAL DEFENSE OF UNIVERSALISM

3. As such, anyone who possesses universal love for all persons and who is aware that some persons are eternally damned cannot possess eternal blessedness (1,2).

4. If anyone is eternally damned, anyone who possesses eternal blessedness would be aware of this.

5. Thus, if anyone is eternally damned, then none possess eternal blessedness (3,4).

6. God, out of benevolent love for his creatures, confers blessedness *at least* on those who earnestly repent and seek communion with Him.

7. Therefore, God does not eternally damn anyone (5,6).

I am not going to provide justification for this syllogism. Reitan and Kronen do that just fine. I shall just levy another argument to support this. To review, if we are aware of the existence of those who are eternally damned, it seems that we cannot possess perfect bliss. If we are not aware of this and yet have perfect bliss, this seems to mean there is a FEB. But consider this. Suppose we grant Florensky his model of free will. If the LFW model is true, then God cannot (or rather, it would be unjust) for God to instill a FEB. This is because it would violate the saved person's autonomy. If not guarding the saved from knowledge pertaining to the existence of the damned would lead the saved to not be in a state of perfect bliss, then that assumes the saved would not regard perfect bliss as fitting if they were aware of the damned. Put otherwise, if the saved were to know of the damned, this would diminish their perfect bliss in a way that remaining in ignorance of the damned would not. In order to maintain their perfect bliss, God must impute a *false belief* onto them. To make someone accept a false belief in the way that God would be doing this is a violation of personal autonomy. This follows from the fact that if a false belief is created, this leaves open the possibility of the saved making a choice that they would not have otherwise made. If we are free by virtue of alternative choices but the knowledge of these alternative choices is diminished by God, this would entail a loss of creaturely freedom that would not exist otherwise. Therefore, since those in heaven have LFW and perfect bliss, God could not put a FEB in place, or else this would violate such LFW. Though since a FEB is that which guards the saved against the knowledge that the damned exist, this entails that the saved would know the damned exist if such a mechanism were not present.

And if the saved *must* know that the damned exist to retain their creaturely freedom, then FEB is not a tenable response. Hence, Florensky's attempt to escape this objection fails. He is forced to accept the untenable proposition that the saved will have knowledge of the damned. Under infernalism, Paradise is an illusion that is never wholly actualized. Only universalism can guarantee total and complete bliss for the saved, that is, analytically necessarily, all people.

Putting aside the untenable philosophical baggage of a FEB, there is no indication in Scripture that we will be unable to know who is damned. There is, however, some sort of indication that Paradise will provide the fullest knowledge to all. Take just two examples. First Corinthians 13:12 in the NKJV reads, "For now we see in a mirror, dimly, but then face to face. Now I am known in part, but then I shall be known just as I am known." There is little dispute in contemporary scholarship about the fact that Paul makes a Platonic reference here. A mirror indicates a fallible understanding, a faulty understanding. Being face-to-face expresses a full understanding. A fullness of knowing. Although Paul does not provide a robust theory of knowledge in this verse, he does indicate how we have incomplete knowledge now and will not have incomplete knowledge in the Age to come. In fact, St Clement of Alexandria used precisely this verse to argue in favor of *apokatastasis*.[26] Taking this into account, it does not seem we can cogently claim that there will be an eternal FEB that prevents the saved from knowing the existence of the damned and perhaps knowing who exactly is among the damned.

Let's now tackle the second part of this verse. Here, Paul is more or less restating what he has already provided through an analogy. In the present, we are known in part, and in the Age to come, we will know just as we are known. I would press into this a speculative hypothesis. If, truly, we have a fullness of knowledge, then this knowledge should correspond not only to growing adoration of God among the saved but a fullness of knowledge in regard to *all* of creation. If a fullness of knowledge in regard to all of creation is given to the saved, and we can suppose that some are eternally damned to burn in their own wrath, then those who are saved would be aware of the existence of those who are burning in their own wrath. Despite being speculative, I argue the conclusion follows from a more expansive interpretation of the verse that builds an eschatological theory of knowledge from what is alluded to in Scripture.

26. Ramelli, "Apophaticism, Mysticism," 550.

PART 3: A PHILOSOPHICAL DEFENSE OF UNIVERSALISM

Now briefly examine Luke 8:17, which reads in the NKJV, "For nothing is secret that will not be revealed, nor anything hidden that will not be known and come to light." Jesus is speaking from, I believe, two contexts here. An eschatological context and a finite context. He means to say that all the things that we hide from others and ourselves will be known by God at the end of days. Jesus also means that the disciples have the task of spreading the knowledge he gave to them. This is why, following the parable, we must never hide the light of God from others.

After examining these two verses, it is plausible to claim that Scripture indicates there will be a fullness of knowledge guaranteed to us in the hereafter. To argue in favor of a FEB does not align with what has been established philosophically and biblically.

But consider a counterargument. If we have full knowledge in heaven, wouldn't this mean we have full knowledge of God and hence know his nature? If we cannot know God's nature, even in heaven, because it is inaccessible, then we do not have full knowledge in heaven. We may have much more knowledge than we have now, but this does not constitute ever reaching full knowledge. If we could reach full knowledge, then God's essence is knowable. Since God's essence is not knowable, we do not reach full knowledge. Indeed, if I were to claim that the fullness of knowledge entails knowledge of God's nature, then this response would have found the Achilles heel of my argument.

Yet I do no such thing. In my brief mention of 1 Corinthians 13:12 above, I *explicitly* say that the fullness of knowledge is in regard to all *created* things. Hell itself is not a created thing as it is the presence of God experienced as the person's own wrath. But the experience of hell is a created thing as it is the ever-present psychological torment of wrath that the for-itself perpetuates on itself. Moreover, those entities in hell, which Florensky says are perishing but will never perish, are created things. Since the psychological torment is a created thing and the entity that is being psychologically tormented is a created thing, this entails that the saved will know of both the existence of the damned and know of the brutal experience of the damned; the saved will know about all created things. Hence, this response can be disregarded because it does not crucially distinguish between three modalities: Hell itself (uncreated). The psychological conditions of wrath the entity inflicts on itself (created). The entity experiencing the psychological conditions of wrath (created). FEB remains untenable. The infernalist is forced to accept that knowledge of the damned will exist for the saved, which necessarily weakens the promise and efficacy of salvation.

Florensky distinctly ends this chapter by being personal with the reader. Worldly passions consumed him one day in July, and he could do nothing but sleep. If he were awake, he feared he would give into the passions. After gathering strength, he eventually took to prayer. He would no longer be a chained slave to these passions. During Vespers that Saturday night, he cried "with agitation through the service."[27] This was his victory over worldly passions. Though he does not interpret it this way, his story has a universalist bend. Florensky cried in agitation after the glorious help of God had aided him in ridding himself of these passions. Why does this glorious help not aid those in hell of ridding their wrathful passions? The tears of joy and excitement that Florensky shed during Vespers are the same that all the damned will shed when the Lord grants them entrance to the blissful kingdom. Tears of joy mark an end to a way of life. A way-of-being. Where once they cried tears of sorrow in hell, the damned will no longer feel humiliated and in pain. Tears of joy will be shed once and for all. There will be no more tears (Rev 21:4). The in-itself and for-itself shall become the Hegelian in-and-for-itself: Exalted *Geist*.

We can conclude this discussion on Florensky with a few words. His chapter is one of the most often cited responses to universalism by Orthodox infernalists. I have shown why this does not need to be a stickler point for any universalist, as the arguments here, by and large, are only justified if the person has accepted the LFW model. And we know this model has many problems that make it practically untenable. What Florensky offers of great value is the concept of an eschatological split. I agree that the allusions in Scripture can justify this, and there doesn't seem to be anything in Scripture that would point us away from this conceptualization. However, what he does not realize about this split is that it by no means entails an everlasting qualifier. The everlasting qualifier can be dismissed, and the qualifier that the split will be mended can be argued. This is not something I will do in this text, but I would be interested in a future text that attempts to do this.

---

27. Florensky, *Pillar and Ground*, 188.

15

Annihilating Annihilationism

As I SAID IN Chapter 8, annihilationism is not popular in Orthodoxy. This is in comparison to its growing numbers in Protestantism and Catholicism. Still, in favor of goodwill towards my opponents, I shall respond to several philosophical arguments for annihilationism. Compared to philosophical arguments for infernalism, arguments for annihilationism are relatively hard to come by. Most engagements with annihilationism, be they positive or negative, seem to focus more on the scriptural basis of the doctrine rather than the philosophical cogency. This is unfortunate because annihilationism presents some fascinating arguments that make a case for themselves far more than philosophical arguments for infernalism do. Yet when put in context to Holy Tradition, and just simply a rational mindset that can evaluate philosophical arguments, they either fall apart entirely or, at the very least, decrease heavily in their relative credence.

In general, I think the choice to adopt annihilationism today stems from one's dissatisfaction with the incoherencies associated with infernalism. Annihilationists see the incoherence of infernalism but hasten to abandon the concept of an unalterable divine punishment altogether. This is in comparison to universalists who see precisely those same incoherencies but realize how they are not mendable; any unalterable divine punishment is against the God we know and love. Infernalists see annihilationism as an optical alternative since so many people are unaware of this position. If an unassuming secularist brings up the obtuse presuppositions associated with a belief in eternal hell, and hence why Christianity is irrational, the annihilationist can respond, "Aha! I agree with you! You see, I don't believe in eternal hell. I believe that some people will cease to exist at a certain point and thus avoid eternal torture." The secularist is probably baffled by this response, having never engaged with a belief like this, and the annihilationist can continue along their merry way. I hasten to think that a situation exactly like this has transpired before, but it certainly doesn't seem to be *that* far from what happens when an annihilationist discusses their beliefs with an unsuspecting victim of ignorance. I hope to equip those victims of ignorance, both Christian and secular, with the tools to respond.

A Limited Immortality

One of the most common philosophical arguments in favor of eschatological annihilationism (in, at least, Evangelical Protestantism) is that immortality is solely guaranteed by one's faith in Christ rather than being guaranteed to all people. The thesis of this argument strikes to the core of universalism and infernalism: Both doctrines hold that the non-saved and saved have immortal souls. Universalism believes all people will eventually be saved, so they must have an immortal soul. Infernalism believes that some people will be saved, and others will not be but will still retain their immortal soul. Annihilationism turns this common assumption on its head and claims that immortality is conditionally guaranteed. If one holds to a punitive form of annihilationism, one may argue that God destroys the soul. If one holds to a non-punitive form of annihilationism, one may argue the soul ceases to exist because the person did not accept Christ in their life. Either way, those who do not accept Christ will not be immortal and, hence, will stop existing at some point in time.[1]

In *Sickness unto Death*, Søren Kierkegaard innovates upon an ancient Socratic argument for why the soul is indestructible/immortal:

---

1. This section, "A Limited Immortality," was presented in an edited form at the Southeastern Regional Evangelical Society Conference in February 2024, held in Toccoa Falls, Georgia, under the title "Is the Soul Immortal? Annihilationism and Conditional Immortality."

PART 3: A PHILOSOPHICAL DEFENSE OF UNIVERSALISM

> "Socrates demonstrated the immortality of the soul from the fact that sickness of the soul (sin) does not consume it as sickness of the body consumes the body. Thus, the eternal in a person can be demonstrated by the fact that despair cannot consume his self, that precisely this is the torment of contradiction in despair."[2]

The original argument from the *Republic* can be formalized as follows: (1) If the natural evil of a thing cannot destroy it, the thing is indestructible/immortal; (2) The natural evil of the soul is vice and wickedness; (3) If vice and wickedness cannot destroy the soul then the soul is indestructible/immortal; (4) Vice and wickedness cannot destroy the soul. Thus, the soul is indestructible/immortal. Kierkegaard's explanation of the argument differs from the above. He "baptizes" the argument: Sin can only ruin the soul; it cannot make the soul cease to exist. This applies a Christian spin to the Socratic claim that may prove more fruitful. Indeed, the non-punitive annihilationist must contend with the above. The soul cannot cease to exist if vice and wickedness cannot destroy the soul. If the soul cannot cease to exist, then non-punitive annihilationism must be disregarded as a viable eschatology. While this may require engagement from the non-punitive annihilationist, the punitive annihilationist can ignore it altogether. It is God who destroys the soul, not the soul itself, due to deterioration over time.

However, regardless of which position one holds, Kierkegaard's argument does not have many legs to stand on and fails to justify why sin cannot destroy the soul. One can easily respond, "Why must I accept that sin cannot destroy the soul?" Before I discuss possible responses to this, another case for the immortality of the soul should be examined.

In *Hell and Divine Goodness*, the annihilationist James Spiegel mentions a contemporary argument by the universalist Mark Mcleob-Harrison and then proceeds to rebut it.[3] Mcleob-Harrison makes the case solely against a punitive annihilationist view. The argument has a few peculiarities that must be mentioned before we examine the premises. (a) He disagrees with the common assumption that God owns humans. Instead, he appeals to what he calls "structural values." These include beauty, justice, and so on. He then says that since God does not own these, humans are also not owned by God. Nobody owns humans because they exist in a communal relationship with one another and God.

---

2. Kierkegaard, *Sickness unto Death*, 20–21.
3. Spiegel, *Hell and Divine Goodness*, 82–85.

(b) He assumes LFW. This is the position that one's action is free if and only if there are alternative choices that can be reasonably made by the agent. His conclusion is that God would never destroy human beings because they are such "structural values." God's destruction of even a single human being is paramount to God's destruction of any other structural values. The premises of his so-called "Master Argument" are as follows:

P1: All other things being equal, if an event interferes with human h's freedom, the event is metaphysically bad.

P2: An event leading to the permanent cessation of human h is an event that interferes with human h's freedom.

C1: Therefore, an event leading to the permanent cessation of human h is metaphysically bad.

P3: Some metaphysically bad events would undermine the divine nature were they to occur.

P4: It is impossible for events to occur that would undermine the divine nature.

P5: The permanent cessation of human h is a metaphysically bad event that undermines the divine nature.

C2: Therefore, the permanent cessation of human h is impossible.

If sound, the argument entails that humans are immortal. Whether some are eternally being tortured or all are enjoying a blissful life is outside the scope of the argument. Spiegel has three main issues with the argument. It assumes an anti-biblical belief that God does not own humans. It assumes LFW. It assumes that the "permanent cessation of a human is a metaphysically bad event that undermines the divine nature." The first assumption is certainly not warranted. If we are truly made in the image of God, then obviously, God owns us in some sense. Sure, there is also a sense of communal relation implied in this, as in, we are not chattel slaves to God, but his ownership over us is still all-encompassing. For just one example, St Paul in Romans 9 compares humans to pots of clay being shaped by a potter. This statement is the basis of Paul's hypothesis, which he pursues in the next few chapters of Romans 9–11: Did God create some to be irredeemable vessels of wrath and others to be everlasting vessels of mercy? We see at the end of Romans 11 that the answer is no. God did not create some to remain vessels of wrath forever. He created all to eventually receive mercy (see Chapter 9). Even with this

PART 3: A PHILOSOPHICAL DEFENSE OF UNIVERSALISM

universalist interpretation that I accept, however, the idea that God owns us is not absolved. God is likened to the potter because, like the potter, he shapes and molds his creation.

The second assumption, if Spiegel is to be believed, may be an issue for those who deny LFW; I will return to this in a moment. The third assumption seems to be where Spiegel puts his stake in the ground. He says that even if we grant the reasoning about "structural values," this does not entail that these values cannot be overridden as in the case where ensuring divine justice would lead to the annihilation of wicked human beings. He goes on to say, logically, that because human wickedness is such an offense against God, the "persistence of rebellion" for all eternity would undermine the divine nature.[4] This leads him to suggest that the "persistence of rebellion" can only be stopped if the non-saved are annihilated or the non-saved are saved. He spends the rest of the chapter explaining why he believes the philosophical problems with universalism should lead us to think that the non-saved will be destroyed instead of saved. One of his major concerns is the problem of justice. I, however, have shown in several past chapters that these alleged philosophical problems are not much of a worry for the universalist; and later in this chapter, I will directly confront the claim that annihilationism can ensure divine justice. If Spiegel's main argument against Mcleob-Harrison's position relies on the follies of universalism, yet universalism seems to lack such follies, then Spiegel's argument collapses.

Leaving this aside, can Mcleob-Harrison's argument itself be saved? Perhaps it can be with some tweaks. I shall examine two here and leave the rest to the reader's discretion.[5] P1 must be changed in some way so as to exclude the entailment of LFW. Suppose we tentatively rephrase it as follows: All other things being equal, if an event interferes with human h's transcendental orientation towards the Good, the event is metaphysically bad. This employs classical free will, a term I explained in Chapter 11. By rephrasing this, the follies of LFW have been removed. P2 can now be rephrased: An event leading to the permanent cessation of human h is an

---

4. Spiegel, *Hell and Divine Goodness*, 85.
5. If I sought to explore this argument further, engaging with the concept of "structural values" would be worth pursuing. This, to me, has some very odd presuppositions baked into it that I disagree with. For one, love and beauty are Divine Names of God and thus do not seem to fit properly under the term "ownership." Two, the concept of communal relation with God, in the way that I understand it, would take us into the realm of *theosis*, which is certainly not something an Evangelical like Mcleob-Harrison sought to do.

event that interferes with a human's transcendental orientation towards the Good. The destruction of the soul removes its transcendental orientation towards the Good since the soul can no longer act. The rest of the syllogism remains valid with these changes. Also, these changes dramatically strengthen the syllogism and bring us back into familiar territory since we are dealing with patristic language rather than contemporary philosophical language, which can sometimes assume too much.[6]

Returning to Kierkegaard is fruitful here. The thesis of Kierkegaard, borrowing from Socrates, is that sin cannot destroy a soul. This argument was applied to non-punitive annihilationism and was found to require a response from the opponent. It was then applied to punitive annihilationism and found to be irrelevant to what the position argues. Paul Griffiths may give us reason to doubt the former. In a 2007 paper, he argues that since sin is the orientation towards non-being, the soul's embracement of stains will eventually lead to self-annihilation. This is why, contrary to infernalism, the wicked soul cannot endure perpetual torture. This is why, contrary to universalism, the wicked soul cannot endure eternal bliss. Griffiths uses the following passage from St Augustine to support his argument.

> "And so it [the soul] turns away from him [God] and slips and slides into what is less and less, which it imagines to be more and more. Neither itself nor anything else suffices for it as it moves away from that one [God] who alone suffices. In its destitution and difficulty, it [the soul] becomes excessively intent upon its own actions, and upon the disquieting delights it gets from them."[7]

To rephrase this with more formal language, (1) Sin is an orientation of the will against God; (2) God is the source of all being; (3) Since sin is an orientation of the will against God and God is the source of all being, a continued orientation towards sin will eventually lead to non-existence. There are several issues with this argument.

---

6. On a brief note, there is a fascinating argument made by Anselm of Canterbury that seems to entail the conclusion that all souls are immortal. If God were to destroy those who have not repented or the unrepentant simply ceased to exist for whatever reason, then the unrepentant would face the same fate as those who have never been born. Those who are most guilty and wicked would face the same state as those who have no guilt or wickedness. In such a case, there is symmetry between the state of being for the most wicked and the least wicked. Does this not preclude divine justice? Seemingly yes. See Walls and Brown, "Annihilationism," 55.

7. Quoted in Griffiths, "On Annihilationism," 426.

PART 3: A PHILOSOPHICAL DEFENSE OF UNIVERSALISM

The most obvious one is that so many historical and contemporary figures embrace the privation view of evil, but very few have been led to the conclusion of annihilationism. I do not mean to bring this up in a fallacious manner, as an argument *ad populum*; I mention this to say that it seems odd to suggest this is a logical entailment of accepting the privation view; indeed, even St Augustine, who is thought to be the first Christian to argue that evil is non-being (though this was really Origen), clearly was not an annihilationist (nor was Origen). Griffiths knows that referring to this as an Augustinian argument does not entail that Augustine would have accepted this consequence, but he does seem to think it is an entailment of the view. I am puzzled by this. Why is this an entailment of the view at all? Suppose there is a person in hell. The person remains in hell because of their continued rejection of God, which extends into the next life. They continue to sin against God and thus orient themselves towards non-being. Say I grant all this. Still, how does this eventually lead the person to stop existing? I struggle to see how an orientation towards non-being will eventually lead to the person ceasing to exist. It seems like the proper language here would rather be along the lines of Fr Pavel Florensky when he says that the damned person is in eternal destruction. The idea is not that the person is *literally* destroyed but that they are so close to being destroyed, on the brink of destruction, that their existence is constituted by an absolute monotony. Indeed, when we commonly think of sin, we tend to think of it as corrupting our capacity for goodness, love, trust, care, and perhaps even cognition. Still, sin does not lead us to non-existence in this life. It may, for instance, if a person were shooting up heroin and having unsafe promiscuous sex daily, one would expect death to befall them soon enough, whether due to an overdose or catching some sort of ferocious sexually transmitted disease, though this situation is out of the ordinary and does not correspond to the experience of many *very* sinful people who have walked this earth and died of natural causes. If sin does not necessarily lead us to non-existence in this life, why should we expect it to do anything different in the hereafter? Why should we expect it will lead us to *true* non-existence (constituted by the destruction of our soul and personhood)? This is an unjustifiable leap in logic.

The universalists John Kronen and Eric Reitan respond to Griffiths in another way. "We think the annihilationist must concede that God could design rational creatures such that they lacked the power to put their souls out of existence."[8] By my lights, this strikes to the core of his argument and, frankly, any other non-punitive annihilationist argument. If God does not destroy the soul but rather the soul destroys itself eventually, then why not just reject that this is metaphysically possible? In other words, the response to the annihilationist on this point may simply consist of denying that a soul can cease to exist if God is not the agent who destroys the soul. Hence, God may very well have created rational creatures without the ability to self-annihilate.[9]

There are several reasons to take the argument from Kronen and Reitan seriously. First, if God is the most good parent, it seems odd for God to create sons and daughters who could very well choose to cease to exist at some point. Sure, perhaps God would allow them to choose eternal torment over blissful union with him, but the possibility that they could choose to stop existing at least seems odd. Second, if God truly desires salvation for all—as 1 Timothy 2:4 says—it seems that if the non-saved cease to exist at a certain point, then God's desire for universal salvation is snuffed out. One cannot be saved if they cease to exist, but one can be saved if they continue existing. This does not entail that they will be saved, that they will accept Christ, but it does entail that this is not completely out of the question *ceteris paribus*. Third, if God created humans with free will, the self-annihilation of a soul would entail a complete loss of freedom. A complete loss of freedom seems to be far from what God intended.

These reasons are certainly debatable, but they and others lead me to believe that God probably did not create humans with the intention that some would cease to exist at a certain point. The argument from Griffiths does not provide a strong enough reason to doubt the ancient Socratic argument employed by Kierkegaard. One can be philosophically justified in contending against the argument that sin can destroy the soul because this seems to go against what God would permit to be in the capabilities of humans.

A final critique of the argument that immortality is not guaranteed can be pursued concerning what is dogmatically held in Christian traditions. This is not exactly a philosophical critique, but still relevant. *The Catechism of the Catholic Church* is probably the clearest on this point. The soul "does not perish when it separates from the body at death, and

---

8. Kronen and Reitan, "Annihilation or Salvation," 138–61.
9. See another approach to this argument in Wild, "Philosophy 1," 73–97.

PART 3: A PHILOSOPHICAL DEFENSE OF UNIVERSALISM

it will be reunited with the body at the final Resurrection."[10] This statement in the *Catechism* probably comes from the Fifth Lateran Council, which said the same. In at least Catholicism, the soul is immortal and does not "perish." For Orthodox Christians, a dogmatic statement on the eternality of the soul, to my knowledge, is not found in any decrees of the ecumenical councils, but if we take the "mind of the Fathers" as having any relevant basis for at least shaping the theological conversion on a topic, then there may indeed be reason to think Orthodoxy is against the view that immortality is not guaranteed. Take several examples of Fathers in the patristic period.

(It is worth noting that a common way the Eastern Fathers argued for the soul's immortality during this time involved them conceiving immortality as a gift. Only God is immortal in the sense that immortality is a necessary condition of God. Humans (and even angels) are only gifted with immortality.[11] Another common way they argued for the soul's immortality was by viewing "ordinary matter" as compiled with parts in comparison to the soul. Concurring with the Socratic argument from earlier, the Fathers taught the soul was simple.)

St Justin Martyr identifies the soul's immortality as one of the great truths in Greek philosophy.[12] St Clement of Alexandria explicitly uses the fact that the fires of hell correct and purge evil in the soul, rather than destroy it, as a case for why the soul is immortal. He then uses this to explore a universalist argument, but that is beyond our scope here. St John Chrysostom draws a symmetry between reason and immortality to say that just as God gave man reason, he gave man immortality. While the Eastern Fathers do not employ the philosophical language with the same exactitude that contemporary proponents for the soul's immortality harp on, it seems clear that the Fathers thought the question of the soul's immortality was not up for debate. Often, annihilationists who care about what early Fathers have to say about the soul's immortality turn towards quote-mining the writings of St Irenaeus of Lyon and St Athanasius of Alexandria. This is laughable. The former is an infernalist, and the latter is *very likely* (like I said in the Introduction) a universalist. Ignorance of the native language is very prevalent in those who argue this. Nobody who seriously studies the early Fathers concludes that they believed the soul was only conditionally immortal. This probably explains why those who

10. *Catechism of the Catholic Church*, 93.
11. Jacobs, "On Whether the Soul Is Immortal."
12. Jacobs, "On Whether the Soul Is Immortal."

argue this rarely engage with scholarship on what these Fathers thought. The early Christians who believed the soul was not necessarily immortal, and indeed there were several, as we know from Tertullian, were mostly heretics or at least were granted little respect from the Church. Certainly, there are no annihilationist saints. This is a very late view with little to no basis in the Fathers who shaped our great faith.

Justice and Annihilation

In Chapter 13, I discussed the debate between infernalism and universalism regarding necessary divine justice (NDJ). Here, I seek to revisit the topic of justice, but this time, I will do so in relation to universalist arguments against annihilationism. In comparison to infernalism, which cannot obtain NDJ by nature of its eternal length, annihilationism can obtain NDJ if we operate *solely* from the earlier argument. This is because annihilationism argues that there is a temporal moment, whether it be known or unknown is irrelevant, at which the souls of the damned will cease to exist; suppose this is t^*. This would *presumably* constitute the moment at which NDJ is obtained. If t^*, there is likewise a temporal moment after t^* when there are no damned souls in existence; suppose this is t^{**}. In that case, t^{**} is the moment at which the only souls in existence are those who are saved. This basic schema shows why we cannot simply repeat the argument against infernalism from earlier. Hence, we must pursue an original investigation as to why annihilationism does not obtain NDJ while universalism does.

I take it that an annihilationist and a universalist agree on a basic foundation when it comes to how they think NDJ is obtained: Evil and suffering must no longer exist. Annihilationism has a dramatic leg-up over infernalism for this reason. Infernalism must accept that there will forever be a torture box where sin and evil will persist, irrespective of the blissful life that other souls experience. Annihilationism is correct in arguing that this is flatly incoherent. This shared foundation entails that all beings who exist after the moment when evil and suffering cease to exist will be experiencing eternal bliss. For the universalist this has a universal scope as it applies to all beings. For the annihilationist this has a limited scope as it applies only to those beings who were not annihilated. In both cases, only beings experiencing the bliss and beauty of God's presence can exist when NDJ is obtained. This is the foundation for

PART 3: A PHILOSOPHICAL DEFENSE OF UNIVERSALISM

NDJ because justice, when thought most elementary (through Aristotle), is the basic belief of ensuring that one is given what one is due. If we tack onto "justice" that it is "necessary and divine," this qualifies that God is the one who ensures one is given what one is due.

The universalist seeks to argue that since God is love and his love is infinite, plentiful, and never-ending, God will ensure that all will eventually experience his love in the end. This is the concrete manifestation of NDJ. As a brief recap from Chapter 12, love will wait for the other to accept it. God does not need everyone to accept his love immediately, that is, during their life on this earth. God expects some will not accept his love due to their imperfection, which leads them to become caught up in worldly passions and disoriented from pursuing God above all else. However, what God expects is that all will eventually accept his love and grace, which he pours out of himself without end and without limit. God respects humans to choose this for themselves in the most basic sense, but he knows that no matter what, all will eventually choose to be united to him. There is simply no greater joy.

The most likely response of the annihilationist is to say that some beings are so beyond wicked that they must be destroyed for NDJ to be obtained. I shall briefly explore several responses.

The first issue is that this flatly contradicts the statements in Scripture that God desires all to be saved (1 Tim 1:15). I do not think this necessarily entails that all will be saved. My point is that the statement has no condition of exemption. There are no mitigating factors where God no longer desires the salvation of all people. The second issue ties into the first because we know that all beings are created in the image of God. If all beings are created in the image of God, however exactly we seek to cache out what this means, it surely does not mean that God would create some beings who he knew would be beyond salvation and must be destroyed. If so, why did he create them in the first place? Disregarding the Calvinist response that these beings "glorify" God in some way through the torture they endure in hell (since this is laughably evil), there is no reason why God would do this.

The third issue ties into both of the former ones. We all fall short of the glory of God, but presumably, at least some of us are still gifted salvation. If true, why are some people so wicked that they will not be granted salvation? We know that God has created us with a gnomic and a natural will, to use the words of St Maximus the Confessor. Our gnomic will is certainly off-balance many times with our natural will but we always retain our natural will, that orientation towards the Good. Even the most wicked retain their natural will, and thus, even the most wicked retain that transcendental orientation to the Good. Going further, why should we even think in these individualistic terms, let alone use them in arguments? The author of 1 Timothy 1:15, presumably mirroring Paul's journey to Christ, considers himself the worst sinner of all. The worst sinner of all, as he goes on to say, was precisely the one chosen by God. The Desert Fathers consistently emphasized that humility is the one thing the demons lack, and this is what will forever give us power over them. An anonymous elder said, "It is impossible to possess Jesus other than by labor, humility, and ceaseless prayer."[13] They also repeatedly instructed the pious to never compare themselves as greater or more holy than another but rather always view themselves as worse than everyone else. After experiencing a demonic attack where he could not think anything but lustful thoughts, a holy anonymous monk said, "Entertaining such thoughts, I am not good enough to be saved."[14] If we are worse than the worst sinner, why do we expect that we will be a part of God's final collection? Why do we assume that *we* will not be annihilated? Thinking in a highly prideful way like this is just food for demons. According to the Fathers, we must embrace humility as it is the greatest virtue in bringing us closer to God.

The final and biggest issue with this argument is that it completely distorts what St Paul teaches, which is the key that unlocks the rest of his musings on eschatology: God will be "all in all" (1 Cor 15:28).[15] DBH poignantly notes:

> "[Annihilationism] would never allow for the reality of God being 'all in all.' *Sub specie aeternitatis*—and God is eternal and transcendent of time, after all there would always be a fixed number of finite histories that ended in a divine absence, and so of inner rational wills where God was present only ever in a relative and partly negative degree."[16]

What he means is that under annihilationism, God may be "over all," that is, express his ultimate authority over all beings, condemning some to non-existence while others to a blissful life, but God will *never* be "all

---

13. Wortley, '*Anonymous*' *Sayings*,' 337.
14. Wortley, '*Anonymous*' *Sayings*,' 395.
15. Hence why I study this verse first in Chapter 5.
16. DBH, *That All Shall Be Saved*, 194.

PART 3: A PHILOSOPHICAL DEFENSE OF UNIVERSALISM

in all." While I agree that this adequately attacks the punitive form of annihilation, it does not address the non-punitive form of annihilation. Yet this is not much of a problem since it can easily be adapted to fit the view that the damned will self-destruct on their own. Consider the following: God can only be "over all" because only those who have chosen him will he be in. The damned will self-destruct since their soul is not immortal, so sin will eventually corrode them into non-being.

Putting this slight critique aside, the core of DBH's argument is insightful: God will never be "all in all" because there will be at least one but likely many more souls who will no longer exist. Now, if we limit God's eternality and transcendence, we could make sense of how God will be "all in all," but if we recognize his eternality and transcendence, and we must, this is simply incoherent. Even in the eschaton, there will be a group of no longer existing souls that constitute the remnant where God was never their *all*. If God is never the *all* of *all* souls, then God will never be "all in all." If God is never "all in all," then annihilationism cannot account for 1 Corinthians 15:28. This is a serious problem for the doctrine that went unmentioned in my biblical exegesis of this verse in Chapter 5.

Annihilationism thus also cannot account for the eschatological dimension of the Eucharist. The Eucharist is the always-already present invitation to believers of the redeemed universe, redeemed matter, such that all things, from ants to slugs to humans, will return to the Godhead of which they were from. The sacrament of the Eucharist displays this truth; when normal bread and wine become the body and blood of Christ, through his spiritual presence of indwelling, the believer progresses on that ontological transformation known as *theosis*. Such transformation, in this life, is a preparatory "leg-up," one can say, on those who do not receive the sacraments and partake in good works; those who will necessarily require purification in Gehenna (not to say that others won't). This is to say, then, that if God cannot be "all in all" because there will eventually be some souls that no longer exist, then the eschatological dimension of the Eucharist is a farce. The Eucharist is not a promise, a sign, that God will be "all in all." The Eucharist may still have many theological implications, such as being the reality of Christ's persistent recurring Incarnation, though even this loses significance and meaning when the eschatological dimension is stripped away. Christ's Incarnation without universalism becomes little more than a blip in history; it fails to express the cosmic interpretation that the Incarnation displays the fundamental ontological (monistic) compatibility between the Creator and the created, of grace and nature. A saying of Jesus in the *Gospel of Thomas* explains this well. "I am the All; the All came forth from me and the All has returned to me. Split the wood and I am there; lift up the stone and I am there."[17] The Incarnation has revealed that God is truly everywhere, enlightening all things. And it is by partaking in the Eucharist we see such redemption to all matter by destroying the enslavement that matter has to decay and death. Under annihilationism, the Eucharist and all the theological truths that the indwelled body and blood of Jesus Christ carry with them are largely rendered null because of the failure to procure God as "all in all."

Finally, and most philosophically relevant to the argument above (as well as to Evangelicals who don't believe in the Real Presence of Christ in the Eucharist; the Gnostics they are!), annihilationism cannot obtain NDJ because the wicked will never *truly* disappear. The logic of annihilationism goes that some entities are so evil that only when they have been rendered into a state of non-existence can NDJ be obtained. Annihilationism's goal is thus the total destruction of the wicked. However, this goal is modally impossible to reach. The wicked under annihilationism become like gum on the bottom of God's shoe that he is unable to scrape off. The remembrance of who the wicked once were in life and the connections they formed with others shall be with God forever and ever. Only universalism can cogently account for and preserve those connections that loved ones have with one another and God, all the while obtaining NDJ. God's justice can *only* manifest when all are saved.

Annihilation of Love

A problem that annihilationism indubitably struggles with is the (problem) of grief among the saved (GAS). If not all people are saved, those who are not saved will cease to exist. Disregard whether they cease to exist due to a punitive act by God or the conditional nature of their soul since the following argument applies to both positions. If a person ceases to exist, they can no longer be loved by those who once loved them. If a person ceases to exist, they can no longer love those who once loved them. Suppose there is at least one person that a saved person loves who will be annihilated. The problem arises: If even one of the loved ones of

---

17. Elliot, *Apocryphal New Testament*, 144.

PART 3: A PHILOSOPHICAL DEFENSE OF UNIVERSALISM

the saved is destroyed, how can those who are saved continue to experience perfect joy and bliss in the absence of their loved one(s)? I discussed this concerning the infernalism of Fr Pavel Florensky, but here I shall tackle it under an annihilationist context. Many arguments from Chapter 14 likewise apply and can stand to anticipate certain annihilationist rebuttals, so this section will be short.

James Spiegel provides an annihilationist response to GAS. He refers to the following argument as the "Love Web" (LW) and believes it solves several underlying problems with the traditional accounts of escaping GAS. Earlier in his chapter on the topic, he examines several responses from infernalists like William Lane Craig and rightly points out how Craig and others fail to escape the core issue with GAS. Spiegel writes:

> "All of the redeemed constitute a closed community or 'web' of love, such that everyone who loves or is loved by a redeemed person will ultimately find salvation."[18]

With a statement like this, one can only presume that all those who are members of the friends and families of a saved person will be saved along with them. However, what if someone is really evil and just happens to be a family member or friend of someone who is saved? Take someone like Jeffrey Dahmer, the serial killer and cannibal who gruesomely murdered seventeen young men between 1978 and 1991. By all measures of goodness and morality according to annihilationism, Dahmer should not be saved. But as anyone who has studied this case knows, Jeffrey's father, Lionel Dahmer, was a good man and a strong Evangelical Christian. Until the day he died, he stood by Jeffrey and sought to care for his son while he was in prison. Lionel was not some sort of psychotic who stood by the crimes themselves, rather he stood by his son since he loved him more than anything. While an annihilationist may not want to say that Lionel will, beyond the shadow of a doubt, be among the saved, he certainly embodied the gospel and lived his life seeking to imitate Jesus in his actions; Lionel's unrelenting forgiveness of his son was the pinnacle of his Christ-like imitation. Suppose, then, that Lionel is counted among the saved. One can only assume that the love he showed Jeffrey in this life will carry on to the next. If Lionel is saved and LW proves to be true, Jeffrey Dahmer, the serial killer and cannibal, will surely be saved as well.

An example like this can show how an annihilationist, although they may claim otherwise, likely does not even grant the most basic

---

18. Spiegel, *Hell and Divine Goodness*, 119.

entailments of LW. If family and friends among the saved are not necessarily saved, so much for overcoming GAS with this approach. Lionel, or any person who fits a similar story to him, would surely miss out on the joy and bliss of Paradise if his son were not to be with him. I realize this is an extreme case, and most of the saved do not have such an extraordinarily evil person they love. Still, this shows how the annihilationist who accepts the LW approach does not realize what they are signing up for.

Moving on from a basic entailment like this, LW has two underlying presuppositions that prove devastating to the argument and lead to universalism when their issues are cached out: (1) There is a meaningful and qualitatively substantial divide between a person whom someone does not love and a person whom someone loves. (2) Salvation is at least in part determined based on the will of other humans. I shall address these individually, but I find that their entailments overlap.

Spiegel addresses the first presupposition but thinks it is fair game. He writes, "The love web proponent may simply grant that even the slightest trace of Christian love would be sufficient to ensure the salvation of the spiritually beloved."[19] However, I struggle to see why this solves the problem. "Christian love," I would presume, is universal love à la Søren Kierkegaard. If Christian love is universal love, given to all people, just as God loves all people, how does the "slightest trace" of it not entail the salvation of all people? Would it not be true that all people are then "spiritually beloved?" If so, this would entail a universalist conclusion. But suppose that "Christian love" is not synonymous with a universal love that extends to all people. If the "slightest trace" of love on behalf of the saved is given to someone who is not saved, and this entails they will then become saved, this still fails to escape the problem that there is no sharp distinction between someone a person loves and someone a person does not love. Even if love is not given to every single person who has ever existed—such that Osama Bin Laden and Adolf Hitler are not included in the range of who I love—surely, I still love many people who I do not particularly "like" from day-to-day as much as I may "like" my family and friends.

For instance, I probably don't like my boss too much because he overloads me with work, yet I would still say that I love him insofar as I love him to the point where he can avoid being snuffed out of existence. The same goes with practically every other person we interact with daily.

---

19. Spiegel, *Hell and Divine Goodness*, 120.

PART 3: A PHILOSOPHICAL DEFENSE OF UNIVERSALISM

If I am walking on a busy street in New York City, it is unlikely I love every person I pass, but I probably still love the businessman who is rushing to work enough to the point where my degree of love meets the criteria for "slightest" trace of Christian love. After all, he's on the phone with his wife. Why would I want to potentially deprive her of her husband forever? Is the businessman saved due to the slightest trace of love I feel towards him? What if it turns out that he was an abusive husband and cheated on his wife many times with prostitutes? Is every person I meet in my life—and do not utterly despise and hate—saved? Presumably, the annihilationist would like to avoid accepting this conclusion.

Now, let's briefly expand this to a much broader scope. Obviously, the annihilationist accepts that more than one person will be saved. I (the hypothetical saved person) am not the harbinger of who is and is not annihilated. Think about all the people who have ever lived and constitute those among the saved in Paradise. Think about all the people they—those who are already saved—interacted with on a daily basis. Think about all those people that those who are already saved did not particularly "like" as much as their friends and family, but still loved enough insofar as they would want them to avoid being annihilated from existence. One can only presume that the number of these people being saved is extremely high. Again, take the example of the boss. Most people have a boss today and most people who have died and are now saved had some sort of authority figure that dictated their labor output. Is the annihilationist seriously going to argue that most people do not love their bosses to the degree that would save them from everlasting non-existence? Surely, our bosses are not that bad. Surely, those people the saved do not particularly "like" will still be counted among the saved due to their slight trace of love for them.

Taken to its logical extreme, this inevitably leads to a universalist conclusion. In the words of the Catholic theologian Emilio Domínguez, "What would communion with God be like if there was a human who did not participate?"[20] One thing is for certain: There would be less love. I shall leave it up to the reader to form further situations that illustrate the drastic universalist entailments of this first presupposition and hence LW as a whole.

Failing to instill a meaningful divide between those who are loved and those who are not loved leads to the second presupposition. LW

---

20. Domínguez, "Pensar Y Decir," 767. My translation.

leaves too much power in the hands of other humans to determine the economy of salvation. If true, this ensures a universalist rather than annihilationist conclusion. In Chapter 13, I explained that the view on free will I accept is what I refer to as classical free will. All people desire the Good (God), and while they may make evil decisions due to their gnomic will, their decisions still require a transcendental orientation toward the Good that underlies the schema of human action. If we assume this roughly corresponds with reality, Spiegel's presupposition surely entails universalism. If all people desire the Good and the best outcome will be the salvation of all people, then those who are saved, when the time comes for the annihilation of the damned to commence, will shield the damned from destruction due to their luscious praise of the Good.

The response from the annihilationist could be that the salvation of all people is not the best outcome. If the best outcome is not the salvation of all people and all people desire the Good, then their desire for the Good does not necessitate universalism, rather it necessitates another eschatological conclusion. It is here where instead of forming a new argument, I can just appeal to the various responses I have made to the claim that universalism is "not the best outcome." In Chapter 13, I showed how infernalism fails to ensure NDJ. In the last section of this chapter, I showed how annihilationism likewise fails to ensure NDJ. If NDJ involves ensuring that the "most good" outcome is obtained, and yet neither infernalism nor annihilationism can ensure this outcome, then universalism ensures the best outcome. The saved will shield the damned from destruction.

At the close of his discussion on LW, Spiegel points out that perhaps when 1 Corinthians 13:8 says, "love never fails," it hints at the salvific efforts that the love of the saved has on the damned.[21] Love never fails because the love of the saved can shield even those marked for annihilation. However, as I have shown, he does not accept the full entailments of LW. All are saved because love is not a touch-and-go, a strict demarcation. Love is the bountiful attitude of the Christian towards the whole world. Even those we do not "like," we often still love in the most basic sense. When the time comes, however and whenever it does, our fundamental orientation towards the Good over the vices of the world will overflow our cognition and ensure the salvation of each and every person. Lionel Dahmer's love for his son will save him from annihilation;

---

21. Spiegel, *Hell and Divine Goodness*, 123.

PART 3: A PHILOSOPHICAL DEFENSE OF UNIVERSALISM

Jeffrey Dahmer will be exalted in Paradise. LW is most certainly not a cogent escape of GAS.

A final point I want to make concerning responses to GAS is not towards any specific person but covers all attempts to escape this problem I have seen. St Gregory of Nyssa understood the whole of humanity to be ontologically connected at the base level such that it forms an image that has eternally been in the hypostasis of the Son in the Trinity. At the end of days, the material history of humanity will fill that image perfectly, which, for Gregory, seems to constitute the contours of the eschaton. All of humanity will be perfectly in this image and will be with/in the Son, eternally experiencing joy beyond their wildest imagination. The pragmatic relevance, or at least the relevance to us in this life, is that all people share a central ontological connection. While we may love and hate one another in a rudimentary finite way, for instance, I hate those who bomb buildings full of innocent civilians, as do most people; this hate is merely that, finite. This hate does not go further than a strong dislike towards the people involved and the hope that they repent for the evils they bring to the world. This hate does not rise to the level where I seek to disconnect them from the ontological *eros,* in the Platonic sense, that stands above and beyond the material relationships we have with one another. Each of us is a token of this *eros*, as Aristophanes says in the *Symposium*, and this *eros* is fundamentally broken, which leads us to search for the one who can mend the tokens together. For Aristophanes, this leads to a further diatribe about the lover and the one who is loved. For our purpose, this nicely ties into the Christian eschatological truth that Gregory taught. All of us are a token of this unbreakable bond that unites all humans—*eros*, or if you prefer the Bulgakovian term, created Sophia—and this bond is only satisfied when the infinite love that resides in all of us is allowed to abound. And we become uncreated gods, enshrined in and through the one God over all. The web of love shall involve all of creation.

A very reasonable case has been made against annihilationism in this chapter. Since the philosophical arguments are pretty weak, and I briefly showed how a specific biblical argument is pretty weak in Chapter 8, the doctrine doesn't seem to have much going for it. Perhaps the fact that there are sparse proponents of annihilationism historically and in contemporary theology is quite telling. Universalism and infernalism certainly win in the numbers game alone.

16

Shall We Only Hope?

THIS IS A SHORT chapter written at the end of the book because I don't consider hopeful universalism (HU) a serious position in Christian eschatology. HU grew to relative popularity in the twentieth century because of Catholic theologians like Hans Urs von Balthasar and Karl Rahner and Protestant theologians like Karl Barth and Jürgen Moltmann. Balthasar's following statement is a basic summary of what all these figures taught. "I would like to request that one be permitted to hope that God's redemptive work for his creation might succeed. Certainty cannot be attained, but hope can be justified."[1] Simply put, we should not be certain that all will be saved, but we can hope that all will be saved. Many later commentators were quick to point out how it is unlikely for someone to genuinely hold this position and not be a private universalist, even if they did not express it explicitly. Debates continue in the scholarship on whether these giants of twentieth-century theology were private universalists, but that is outside my scope. Whatever the case may be about the private logical implications of their positions, I argue that HU arises from a refusal to take a definite stance in either the universalist or non-universalist camp. Such a refusal is not tenable.

1. Balthasar, *Dare We Hope*, 72.

PART 3: A PHILOSOPHICAL DEFENSE OF UNIVERSALISM

A Kierkegaardian Hopeful Universalism

Søren Kierkegaard's theology is a heavily discussed topic in all Christian traditions. However, an aspect of his theology that goes unnoticed by many is his eschatology. In this brief section, I argue that Kierkegaard can be classified as a hopeful universalist. If he were alive today, he would not accept this label because, as we will see, he didn't think eschatology should be focused on by any Christian. Regardless of his feelings towards eschatology, I argue this classification is accurate and will briefly explain why.

In *Works of Love*, Kierkegaard writes, "Blessed is the one who loves—he hopes all things. Even in the final moment he hopes for the possibility of the good for the worst reprobate!"[2] By this statement alone, Kierkegaard reads like a hopeful universalist. He is not clear that God will save those who are the worst and does not make a clear statement that by praying for the worst they will be saved, but he makes a hopeful statement. A few pages later, he writes: "Yet if one hopes for something for which it is a shame to hope, regardless of whether the hope is fulfilled or not, one does not really hope. It is a misuse of the noble word 'hope' to bring it into connection with something like that, because hope relates essentially and eternally to the good—therefore one can never be put to shame by hoping." When put in context to the question of universal salvation, although by no means can we be sure he was thinking about the destiny of the damned, Kierkegaard reads like Balthasar or Barth: Hope is directed towards the Good, the will of God. We should hope that the damned will be saved, and we should not be shamed for this hope. We should hope that the glory and mercy of God will truly extend to all, and this is not a mere metaphor. Yet we cannot be sure of this, nor should we pretend to be sure of it. We are finite humans. We lack the foresight of our Lord, and to claim that we know his predestination, ordained and ratified eternally in the Trinity, is mere speculation.

In order to be charitable to Kierkegaard and represent him fairly, let us turn to a text where it seems he expresses beliefs about damnation. In *Sickness Unto Death*, he writes, "Eternity nevertheless will make it manifest that his condition was despair and will nail him to himself so that his *torment* will still be that he *cannot* rid himself of his self, and it will become obvious that he was just imagining that he had succeeded in doing so."[3] The sinful man who dies sick in sin has nailed himself

---

2. Kierkegaard, *Works of Love*, 260.
3. Kierkegaard, *Sickness unto Death*, 21. My emphasis.

to the torment that awaits him. As Friedrich Nietzsche wrote in his last journal entry before his death, "Sickness is a powerful stimulant—but one has to be healthy enough for it."[4] The man who is sick with sin has to live through the torment that awaits him. Kierkegaard's use of "nail" here seemingly indicates an eternal state of torment. A state that the man cannot rid himself of because he has willed it on himself. He indeed affirms this, "Despairing lies in man himself."[5] The despairer is in despair because they rejected themselves. Most in despair do not realize they are in despair until it is too late. What is said here leaves a sordid picture. Some commentators may say that since the pseudonyms of Kierkegaard are different, this could depict different "sides" of his thinking, some of which he does not hold to the same credence as others. While that is true, I still argue that Kierkegaard's statement on ECT is pretty clear.

He then follows this statement with the following. "Eternity is obliged to do this, because to have a self, to be a self, is the greatest concession, an infinite concession, given to man, but it is also eternity's claim upon him." Being a person with the ability to engage in free acts and thus the ability to fall into sin is both the greatest and scariest aspect of our existence. When we reject the self, we delude ourselves into thinking we are not in despair when the fact of the matter is that we are in complete despair. This is because by rejecting the self, we reject God. We might reject the self because of the anxiety we feel because of existing and not particularly reject the self because we choose to reject God. But when we do reject the self, this ends up as a rejection of God. As such, when a person is taken to hell by God, they must come to the realization that they are nailed to their selfhood. All their attempts to rid the self and their belief in the acceptance that followed this was illusory. They have made their bed in life and now must lay in it. What we find here is a proto-Lewisian view of ECT, where the defiance of the damned soul is what keeps them in hell. In this sense, damnation is caused by the person in their life. Once they are "nailed" to this condition after death, the issue is completely out of their hands.

The issue with this stance from Kierkegaard tracks back to what was outlined earlier in Chapter 11 concerning the inability to choose whether or not we follow Christ in this life. In his words, this is more or less whether we accept the self or attempt to rid ourselves of it. As a Lutheran,

---

4. Nietzsche, *Writings from the Late Notebooks*, 276.
5. Kierkegaard, *Sickness unto Death*, 16.

PART 3: A PHILOSOPHICAL DEFENSE OF UNIVERSALISM

Kierkegaard believed in *sola fide*. So, the step of faith itself, what he called the "leap of faith" in other texts, is all that is needed to be saved. Yet, since one does not choose to follow Christ in the same way that we choose to sit in a chair, this argument flounders. He even says that many in despair do not know they are in despair. In that sense, he believes those in despair tend to have a relative ignorance about their condition. Moreover, as a Christian existentialist, Kierkegaard should know that following the Word of God is not so easy as simply picking from an array of options. One does not become faithful in this way. As he duly notes, one takes a "leap of faith," a temporary suspension of reason, that then leads the person to the ultimate reason, which is God. Since taking the leap of faith is qualitatively distinct in every possible way from taking a literal leap in the air or performing another bodily action, this argument cannot be thought to hold up under scrutiny. We do not choose to follow Jesus nor do we choose to reject Jesus. To choose either one of these entirely is not possible. In fact, Kierkegaard can even aid our understanding, established earlier in Chapter 13, of why coercion is alien to God and God can never be coercive. In one of his unpublished journals, he writes, "God is not a person in the external, palpable sense a power who, face to face with me, asserts his rights." God is not an external cause of my deliberation or my will. God is part and parcel of my deliberation and will. Hence, to say that God can engage in coercion against me is to engage in a category error. God cannot coerce me because God is not a third party who approaches me externally. God is the motor of which all my will, whether gnomic or natural, flows through and in.

As far as I can tell, Kierkegaard adopts a position of HU because he believes some may not be saved because they bring damnation on themselves in life. But what about when it comes to the saved? In *Works of Love*, he writes, "Eternally and happily—yes, because only that person is saved from despair who is eternally saved from despair."[6] He does not write this in context to the question of damnation, but he expresses an eternal sense of salvation. The person saved from despair, saved from being nailed to the condition of torment, is eternally saved and in God's Kingdom. This seems plausible and is in line with the majority tradition of Christianity, so not much more needs to be said. What I want to note here at the end are some nuanced stipulations to what we have determined here.

6. Kierkegaard, *Works of Love*, 42.

There is nowhere in any texts or journals from Kierkegaard where he gives direct statements concerning his eschatological commitments. It is clear he certainly believes in hell, as seen from the statements mentioned earlier, and that some people will end up in this hell. However, it is unclear if those people will remain eternally in hell. Older Lutheran theologians before Kierkegaard were much more forceful with their views of hell, justifying them along the lines of what I have referred to in other chapters as the status argument. Kierkegaard never once makes this argument and, in fact, he rebukes older theologians for doing so.[7] Yet, he still makes a proto-Lewisian argument, as explained earlier. Since there is so much in the air regarding his eschatological commitments, we are left picking up the pieces of eschatological wisdom scattered among his many monographs and pseudonyms to declare he is a part of any eschatology. In this section, I have tried to show that Kierkegaard can be classified as a hopeful universalist. This is because he adopts positions that speak to the hope of those who will be damned, and he adopts positions that seemingly leave open the possibility of eternal torment for some.

A Depressing Antinomy... Or Not?

We can end this chapter with an antinomy related to HU, noted by the Orthodox theologian Met Kallistos Ware. Ware finds himself in the camp of HU alongside Balthasar and others, but he notes that the position itself is maintained by a fundamental antinomy:

> "If the strongest argument in favor of universal salvation is the appeal to divine love, and if the strongest argument on the opposite side is the appeal to human freedom, then we are brought back to the dilemma with which we started."[8]

The infernalist argues for human freedom. The universalist argues for God's love. The infernalist believes these can be reconciled. The universalist is starkly against the reconciliation of divine love and eternal damnation. We are at a fork in the road. Where do we go from here?

Ware doesn't think we go anywhere. We must not apply certainty in our belief that God will save all. In the words of the Catholic theologian

---

7. Kierkegaard, *Journals and Notebooks*, 551.
8. Ware, *Inner Kingdom*, 214.

PART 3: A PHILOSOPHICAL DEFENSE OF UNIVERSALISM

Juan Alfaro, it is only acceptable to have the "certainty of hope."[9] However, when we speak of hope, what do we imply by this? Hope is often synonymous with "good wishes" or "good luck" or something along those lines. Our family member gets chosen for a job interview and we hope they do well in the interview. Our friend gets chosen to compete in a contest at school and we hope they win. We might also use the phrase "hope in" or "hope that." These have a more specific referent. Suppose you are undergoing some sort of medical procedure. Your family members might say they have hope in the doctor's abilities. If I book dinner for a date, I hope she will show up on time. These latter two uses denote an object that is being taken as the referent for what we hope.

Sometimes we use "hope" to be synonymous with "wish." I wish I won the prize, or I hope I won the prize. This is often employed to be synonymous, but we can draw a relevant distinction. I can wish that an event had not happened, but I cannot hope that an event did not happen. If an event happens and I do not know the result of the event, even though it has already happened, I can hope that x outcome would have been obtained, but this is a past-oriented referent. Once I know what has been obtained in the event, I will no longer use the term "hope" in this context. *Hope is future-oriented.* We might also add that the concept of hope does not seem to apply to events that, for all intents and purposes, are impossible. For example, I can wish to teleport to Tokyo to eat lunch, but I cannot hope to teleport to Tokyo to eat lunch.

We can now turn once more to Kierkegaard, who offers some wisdom on understanding hope. "To relate oneself expectantly to the possibility of the good is to hope, which for that very reason cannot be any temporal expectancy but is an eternal hope."[10] The Good is God, and to relate ourselves to him in a way where it is expected x will obtain is hope. Kierkegaard strengthens what was said above about hope being future-oriented. We fear when we relate ourselves to what is not God. A Kierkegaard scholar comments on this. "His intent is clear: the definition is to apply only to Christian hope, since strictly speaking, there is no other hope."[11] Indeed, Kierkegaard is not dealing with the colloquial "hope" I described above. This is a divine hope, a hope we see in the Scriptures. Take Matthew 12:25, which reads in the NKJV, "In his name the nations will put their hope." The once pagan-worshiping nations will

9. Quoted in Ladria, "El Cristianismo Y La Universalidad," 363.
10. Kierkegaard, *Works of Love*, 249.
11. Bernier, *Task of Hope*, 88.

look to the Messiah, Jesus, with assurance. It does not say that they will kind of beckon and look forward to Christ. No, they will put their assurance and trust in him. This is indeed what the Greek word for hope [*elpis*] means. This term brings with it the recognition of trust in what is hoped for and looking forward to that hope becoming manifest. Hence, HU claims to be hopeful about the universalist hypothesis but does not in any way accept the concept of hope laid out in the Scriptures. If HU were to hope for all people, then HU would relate the quality of expectancy of hope to the possibility between a person and God. HU would take a clear stance on the issue of eschatology. The hopeful universalist would be a universalist.

When pressed, I believe the HU defender must accept one of three propositions: (1) It would be good for God to make universal salvation obtain *ceteris paribus*, but God *cannot* cause this for whatever reason; (2) God does not make universal salvation obtain because it would be *sacrificing* some sort of *greater good*; (3) God does make universal salvation obtain. Acceptance of (1) would entail a denial of God's omnipotence and presumably entail infernalism or annihilationism. Acceptance of (2) would also entail the position of an infernalist or annihilationist who believes that free will, justice, or some other reason is why God does not make universal salvation obtain; all problems that I responded to in this book. Acceptance of (3) would entail universalism. The HU defender has a tricky situation on their hands. Do they capitulate to the proposition of a finite God, claim that universal salvation will not be obtained under a free will or justice defense, or commit themselves to universalism? Only time will tell.

Postscript
Grace Will Abound

THIS BOOK HAS ARGUED that universalism and its theological commitments are justified when viewed from the holistic lens of Holy Tradition and philosophy. By studying the Scriptures, early Christian apocrypha, Orthodox liturgical texts, decisions from local and ecumenical councils, patristic interpretations of crucial terms and verses, and the relevant philosophical debates through the years, including but not limited to free will, God's justice, God's sovereignty, post-mortem memory, the extent of grace, and so on, the above conclusion has been confidently reached. However, one lingering thorn in the side of universalism must be addressed: God's providential will in history.

The universalist has an admittingly difficult situation on their hands. They must argue that despite the broad consensus throughout Church history (after the patristic period) on the truth of infernalism, universalism, despite being a minority position, is, in fact, the correct eschatological viewpoint. If universalism were true, would this not mean the Church has been wrong in its faithful consensus for at least a millennium? Would this not then constitute that the Church has seen the "gates of Hades?" Would this not mean that Christ's declaration in Matthew 16:18 was wrong? Did it really take over a millennium for the Church to produce "prophets" like DBH and others, those few who have seen clearly through the mist of confusion that the Church had fallen into?

On the face of it, these are very difficult bullets to bite for the universalist, though they should not be.

Jesus Christ was born almost two thousand years ago. Since we live finite lives that end, at the very most today, around one hundred years of age, this is an unthinkably long time. Indeed, it is recognized by psychologists that humans cannot comprehend such time spans coherently because of how long they are compared to how short our lives are; our temporal experience of the world greatly shapes the possibilities of our cognition of time. So, it should be no surprise that in almost all moments of Church history, one can find the fervorous belief that history is at an end. St Paul believed this for most (all?) of his life, as seen in his exhortations of the coming apocalypse in 1 Thessalonians 4 and later 1 Corinthians 7. Then there are others much later like Martin Luther, who fell into a similar belief, which for him was so extreme that he had to abandon his interpretation of Romans 9–11 that the Jews would become Christian in an episode of mass conversion; subsequently leading to his most extreme antisemitic screeds. These men should not be faulted for such a belief. It is natural to think, due to the extreme world-ending words of our Lord in the gospels—especially Matthew 24:32—that an apocalypse is surely just over the horizon. His disciples very probably thought so. However, taking a step back, what if we are still in the early days of Church history?

What if, instead of the end just being around the corner, we are still in the beginning throngs of God's providence over this Age? Because we judge history from the view of the present—such that what has "already happened" is in juxtaposition to what is "happening now"—we often are led to consider that *this* time, this present time, *must* be it. Yet this assumes that God's operation and dynamic presence in history functions according to our temporal moment. Just because the broad witness of the Church has been incorrect on eschatology for over a millennium does not mean that the broad consensus of the Church *cannot* change or *will not* change. I am sure this sounds untenable for those whose approach to Church history is like that of the nineteenth-century Catholic convert, John Henry Newman. For them, there is marked difficulty in recognizing that the Church must be allowed to freely correct and, if need be, amend her errors.

This is ahistorical and even tautological. It is, after all, only through recognizing an innovative solution to the variant uses of "Father," "Son," and "Holy Spirit" (or, perhaps sometimes, just "Spirit" as in Paul's epistles) that we have the trinitarian dogma accepted at Nicaea I. It is only through the *creative* and *speculative* and *daring* thought of figures like St Clement of Alexandria, Origen of Alexandria, St Gregory of Nyssa, and St Basil the Great, to name a few, that an official trinitarian formula made it to the steps of an ecumenical council and was then dogmatically decided upon. The trinitarian dogma accepted at Nicaea was not the "vast consensus of the Church" at the time, nor did it become so for at least a century after; and even then, there were many dissenters until the end of the Arian kingdoms around the eighth century. What if we, instead of living in the twenty-first century with two thousand years of Church history behind us, lived in the fourth century? What if we, instead of having a "vast consensus of the Church" for sixteen hundred years that the Persons in the Trinity are consubstantial and co-eternal with one another, lived at a time when this was *not* the consensus? What would we say to ourselves then?

Would we say, "Look back at the ancients like Melito of Sardis, Justin Martyr, Tatian the Syrian, Irenaeus of Lyon, Polycarp of Antioch, Ignatius of Antioch... they didn't teach this trinitarian formula that these *speculative* and *daring* theologians are teaching! My word, are we not living three hundred years after the birth of Christ? And are we not only a number of generations separated from Moses? Good heavens, would we not have figured out *by now* who God is and the relation between the Father and Jesus the Christ! Christ isn't God! And the 'Holy Spirit,' who is he? Why is he also distinct from the Father? Do you hear yourself? Are you saying that the Church has been wrong for almost three hundred years? You are contradicting the words of the great prophet Jesus in Matthew 16:18! God's providential care over the history of our Church has ensured that error cannot be accepted for long portions of time. Three hundred years? My father only lived to fifty-five and my mother to fifty-two. Three hundred is practically unthinkable!" Forgive the theatrics, but if you take the rigorist providential view of those like Newman, this probably would have resembled your view if you lived in the fourth century. The reader should be able to see the glaring flaw in this response and, thus, the ultimate flaw in the argument against universalism from God's providence in history.

Briefly take another example that is far more agreeable and even a stronger analogy—slavery. Early Fathers were split regarding the morality of forced labor. The only apostle to comment on slavery that we know of is St Paul, and he was seemingly against the institution (though it could have been in just that particular case of Onesimus). In the third century,

POSTSCRIPT

Origen was hotly opposed to it, as was St Gregory of Nyssa in the fourth century and St Augustine of Hippo in the fifth century, but then there were others like St Gregory the Theologian in the fourth century and St John Chrysostom in the fifth century who upheld the institution as just. The issue of slavery was never condemned at a single ecumenical or even local council. However, minor debates were had regarding slavery at twelve Western local councils stretching from the fourth century to the twelfth century.[1] Due to slavery's ambiguous ecclesial reception at several local councils and its contentious reception among the early Fathers, one that soon became (or already was) a Church *consensus* in support of slavery, it is in a very similar spot in terms of its ecclesial judgment to universalism. Certain iterations of universalism were definitionally condemned at several local councils in the fourth century, and then a nasty variant was condemned at Constantinople II in 553. However, there has not been a single uniform denunciation of universalism at any ecumenical council. A similar thing is true about slavery. Some councils, such as the Council of Gangra in 341, upheld slavery and declared that priests who teach slaves to despise their masters under the pretext of religion are anathematized. The Council of Aix-La-Chapelle in 816, went so far as to justify the institution of slavery by using the doctrine of original sin, such that the punishment of servitude was bestowed upon the human race as a consequence of Adam's sin. On the other hand, others, like the Council of Narbonne in 589, declared that every person, whether slave or free, is prohibited from working on Sunday because it is the Lord's Day.

Like universalism then, there has never been a uniform denunciation of slavery at any ecumenical or local council. There have just been denunciations about the minutia positions surrounding the acceptance of the institution of slavery. (This can be analogized to the denunciations at Constantinople II of doctrines like "the kingdom will come to an end" in Anathema 12. This is a minutia external position to the belief that all will be saved.) Indeed, there is still no official dogmatic statement from the Church denouncing slavery as an institution, but it is accepted today by Orthodox Christians and Christians in practically every communion that slavery is *definitionally* unjust. This uniform opinion, however, is, at most, only two centuries old. From the position of the Christian who argues that it would be very unlikely for the Church to have remained, for more than a millennium, in complete error regarding the eschatology

---

1. Roper, "Views of the Early Church on Slavery."

of universalism, to be consistent, the same position would have to follow when it comes to the moral evil of slavery: The Church could not have been wrong for over a millennium about slavery. This is surely untenable; therefore, the argument against universalism from God's providential will in history should again be disregarded.

The history of the Church has just begun for both those in the first century, the fourth century, and even those in the twenty-first century. Let us stay hopeful that, like when it came to trinitarian dogma and (later informally) the institution of slavery, our Lord, through his providence in history, will correct the eschatological errors of earlier generations. The Church will *never* see the gates of Hades. When the end of days eventually comes, we will transcend to God and enter into an ever-becoming state of glory as his *logoi* fills all creation. The cherubim will no longer guard Eden since all will be brought into it. We will become uncreated, as all beings will know each other and know God just as they are known by God. The dim mirror that we know each other and God through will be whisked away (1 Cor 13:12); like all symptoms of fallenness, this too cannot subsist in the pneumatical life. *Apokatastasis* is the only conclusion to *theosis*. Grace will abound.

Appendix

A Few Thoughts on Ibn Taymiyya and Islamic Universalism

I IMAGINE THAT MOST Christians are not aware of the historical debates in Islamic eschatology over universalism. Most Christians would even be surprised to learn that Islam has a universalist tradition. Many Muslims today would be surprised as well. The orthodox literalist interpretation of the Qur'an has long overshadowed the universalist message.[1] The literalist approach to the Qur'an is held to be the most honest to the text by most Islamic scholars today. Yet while most Christian universalists today disagree with a literalist reading of the Bible, Islamic universalists have historically leaned into a literalist reading of the Qur'an. They need not, as some in the Sufi tradition outright reject literalism, but the more orthodox universalists, that is, before a group of elite Muslim scholars decided that universalism is now against the consensus of tradition, often argued that a literal reading of the Qur'an teaches universalism. This takes us to our man of the hour, Ibn Taymiyya.

Taymiyya was a thirteenth-century Muslim theologian still regarded today as one of the greatest voices in Muslim history. Taymiyya agreed wholeheartedly with a literalist hermeneutic of the Qur'an. Following scholars before him, he rightly saw that there was no consensus

---

1. English translations of the Qur'an follow the Quran.com. I don't read Arabic, so I cannot judge the translation quality of this resource.

APPENDIX

[*ijima*] in Salaf (the first three generations of Islam) regarding universalism. He reasoned that the question was left open to public debate and the sovereign knowledge of Allah. While he was right that there was not a consensus in Salaf, if going by the dominant Sunni standards of his time (which are no longer relevant to Muslims today), this was irrelevant. Thirteenth-century Sunni orthodoxy did not base consensus solely in terms of what was considered to be so in Salaf, rather consensus involved all generations of scholars up to the current one.[2] At the very least, this would make Taymiyya's approach heterodox, though not outright heretical. Yet this did not deter him as it would many others. Since there was not a consensus in Salaf, the Qur'an seems to teach universalism, and there are weighty philosophical reasons to be in favor of it, he felt justified in propagating the view that all people will be saved and brought into Paradise once some undergo temporary torment in hell; see passages like 14:16; 25:14; 69:30–31 for descriptions of the brutal punishments undergone in hell.[3]

Most admiration paid to Taymiyya in the now-dominant Salafi school—which views Taymiyya like how Christian Neo-Thomists view Thomas Aquinas—would be severely undercut if those scholars took the time to seriously contend with the universalist arguments raised by Taymiyya. He was, for all intents and purposes, a proto-Salafi theologian. The moral rigidity of his theology, his somewhat heterodox utilitarian ethics, and his unapologetic jihadist attitude to those of other faiths are hard to rival today, even by some of the more extremist Salafis. While his very early writings portray an infernalist eschatology, as he grew older, he began to see the validity of universalism. He saw the flaw in his earlier arguments, many of which were ironically recycled without recourse to his own response to them by infernalist Muslim theologians soon after his time. We might say that his eschatological development is the inverse of St Augustine of Hippo, who went from professing universalism to teaching one of the most consequentially abhorrent eschatologies of the early Church. And the adoption of universalism did not lessen the moral rigorousness of Taymiyya's theology in the slightest. As discussed

---

2. Hoover, "Islamic Universalism," 181–201.

3. Mircea Eliade was clearly mistaken when he said that Islam was more concerned with describing the state of the blessed than the state of the damned when compared to Christianity. See Eliade, *History of Religious Ideas*, 67–68. The Qur'anic descriptions of post-mortem punishments are graphic and specific. Such a tradition was absent in early Christianity and only developed through apocryphal texts.

A FEW THOUGHTS ON IBN TAYMIYYA AND ISLAMIC UNIVERSALISM

in Chapter 12, it is a pervasive misunderstanding to think universalism is synonymous with moral and theological tolerance. While many universalists otherwise have liberal positions, this is not necessarily due to universalism but likely a host of other proclivities they hold dear to their heart. Universalists can be just as theologically, morally, and socially rigorous as the most heinous Calvinist who believes that double-predestination is enshrined in the fabric of reality. They need not be, but they can very well be. I hope most are closer to the former. Origen of Alexandria and St Gregory of Nyssa—both opponents to slavery and the subordination of women—surely were.

In this appendix, I study three similarities in argumentation that Taymiyya's Islamic Qur'anic universalist arguments have to the Christian biblical universalist arguments seen earlier in this book. The attempted rebuttals to Taymiyya, the many there are, are irrelevant to my purpose and only deserve a brief mention. Many of his scriptural arguments stand the test of time, and the philosophical rebuttals given are implicitly answered in this book. Christians and Muslims both come from a broadly Aristotelian and Platonist standpoint, some closer to one side than the other; still, the philosophical contentions against universalism are almost 1:1; excluding some more niche Orthodox critiques that center on the Person vs. Nature distinction, but I responded to these and others in Chapter 14. After studying Taymiyya's arguments, I provide further information by examining several universalist traditions that date back to some of the earliest years of Islamic scholarship. This leads me to conclude that Islam certainly has a universalist undercurrent that, like Christianity, stretches back to the earliest years of the respective faiths. I hope this exercise is informative to Christians and Muslims alike.

In Chapter 1, I explained how the Divine Names of God from St Dionysius the Areopagite involve titles like "the Good," "Love," "Beauty," and "Truth." These are not attributes or parts of God, but rather the closest linguistic articulation available that allow us to speak of his being as we experience him in creation. As I asked in Chapter 12 and answered in Chapter 13, if God is Love, why would a loving God allow those who are images of him to be subject to eternal damnation? Why were they created in the first place? Is the rest of creation merely a contextual boundary for those who are saved? The answer is that a loving God would not do this. A loving God would take every possible step so that we, of our own free will, come to repentance and salvation. Taymiyya takes a similar line of reasoning by referencing the Ninety-Nine Names of Allah as understood

APPENDIX

in Islamic tradition, partly through the Qur'an and several well-reported hadiths, which will be discussed later.[4] If Allah is the Most Merciful, the Most Good, the Most Loving, and the Most Forgiving, would Allah truly subject creation, those whom he freed from the shackles of non-being, to eternal damnation? Taymiyya sees it to be unquestionable that Allah would not do this if he were truly who Muslims claim him to be. However, this argument was not without naysayers. Several years after he put it forward, Al-Subki, a great theologian in his own right, responded that there are other Names in the Ninety-Nine that Taymiyya has forgotten, which seems to at least muddy the waters of his analysis.[5] Is Allah not also the Compeller? Indeed, I am sure he would say, Allah is both the Subduer and Compeller, but this does not in any way necessitate a wrath that condemns some to eternal damnation. At first, some will be subdued and compelled into hell, but eventually, all will be delivered into Paradise. After all, Allah is called *Ar-Raḥīm* (Most Merciful) in practically every chapter of the Qur'an and only called the Compeller six times.[6] This is perhaps the only adequate way to balance all the consequences stemming from Allah's Names.

In Chapter 9, I explained that the adjective *aiōnios* often means "in the Age to come," and divine punishment in the New Testament (NT) is never once put in connection to the adjective *aïdios* or any other determinative term for eternal or everlasting. After investigating several other verses, I concluded that nowhere in the NT is divine punishment said to be eternal. Taymiyya makes a parallel to this when he invokes Qur'an 78:21–23. "Indeed, Hell is lying in ambush as a home for the transgressors, where they will remain for ages." A universalist would be quick to point out that "ages" seems very similar to the Greek singular noun *aiōn*, what we saw as age, which then in an adjectival form can become *aiōnios*, as in "in the Age to come." The Arabic here is likewise fascinating. The term *aḥqāb* (age) denotes finitude, and thus, according to him, there will only be a durational period of punishment for unbelievers or infidels. Since the Qur'an is the Word of God, according to Islam, that was dictated precisely by Allah, impervious to human editors who would seek to corrupt the holy book (unlike the Gospel and the Torah), it would surely not make much sense for him to employ a term for finitude when describing damnation if indeed Allah did not intend on damnation to

4. Taymiyyah, "Response."
5. Khalil, "Is Hell Truly Everlasting?," 171.
6. Aijaz, "Unreality of Traditional Islamic Theism's Views," 17.

be only durational. If Allah sought to emphasize the eternality of hell, would he not, as he is the Most Knowledgeable and Most Wise, employ a term that more properly means infinity in context to the duration of hell? As Taymiyya admits, there are several uses of *khālidīna* and *abadan* (2:95; 43:77; 72:23), which properly do mean "forever" and can mean "eternality" in Arabic. For him, however, these do not refer to the eternal length of hell but that insofar as hell exists, however long that may be, it is inescapable for those who are trapped there.[7]

However, the term is likewise used to modify the temporal length of Paradise (98:8). Is Paradise also purely durational? No, the point is not that these terms denote duration qua duration, that is, finitude, rather they refer to a perpetual state of being that is inescapable insofar as it exists. Since Paradise will exist forever, as other verses clearly indicate (13:35; 41:8; 68:3), Paradise is eternally inescapable for those already in it. But hell is not eternally inescapable. Hell is escapable only once hell has ceased to exist. Insofar as hell exists, hell is inescapable.[8] It is left up to the Mercy of Allah, as we will see further down, to determine when hell will cease to exist so Paradise can be that which permeates all creation. Even the unbelievers like the "People of the Book" (Christians and Jews) and pagans will be brought into it.

In Chapter 9, I explained that the invocation of *aiōnios* punishment and *aiōnios* life in Matthew 25:46 does not imply eternality in this context. This led me to conclude that while life in the Age to come will be eternal, the duration of the punishment in the Age to come will not be eternal, but it will occur in the Age to come, as denoted by *aiōnios*. Tayimyya references Qur'an 11:106–8, which shows a similar parallel. "As for those bound to misery, they will be in the Fire, where they will be sighing and gasping, they remain as long as the heavens and the earth will endure, except if your Lord wills otherwise. Surely your Lord does what He intends. And for those destined to joy, they will be in Paradise, staying there as long as the heavens and earth will endure, except if your Lord wills—a gift without end." The discussion earlier leads nicely into the verse above. For Taymiyya, it teaches that the damned will remain in hell forever, that is, at least if Allah does not "will otherwise."[9] Another thirteenth-century Muslim theologian, Ibn 'Arabi, who may have been a universalist himself, but the evidence is unclear, also highlighted the

7. Taymiyyah, "Response."
8. Hoover, "Muslim Argument," 163.
9. Taymiyyah, "Response."

APPENDIX

importance of the statement that Allah could very well "will otherwise."[10] Some infernalists may not see a statement like this as a big deal for someone to grant. After all, if Allah is all-powerful, then of course he could "will otherwise." The infernalist would just counter that he would not for any number of reasons I have discussed in this book. Yet Taymiyya is not engaging in semantics here. He does not just mean that Allah has the power to do this in a purely ontological modal framework, but that Allah will do this because he is the Most Merciful, Most Good, Most Forgiving, and so on.

This view was very controversial since it put Taymiyya squarely in opposition to the dominant pervasive Ash'ari theology of his time. Classical Ash'arism roughly taught that one should not employ reason to explain Allah's actions. The simple explanation is that Allah will do what he will, and humans should not question or make predictions about his actions. Although he expressed goodwill toward contemporary Ash'ari theologians at various points in life, he maintained a philosophical optimism that upset many of them. Taymiyya was not about to sit by and watch his fellow Muslims teach that Allah would perform actions that he saw as against the nature of Allah. He proudly taught that Allah created all things to be good and wise and that the evils that exist are not created on purpose but persist only in relation to the good in the world. This privation view of evil—which in Christianity stemmed from Origen of Alexandria and was popularized by St Augustine of Hippo—did not catch on as easily in Islam as it did in Christianity. Over time, it found its footing, but by the thirteenth century, it was still looked at wearily by the theological orthodoxy.

Later in life, the question of eternal punishment was also a major underlying concern in Taymiyya's writings against Ash'arism. His Ash'ari opponents could not provide a coherent answer for why Allah created some humans to experience eternal hell, and he seized this opportunity to argue the reason why Allah would permit the existence of a temporary hell but not the former.[11] His central philosophical argument was an adaptation of the Soul-Making Theodicy from St Irenaeus of Lyon, briefly discussed in Chapter 13. Even Taymiyya's fellow Hanbali Athari theologians, who followed a literalist hermeneutic and were not afraid of reasoning about Allah's will, held strong to a belief in eternal hell. Thus,

10. Khalil, *Islam and the Fate of Others*, 63.
11. Hoover, *Ibn Taymiyya*, 146–47.

A FEW THOUGHTS ON IBN TAYMIYYA AND ISLAMIC UNIVERSALISM

Taymiyya's eschatology stood out against his Ash'ari opponents and the background of Hanbali Athari orthodoxy—the latter, whom he certainly dealt with more sympathetically but maintained strong disagreements with on this issue.

Now we can return to Qur'an 11:106-8. There is not a single NT text which comes close to the meaning expressed here. The Qur'an pays much more attention to the motif of divine sovereignty, which, while a common polemical motif in the OT, is not as prevalent in the NT. From a historian's perspective, this polemical attitude towards sovereignty in the OT and the Qur'an was needed because pagan beliefs were widespread in the respective regions and periods in which these texts were compiled. Once Yahwism became the dominant cult in the Levant region, OT scribes sought to magnify the sovereignty of YHWH over all the other gods and lords of the surrounding nations. The Qur'an was likewise compiled in a region where Believers constantly interacted with various pagan cults.[12] This is to say, then, that in the Qur'an, there was a pragmatic imperative in bolstering Allah's sovereignty to the extreme point of him having the "final say" on who is saved and who is not saved. This invocation of extreme sovereignty on behalf of Allah would rebut any belief that intermediary deities could issue salvation unbeknownst to Allah; hence, the attitude of disgust that orthodox Sunnis have toward the veneration of saints in Christianity, and a little closer to home, Sufism.

The image in Quran 11:106-8 may have its message emboldened by verses like 7:156, where Allah says, "My mercy is extended to all things." There is not a single verse in the Qur'an where Allah's wrath is said to extend to all things. The wrath is always focused on a particular person or group. Such wrath is never universal. As the verse continues, Allah says that his mercy will especially be directed at those who believe in him.[13] For a universalist like Taymiyya, I hesitate to think the second part of the verse would eliminate the clarity of the first part. His literalism would

---

12. For more on how early faithful Muslims saw themselves in cohabitation with loyal monotheistic Christians and Jews, but against pagans, see the scholarly staple Donner, *Mohammad and the Believers*. For how apocalyptic expectations were a major influence in the growth of Islam out of Arabic Christian-Jewish communities, see Shoemaker, *Apocalypse of Empire*, 116-46.

13. A well-known hadith from Bukhari records that Mohammad said that all children are born in such a natural state that they want to worship Allah alone. Since Islam does not have a doctrine like Augustinian original sin (because Adam repented; Qur'an 7:23), perhaps this hadith and Qur'an 7:156 can be brought together to argue against the idea of infant damnation.

not permit it. Like many Christian universalists, he could just as well say that those in the Age to come will indeed be given "clear" confirmation of Allah's existence, mercy, and love, due to the belief that all desire Allah as their end or *telos*; the realization of their *fiṭrah*. Following Taymiyya's earlier analysis, before the person has clear confirmation, they must persist in that state of hell until Allah decides to banish the hellish state of being altogether. Once the hellish state has altogether ceased to exist, it is necessarily true that all people will already have desired to be brought into Paradise and thus recognize Allah as their *telos*. This is the line of argumentation that the most loyal student of Taymiyya, Ibn al-Qayyim, took when arguing for universalism in his early-middle period.[14]

Christian universalists follow very similar reasoning, and nothing in the Qur'an contradicts what is said here. Many statements indicate the existence of a tortuous afterlife for unbelievers and sinners, just as there are in the NT. However, there are no statements that indicate this is definitionally irrevocable. Can a Muslim be a universalist, then? Of course, this isn't for me to say, but I think those who are Muslim universalists can feel comfortable in their position. Still, however, I argue the scriptural case in favor of infernalism is stronger in Islam than it is in Christianity. This is *not* to say that the Qur'an entails an infernalist eschatology, which I don't think is true, but it is to say that the case to be made in favor of infernalism is *stronger* for Muslims than it is for Christians.

The central reason for why I believe this is that in the Qur'an, the Arabic word for "forever" (or "never" if preceded by a negation), *abadan*, is used to modify "hell" and "Paradise" multiple times. While Taymiyya's argument examined earlier is scripturally and logically coherent—that Allah, because he is the Most Merciful, will choose to save all people in the end, and the Qur'an teaches Allah will elect the People of the Fire into salvation eventually—even in a universalist framework, an Islamic eschatology must accept that infidels (non-Muslims)[15] will *remain* in the Fire until the very end. Even Taymiyya believed that only in the end is anybody in the Fire—who was not already a Muslim in life—saved from the Fire. This acceptance strikes against what an Orthodox, and practically

14. Hoover, "Islamic Universalism;" "Muslim Argument," 165–67.

15. This does not mean all those who were historically non-Muslims before the time of Mohammad. The Qur'an in 5:69 and several other places teaches that all the great prophets of the Hebrew Bible (plus or minus a few), Jesus, and his disciples were Muslims. They worshipped Allah, who is the one and only God. Thus, the idea is that all those who were truly Muslims before or after Mohammad delivered the final revelation of Allah can be saved from the Fire before the end of the Age.

A FEW THOUGHTS ON IBN TAYMIYYA AND ISLAMIC UNIVERSALISM

every other Christian universalist, believes to be true. Christian universalism teaches that those in hell can be released from the shackles of damnation. This is shown by Christ's victory over Hades, which, as argued in Chapter 7, is an ongoing promise that the damned can and do exit hell. Islamic universalism does not have such a mechanism. It does not accept the promise that all *kinds* of damned souls—sinful Christians, atheists, Jews, pagans—can exit hell before the end of the Age. From a Christian universalist's perspective, there is thus an extremely detrimental, and need I say, tragic, flaw at the core of Islamic universalism.

To make a broad statement about the history of universalism in Islam, I have to say that as my research became more centered around this topic, I noticed how the historical development of Islamic eschatology parallels the eventual denouncement of universalism that occurred in Christianity. Christian eschatology began, high and mighty, with the writings of St Paul, who I have shown in Chapter 5 to be a universalist for most of, if not all, his life. As time passed, the Good News began to lose ground in debates over what was considered Christian orthodoxy. By the sixth century, universalists learned that they had to hide their beliefs or face ridicule in the public eye. Many chose to maintain an honorable silence, famously St Maximus the Confessor, but there were some even after who stuck true to Paul's universalist sentiment, such as St John Dalyatha and St Isaac the Syrian.[16]

Islam saw a similar pattern. The teachings of universalism undoubtedly stretch back to some of Mohammad's closest companions and perhaps, if certain hadith traditions are believed, Mohammad himself. The particular Bukhari hadith that comes to mind is quoted in full by Taymiyya. "After they [disbelievers] have crossed the sirat they will be confined at a bridge between the Garden and the Fire. Then when they have been cleaned and purified they can enter the Garden."[17] This eschatological imagery is similar to what we saw earlier in Revelation 21. In Chapter 9, I discussed the eschatology of Revelation. I concluded that a universalist need not avoid the text since it very well could—if an eschatological lens is valid—teach universalism, or at the very least, leave open the universalist conclusion. In Revelation 21, there is a Garden, and there are those outside the Garden—the nations—who were cast into the lake of fire.

---

16. St Isaac the Syrian was revered by several Syrian Muslim universalists as somewhat of a sage in Christian thought. Syrian non-universalist Muslims were also very familiar with him. See Zaleski, "Universal Salvation," 89–92.

17. Taymiyyah, "Response."

This, however, is only for a temporary period. As we read in 21:26, in the NKJV, "The nations shall walk in its light, and the kings of the earth bring their glory and honor into it." The next verse says that the gates to the Garden will never be shut since there is no night in the Garden. Since the gates are never shut, all those in the lake of fire are not necessarily doomed forever. The Bukhari hadith's imagery seems to bring a similar message. There is the Garden and the Fire with a bridge that separates the two of them. Yet once those in the Fire are cleansed—which uses roughly the same language as Revelation 22:2—the "People of the Fire" are admitted into the Garden. And as we know from several Qur'anic verses studied earlier, once one is admitted into the Garden, they remain there forever. Paradise does not end.

Many could dismiss this without much thought if it were merely a one-off hadith. Yet at least two more hadiths are relevant, both from Sahih al-Bukhari's collection. Al-Bukhari is universally seen as the greatest hadith scholar in the history of Sunni Islam. While not all the hadiths in his collection are considered to have a strong transmission, many are. There is no reason to think this one does not have a strong transmission since it is included in the main collection of Bukhari hadiths. Hence, the fact that there are at least two hadiths in Bukhari that *prima facie* lend evidence to the universalist hypothesis is certainly worth mentioning. *Bukhari 3194* reads, "When Allah completed the creation, He wrote in His book which is with Him on His Throne, 'My Mercy overpowers My Anger.'"[18] Earlier, we examined Qur'an 7:156, which says Allah's mercy extends to everything. When read in tandem with *3194*, one can argue that it applies even to eschatological concerns regarding eternal hell. The universalist can then stipulate that while Allah's anger will be directed towards those in the Fire for an extended period, since his mercy always overcomes anger, his mercy and love will prevail. (Again, because Allah is said to be the Most Merciful in almost every chapter of the Qur'an.) Fire will not exist forever. While I do not consider this evidence to directly support universalism, it surely leads to a universalist conclusion.

A more likely contender for a universalist hadith is *Bukhari 6571*:

> "The Prophet said, "I know the person who will be the last to come out of the Fire, and the last to enter Paradise. He will be a man who will come out of the Fire crawling, and Allah will say to him, 'Go and enter Paradise.' He will go to it, but he will

---

18. "Sahih Al-Bukhari 3194—Beginning of Creation."

imagine that it has been filled, and then he will return and say, 'O Lord, I have found it full.' Allah will say, 'Go and enter Paradise, and you will have what equals the world and ten times as much.'"[19]

This is much more detailed than 3194 and is explicitly an eschatological statement. The hadith clearly discusses what will occur for the "last" person to exit the Fire, who is the "last" person to enter Paradise. It is clear that the person has been in the Fire for a very long time, as denoted by the "crawling" performed by the man. Tortured for centuries but not forever.

However, the problem with 6571 is that it does not specify who the "last" man is. All classical Sunni creeds of faith specify that at least one damned group will be saved from the Fire.[20] Sometimes, it is the salvation of sinful Muslims, but other times, it is even the salvation of all monotheists. Taking this into account still does not clarify the possible referent of 6571. Is the last man a sinful Muslim? Is the last man a disbelieving monotheist? Could the last man even be a pagan? The reader is left with these three questions that do not have a definitive answer, and the answer could very well drastically shape the likelihood that this hadith is universalist. While I would like to think the "last" man is quite literally the last person in hell, a *prima facie* reading would surely indicate this, I cannot say for sure, nor do most who comment on this. Since the referent of this hadith's "last man" is notoriously debated (while the authenticity is not) and all sides often rely on not much more than circumstantial evidence, it would be irresponsible to claim this is in direct favor of universalism. It very well may be, and as we have seen, there is reason to believe this, but I am unsure; at the very least, I would bet that it indicates the salvation of all disbelieving monotheists. We Christians will be fine!

There are also at least two companion reports that seem to teach universalism. In Islam, although they are not scholars in the modern sense of the word, the companions of Mohammad are seen as among the most respected scholars for matters of faith and morals. They were the ones who knew Mohammad the Prophet as a person and conversed with him on these matters. The companion ʿUmar al-Khaṭṭāb—revered in Sunni Islam for being the second greatest companion behind Abu Bakr—taught that even if the People of the Fire stay there for many years,

19. "Sahih Al-Bukhari 6571—To Make the Heart Tender."
20. Hamza, "Temporary Hellfire," 371–73.

there will eventually be a day when they will come out. Umar is one of the closest sources to Mohammad, and it is extremely telling that he was a universalist. As Muslim universalists have repeated for centuries, if Umar was a universalist and one of the closest companions of Mohammad, it is very unlikely that Mohammad did not at least share similar sympathies. The report above should lead us to think he did.

Yet some argue the transmission history is shaky, and the report may even be a forgery. Assuming for the sake of the argument that the science of hadith authenticity is valid (which can certainly be debated), I consider this pretty unlikely for two reasons: (1) Umar was a very strict and harsh teacher on matters of faith and was not one to say certain statements just to make others happy or to sound nice. It is unlikely that a late forger would attribute this sentiment to Umar if he did not believe it. It would be more likely for the sentiment to be falsely attributed to someone like Abu Bakr, who was more known for statements that appealed to the emotions of others and their personal sensitivities. (2) This is widely attributed to Umar and agreed upon by many voices throughout the history of Islam. While this is not decisive evidence favoring its authenticity, a fabricated report over time tends to lose its precedence in Islamic scholarship. This has been seen time and time again. Adding to the fact that almost all of these same scholars disagree with universalism yet uphold the authenticity of this report, it is unlikely if it truly were a fabrication that, scholars would not harp on this to further discredit the heterodox belief in universalism. These reasons lead me to conclude that the report is authentic.

The companion ʿAbdullah Ibn Masʿūd—who is seen as the second greatest interpreter of the Qurʾan ever—also taught that there will be a day in hell where nobody will remain in it after they have dwelt there for "ages" [aḥqāb]. Here, we find the use of "ages" by a companion of Mohammad to denote finitude in the Age to come. This should heavily raise the credence that Qurʾan 78:21–23 likewise points to a durational period of punishment for the People of the Fire, not an everlasting punishment in the coming Age. Not only is this a companion of Mohammad using "ages" to denote finitude in an eschatological context, but this is the second greatest interpreter of the Qurʾan to have ever lived. This also points further in the direction that Mohammad himself was a universalist.

While there are only two companions who were undoubtedly universalists, it is worth noting that there was not a single companion who reportedly taught the belief in eternal hell. Early Muslim groups were

A FEW THOUGHTS ON IBN TAYMIYYA AND ISLAMIC UNIVERSALISM

aware of these universalist seedlings. *The Sunnah*, a holy book that compiles many of the practical ways to worship as taught by Mohammad and passed down the generations, already indicates that sinful Believers will not face eternal damnation. There is no mention of the fate of unbelievers. Still, this shows that very early Muslims were already thinking about eschatology; and in enough depth to note how there will be different interim fates for sinful Believers and Believers who died without sin on their hearts before both are brought to Paradise. By the time 'Abd al-Razzaq was compiling his *Mussanf* around the late eighth century, the question of who would exit the Fire was being contested and had been contested by various proto-Sunni and other Muslim groups.[21] The thirteenth century was the high point of Islamic Universalism, but this high point coincided with the last gasp of the doctrine. As the pressure of orthodoxy grew, the view became less and less popular among the pious. If the hadiths and companion reports convey accurate attestation, however, many no longer extant universalist writings probably stem from the earliest years of Islam. Many early accounts could have been lost to the tumultuous tide of history—Minerva. An owl that, à la Hegel, only takes flight at dusk.

There is still much to study and debate regarding the early history of Islamic universalism. I hope this brief appendix has contributed in some way to that debate and that it has shown the similarities between Christian and Muslim proponents of universalism. This is not to spark some sort of illusionary "Abrahamic" unity between the faiths—the dogmas associated with the Trinity and Christology are foundational and irreplaceable—but it is to examine how Christians and Muslims reasoned in very similar ways about controversial eschatological claims that often share similarities in their respective holy books. What this can tell us is beyond what I am willing to offer here. All I can say is that if St Nikolai Velimirovich is an authoritative voice (see Chapter 4), then perhaps as universalists, we should feel comfortable adding St Ibn Taymiyya to a list of saintly figures outside the Church.

---

21. Hamza, "Temporary Hellfire," 381–82.

Bibliography

Aijaz, Imran. "The Unreality of Traditional Islamic Theism's Views on Belief, Providence, and Eschatology: A Rejoinder to Tabur." *Religious Studies* (2024) 1–21.

Alfeyev, Hilarion. *Christ the Conqueror of Hell: The Descent into Hades from an Orthodox Perspective*. Crestwood: St. Vladimir's, 2009.

———. *The History and Canonical Structure of the Orthodox Church*. St. Vladimir's, 2011.

———. "The Reception of the Ecumenical Councils in the Early Church." *St. Vladimir's Theological Quarterly* 47 (2003) 413–30.

Allin, Thomas. *Christ Triumphant*. Wipf and Stock, 2015.

Allison, Dale. *The Resurrection of Jesus: Apologetics, Criticism, History*. Bloomsbury, 2021.

Anastasius. "The Letter of Anastasius, Bishop of the Church of Rome to John Bishop of Jerusalem Concerning the Character of Rufinus." https://catholiclibrary.org/library/view?docId=Fathers EN/npnf.000073.LifeAndWorksOfRufinusWithJeromes ApologyAgainstRuf.TheLetterofAnastasiusBishopoftheChurchofRometo JohnBishopofJerusalemConcerningtheCharacterofRufinus.html&chunk.id=00000003.

Arendt, Hannah. *Between Past and Future: Six Exercises in Political Thought*. Translated by Jerome Kohn. New York: Penguin, 2006.

Armstrong, Karl Leslie. *Dating Acts in its Jewish and Greco-Roman Contexts*. Bloomsbury, 2021.

Artman, David. "Bible." *Grace Saves All: The Necessity of Christian Universalism*. Wipf and Stock, 2020.

———. "Hell." *Grace Saves All: The Necessity of Christian Universalism*. Wipf and Stock, 2020.

———. "Mystery and Free Will." *Grace Saves All: The Necessity of Christian Universalism*. Wipf and Stock, 2020.

BIBLIOGRAPHY

Athanasopoulos, Constantinos, and Christoph Schneider. *Divine Essence and Divine Energies: Ecumenical Reflections on the Presence of God in Eastern Orthodoxy.* Cambridge: James Clarke, 2013.

Augustine. *The City of God. Books XVII-XXII.* Translated by Daniel J. Honan and Gerald Walsh. Washington, DC: Catholic University of America Press, 2008.

Badiou, Alain. *Saint Paul: The Foundation of Universalism.* Translated by Ray Brassier. Stanford University Press, 2003.

Baghos, Mario. "The Conflicting Portrayals of Origen in the Byzantine Tradition." *Phronema* 30 (2015) 69–104.

Baker, Sharon L. *Razing Hell.* Louisville: John Knox, 2010.

Ball, Phillip. "Agency," In *How Life Works: A User's Guide to the New Biology.* University of Chicago Press, 2023.

Balthasar, Hans Urs. *Dare We Hope 'That All Men Be Saved?'* San Francisco: Ignatius, 2014.

Banev, Krastu. *Theophilus of Alexandria and the First Origenist Controversy: Rhetoric and Power.* New York: Oxford University Press, 2015.

Barkay, Gabriel. "The Riches of Ketef Hinnom: Jerusalem Tomb Yields Biblical Text Four Centuries Older than Dead Sea Scrolls." *Biblical Archeology Review* (2009) 26.

Bauckham, Richard. "Monotheism and Christology in the Gospel of John." In *Contours of Christology in the New Testament,* edited by Richard N. Longenecker, 148–69. Grand Rapids: Eerdmans, 2005.

Behr, John. "Introduction." In *On First Principles.* Translated by Fr John Behr. Oxford University Press, 2018.

———. "The Rational Animal: A Rereading of Gregory of Nyssa's De hominis opificio." *Journal of Early Christian Studies* 7 (1999) 219–47.

Behr-Sigel, Elisabeth. *The Ministry of Women in the Church.* Translated by Steven Bigham. Crestwood: St. Vladimir's, 1991.

Berghaus, Margitta, and Volker Drecoll, eds. *Gregory of Nyssa: The Minor Treatises on Trinitarian Theology and Apollinarism.* Boston: Brill, 2011.

Bergsma, John. *Jesus and the Old Testament Roots of the Priesthood.* Steubenville, Ohio: Emmaus Road, 2021.

Bernier, Mark. *The Task of Hope in Kierkegaard.* Oxford University Press, 2015.

Biesen, Kees D. "The Irresistible Love of God: Two Syrian Church Fathers on Universal Salvation in Christ." In *Between the Cross and the Crescent,* edited by Zelijko Pasa, 437–49. Rome: Orientalia Christiana Analecta, 2018.

Bird, Michael F. *Colossians and Philemon.* Wipf and Stock, 2009.

———. *Jesus Among the gods.* Baylor University Press, 2022.

Bird, Michael, Nijay K. Gupta. *Philippians.* Cambridge: Cambridge University Press, 2020.

Blocher, Henry. "Everlasting Punishment and the Problem of Evil." In *Universalism and the Doctrine of Hell: Papers Presented at the Fourth Edinburgh Conference in Christian Dogmatics,* edited by Nigel de S. Cameron, 281–313. Paternoster, 1992.

Bowens, Lisa M. *An Apostle in Battle: Paul and Spiritual Warfare in 2 Corinthians 12:1–10.* Mohr Siebeck, 2017.

Boyarin, Daniel. *The Jewish Gospels: The Story of the Jewish Christ.* New York: The New, 2013.

BIBLIOGRAPHY

Bradshaw, David. *Aristotle East and West: Metaphysics and the Division of Christendom* Cambridge: Cambridge University Press, 2004.

Bradshaw, David. "Patristic Views on Why There is No Repentance after Death." In *The Unity of Body and Soul in Patristic and Byzantine Thought*, edited by Anna Usacheva, Siam Bhayro, and Jörg Ulrich, 192–213. Netherlands: Brill, 2021.

Bray, Gerald Lewis. *God Is Love: A Biblical and Systematic Theology*. Wheaton, Illinois: Crossway, 2012.

Bremmer, Jan N. "Descents to Hell and Ascents to Heaven in Apocalyptic Literature." In *The Oxford Handbook of Apocalyptic Literature*, edited by John J. Collins, 340–58. Oxford, 2014.

Bruce, F. F. *The Canon of Scripture*. Glasgow: Chapter House, 1988.

———. *The Epistles to the Colossians, to Philemon, and to the Ephesians* 2nd Edition. Grand Rapids, Michigan: Eerdmans, 2007.

Bulgakov, Sergius. *The Apocalypse of John: An Essay in Dogmatic Interpretation*, edited by Barabra Hallensleben and Regula M. Zwahlen. Translated by Mike Whitton. Germany: Aschendorff Verlag, 2019.

———. "Apocatastasis and Theodicy." In *Sophiology of Death: Essay on Eschatology, Personal, Political, Universal*. Translated by Roberto J. De La Noval. Eugene, Oregon: Cascade, 2021.

———. *The Bride of the Lamb*. Translated by Boris Jakim. Grand Rapids: Eerdmans, 2002.

———. "Dogma and Dogmatic Theology." In *Living Tradition*, edited by Peter Bouteneff. Paris: YMCA, 1937.

Campbell, Douglas A. *Pauline Dogmatics: The Triumph of God's Love*. Grand Rapids: Eerdmans, 2020.

Camus, Albert. *Christian Metaphysics and Neoplatonism*. Translated by Ronald D. Srigley. University of Minnesota Press, 2007.

Casiday, Augustine. *Reconstructing the Theology of Evagrius Ponticus*. Cambridge University Press, 2013.

Catechism of the Catholic Church 2nd Edition. Washington, DC: U.S. Catholic Conference, 1997.

Chesterton, G. K. *Orthodoxy*. California: John Lane, 1908.

Clark, Elizabeth A. *The Origenist Controversy: The Cultural Construction of an Early Christian Debate*. Princeton: Princeton University Press, 1992.

Coates, Hunter. *Conspiracy and the Subject: A Lacanian Enterprise*. Chicago: GGV, 2023.

———. "Fairies Exist: A Christian Inquiry." https://copiousflowers.substack.com/p/fairies-exist-a-christian-inquiry

———. "Toward a Hegelian Mariology: The Marian Concept." https://www.theophaneia.org/toward-a-hegelian-mariology-the-marian-concept/

Cousar, Charles B. *Philippians and Philemon*. Louisville: John Knox, 2013.

Corduan, Winfried. *In the Beginning God: A Fresh Look at the Case for Original Monotheism*. B&H, 2013.

Craig, William Lane. *The Son Rises: The Historical Evidence for the Resurrection of Jesus*. Eugene, Oregon: Wipf and Stock, 2000.

Culpepper, Alan R. *Matthew: A Commentary*. Louisville: John Knox, 2021.

BIBLIOGRAPHY

Daley, Robert. "The Discovery of the True Origen by Twentieth-Century Scholars." In *The Oxford Handbook of Origen*, edited by Ronald Heine and Karen Torjesen, 546–62. Oxford: Oxford University Press, 2022.

Daley, Robert. *The Hope of the Early Church: A Handbook of Patristic Eschatology*. Grand Rapids: Baker Academic, 2010.

Danker, Frederick, and Kathryn Krug. *The Concise Greek-English Lexicon of the New Testament*. Chicago: The University of Chicago Press, 2009.

Davies, Margaret. *Matthew 2nd Edition*. Arizona: Sheffield Phoenix, 2009.

Davies, W. D. *The Setting of the Sermon on the Mount*. Cambridge University Press, 1964.

De Boer, Martinus. *The Defeat of Death: Apocalyptic Eschatology in 1 Corinthians 15 and Romans 5*. Burns & Oates, 1988.

———. "The Story of the Johannine Community and its Literature." In *The Oxford Handbook of Johannine Studies*, edited by Judith M. Lieu and Martinus De Boer, 63–83. Oxford: Oxford University Press, 2018.

Dewrell, Heath D. *Child Sacrifice in Ancient Israel*. Penn State University, 2017.

De Young, Stephen. *The Religion of the Apostles: Orthodox Christianity in the First Century*. Chesterton, Indiana: Ancient Faith, 2021.

Diekamp, Franz. *Die Origenstischen Streitigkeiten Im Sechsten Jahrhundert Und Das Fünfte Allgemeine Concil*. Münster: Aschendorff, 1899.

Domínguez, Emilio-José Justo. "Pensar Y Decir La salvación Cristiana." *Estudios Eclesiásticos* 97 (2022) 745–71.

Donner, Fred. *Mohammad and the Believers: At the Origins of Islam*. Harvard University Press, 2010.

Dudley, Robert et al. "Prevalence and Nature of Multi-Sensory and Multi-Modal Hallucinations in People with First Episode Psychosis." *Psychiatry Research* 319 (2022) 1–6.

Dunn, James D. G. *The Epistles to the Colossians and to Philemon: A Commentary on the Greek Text*. Grand Rapids, Michigan: Eerdmans, 2014.

———. *Jesus Remembered*. Eerdmans, 2003.

Ehrman, Bart. "Did Paul Write Colossians?" https://ehrmanblog.org/the-more-scholarly-argument-that-paul-did-not-write-colossians/.

———. *Forgery and Counterforgery: The Use of Literary Deceit in Early Christian Polemics*. New York: Oxford University Press, 2014.

———. *How Jesus Became God: The Exaltation of a Jewish Preacher from Galilee*. New York: HarperOne, 2015.

———. *Heaven and Hell: A History of the Afterlife*. Simon & Schuster, 2021

———. *Journeys to Heaven and Hell*. Yale University Press, 2023.

Eliade, Mircea. *History of Religious Ideas, Volume 3*. University of Chicago Press, 2013.

Elliott, J. K., ed. *The Apocryphal New Testament: A Collection of Apocryphal Christian Literature in an English Translation*. Oxford: Oxford University Press, 1993.

Emerson, Matthew Y. *'He Descended to the Dead' an Evangelical Theology of Holy Saturday*. InterVarsity, 2019.

Engels, Friedrich. "The Book of Revelation." In *On Religion*. Chico, California: Scholars, 1964.

Evagrius. *Les Six Centuries Des Kephalaia Gnostica d'évagre Le Pontique*. Translated by Antoine Guillaumont. Turnhout: Brepols, 2003.

BIBLIOGRAPHY

Evans, Craig A., and Emanuel Tov. *Exploring the Origins of the Bible: Canon Formation in Historical, Literary, and Theological Perspective.* Grand Rapids: Baker Academic, 2008.

Florensky, Pavel. *The Pillar and Ground of the Truth an Essay in Orthodox Theodicy in Twelve Letters.* Translated by Boris Jakim. New Jersey: Princeton University Press, 2018.

Foster, Paul. "An Apostle Too Radical for the Radical Perspective on Paul." *Expository Times* 133 (2021) 1–11.

Fowl, Stephen E. *Philippians.* Eerdmans, 2004.

Fudge, Edward. *The Fire that Consumes Third Edition: A Biblical and Historical Study of the Doctrine of Final Punishment.* Lutterworth, 2012.

Gadamer, Hans-Georg. *Truth and Method.* London: Bloomsbury, 2013.

Gallagher, Edmon L., John D. Meade. *The Biblical Canon Lists from Early Christianity.* Oxford University Press, 2017.

Gathercole, Simon. *The Gospel of Thomas: Introduction and Commentary.* Boston: Brill, 2014.

Gavrilyuk, Paul L. "Divine Judgement in Pavel Florensky and Sergius Bulgakov." *International Journal of Orthodox Theology* 9 (2018) 9–31.

Gleaves, G. S. *Did Jesus Speak Greek? The Emerging Evidence of Greek Dominance in First-Century Palestine.* Wipf and Stock, 2015.

Graieg, David. *Resurrection Remembered: A Memory Approach to Jesus's Resurrection in First Corinthians.* New York: Routledge, 2024.

Griffiths, Paul J. "Self-Annihilation or Damnation? A Disputable Question in Christian Eschatology." *Pro Ecclesia* 16 (2007) 416–44.

Hadas-Lebel, Mirielle. *Philo of Alexandria: A Thinker in the Jewish Diaspora.* Boston: Brill, 2012.

Hagner, Donald A. *Matthew 1–13.* Dallas: World, 1993.

Hainsworth, Kaleeg. "Infant Baptism: What the Church Believes." Antiochian Orthodox Christian Archdiocese. https://www.antiochian.org/regulararticle/1899.

Hamza, Feras. "Temporary Hellfire Punishment and the Making of Sunni Orthodoxy." In *Roads to Paradise: Eschatology and Concepts of the Hereafter in Islam,* edited by Sebastion Gunther and Todd Lawson, 371–406. Boston: Brill, 2017.

Hart, David Bentley. *The Doors of the Sea: Where Was God in the Tsunami?.* Eerdmans, 2005.

———. *The New Testament.* Yale University Press, 2023.

———. "The Theotokos Visits Hell." In *Roland in Moonlight.* Angelico, 2021.

———. *That All Shall Be Saved: Heaven, Hell, and Universal Salvation: With a New Preface.* Yale University Press, 2021.

———. *You Are Gods: On Nature and Supernature.* Notre Dame: University of Notre Dame Press, 2022.

Harvey, Katherine. *The Fires of Lust: Sex in the Middle Ages.* Reaktion, 2019.

Hawthorne, Gerald, and R. P. Martin. *Philippians.* Zondervan, 2004.

Hegel, G. W. F. *The Science of Logic.* Translated by George Di Giovanni. Cambridge: Cambridge University Press, 2015.

Hengel, Martin. *Acts and the History of Earliest Christianity.* Eugene, Oregon: Wipf and Stock, 2003.

Henning, Meghan. *Educating Early Christians through the Rhetoric of Hell.* Tübingen: Mohr Siebeck, 2014.

BIBLIOGRAPHY

———. *Hell Hath No Fury: Gender, Disability, and the Invention of Damned Bodies in Early Christian Literature*. New Haven: Yale University Press, 2021.
Hick, John. *Death and Eternal Life*. Louisville: John Knox, 1994.
Hombergen, Daniel. *The Second Origenist Controversy*. Roma: Centro Studi Sant'Anselmo, 2001.
Hoover, Jon. *Ibn Taymiyya*. Simon and Schuster, 2019.
———. "Islamic Universalism: Ibn Qayyim Al-Jawziyya's Salafi Deliberations on the Duration of Hell-Fire." *The Muslim World* 99 (2009) 181–201.
———. "A Muslim Argument for Universal Salvation." In *Alternative Salvations: Engaging the Sacred and the Secular*, edited by Hannah Bacon, et al., 165–75. Bloomsbury, 2015.
Hronich, Andrew. *Once Loved Always Loved*. Oregon: Wipf and Stock, 2023.
Hundley, Michael. *Yahweh Among the Gods*. Cambridge: Cambridge University Press, 2022.
Hurtado, Larry W. *One God, One Lord: Early Christian Devotion and Ancient Jewish Monotheism*. London: Bloomsbury, 2015.
Hunsinger, George. *Philippians*. Baker, 2020.
Irenaeus. *The Scandal of the Incarnation*. Translated by Hans Urs von Balthasar. San Francisco: Ignatius, 1990.
Isaac. *The Ascetical Homilies of Saint Isaac the Syrian*. Boston: The Holy Transfiguration Monastery, 2011.
Izydorczy, Zbigniew. *The Medieval Gospel of Nicodemus: Texts, Intertexts, and Contexts in Western Europe*. Tempe, AZ: Medieval & Renaissance Texts & Studies, 1997.
Jacobs, Nathan A. "On Whether the Soul Is Immortal according to the Eastern Church Fathers." *St. Vladimir's Theological Quarterly* (2020) 1–38.
Jersak, "Gehenna." In *Her Gates Will Never Shut: Hope, Hell, and the New Jerusalem*. Oregon: Wipf and Stock, 2010.
———. "Lake of Fire." In *Her Gates Will Never Shut: Hope, Hell, and the New Jerusalem*. Oregon: Wipf and Stock, 2010.
Jewett, Robert. *Romans: A Commentary*. Minneapolis: Fortress, 2007.
John Chrysostom. *The Love Chapter*. Paraclete, 2009.
John of Damascus. *On the Divine Images*. Translated by Fr Andrew Louth. St. Vladimir's, 2003.
Johnston, Philip S. *Shades of Sheol: Death and Afterlife in the Old Testament*. Downers Grove: InterVarsity, 2002.
Josephus. *The Works of Flavius Josephus*. Translated by William Whiston et al. 1895. https://www.perseus.tufts.edu/hopper/text?doc=Perseus%3Atext%3A1999.01.0148%3Abook%3D2%3Asection%3D154
Keener, Craig S. *Acts, Vol. 4, 24:1—28:31: An Exegetical Commentary*. Grand Rapids: Baker Academic, 2015.
Keizer, Heleen. *Life, Time, Entirety. A Study of AION in Greek Literature and Philosophy, the Septuagint and Philo*. Heleen M. Keizer, 2010.
———. Review of *Terms for Eternity*, by Ilaria Ramelli and David Konstan. *The Studia Philonica Annual* 23 (2011) 200–206.
Khalil, Mohammad Hassan. *Islam and the Fate of Others: The Salvation Question*. Oxford University Press, 2012.

BIBLIOGRAPHY

———. "Is Hell Truly Everlasting? An Introduction to Medieval Islamic Universalism." In *Locating Hell in Islamic Traditions*, edited by Christian Lange. Boston: Brill, 2016.

Khramov, Alexander. "Fitting Evolution into Christian Belief: An Eastern Orthodox Approach." *International Journal of Orthodox Theology* 8 (2017) 75–105.

Kierkegaard, Søren. *Kierkegaard's Journals and Notebooks, Volume 11, Part 2*. Translated by Niels Jørgen Cappelørn, et al. Princeton University Press, 2020.

———. *The Sickness unto Death: A Christian Psychological Exposition for Upbuilding and Awakening*. Translated by Howard Hong and Edna Hong. Princeton: Princeton University Press, 1983.

———. *Works of Love*. Translated by Howard Hong and Edna Hong. Princeton University Press, 1995.

Kimel, Aidan Jr. *Destined for Joy: The Gospel of Universal Salvation*, edited by Brad Jersak. New Haven: The Works of Gregory Macdonald, 2022.

———. "Divine Retribution, Hell, and the Development of Dogma." https://afkimel.wordpress.com/2020/06/06/divine-retribution-hell-and-the-development-of-dogma/.

Klaassens, Harry. "The Reformed Tradition in the Netherlands." In *The Oxford History of Christian Worship*, edited by Geoffrey Wainwright and Karen B. Westerfield Tucker, 463–73. Oxford University Press, 2005.

Kloppenborg, John S. *Q, the Earliest Gospel*. Louisville: Presbyterian, 2008.

Koisor, Wojciech. "The Underworld or its Ruler? Some Remarks on the Concept of Sheol in the Hebrew Bible." *The Polish Journal of Biblical Research* 13 (2014) 29–40.

Koperski, Andrew R. "Eusebius, Revelation, and Its Place in the New Testament Canon." *Journal of Early Christian History* 11 (2021) 79–94.

Kronen, John, and Eric Reitan. "Annihilation or Salvation? A Philosophical Case for Preferring Universalism to Annihilationism." *Religious Studies* 58 (2020) 138–61.

———. *God's Final Victory*. Bloomsbury Academic, 2013.

Kurkilamkatt, James. "Mission of St. Thomas the Apostle in India: Archeological, Epigraphic, and Numismatic Evidences." In *St. Thomas and India: Recent Research*, edited by K. S. Matthew et al., 55–68. Fortress, 2020.

Kyrtatas, Dimitris J. "Historical Aspects of the Formation of the New Testament Canon," edited by Einar Thomassen, 29–45. Norway: Museum Tuscalanum, 2010.

Lacan, Jacques. *Transference: The Seminar of Jacques Lacan Book VIII*. Translated by Bruce Fink. Polity, 2015.

Ladria, Luis F. "El Cristianismo Y La Universalidad De La Salvación." *Estudios Eclesiasticos* 81 (2006) 353–81.

Lee, Justin J. *Origen and the Holy Spirit*. Vandenhoeck & Ruprecht, 2023.

Licona, Mike. *The Resurrection of Jesus: A New Historiographical Approach*. Nottingham: Apollos, 2018.

Louth, Andrew. "Eastern Orthodox View." In *Five Views on the Extent of the Atonement*, edited by Adam J. Johnson and Stanley N. Gundry, 19–44. Zondervan, 2019.

———. "Response to Tom Greggs." In *Five Views on the Extent of the Atonement*, edited by Adam J. Johnson and Stanley N. Gundry, 218–23. Zondervan, 2019.

———. *Greek East & Latin West: The Church AD 681–1071*. Crestwood, New York: SVS, 2007.

Ludlow, Morwenna. *Universal Salvation: Eschatology in the Thought of Gregory of Nyssa and Karl Rahner*. Oxford University Press, 2000.

BIBLIOGRAPHY

Lundhaug, Hugo, and Lance Jenott. *The Monastic Origins of the Nag Hammadi Codices*. Mohr Siebeck, 2015.
MacDonald, George. *Unspoken Sermons*. CreateSpace, 2014.
MacDonald, Margaret. *Sacra Pagina: Colossians and Ephesians*. Collegeville: Liturgical, 2000.
MacGregor, George H. C. "Principalities and Powers: The Cosmic Background of Paul's Thought," *New Testament Studies* 1 (1954) 17-28.
Martin, R. P. *A Hymn of Christ*. Downers Grove: Intervarsity, 1997.
McDonald, Gregory. *The Evangelical Universalist* 2nd Edition. Eugene, Oregon: Cascade, 2012.
McDonald, Lee Martin. *The Biblical Canon: Its Origin, Transmission, and Authority*. Peabody, Massachusetts: Hendrickson Publishers, 2006.
———. *The Canon Debate*. Peabody, MA: Hendrickson Publishers, 2001.
"Forming Christian Scriptures as a Biblical Canon." In *Ancient Jewish and Christian Scriptures: New Developments in Canon Controversy*, edited by John J. Collins et al., 121-45. Westminster John Knox, 2020.
McDowell, Sean. *The Fate of the Apostles*. Routledge, 2016.
McGrath, James F. *Christmaker: A Life of John the Baptist*. Eerdmans, 2024.
McGrew, Timothy. "The Argument from Silence." *Acta Analytica* 29 (2014) 215-28.
McGuckin, John Anthony. *The Eastern Orthodox Church: A New History*. New Haven: Yale University Press, 2020.
———. *Origen of Alexandria: Master Theologian of the Early Church*. Lexington Books, 2022.
Medham, John, ed. *The Seventh General* Council. Translated by John Medham. Oxford University, 1849.
Metzger, Bruce M. *The Canon of the New Testament: Its Origin, Development, and Significance*. Oxford: Clarendon, 2009.
Milbank, John. *Being Reconciled: Ontology and Pardon*. London: Routledge, 2008.
Milbank, John. "Paul against Biopolitics." In *Paul's New Moment: Continental Philosophy and the Future of Christian Theology*, edited by John Milbank et al., 21-74. Grand Rapids: Brazos, 2010.
Milton, John. *Paradise Lost*. New York: Oxford University Press, 2008.
Moltmann, Jürgen. *The Coming of God*. Fortress, 2004.
Montagnese, Marcella et al. "A Review of Multimodal Hallucinations: Categorization, Assessment, Theoretical Perspectives, and Clinical Recommendations." *Schizophrenia Bulletin* 47 (2020) 237-48.
Moo, Douglas J. *The Letters to the Colossians and to Philemon*. Grand Rapids: Eerdmans, 2008.
———. *The Letter to the Romans* 1st Edition. Michigan: Eerdmans, 1996.
———. *A Theology of Paul and His Letters*. Zondervan, 2021.
Moss, Candida R. *Ancient Christian Martyrdom: Diverse Practices, Theologies, and Traditions*. New Haven: Yale University Press, 2012.
———. *Divine Bodies: Resurrecting Perfection in the New Testament and Early Christianity*. London: Yale University Press, 2019.
———. "Curators of the Word." In *God's Ghostwriters: Enslaved Christians and the Making of the Bible*. Little Brown, 2024.
Moule, C. F. D. *An Idiom Book of New Testament Greek*. Cambridge: Cambridge University Press, 1959.

BIBLIOGRAPHY

Nanos, Mark D. "The Question of Conceptualization: Qualifying Paul's Position on Circumcision in Dialogue with Josephus's Advisors to King Izates." In *Paul Within Judaism: Restoring the First Century to the Apostle*, edited by Mark D. Nanos and Magnus Zetterholm, 105-53. Minneapolis: Fortress, 2015.

Nida, Eugene A., and J. P. Louw. *Lexical Semantics of the Greek New Testament*. Society of Biblical Literature, 1992.

Nietzsche, Friedrich. *Human, All Too Human*. Translated by R. J. Hollingdale and Richard Schacht. Cambridge: Cambridge University Press, 1996.

———. *On The Genealogy of Morals*. Translated by Michael A. Scarpitti. Penguin, 2013.

———. *Untimely Meditations*. Translated by Daniel Breazeale and Daniel Hollingdale. Cambridge University Press, 1997.

———. *Writings from the Late Notebooks*. Translated by Bittner Rüdiger and Kate Sturge. Cambridge University Press, 2009.

O'Brien, Peter. *Colossians, Philemon*. Thomas Nelson, 1982.

O'Ceallaigh, G. C. "Dating the Commentaries of the Gospel of Nichodemus," *Harvard Theological Review* (1963) 21-58.

O'Leary, Joseph. "Socrates and Plato in the Fathers." In *Routledge Handbook of Early Christian Philosophy*, edited by Mark Edwards, 191-206. Routledge, 2021.

Origen. *Commentary on the Epistle to the Romans Books 1-5*. Translated by Thomas P. Scheck. Washington, DC: Catholic University of America Press, 2002.

———. *Contra Celsum*. Translated by Henry Chadwick. Cambridge University Press, 1980.

———. *New Fragments from the Commentary on Matthew*. Translated by P. Tzamalikos. Paderborn: Brill, 2020.

———. *On First Principles*. Translated by Fr John Behr. Oxford: Oxford University Press, 2018.

Ortlund, Dane. *Gentle and Lowly*. Crossway, 2020.

Ortlund, Gavin. *What It Means to Be Protestant: The Case for an Always-Reforming Church*. Zondervan, 2024.

Osborne, Grant R. *Philippians: Verse by Verse*. Bellingham: Lexham, 2017.

Overbeck, J. J., ed. *The Acts and Decrees of the Synod of Jerusalem*. London: AMS, 1899.

Overton, Shawna, and Richard Friedman. "Death and the Afterlife: The Biblical Silence." In *Judaism in Late Antiquity: Death, Life-After-Death, Resurrection and the World-To-Come in the Judaisms of Antiquity*, edited by Alan J. Avery-Peck and Jacob Neusner, 35-61. Leiden: Brill, 1999.

Oxenham, Henry. *Catholic Eschatology and Universalism: An Essay on the Doctrine of Future Retribution*. London: W.H. Allen, 1878.

Oxford News Editors. "Ancient Carthaginians Really Did Sacrifice Their Children." https://www.ox.ac.uk/news/2014-11-23-ancient-carthaginians-really-did-sacrifice-their-children#:~:text=Children%20%E2%80%93%20both%20male%20and%20female,in%20Sicily%2C%20Sardinia%20and%20Malta.

Palmer, G. E. H., et al., eds. *The Philokalia Volume 2*. Translated by G. E. H. Palmer, et al. London: Faber and Faber, 1984.

Pao, David W. *Colossians and Philemon*. Grand Rapids: Zondervan, 2012.

Parry, Robin. "A Universalist Response." In *Four Views on Hell* 2nd *Edition*, edited by Preston Sprinkle. Zondervan, 2016.

Pederson, Nils Arne. "Ilaria Ramelli's History of the Apokatastasis Doctrine: A Critical Assessment of Evidence from before Origen." *The Journal of Theological Studies* (2024) 134–47.
Perczel, Istvan. "Pseudo-Dionysius and Palestinian Origenism" In *The Sabaite Heritage in the Orthodox Church from the Fifth Century to the Present*, edited by Joseph Patrich, 261–83. Peeters, 2001.
Perrone, Lorenzo. "Palestinian Monasticism, the Bible, and Theology." In *The Sabaite Heritage in the Orthodox Church from the Fifth Century to the Present*, edited by Joseph Patrich, 245–61. Peeters, 2001.
Philaret. "The Catechism of St Philaret of Moscow." http://www.pravoslavieto.com/docs/eng/Orthodox_Catechism_of_Philaret.htm
PhilPapers editors. "Survey Results: Free Will." https://survey2020.philpeople.org/.
Plotinus. *Enneads*, edited by Lloyd P. Gerson. Translated by Lloyd P. Gerson, et al. Cambridge: Cambridge University Press, 2017.
Plutarch. *Lives: Theseus and Romulus, Lycurgus and Numa, Solon and Publicola*. Translated by Bernadotte Perrin. Harvard University Press, 1967.
Poirier, John C. *The Invention of the Inspired Text*. Bloomsbury, 2021.
Polybius. *Histories*. Translated by Evelyn S. Shuckburgh. London: Macmillan, 1889.
Porter, Stanley E. "Did Jesus Ever Teach in Greek?" *Tyndale Bulletin* 44 (1993) 218–22.
Price, Richard, and Michael Gaddis, trans. *The Acts of the Council of Chalcedon*. Liverpool: Liverpool University Press, 2007.
———. *The Acts of the Council of Constantinople of 553*. Liverpool University Press, 2010.
Price, Richard, and Mary Whitby, eds. *Chalcedon in Context: Church Councils, 400–700*. Liverpool: Liverpool University Press, 2011.
Price, Richard, ed. *The Acts of the Second Council of Nicaea (787)*. Oxford: Oxford University Press, 2020.
Quran. https://quran.com/.
Radde-Galwitz, Andrew. "The One and the Trinity." In *Christian Platonism: A History*, edited by Alexander Hampton and John Peter Kenney, 53–79. Cambridge University Press, 2020.
Rahner, Karl. *Theological Investigations: Volume 4*. Baltimore, Maryland: Helicon, 1966.
Ramelli, Ilaria. "Apophaticism, Mysticism, and Epoptics in Ancient and Patristic Philosophy: Some Important Examples." *Verbum Vitae* 41 (2023) 547–86.
———. *The Christian Doctrine of Apokatastasis*. Brill, 2013.
———. *A Larger Hope?: Volume 1*. Eugene, Oregon: Wipf and Stock Publishers, 2019.
———. "Origen, Greek Philosophy, and the Birth of the Trinitarian Meaning of Hypostasis." *Harvard Theological Review* 105 (2012) 302–50.
———. "Origen, Patristic Philosophy, and Christian Platonism: Re-Thinking the Christianisation of Hellenism. *Vigiliae Chrisianae* 63 (2009) 217–63.
———. "Origen's Anti-Subordinationism and its Heritage in the Nicene and Cappadocian Line." *Vigiliae Christianae* 65 (2011) 21–49.
———. "Patristic Readings of Scripture in Support of *Apokatastasis*, Straw Men, and Titus of Bostra's Refraining from Advocating Eternal Punishment: A Response to Nils Arne Pedersen." https://afkimel.wordpress.com/2024/08/06/patristic-readings-of-scripture-in-support-of-apokatastasis-straw-men-and-titus-of-bostras-refraining-from-advocating-eternal-punishment-a-response-to-nils-arne-pedersen/

BIBLIOGRAPHY

Ramelli, Illaria, and David Konstan. *Terms for Eternity: Aiônios and Aídios in Classical and Christian Texts*. Piscataway: Gorgias, 2013.
Reif, Stefan C. "Some Notions of Restoration in Early Rabbinic Prayer." In *Restoration: Old Testament, Jewish, and Christian Perspectives*, edited by James M. Scott, 281–305. Boston: Brill, 2000.
Reitlinger, Joanna. "The Final Days of Father Sergius Bulgakov: A Memoir." In *Sergius Bulgakov: Apocatastasis and Transfiguration*, edited by Boris Jakim. New Haven: Variable, 1995.
Ricœur, Paul. *Time and Narrative Volume 1*. Chicago: University of Chicago Press, 1984.
Roper, Gary Lee. "Views of the Early Church on Slavery." In *Antebellum Slavery: An Orthodox Christian View*. Xlibris, 2009.
Rose, Seraphim. *Genesis, Creation, and Early Man: The Orthodox Christian Vision*. Alaska: St Herman of Alaska Brotherhood, 2011.
Rubenson, Samuel. "Asceticism and Monasticism, I: Eastern." In *Christianity: Constantine to 600 c.*, edited by Augustin Casiday and Frederick W. Norris, 637–68. Cambridge: Cambridge University Press, 2007.
Rubenson, Samuel. "Why Did the Origenist Controversy Begin?: Re-thinking the Standard Narratives." *Modern Theology* 38 (2022) 318–37.
Russell, Bertrand. *Why I Am Not a Christian: And Other Essays on Religion and Related Subjects*. London: Routledge Classics, 2004.
"Sahih Al-Bukhari 3194—Beginning of Creation." https://sunnah.com/bukhari:3194.
"Sahih Al-Bukhari 6571—To Make the Heart Tender." https://sunnah.com/bukhari:6571.
Schelling, F. W. J. *Philosophie der Offenbarung 1841/42*. Suhrkamp Verlag, 1993.
Seijas, Carlos Miramontes. "La Apocatatasis O Restauración Universal Como Tradición Teológica En La Obra De Ilaria Ramelli." *Proyección: teología y mundo actual* (2019) 423–53.
Segal, Alan F. *Two Powers in Heaven: Early Rabbinic Reports about Christianity and Gnosticism*. Waco, Texas: Baylor University Press, 2012.
Shariff, Azim F., and Lara B. Aknin. "The Emotional Toll of Hell: Cross-National and Experimental Evidence for the Negative Well-Being Effects of Hell Beliefs." *PLoS ONE* 9 (2014) 1–8.
Shoemaker, Stephen J. *Ancient Traditions of the Virgin Mary's Dormition and Assumption*. Oxford: Oxford University Press, 2010.
———. *The Apocalypse of Empire: Imperial Eschatology in Late Antiquity and Early Islam*. University of Pennsylvania Press, 2018.
———. *Mary in Early Christian Faith and Devotion*. New Haven: Yale University Press, 2016.
Siecienski, Edward A. *The Filioque: History of a Doctrinal Controversy*. New York: Oxford University Press, 2013.
Silva, Moisés. *Philippians*. Grand Rapids: Baker Academic, 2005.
Sophrony. *Saint Silouan the Athonite*. Translated by Rosemary Edmonds. Essex: Stavropegic Monastery of St. John the Baptist, 1991.
Spiegel, James S. *Hell and Divine Goodness*. Wipf and Stock, 2019.
Sproul, R. C. *Chosen by God*. Illinois: Tyndale, 1994.

BIBLIOGRAPHY

———. *God's Love: How the Infinite God Cares for His Children.* Colorado Springs: David C. Cook, 2012.

Stăniloae, Dumitru. *Eternity and Time.* Oxford: SLG, 2001.

———. *The Experience of God Volume 1.* Translated by Ioan Ionita and Robert Barringer. Brookline: Holy Cross University Press, 1998.

Stamps, John. "St Symeon the New Theologian and the Quest of the Historical Jesus." https://afkimel.wordpress.com/2016/09/26/st-symeon-the-new-theologian-and-the-quest-of-the-historical-jesus/

Strachan, Owen. *The Warrior Savior.* P&R, January 2024.

Sumney, Jerry L. *Reading Paul's Letter to the Romans.* Atlanta: Society of Biblical Literature, 2012

Swinburne, Richard. "A Theodicy of Heaven and Hell. In *The Existence and Nature of God*, edited by Alfred Freddoso, 37. Notre Dame University Press, 1983.

———. *Was Jesus God?.* Oxford University Press, 2008.

Talbert, Charles H. *Ephesians and Colossians.* Michigan: Baker Academic, 2007.

———. *Matthew.* Grand Rapids: Baker Academic, 2010.

Talbott, Thomas B. *The Inescapable Love of God* 2nd *Edition.* Eugene, Oregon: Cascade, 2014.

———. "A Pauline Interpretation of Divine Judgement." In *Universal Salvation? The Current Debate*, edited by Robin Parry and Christopher Partridge, 32–55. Michigan: Eerdmans, 2004.

Tanner, Norman P. *Decrees of the Ecumenical Councils: Nicaea to Lateran V.* Georgetown: Georgetown University Press, 2016.

Taubes, Jacob. *The Political Theology of Paul.* Translated by Dana Hollander. California: Stanford University Press, 2003.

Taymiyyah, Ibn. "Response to Those Who Say That Heaven & Hell Will Pass Away." Translated by Hassan Radwan, 2020. https://drive.google.com/file/d/1j8by6wMqLUu6oVGtMoO9anBMD7w1SDa7/view.

Telea. Marius. "Origenism in the Vision of Emperor Justinian I (527–65)." *International Journal of Orthodox Theology* 13 (2022) 28–56.

Theopan. "What is an Anathema?" https://www.orthodox.net/articles/anathema-bp-theophan.html

Tomlin, Graham. *Philippians, Colossians.* Downers Grove, Illinois: Intervarsity, 2013.

Trombley R., Frank. "Christianity and Paganism, II: Asia Minor." In *Christianity: Constantine to 600 c.*, edited by Augustin Casiday and Frederick W. Norris, 189–209. Cambridge: Cambridge University Press, 2007.

Trumbower, Jeffery A. *Rescue for the Dead the Posthumous Salvation of Non-Christians in Early Christianity.* Oxford: Oxford University, 2001.

Tzamalikos, P. *Anaxagoras, Origen, and Neoplatonism.* De Gruyter, 2016.

———. *Origen: Philosophy of History and Eschatology.* Leiden: Brill, 2007.

———. *The Real Cassian Revisited: Monastic Life, Greek Paideia, and Origenism in the Sixth Century.* Leiden: Brill, 2012.

Villanueva, Rodrigo Ballon. "Apocatástasis: La Relación Dios-criatura en el Retorno Eriugeniano." *Enrahonor* (2018) 25–34.

Vincent, Martin R. *Word Studies in the New Testament: Volume IV.* Peabody: Hendrickson, 1991.

Wallace, Daniel B. *Greek Grammar Beyond the Basics.* Zondervan, 1996.

BIBLIOGRAPHY

Walls, Jerry L., and Claire Brown. "Annihilationism: A Philosophical Dead End?" In *The Problem of Hell: A Philosophical Anthology*, edited by Joel Buenting, 45–65. Routledge, 2016.
Walter, G. W. *The Letter to the Philippians*. Grand Rapids: Eerdmans, 2009.
Ware, Kallistos. *The Inner Kingdom*. Crestwood: St. Vladimir's, 2001.
Wessel, Susan. *Cyril of Alexandria and the Nestorian Controversy*. Oxford University Press, 2004.
Wild, Robert. "Philosophy 1." In *A Catholic Reading Guide to Conditional Immortality: The Third Alternative to Hell and Universalism*. Eugene, Oregon: Resource, 2016.
Williams, Rowan. *Looking East in Winter: Contemporary Thought and the Eastern Christian Tradition*. London: Bloomsbury Continuum, 2021.
Witherington, Ben, and Darlene Hyatt. *Paul's Letter to the Romans: A Socio-Rhetorical Commentary*. Grand Rapids: Eerdmans, 2004.
Wortley, John, ed., *The 'Anonymous' Sayings of the Desert Fathers*. New York: Cambridge University Press, 2013.
Wright, N. T. *Colossians and Philemon: An Introduction and Commentary*. Tyndale, 2008.
———. *Jesus and the Victory of God*. Minneapolis: Fortress, 1996.
———. *The Resurrection of the Son of God*. Minneapolis: Fortress, 2003.
———. *Surprised by Hope*. New York: HarperOne, 2008.
Yogev, Jonathan. *The Rephaim: Sons of God*. Brill, 2021.
Young, Stephen. "Protective Strategies and The Prestige of the Academic: A Religious Studies and Practice Theory Redescription of Evangelical Inerrantist Scholarship," *Biblical Interpretation* 23 (2015) 1–35.
Zaleski, John. "Universal Salvation in Christian and Islamic Thought: The Arabic Reception of Isaac of Nineveh." *Journal of Orthodox Christian Studies* 5 (2022) 71–94.
Žižek, Slavoj. *Christian Atheism: How to Be a Real Materialist*. Bloomsbury, 2024.
Zizioulas, John. "One Single Source: An Orthodox Response to the Clarification of the Filioque." http://www.orthodoxresearchinstitute.org/articles/dogmatics/john_zizioulas_single_source.html.

Subject Index

Adam, Adamic, 13–14, 17, 50, 56, 68–70, 88, 98, 100–103, 123–24, 153, 158–159, 161, 166–69, 213, 244, 279, 292, 302, 325, 367, 375n13
aenaōn, 190
aïdios, 11, 180, 182, 186–90
aiōn, 179–80, 186–90, 372
aiōnion, 11, 53, 187
aiōnios, 179–91, 203, 372–73
Alfeyev, Hilarion, 155, 165–71, 249n89
Allin, Thomas, 81–82
Allison, Dale, 64
Ambrose of Milan, 5, 12, 93
Anathema 9, 223–25
Anathema 12, 219, 228–29, 229n51, 367
Angel of the Lord, 39, 46–47, 49, 77, 192
annihilationism, vii–iii, 73, 97, 173–77, 300, 306, 338–56, 363
Anselm of Canterbury, 50, 53, 292, 343n6
apokatallaxai, 112, 114–17
apokatastasis, 2–5, 8, 18, 70, 87, 94, 163, 189, 204–12, 230–239, 250, 287, 318, 335, 368
apophatic, 25–27
Aquinas, Thomas, 13, 172, 370
archeological, 44, 133n8, 181n6, 195

Aristotle, 4, 183, 190, 348
Artman, David, 140n23, 267, 290n10
asbestō, 190, 194–97
Athanasius of Alexandria, 4, 32, 36, 53, 125, 190, 346,
Augustine of Hippo, 5–6, 12, 79, 83, 95, 101, 141, 163–64, 182, 197, 229, 232, 287, 318, 333, 367, 370, 374

Ba'al, 48–49, 139, 139n15
Babylon, 206–7
Balthasar, Hans Urs von, 168, 357–58, 361
Barth, Karl, 82, 357
Basil the Great, 5, 13, 24, 32n3, 33, 53, 66, 84, 171, 184, 232, 310, 366
Bethlehem, 42
Bradshaw, David, 170
Bray, Gerald, 294–96, 303, 305–6, 313–16
Bulgakov, Sergius, Bulgakovian, 18n15, 68, 134n9, 185, 205, 250, 356
Byzantine, 42, 79, 140, 212

Calvin, John, Calvinism, Calvinist, 50–51, 99, 178, 197, 200, 243, 268, 287–88, 288n8, 290, 291n12, 292, 348, 371

SUBJECT INDEX

Catholicism, 74, 101, 242–43, 245, 338, 346
Celsus, 46n18, 61n42, 64n49, 78
Christology, 46–50, 111n51, 227, 227n44, 324, 381
Christ Hymn, 103, 110, 112, 125
Clark, Elizabeth, 221, 224, 236
classical free will, CFW, ix, 257, 258n3, 259–63, 263n8, 265, 267, 270, 272–73, 276, 342, 355
Clement of Alexandria, 4, 48, 78, 184, 189, 335, 346, 366
conciliatory fundamentalism, 248–49
Constantinople II, vii, 163, 209, 212, 214–15, 215n11, 215n13, 216, 222, 225–30, 234, 237–40, 249, 252, 367
Constantinople III, 215n13, 237–38, 240
consubstantial, 43, 80, 218–20, 228, 366
Council of Carthage, 35, 205
Council of Chalcedon, 52, 128, 234, 248, 249n91
Council of Ephesus, 52, 241
Council of Hippo, 35, 205
Craig, William Lane, 57, 262, 352
Cyril of Alexandria, 5, 32n3, 79, 104
Cyril of Scythopolis, 214, 215n11, 228

Definition 18, 240–242, 245–46
determinism, 258
Didymus the Blind, 5, 79, 204, 223
Dionysius the Areopagite, 8, 22–23, 124, 227, 276–77, 280, 371
divine hiddenness, 266
Divine Liturgy, 9–11, 84
Divine Names, 22–25, 277, 342n5, 371
divinization, *theosis*, 54–55, 66–68, 79–80, 251, 262, 308, 325, 329, 342n5, 350, 368
dogma, 217, 248–52, 285, 312, 327, 329, 365–66, 368
Dormition, 23, 42–45

ecclesial, ecclesiastical, 9–10, 30–31, 126–27, 221, 226, 229, 236, 250, 367
Edwards, Johnathan, 285, 292
eirēnopoiēsas, 117–21, 121n70, 122

Ehrman, Bart, 63, 110n51, 112, 113n55, 153–54, 157–58, 161, 174, 309
elect, 199–200, 290–291, 376
eph'hō, 101–2, 102n31
Epiphanius of Salamis, 233, 236
eternal conscious torment, ECT, infernalism, vii, ix, 73–74, 86–129, 173, 178–211, 247, 265, 267–68, 284–317, 329, 332–37, 338–39, 347, 352, 355–56, 359, 363, 376
Eucharist, 8, 10, 84–85, 127, 246–47, 250, 350–351
Evagrius Ponticus, 5, 124, 223, 227–28, 237–40
exomologēsētai, 103, 105n40, 106–9

Fall, 10–15, 17–18, 53, 70, 101, 235, 236n65
Father of Fathers, 241
fifteen anathemas, 214–30
Final Judgment, 145, 185–86, 306, 327, 331
Florensky, Pavel, viii, 26, 245, 318–26, 326n12, 327–37, 344, 352
for-itself, 325–27, 329, 331, 336–37
free will, vii, ix, 10, 171, 177, 257–76, 288, 297, 321–25, 334, 342, 345, 355, 363–64, 371
Freud, Sigmund, 26, 252
fundamental epistemic block, FEB, ix, 332–35

Gehenna, 130, 137–46, 161, 174, 194–96, 271, 302, 318, 321, 326, 332, 350
Gentile, 50, 65n51, 99–100, 107, 144, 199–202, 205
Gregory of Nyssa, 5, 13, 24, 25n4, 32n3, 33, 53, 68–69, 83, 88, 93–94, 95n20, 104, 164, 184, 190, 197, 197n36, 225, 229, 241, 261, 276, 323, 356, 366–67, 371
Gregory the Theologian, 5, 13, 78, 93–94, 157, 184, 367
grief among the saved, GAS, ix, 351–56
guaranteed certainty, GC, ix, 297–301

SUBJECT INDEX

Harrowing, 132, 136, 148–72, 298n22
Hades, vii, 10, 29, 130–32, 134–37, 145,
  148–52, 152n5, 153–72, 207,
  247, 298n22, 364, 368, 377
Hart, David Bentley, DBH, ix, 5n5, 51,
  109, 116n64, 135, 140–141, 172,
  174, 180–181, 195, 251, 257,
  268–70, 323–25, 349–350, 364
Hegel, G. W. F., 41n5, 320–321, 337, 381
Heidegger, Martin, Heideggerian, 56,
  75n1
hesychasm, hesychast, 76, 77, 185
Hinnom, 137–42, 145
hopeful universalism, HU, ix, 73, 96,
  310, 357–63

Ibn Taymiyya, viii, 369–81
idolatry, 109, 193, 195–96, 199
Incarnation, vii, 37–70, 110n51, 115,
  126, 198n37, 213, 223, 225, 238,
  290, 313–14, 324, 350–351
in-itself, 325–27, 329–31, 337
Irenaeus of Lyon, 55–56, 346, 366, 374
Isaac the Syrian, 2, 8, 377
Isochrists, 124, 216n14, 226–29, 234, 240
Israel, Israelite, 15, 15n13, 41, 46n16,
  47, 60, 67, 78–79, 87, 109,
  126, 132, 132n6, 137, 139–42,
  144–45, 150, 175–76, 181, 186,
  192–93, 198, 198n37, 199–202,
  202n42, 265, 315n43

Jerome the Great, 5, 152n4, 209, 221,
  233, 236–37
John Chrysostom, 10, 53, 78, 81, 91n14,
  95, 98n24, 111, 157, 167, 178,
  190, 278, 346, 367
John of Damascus, 66, 166, 190, 323
John Scotus Eriugena, 8, 12, 95
John the Forerunner, 39–40, 172, 185,
  192
Josephus, 40, 58n36, 140n23, 180, 206
Justinian I, 212, 226, 232, 236, 249
Justin Martyr, 33, 42, 46n18, 48, 64n49,
  78, 156, 346, 366

kampsē, 103–4
katargeō, 92–93

Khimi, David, 139–40
Kierkegaard, Søren, 339–45, 353–62
Kimel, Aidan, 7, 82n12, 180, 225, 242
kolasis, 183–84
Kronen, John, 273–76, 333–34, 344–45

Lazarus, 135–36, 279
Lewisian model, LM, ix, 74, 276n17,
  296–98, 305
libertarian free will, LFW, ix, 257–76,
  288, 297, 300, 321–25, 334, 337,
  342
love web, LW, ix, 352–56
Luther, Martin, 104, 204, 243, 292, 365

MacDonald, George, 82, 84
Macrina the Younger, 5, 197
Marcarius II, 226
martyrdom, 44, 54, 114, 175
Mary, Theotokos, 12, 23, 40–45, 152n6,
  172, 185, 213, 251, 305
Mary Magdalene, 62, 64, 64n48, 64n49
Maximus the Confessor, 8, 13, 17, 40,
  42, 54, 66, 120, 258, 276, 282,
  311, 348, 377
Milbank, John, 202n42, 271
Milton, John, 112
Mohammad, 128, 375n13, 376n15, 377,
  379–81
Moltmann, Jürgen, 82, 310n35, 357
Moo, Douglas, 99, 102
Moses, 25, 47, 66–67, 78, 83, 131, 148,
  161, 192, 202, 266, 302, 366
Moss, Candida, 54, 194–95

necessary divine justice, NDJ, ix, 297,
  303–5, 347–51, 355
Nietzsche, Friedrich, Nietzschean, 52,
  139, 278, 291, 359
Nicaea I, 50, 365–66
Nicaea II, 212, 237–43, 243n80, 245–46
Nicene, 39n1, 43, 49, 80, 111n51,
  111n52, 126, 128, 220–221, 251
nine anathemas, 222–26, 230
Nephilim, 132, 146–47, 149, 192, 202
Nestorianism, 213, 225–27, 238

ʿolām, 181, 186

SUBJECT INDEX

Origenist Christology, 225–26
Origen, Origenism, Origenist, 4, 8–9,
  12–13, 24, 39–40, 43n11, 53,
  61, 64n49, 78, 83–84, 88, 88n4,
  94, 95n20, 98, 98n24, 102–3,
  104n36, 111n51, 124, 163–64,
  182, 188–90, 194, 207, 213–15,
  215n13, 216–17, 220–222,
  222n24, 223–24, 224n31, 225–
  29, 229n49, 230–235, 235n64,
  236, 236n65, 236n67, 237–43,
  311, 316, 331, 344, 366–67, 371,
  374
original sin, OS, x, 292, 292n14,
  292n15, 293
Ortlund, Dane, 284–87, 316

panta en pasin, 94–96
Parry, Robin, 82, 90, 110, 207n51,
  293n18
penal substitutionary atonement, PSA,
  x, 50–56
perpetual sin hypothesis, PSH, x, 284,
  296–305
Philaret of Moscow, 247
Plato, Platonic, Platonism, Platonist, 4n3,
  8, 22, 25, 68, 76, 78–79, 79n8, 90,
  189–90, 228n49, 258, 276, 335,
  356, 371
Plotinus, 79n8, 291n12
possible world, x, 275–76, 298, 314–16
predestination, 197–202, 251, 290, 358,
  371
Price, Richard, 215, 229n51, 241, 248
Proclus, 276
Protestantism, 74, 243, 251, 338–39
Protochrists, 226–28
psychoanalysis, psychoanalytic, 26,
  75n1, 162, 261, 263

Qumran, 97, 143–45, 201
Qur'an, 128, 369, 369n1, 370, 370n3,
  371–75, 375n13, 376, 376n15,
  377–81

Rabbinic, 47, 143–45
Rahner, Karl, 86, 357

Ramelli, Ilaria, 6–7, 87, 186–88, 188n21,
  189n26, 214, 232, 234–35
Reitan, Eric, 273–76, 333–34, 344–45
Rephaim, 132, 147
resurrection, 23, 43, 54, 57–65, 84,
  89–90, 113, 132, 137, 148, 155,
  165, 219–20, 223–24, 239–40,
  266, 346

Satan, 53, 130, 143, 156–61, 168, 190,
  202, 207, 328–29
Second Temple, 46n17, 47, 76–77, 81,
  87, 97, 119n69, 136, 140–41,
  144, 201, 205–6, 281
Sheol, 130–32, 132n6, 133–34, 136–37,
  146–47, 149
Socratic, 198, 200, 339–40, 345–46
soul-making, 306–8, 374
Spiegel, James, 101, 263–64, 308, 340–
  342, 352–56
Sproul, R. C., 287–91, 294, 316
Stăniloae, Dumitru, 69, 229, 250
status argument, SA, x, 284, 291–94,
  305, 329, 361
Swinburne, Richard, 299, 299n23,
  300–301
Synod of Alexandria, 230–231, 233,
  235–36
Synod of Jerusalem, 243–48

Talbott, Thomas, 89–90, 91n13, 182,
  262–64, 272
Tartarus, 130, 144, 146–47, 149, 160, 187
telos, 18, 55, 70, 90, 91n13, 95–96, 103,
  259, 290, 299–300, 376
Theodore of Mopuestia, 5, 84, 213, 224,
  237, 239
Theophilus of Alexandria, 5, 231–36
timōria, 183–84
Transfiguration, 66, 148

unconscious, 26, 261, 263, 269, 279,
  309, 312, 322, 322n7, 323

value-correspondence, VC, x, 292–94,
  297, 304

Ware, Kallistos, 74, 96, 361

Ancient Document Index

Genesis

1–3	10–12
1:1	125–26
1:26`	14, 69, 158
1:28	14
2:20	14
3:5	14
3:6	14
3:22	14
6:6	149
9:16	186
15:17	192
17	200
19:24	192
19:24–29	202
21:33	186
33:10	200

Exodus

3	192
14:24	192
32:6	196
33	25
34:29	66–67

Leviticus

19:31	133

Numbers

6:25	67
13	198
25	196

Deuteronomy

4:11	192
4:24	151, 192
12:9	55
17:8–13	29
18	133
29:22	202
32:8–9	15n13

Joshua

5	47
15:8	137

Judges

6:11–23	47

ANCIENT DOCUMENT INDEX

1 Samuel
1–2	39
16:14	207
18:10	207
28:15	133

2 Samuel
15	279

1 Kings
19:11–20	39

2 Kings
23:10	138

1 Chronicles
29:13	106

2 Chronicles
28:3	137n12

Nehemiah
11:30	137n12

Tobit
3:6	186
4:7	195

Judith
8:14	323

Esther
4:1	186

2 Maccabees
1:5	116n63
4:38	183
5:20	116n63
7:23	35
12:45	133, 136

3 Maccabees
1:3	183
2:1	103
2:5	203

Job
5:17–18	192
11:8	131
16:22	132
21:13	132
24:19	132
33:4	35
38:17	150

Psalms
8:6	93
9:17	132
15:10	150
18:49	107
23	157
27	139
30:4	107
40:3	271
66:10–12	192
88:11	132
103:9	303
110:1	93
127:2	55
129:4	332
139:7	269
139:8	131
150	94, 241

Proverbs
5:5	132
8:22	47, 126
9:18	132, 135
10:10	117
10:31	332

Song of Songs
1:4–5	261–62

Wisdom

1:4	47
2:1	133
4:12	195
7:26	126
7:28	47
11:3	183
14:7	31
15:11	35

Sirach

1:4	126
24:9	126
25:11	277

Isaiah

1:10	203
1:25	193
3:9	203
5:14	135
7:11	131
10:17–18	175
19	175
26:19	132
27:13	175
30:33	138
38:10	132
38:18	132n6
41–45	105
41:13	105
42:5	35
42:8	105
42:17	109
43:11	105
44:6	105
44:9	109
45:20–25	109–10
45:22	105
45:23	104n36, 105, 105n40, 109
45:24	106n41, 109
49:6	30, 200
57:16	302
60	208
65:25	12
66:24	139, 142

Jeremiah

17:27	194
18	199, 201
18:20	183
19	139–41
24:14	203
31:3	274, 277

Lamentations

3:23	274

Ezekiel

16:53–55	203
16:63	109
18:30	183
20:47	193–94
37	150
37:5–10	35
43:11	183

Daniel

7	48–49
12:3	143

Hosea

2:16	139n15
13:14	150

Amos

5:6	193

Jonah

2:6	132

Micah

2:12	201
4:7	201

Habakkuk

1:12	192
3:4	67

Zechariah
8:12 — 201

Malachi
3:1 — 39
4:5 — 39

1 Enoch
10 — 146
27 — 141
46 — 49
54:1–2 — 141
67:4 — 141
67:13 — 30
91:17 — 117n65

2 Enoch
22 — 202

Jubilees
1:29 — 117n65
10 — 207
23:26–29 — 117n65

4 Maccabees
12–13 — 174–75
13 — 175
13:9 — 175
13:14 — 174
13:15 — 186

4 Ezra
7:36 — 141

Matthew
3:6 — 107
3:12 — 191–97
5:9 — 117, 122
5:22 — 142–43, 196
5:29 — 142, 332
5:30 — 142
5:38–42 — 184
5:47 — 184
5:66 — 92
6:22 — 195
7 — 330
8:12 — 192
10:15 — 203
10:28 — 142, 174–77, 306
11:23 — 134–36
11:25 — 107
11:27 — 24
11:28 — 55
12:25 — 362
12:40 — 150
15:25 — 103
16:18 — 29, 134, 364–68
16:20 — 310n34
16:23 — 143
17:2 — 66
17:10–13 — 39
18:9 — 142
18:18 — 29
18:20 — 105–6
19:16 — 187
22:13 — 272
23:15 — 142
23:32 — 142
24 — 331
24:30 — 49
24:32 — 365
25:46 — 178–86, 190, 373
27 — 150
27:29 — 103

Mark
3:29 — 187, 302
7:22 — 195
8:27–30 — 310n34
9:11–13 — 39
9:43 — 142, 192, 194–96
9:45 — 142
9:47 — 142
10:30 — 187
12:30–31 — 319–20
14 — 49
15:18 — 103

Luke
1:3 — 58n36
1:42 — 41

ANCIENT DOCUMENT INDEX

3:17	194	3:21	2
6:35	92	4	53
8:17	336	7:55	66
8:31	146	17	22–23
9:18–22	310	17:25	35
10:15	134	17:28	18, 288
11:1	40	20:35	59
12:5	142	27	58n36
12:46	331		
12:47–48	303	**Romans**	
16:16	88, 88n4	1:20	187
16:23	134–36	2:15	266
21:27	49	3:23	293, 325
22:3	158n20	3:25	118
23:43	76	4:17	89n8
34:30–31	84	5	100
		5:10	91, 115
John		5:11	115
1:3–4	126	5:12	50n23, 101–3
1:5	67	5:12–20	98–103
1:14	110	5:15	102–3, 124
1:18	25	5:16–17	103
1:46	153	5:17	99n26, 99–100
3:17	88, 176	5:18	87, 88n6, 98–103,
4	210, 301		149
5:21	89n10	5:19	98n24, 99, 102
6:47	187	6:23	12
6:63	89	7:15	322n7
10:34–35	18	8:11	89n8
12:32	7, 88	8:20˙	17
13:27	158n20	8:22	103
14:6	77	8:32	99
15:18–19	289	8:38	289
16:13	29	9–11	197–202, 341, 365
16:33	289	9	198–99, 202
19	41, 313	10	199–201
19:3	103	11	200–202
19:30	18	11:15	115
20:17	69–70, 93	11:32	88, 176, 192, 201
21:24	114	12:4	126
21:25	62	12:17	99
		13:8	312
Acts		14:2	99
2	53, 192	15:9	107
2:27	134	16:19	99
2:31	134	16:25–26	187

405

1 Corinthians

1:8	331
1:28	92
3:10–15	330–332
3:12–15	193, 336
7	365
7:11	115–16
8:6	125n73
10	47
11:25	118
12:3	108
12:30	126
13	278–81, 264
13:6	24
13:8	274, 355
13:9	282
13:12	11, 336, 368
13:13	66
14:40	195
15:3–7	63–65
15:14	57
15:20–24	89
15:20–28	87–98
15:22	87–89, 96–99, 123–24
15:23–24	89–93, 96–97
15:25–28	90–98
15:27	91, 93, 97
15:28	18, 66, 90–98, 112, 129, 149, 189, 349–50
15:36	89n8
15:45	89n9
15:49	70
15:50	70

2 Corinthians

3:3	266
3:6	83, 89, 234
3:7–8	67
3:15	137
3:18	12, 264, 282
5:2	70
5:14	88
5:18	115
5:19	88, 115–16
6:15	201

Galatians

1:3	195
2:9	66
3:21	89n8
3:28	65n51, 99, 313
4:3	289
5:11	118

Ephesians

1:9–10	88
1:20–22	93
1:21	23
1:23	18, 30
2:2	289
2:15	117
2:16	115, 116n63
3:11	53
3:14	104
3:18	285
4:9	150
4:14	9
6:13	331

Philippians

1:28	106n41
2	125
2:5–11	103–12
2:6	110–11
2:7	110–11
2:8	110–11, 118
2:9	110–11
2:10–11	87, 105n40, 109, 112, 124, 129, 149, 271
2:10	103–4, 105, 105n40, 106, 110, 112
2:11	103, 105n40, 106, 106n41, 106n42, 108–12

Colossians

1:13	115
1:15–17	48
1:15–18	125–27
1:16	115, 126, 289

1:17	126	
1:18	126–27	
1:19–21	127–28	
1:19	127–28	
1:20	87, 112, 114–29, 149	
1:21	127–29	
1:22	115	
1:28	88	
3:13	286	

1 Thessalonians

4	365
5:14	281

2 Thessalonians

3:6	30

1 Timothy

1:15	348–49
2:3–6	88
2:4	274, 345
2:5–6	54
3:15	30
4:10	88
6:13	89n8
6:16	25, 187

2 Timothy

3	36–37
3:16	16, 31–37, 82

Titus

2:11	88

Hebrews

1:3	48, 126
2:6	93
3:8	331
2:14	92
4:10	55
9:27	273
12:28–29	192
12:29	70

James

3:6	142, 145, 196

1 Peter

2:5	9
2:12	331
3:18–20	149
3:18	89n8, 136
4:6	132, 137, 149, 169
4:12	193
5:13	207

2 Peter

1:11	187
2:4	146
2:6	203
2:9	184
3:8	2, 274
3:9	88
3:16	198

1 John

1:2	187
2:2	88
2:9	319
4:8	277
4:9–10	274
4:12	23, 25, 320
4:14	88
4:18	183, 185, 310
4:19	91

Jude

5	47, 192
6	187
7	187, 202–4

The Apocalypse of John/Revelation

1:4	210
1:8	205
1:18	134
4	77
6:8	134

**The Apocalypse of John/
Revelation** (*cont.*)

12	41–42
14:11	207
17:6	206
17:11	206
20:10	150–51, 306
20:13	134
20:14	134
21–22	207–11
21	207–9, 328, 377
21:2–3	207–8
21:4	337
21:7–8	208
21:8	208
21:22–27	208
21:27	3, 208–9
22	209–11
22:1–2	209
22:5	209
22:13	205, 209
22:15	209
22:17	210
22:21	210

www.ingramcontent.com/pod-product-compliance
Lightning Source LLC
Chambersburg PA
CBHW072117290426
44111CB00012B/1693